Reasoning beyond Reason

Reasoning beyond Reason

Imagination as a Theological Source in the Work of C. S. Lewis

J. T. SELLARS

☙PICKWICK *Publications* · Eugene, Oregon

REASONING BEYOND REASON
Imagination as a Theological Source in the Work of C. S. Lewis

Copyright © 2011 J. T. Sellars. All rights reserved. Except for brief quotations in critical publications or reviews, no part of this book may be reproduced in any manner without prior written permission from the publisher. Write: Permissions, Wipf and Stock Publishers, 199 W. 8th Ave., Suite 3, Eugene, OR 97401.

Pickwick Publications
An Imprint of Wipf and Stock Publishers
199 W. 8th Ave., Suite 3
Eugene, OR 97401

www.wipfandstock.com

ISBN 13: 978-1-60899-503-5

Cataloging-in-Publication data:

Sellars, J. T.

    Reasoning beyond reason : imagination as a theological source in the work of C. S. Lewis / J. T. Sellars.

    x + 256 p. ; 23 cm. Includes bibliographical references and indexes.

    ISBN 13: 978-1-60899-503-5

    1. Lewis, C. S. (Clive Staples), 1898–1963—Philosophy. 2. Lewis, C. S. (Clive Staples), 1898–1963—Theology. 3. Imagination. I. Title.

BX5199 L53 S3 2011

Manufactured in the U.S.A.

To Hollie, Eliana, Linda, Tom, Jen, Alyssa and Jordan with love

Contents

Acknowledgments / ix

Introduction / 1

one   The Nature and Limits of Rationalistic Reason / 9

two   The Function of the Imagination / 45

three   The Imaginative Drive / 58

four   Desire and Longing in Lewis, Plato, and Augustine / 77

five   The Ethics of Fairyland / 107

six   Poetic Labors / 138

seven   The Theological Imagination / 192

Bibliography / 217

Subject Index / 239

Name Index / 252

Acknowledgments

I would like to thank my friends and family for their support and encouragement through the years. To my students: I thank you for challenging and teaching me. To my friends and colleagues: I thank you for your help and criticism. I must single out and thank Dr. Simon Oliver for his advice, guidance, criticism, and wisdom.

Introduction

*I*NTEREST IN C. S. Lewis shows no current signs of slowing down, especially given the renewed attention stirred by the cinema adaptations of the Chronicles of Narnia. What we often find is that Lewis is championed as the "Christian knight," the hard-nosed rational defender of the faith. But this popular view really diminishes Lewis' reach and ignores the deepest aspect of his contribution and personality—namely, the imaginative poet. The recent films of Lewis' Chronicles help to remind us of the great imagination Lewis displayed—and also remind us to look for that imaginative side within his more "rational" work. Despite his massive popularity, it might be well advised to begin with some stage setting, in order to see Lewis' motivation for becoming that "Christian knight," and to see how even this aspect of himself found its beginnings in imagination.

Clive Staples Lewis was born on November 29, 1898, in Belfast, Ireland. His father, Albert Lewis, was a solicitor, setting up his own practice in Belfast. His mother, Flora Lewis (maiden name Hamilton) was a college-educated woman. She read mathematics and logic at Queen's University, Belfast, receiving a first in logic and a second-class honors degree in mathematics.

Lewis was raised in the Church of Ireland. The family worshipped at St. Mark's Church, where Flora's father was rector. Lewis was taken to church by his parents, and became familiar with the services, but they held little meaning for him.[1] What faith Lewis had was lost completely when his mother died of cancer in 1908. Lewis was just nine at the time. He had prayed fervently for his mother's recovery, but his prayers went unanswered. This was the beginning of Lewis' agnostic and atheistic feelings, which lasted until his early thirties.

Lewis' definitive change in attitude towards religion can clearly be seen to pick up steam once he became engaged in the "great war" with Owen Barfield. Barfield and Lewis became friends at Oxford and, in approximately 1922, they began a dialogue on imagination and poetic insight.[2] The debate ended in 1931 with Lewis' conversion to Christianity. Lewis had argued that there was no meaning to be found in the imagination and that contemporary philosophical ideas were superior to those of the past (on the grounds that either modern thought was a progression on past thought or that past thought had been refuted in the process of this progression). Barfield argued "that there is a poetic element in all meaningful language. . . . Barfield jokingly said to his friend after their 'war' was over that while Lewis had taught him *how* to think, he had taught Lewis *what* to think."[3]

Another key moment in Lewis' religious and intellectual life occurred in September 1931, a moment that would help trigger his conversion to Christianity. Lewis and his friends J. R. R. Tolkien and Hugo Dyson had a conversation one evening. Lewis had understood the power of myth and imagination (the draw of fairyland) from an early age, but in the end decided that these "calls to fairyland" were mere fantasy, signifying nothing of ultimate importance. They may appear beautiful to the human mind, but they are merely lies, "breathed through silver." Tolkien countered this by arguing that they are not lies but are instead the best way of conveying truths, truths that are incomprehensible in any other medium.[4] Furthermore, Tolkien argued, if we come from God and if myths are woven by us (even though they may contain error), then they contain at least a glimmer of divine light.[5] And, Tolkien continued, the myth of Christ is a "true myth." It is a myth that works the same way as other myths but with the added detail that it actually happened.[6] Lewis was much indebted to his friends Tolkien and Dyson for his acceptance of Christianity, and they were instrumental in helping Lewis to realize that myths could be seen as prefigures of the unique myth-become-fact of Christianity.

Lewis' conversion was clearly no overnight event. However, the long road to the Christian faith had given him a strong foundation, and "he devoted himself to developing and strengthening his belief, and almost from the year of his conversion, he wanted to become an evangelist for the Christian faith."[7] In his popular apologetics, Lewis was very careful to state that he was not a theologian.[8] However, this certainly depends upon one's definition of the term. Clearly, in a certain sense, we are all theologians. That is, we participate, at least in some fashion, in "God talk"—we decide on theological issues for ourselves. Of course, not all of us are professional theologians, academically trained in the discipline— and clearly Lewis, too, falls into this category.

The two aspects of Lewis, the defender (and translator of Christian doctrine into the language of the everyday[9]) and the mythopoeic Christian author (the "imaginative evangelizer" or "pre-figurer" of the gospel message, if you will) appear at first glance to be dichotomous— and even Lewis thought they were before he became a Christian. When he was a rationalist and an atheist he found that two sides of him were pulling in different directions. On the one hand, his rationalistic side told him that the material universe was all there was and that his love of fiction and fantasy was ultimately meaningless: he could find no ultimate meaning or truth in the imagination, for the images were mere creations (fancies) of his own mind. On the other hand his imagination (through his own work and through the work of others) presented him with images and ideas that seemed full of meaning. Ultimately, when he became a Christian, he found that his rationalistic side was leaving out a vast amount of reality. When he was an atheist and rationalist he believed that his rationalist side could not be reconciled with his imaginative side. Once he became a Christian, he eventually found a means of marrying the two—mainly through story or myth-making.

The notion of Lewis as a lay theologian or a translator also raises the question, "From where did Lewis learn his theology?" He claimed that he initially learned his theology from literature—i.e., specifically through reading works of literature by authors who where Christian.[10] Once he became a Christian, Lewis turned to the classics of Christian theology.[11] He claimed almost no knowledge of (and no debt to) "modern" theologians.[12] The initial stage of Lewis' theological learning is indeed very telling. One can discern the prominence and primary importance of the imagination in his acceptance of Christianity—and not only this but also an acceptance of the Christian imagination before a rationalist assent was made. This, too, is a reasoned deliverance of the imagination, a reason which fills the gaps between the merely rationalistic—a reasoning beyond reason, at least beyond "reason" in its more restricted, modern sense.

Lewis' admitted lack of debt to modern theology places him firmly in a premodern setting. Foremost, Lewis was a medievalist and classicist; he was a professor of classical literature; he studied ancient philosophy as a student and taught it as a tutor. It is this world that informed his teaching, writing, and research. It is to and through these classicist lenses that we find him referring as he tackles the intellectual and social climate of his times. Lewis might also be placed at the fringe of a wider trend. We might place him, in his reference to these classical sources, at the far edges of the Oxford Movement of the nineteenth and early twentieth centuries—the movement was still influential in the Church of England in Lewis' day and in Oxford and Magdalen in particular.[13] The movement called for a return to patristic sources, which also necessitated a return to ancient Greek philosophy and Hebrew narrative. It is through this wider trend that we can see Lewis has a strong precedent for the unity of reason and narrative in the discernment of truth. Long before the Ressourcement movement within Roman Catholicism during the Second Vatican Council,[14] Anglicans were leading their own return to the church's classical roots. Lewis' work and thought could be viewed as falling somewhere within this wider trend. It is, therefore, through these classical sources that we will first look to find Lewis' position on reason and imagination.

In chapter 1 of this book I attempt to place Lewis in a premodern (non-Enlightenment) framework by exploring and rejecting the book that Lewis retreated from reason into imaginative works. How are we to understand "reason" and "imagination" in this context? This common "retreat" argument about Lewis resets upon an assumption about rationality that relies heavily upon Enlightenment notions of what it means to be rational. I argue that the notion that Lewis is a modern rationalist, following the Enlightenment paradigm of rationality, is incorrect. Lewis is to be seen as finding his influence and sources in ancient thought, not modern. The Enlightenment program of rational enquiry (i.e., unbiased, universally accepted rational principles) is at odds with Lewis' own premodern notions of rationality. Lewis' own specific program in his imaginative and explicitly argumentative works is to be seen in light of Platonic persuasion. Lastly, I examine Augustine's conception of faith and Aquinas' notions of revelation and reason in an effort to bolster Lewis' kinship with premodern ideas of rationality.

In chapter 2, I continue on the trajectory set in chapter 1. I attempt to place Lewis on a premodern trajectory in regards to the function of the imagination and its relation to reason. Having looked at Lewis' view of reason through premodern sources, we must explicitly turn to the question of the imagination. What is it and what is its function? Lewis' views are explored by way of Aquinas (viewed at his most Augustinian). Lewis' views are also reflected in his contemporaries Austin Farrer and Dorothy Sayers, and in one important antecedent, namely, George MacDonald. These writers all shared a sense of the imagination as being funded and founded by divine transcendence. It is no surprise that the critique of their positions comes in the form of a denial of said transcendence and a decidedly Enlightenment-bound program that views the imagination as purely phenomenologically funded.

In chapter 3, I continue the argument that Lewis' move into fiction should be seen as a deepening of his intellectual powers: it is the older, premodern, and more operative man coming to light. What are we to make of Lewis turn to children's fiction? Is it a psychological retreat from reasoned work? I examine this largely psychological critique brought against Lewis' fiction for children through an exploration of his own ideas about literary criticism. This is done in an attempt to oppose the idea that Lewis' turn to writing children's fiction is to be seen primarily in terms of outside influence (principally, the Anscombe debate) or a sublimated psychological problem (e.g., a projection of fear). I also consider Lewis' own reasons for writing his children's fiction, which are often ignored or simply rejected in such psychological accounts of Lewis. Lastly, I look at Lewis' own ideas about his personal make-up—how he viewed his "older," imaginative self coming to fruition.

In chapter 4, I examine the role of desire or longing within the work of Lewis, Plato, and Augustine. What role does longing or desire have to do with reason and imagination? How is longing a source of delivered reason and imagination? The answers lie in the effort to place Lewis firmly within a premodern framework, and particularly the Platonic-Augustinian tradition. Through this effort a connection can be found between the Platonic-Augustinian conception of desire and the function of imagination and its role in art and thought: that is, the focus on the role and function of imaginative work is to see it as reasoned work and to recognize that it gains its *telos* and meaning when it reverts back to (participates in) its higher, divine source.

In chapter 5, I argue that Lewis rejected a purely rationalist ethical paradigm, namely because a purely rationalist ethic is troubling due to its commitment to "universal rational consent" and due to its reliance upon a more fundamental, unspoken reasoning beyond rationalistic conceptions of reason. What are the connections between reason, imagination, and ethics? Lewis' relational ethic gives us a clue to this by alerting us to our own stories. I argue that Lewis advocated a relational ethic that develops most explicitly in his narrative work. This narrative framework implicitly indicates that we are all part of a narrative framework and that we find our ethic when we first recognize the narrative of which we find ourselves a part.

In chapter 6, I begin by exploring Lewis' debt to George MacDonald and his theory of the work of phantasm and fairy. How does narrative (explicitly imaginative effort) disclose reasoned work? Lewis' focus on narrative as a means to communicate his chief ideas is one such way this is played out in his corpus. Lewis' focus on story also demonstrates a dual function of narrative: it is a looking *along* (experiencing, learning, knowing through the narrative) and a looking *at* (reasoning from the narrative). It is a disclosure of a reasoning beyond reason—reasoning that fills the gaps between the supposed step-by-step process of modern, rationalistic reason. This view of imaginative works brings with it a sense of the Other—which is an epiphenomenon of the work. This is seen especially, for Lewis, with myth. Myth communicates a special knowledge: it goes beyond the expression of things already known. The imagination is connected with myth through this epiphenomenon—that is, through joy or desire. We gain this special knowledge through participation in the work and in the attempt at authorial discernment. However, we must be in the right place spiritually to receive these spiritual gifts. This applies, for Lewis, to Scripture as well. All language is poetic expression, and as such is deeply connected to thought and imagination. An examination of Owen Barfield's notion of poetic diction explicitly advocates seeing language as essentially poetic, which requires this aforementioned deep connection between thought and imagination: the imagination is a reason-funding (motivational) faculty. But there is a limit to language when approximating the divine: in general, the concessions of poetic language are that the finite cannot fully express the infinite; transcendence cannot be reduced to immanence. But if there is a relationship between God and humanity, it must be apprehended somehow, must have a point of connection—and analogy is just such a connection. Lewis' view opens up works of art by revealing their divinely gifted nature, revealing their analogous connections, all in an effort to lead one back to their source.

In chapter 7, I examine Lewis' view of imagination through his essay "Transposition," where there lies a veiled Lewisian theory of imagination. How is the imagination theological? If it is theological, how does this (either explicitly or implicitly) theology reveal itself? There is a necessary transposition of the higher, divine life to the lower, "mundane" life. In this process, however, the lower life is saved by being brought up into the higher life. The imagination is also to be seen as the organ of meaning: we gain our *telos* and meaning from a reliance upon transcendence. The "untheological" imagination is surreptitiously relying upon transcendence to fund its work: its narrative framework is ultimately nihilistic, terminating on the merely phenomenologically given, and losing, in the long run, what it attempts to hold up. The "untheological" imagination is an unorthodox theological view, in that it is funded by a meaning-filled narrative structure while attempting to communicate a narrative of meaninglessness. Thus, the narrative framework is still theological in its reliance upon a transcendent meaning or *telos*.

Notes

1. Sayer, *Jack*, 61.
2. Duriez, *C. S. Lewis Chronicles*, 147.
3. Ibid.
4. Grace, "Praising God in Myth," 3.
5. Ibid.
6. Ibid.
7. Sayer, *Jack*, 231.
8. Lewis freely admitted that he was not a professional theologian. He was an outsider. However, he noted that there are two kinds of outsiders: uneducated and educated (i.e., those who are educated in some other discipline but not in theology). For this distinction, and an example of one of his many claims of not being a theologian, see Lewis' essay "Modern Theology and Biblical Criticism" in his *Christian Reflections*.
9. For example, Lewis noted that "My task was therefore simply that of a *translator*—one turning Christian doctrine, or what he believed to be such, into the vernacular, into the language that unscholarly people would attend to and understand . . ." (*God in the Dock*, 183).
10. Lewis noted, "Christendom, you see, reached me at first almost entirely through books I took up not because they were Christian, but because they were famous as literature. Hence Dante, Spencer, Milton, the poems of George Herbert and of Coventry

Patmore, were incomparably more important than any professed theologians" (*Collected Letters*, 3:978).

11. For example, "Later, when I had become interested in Christianity—been *caught* by truth in places where I sought only pleasure—came St. Augustine, Hooker, Traherne, Wm. Law, *The Imitation*, the *Theologia Germanica*" (ibid.).

12. For example, "You pay a wholly undeserved compliment to my erudition by supposing that my debt to modern theologians might be too complicated to sort out! There are hardly any such debts at all" (ibid.). For an overview of Lewis' possible influences and reading habits see James Bell and Dawson, eds., *Library of C. S. Lewis*.

13. Some of Lewis' friends could also be placed in this trend of championing the historic sources of the church: for instance, Charles Williams (e.g., in *The Place of the Lion*, where the Platonic forms enter into the world); Dorothy Sayers (e.g., in "The Lost Tools of Learning," where she advocates a return to the "syllabus of the Middle Ages"); and Austin Farrer (e.g., his advocacy of God's "double agency" in Faith and Speculation—which can be seen as a restatement of Aquinas's notion in the *Summa Theologiae*, for example 1a2ae.10.4 and 1a.83.1, that there is no competition between divine and human action).

14. Championed, for example, by theologians such as Henri de Lubac, Yves Congar, and Jean Daniélou.

one

The Nature and Limits of Rationalistic Reason

The common reception of C. S. Lewis has been divided into two camps: philosophical and theological Christian apologetics on the one hand and imaginative myth and narrative on the other. This suggests a particular interpretation of Lewis' work based upon certain assumptions regarding the nature of reason and theology. It appears that the "two Lewises" are distinct and divisible into an early and late Lewis, with the Anscombe debate forming the convenient watershed moment. Contrary to this common reception, Lewis does not divide easily into an early Lewis and a late Lewis (though there is undoubtedly growth)—for he does not fit into the modern, Enlightenment paradigm of reason separated from imagination, which would permit such an interpretation of his work. This is seen clearly in Lewis' teaching: he taught the ancient Greeks and antique literature, and it is from these sources that his work emerges. By his own admission he was a "dinosaur." In his inaugural Cambridge address for his appointment to the Chair of Mediaeval and Renaissance Literature, Lewis noted the loss of ancient knowledge in modern times. There is a great division between the Christian and the post-Christian: "A post-Christian man is not a Pagan. . . . The post-Christian is cut off from the Christian past and therefore doubly from the Pagan past."[1] Lewis' own *modus operandi* is ancient, not modern: "And here comes the rub. I myself belong far more to that Old Western order than to yours."[2] In this chapter I will attempt to place Lewis outside of Enlightenment notions of rationality through a presentation of Lewis in a premodern context. This will be done, first, by challenging A. N. Wilson's "retreat" thesis and then moving on to Lewis' own views of the limits of rationalist reason. I will explore an alternative to Enlightenment, rationalist enquiry by way of Alasdair McIntyre's assessment of rationality. I will then examine the notion of persuasion as presented by Plato to place Lewis in the context of premodern rationality. This will be followed by an analysis of Augustine's concept of faith and Aquinas' view of reason and revelation.

The Wilsonian Thesis

There is an apparent dichotomy in C. S. Lewis' writing. On the one hand we see the Christian apologist: the writer of such argumentative works as *Mere Christianity, Miracles, The Abolition of Man*, and *The Problem of Pain*; and the literary critic, the writer of such books as *The Allegory of Love, The Discarded Image, Studies in Words*, and *An Experiment in Criticism*. On the other hand we have the imaginative poet, the writer of the Chronicles of Narnia, *Out of the Silent Planet, Perelandra, That Hideous Strength*, and *Till We Have Faces*. Even Lewis' close friend Owen Barfield noted that there were two Lewises: "Lewis the dialectician and the 'mythopoeic Lewis.' A comprehensive view of the two Lewises reveals that there was in Lewis, as he himself admitted in his reply (undated) to the Milton Society of America, a central man trying to 'get out,' trying to assert himself over Lewis the dialectician."[3] Barfield also noted that the two Lewises can be seen as not quite uniting but joining hands in *The Great Divorce*.[4] One can see much more than a "joining of hands" in most of Lewis' fiction, not least in his Chronicles of Narnia. Lewis unites and communicates much of his central views in this imaginative world. In Lewis' fiction we often see the scholar and the storyteller fused; in fact, one of the "best ways to understand the intellectual and imaginative context of his children's stories is to read his other books."[5] The fictive writing of Lewis gives a clue as to his *modus operandi*: he saw the symbolic, mythic elements of story as the best way to say what he needed to say.[6]

One of the most striking expressions of the view that there are two Lewises, which also seems to suggest a dichotomy between reason and imagination, can be found in A. N. Wilson's biography of Lewis. He suggests that Lewis retreated from strict reasoned argument into the world of children's fantasy, specifically because of "Lewis's experience of being stung back into childhood by his defeat at the hands of Elizabeth Anscombe at the Socratic Club."[7] According to Wilson, Lewis was awakened to "all sorts of deeply seated fears," and now that the "bullying hero of the hour had been cut down to size, he became a child, a little boy who was being degraded and shaken by a figure who, in his imagination, took on witch-like dimensions."[8] So, the Anscombe debate "about Supernaturalism had stung Lewis into a quite different sort of writing . . ."[9]

Indeed, Wilson is not alone in this assessment. Humphrey Carpenter also reports that Lewis' imagery about the Anscombe debate "'was all of the fog of war, the retreat of infantry thrown back under heavy attack,'"[10] and states that "Lewis had learnt his lesson: for after this he wrote no further books of Christian apologetics for ten years . . ."[11] However, it is clear if one looks at Lewis' publishing record that he continued to engage in Christian apologetics.[12] Even if it is true that Lewis's encounter with Anscombe severely dampened his intellectual spirits at the time and made him feel as if he had been defeated in that particular debate, there remains the issue of Lewis' supposed retreat into children's fantasy, and, crucially, the relation of that fantasy to his theological and philosophical apologetics. Lewis did not focus on narrative and myth as an act of retreat from the "hard-nosed" reasoned philosophical attack; rather, Lewis focused on narrative and myth because he thought they might move us further along than strict rationalistic reasoning.[13] If it is true that the best way "to understand the intellectual and imaginative context of his children's stories is to read his other books," then the charge that Lewis "retreated" into children's books becomes very troublesome.[14]

Given the number of commentators who refer to Lewis' encounter with Elizabeth Anscombe—one of the most prominent philosophers in Oxford, and later one of Ludwig Wittgenstein's literary executors, and a devout Catholic—it is important to examine the nature of this debate in more detail. Lewis' case of the function of reason is in his book *Miracles*, where he presents an argument from reason for the existence of the supernatural.[15] Lewis saw the process of reasoning as an indication of something beyond our faculties that allows us to reason in the first place. He presented his argument as a case against naturalism. Lewis defined naturalism as the belief in an "ultimate Fact," or a "thing you can't get behind," that "is a vast process in space and time which is *going on of its own accord*. Inside that total system every particular event . . . happens because some other event has happened; in the long run, because the Total Event is happening."[16] So, "If Naturalism is true, then every finite thing or event must be (in principle) explicable in terms of the total system." If everything must be explained in terms of the whole system, then anything that exists that cannot be explained in terms of the whole system of naturalism could contradict the claims of naturalism: ". . . if any one thing makes good a claim to be on its own, to be something more than an expression of the character of Nature—then we have abandoned Naturalism."[17]

Lewis' "argument from reason" has been given much attention. Victor Reppert talks about an "Anscombe legend" that has arisen around Lewis' argument from reason. Lewis was president of the Oxford Socratic Club from 1942 to 1954. During this time he debated with many important thinkers about issues concerning the Christian faith. One such debate, on February 2, 1948, was with philosopher G. E. M. Anscombe. Anscombe rejected the argument given by Lewis in the third chapter of *Miracles*. Anscombe was herself a Roman Catholic, but found serious problems with Lewis' argument. A commonly held belief has been that Lewis was utterly devastated by his encounter with Anscombe and that he gave up and stopped producing apologetic work (and retreated into children's literature) because of this encounter.

Victor Reppert, a Lewis scholar and philosopher, insists that much biographical speculation has occurred in regards to this issue. Specifically, Reppert cites Humphrey Carpenter and A. N. Wilson.[18] While some believe that Lewis was so devastated by his encounter with Anscombe that he felt his apologetic arguments were abject failures and that he subsequently stopped writing apologetics for this reason, Reppert insists that neither of these assessments is entirely true,[19] and even if Lewis was initially upset we may ask, "Upset over what?" As Christopher Mitchell suggests,

> Anscombe's experience not withstanding, it does not seem possible to reduce the perceptions of Brewer and Sayer to mere "projection." Lewis was clearly troubled. But the question is over what? Sayer's recollection of Lewis' struggle strikes to the heart

of the matter. When Lewis told Sayer that his defeat was a serious matter, he said it was because in the minds of many people, "the disproof of an argument for the existence of God tended to be regarded as a disproof of the existence of God." At the center of Lewis' struggle, was a concern for the faith of the Christians he represented. He could live with the fact that he had been bested; but he continued to struggle with the implications his defeat may have had for the faith of others.[20]

Additionally, John Beversluis, a Lewis critic who once used the Anscombe legend as a means to discredit Lewis' argument, acknowledges the overblown status of the Anscombe encounter.[21] Lewis clearly did not stop writing argumentative works. He revised *Miracles* in 1960, from which the argument debated with Anscombe arose, to deal with Anscombe's criticisms, and he published articles dealing with other philosophical issues. The idea that Lewis gave up on reasoned work is also betrayed not least by his use of reasoning (and argument) within his fictive works. In addition, Lewis continued to hold to his beliefs on this issue of reason and naturalism.[22] Another commonly overlooked fact is Lewis' continuation as the Socratic Club president. As president, Lewis continued (until 1954, when he moved to Cambridge) to participate in the debates held by the club—hardly the act of someone in retreat from reasoned discourse.

Furthermore, Anscombe did not remember a devastating encounter with Lewis: she acknowledged Lewis' revisions, and the depth of those revisions, while still seeing elements to question. Anscombe recounted the debate as follows:

> The fact that Lewis rewrote that chapter, and rewrote it so that it now has those qualities, shows his honesty and seriousness. The meeting of the Socratic Club at which I read my paper has been described by several of his friends as a horrible and shocking experience which upset him very much. Neither Dr. Havard (who had Lewis and me to dinner a few weeks later) nor Professor Jack Bennet remembered any such feelings on Lewis's part.... My own recollection is that it was an occasion of sober discussion of certain quite definite criticisms, which Lewis's rethinking and rewriting showed he thought was accurate. I am inclined to construe the odd accounts of the matter by some of his friends—who seem not to have been interested in the actual arguments of the subject-matter—as an interesting example of the phenomenon called projection.[23]

While Lewis did revise his argument, Reppert does believe that Lewis "dropped out of the game" (borrowing Austin Farrer's phrase) to some degree. Reppert argues that Lewis felt somewhat ill-equipped to deal with the philosophy of his day. Lewis was not a professional philosopher, and did not keep up with the current trends of philosophical debate.[24] During the 1940s and 50s, logical positivism was a prominent philosophical movement. Unlike professional philosophers who write journal articles and deal with current trends in philosophy, Lewis did not "develop a detailed response to logical positivism, or to Wittgenstein's philosophy, or to other current developments, and so one could say with Austin Farrer that he 'dropped out of the game.'"[25] Lewis was not a professional philosopher in this sense, but avenues of response are available to Lewis' line of thought that might help defend it against modern criticisms.[26] However, in a general sense, Lewis' response is also found in his fictive works, where the imagination makes its own case through argument and image. Lewis' fiction, particularly the Chronicles of Narnia, might be seen as Lewis' *Summa*: while Aquinas "articulated his entire worldview and philosophy of life in his weighty and laborious *Summa Theologica*," Lewis can be seen as offering his "*Summa* in the sprightly and spontaneous chronicles."[27] We must be careful here too, for there is certainly much to be wary about in any account of an author's intentions and motivations. At most, here, I am advocating some restraint—a sense of the middle ground. The case has often been made, on both sides of this argument, in a rather extreme fashion (though the balance has tilted towards accounts of it affecting Lewis dramatically). We should not come to the conclusion that Lewis' encounter with Anscombe was the only (or even the overriding) factor in his imaginative work, but neither should we view it as simply another blip along his path. As Michael Ward has argued in *Planet Narnia: The Seven Heavens in the Imagination of C. S. Lewis*, Lewis did not simply retreat into romance from apologetics; his romance makes its own case in imaginative form.[28] Although, Ward makes the case that Lewis' first chronicle is a form of direct response to Anscombe's criticisms,[29] which has not been forwarded with the same vigor in these pages. What Ward calls the "problem of occasion" (i.e., the question of why Lewis wrote his fairy tales for children) I see slightly differently than he does. Of course, the Chronicles of Narnia are an imaginative response to criticisms of various kinds, but I do not think we can attribute to the Anscombe debate the sole reason of motivation in composition of his children's tales. Lewis himself gives no such indication explicitly, and his view of his own imaginative processes, as noted by Ward himself, lends itself to a much more murky tale of origins:

> However, [Lewis'] comment about not being "quite sure" what motivated him to write... need not mean he was entirely unsure; a lack of complete certainty is different from a complete lack of certainty. Likewise with the argument I am about to make. Since Lewis was fond of pointing out that human life exceeds Contemplative awareness... we should not be surprised that he does not claim total understanding of his own creative processes.[30]

To borrow Ward's phrasing, it is likewise with the argument I am making here: we need not assert from that fact that Lewis was unsure about his motivation that he was therefore completely (psychologically) motivated to respond to Anscombe.

It is also clear that others viewed the debate between Lewis and Anscombe in a different light than utter failure by Lewis or psychological reactionism.[31] It is interesting to note that a second debate took place sometime around February 2, 1967, with Anscombe taking her original position and philosopher John Lucas taking Lewis' position. Basil Mitchell (the succeeding president of the Socratic Club after Lewis) notes that Lewis' position had been successfully sustained by John Lucas.[32] At the very least, it seems that Lewis' points may be defendable and not simply and hopelessly "wrong."[33] Other modern philosophers have also used a version of Lewis' argument to make a case against physical determinism, e.g., James Jordan, William Hasker, Richard Purtill, J. P. Moreland, Alvin Plantinga, and Victor Reppert.[34] In Reppert's version of the argument, he suggests that we view Lewis' argument as an argument from rational inference. Reppert argues that Lewis' argument assumes that we do not start by doubting reasoning. Instead, we presuppose that there is such a thing as reasoning. Lewis' argument points to the fact that the problem with reasoning (in its rationalist, materialist form) occurs when we try to reconcile our ability to reason with materialism.[35]

While I am clearly not alone in questioning the emphasis placed on the Anscombe debate, there is a theme that has gone unnoticed by Lewis commentators, and it is just this theme that I am trying stress in this book: there is premodern, pre-Enlightenment emphasis in Lewis' thought about the relation of reason and imagination. Lewis' argument from reason demonstrates this premodern, pre-Enlightenment focus:

the phenomenologically given is not the stopping point. Lewis saw reason as suggesting something other than itself—implicitly referencing a meaning or reality beyond the mere occurrence of rationality. For Lewis, the materialist view leads ultimately to nihilism because the materialist or naturalist position makes the cosmos one-dimensional, *only* material. Once we have done this, once we have separated the immanent from the transcendent, a curious thing happens: we lose the immanent by jettisoning the transcendent. When we separate the created order from the Creator we have lost ourselves in nothingness; creation is nothing without participation in transcendence. And even here we see the curious wording (viz., that creation *is* nothing): to say that creation is nothing, to give the nothing an *is*-ness, to appeal to creation without transcendence, we lose our ability to say or recognize any significance of such a statement—without God, without transcendence, the utterance becomes incoherent.[36] We have, in the materialist or naturalist position, taken created things as "independent realities. But these 'nothings-in-themselves' were also unhooked from the something (or someone) that granted them being. Thus, the 'logic of nihilism' . . . is 'a sundering of the something, rendering it nothing, and then having the nothing be after all *as* something.'"[37] The ontology of nihilism lends itself to this inherent contradiction, as Lewis points out in his "argument from reason." Ultimately, materialism or naturalism "denies the depth of things, shutting us up in a suffocating immanance."[38] Lewis' argument here is not forwarded as a rationalistic, universally acceptable proof. Rather, it is largely a rejection of the notion of rationality as an independent reality with no transcendent funding. There is larger reality that undergirds the ability to think: it is theologically grounded in divine participation, the notion that because God is, I am able to be and do. Again, Michael Ward hints at something similar: "Lewis's central point in *Miracles* (in both the first and second editions) was that if the human mind gives access to truth about the world it must be because our thinking is not merely cerebral biochemistry, not simply a process going on inside our own heads, but a participation in a cosmic *logos*."[39] We share in a supernatural Reason that funds our ability to think at all. And although our reason "is dependent on Divine Reason, the two are distinct: 'human thought is not God's but God-kindled.' Whereas Descartes famously concluded, 'I think, therefore I am,' we might sum up Lewis's position with the dictum: 'I AM, therefore *I* think.'"[40]

Limits of Rationalism

Many have claimed that Lewis' arguments were forwarded as conclusive proofs, to be viewed from a strong rationalist position.[41] As a young man, Lewis did study under W. T. Kirkpatrick, the "epitome of nineteenth-century rationalism," but "while [Kirkpatrick] greatly assisted Lewis's ability to think clearly, Lewis came to reject [Kirkpatrick's] rationalism."[42] There is also an implicit reference to the inherent problem of unbiased rationalism or reason—namely, the assertion of a "universal," "secular" reason recognized to be unbiased and uncommitted. There was clearly a place for reason in Lewis' thought, but he thought that it was possible to make a role for reason without claiming a rationalist philosophy; rejecting rationalism does not mean that one needs to reject rationality.[43] Consequently, Lewis thought "that there was enough evidence for Christ to lead to the psychological exclusion of doubt, but not the logical exclusion of dispute."[44] However, Lewis is often accused of putting forward his arguments as if they are the last word on the subject. For example, "My complaint about the Broadcast Talks is not that Lewis fails to be as thorough as his subject matter demands, but that he gives the impression of being thorough."[45] But is this really the case? Does Lewis present his arguments as the last and final word?

As early as 1926, Lewis was pushing the idea of imagination and warning against the spellbinding powers of the merely "rational." In a letter to his friend Cecil Harwood, in which Lewis is rejecting the anthroposophy Harwood accepted, Lewis had this to say:

> About powers other than reason—I would be sorry if you mistook my position. No one is more convinced than I that reason is utterly inadequate to the richness and spirituality of real things: indeed this is itself a deliverance of reason. Nor do I doubt the presence, even in us, of faculties embryonic or atrophied, that lie in an indefinite margin around the little finite bit of focus which is intelligence—faculties anticipating or remembering the possession of huge tracts of reality that slip through the meshes of the intellect. And so, to be sure, I believe that the symbols presented by the imagination at its height are the workings of that fringe and present to us as much of the super-intelligible reality as we can get while we retain our present form of consciousness.[46]

Imagination and reason are intertwined in a fundamental way: they are different expressions of a single divine source of truth. But with the work of the imagination there is an ability to grasp truths that might otherwise be unintelligible.[47] In this affective side of human knowledge there is a reason "more profound and prior to rationality."[48] Implicitly, then, "pure reason" is non-existent. Indeed, reason itself suggests a "space" that must be filled in—between the gaps of foundational shortcomings, the initialization of ideas and concepts, the passage from idea-to-idea, inferential leaps, jumping out from the known to the unknown, to the possible. We can also see, in the above quote, Lewis's debt to Platonic thought, especially the idea of the Forms and of learning as remembering or anamnesis.[49] There is a Platonic desire, a longing that connects the imagination to reason: to know we must have the desire gifted through transcendence. Lewis continued:

> My skepticism begins when people offer me explicit accounts of the super-intelligible and in so doing use all the categories of the intellect. If the higher worlds have to be represented in terms of number, subject-and-attribute, time, space, causation etc (and thus they nearly always are represented by occultists and illuminati), the fact that knowledge of them had to come through the fringe remains inexplicable. It is more natural to suppose in such cases that the illuminati have done what all of us are tempted to do: —allowed their intellect to fasten on those hints that come from the fringe, and squeezing them, has made a hint (that was full of truth) into a mere false hard statement. Seeking to know (in the only way we can know) more, we know less. I, at any rate, am at present inclined to believe that we must be content to feel the highest truths "in our bones": if we try to make them explicit, we really make them untruth.[50]

The magnificence of sublime transcendence is communicated through the imagination, which for Lewis consists in the soul. The longing we feel at the "fringe" is, at best, the suggestion of something "other" and certainly something more. When we merely rationalize the sublime, we limit ("squeeze") our reception of its reality, its genuineness and its veracity. We are tempted to take the knowledge we might gain from spiritual matters and run with them—making them "hard statements." Our reason can squeeze these moments (that are better grasped by the imaginative and intuitive aspects of our minds) into supposed "bare facts." However, this was clearly not Lewis' intention with argumentation. In *Mere Christianity*, a book that is often cited as a place were Lewis makes his most triumphalistic claims, he wrote in the preface that

> ... in this book I am not trying to convert anyone to my own position. Ever since I became a Christian I have thought that the best, perhaps the only, service I could do for my unbelieving neighbors was to explain and defend the belief that has been common to nearly all Christians at all times.[51]

And again Lewis wrote in *Mere Christianity* that he was "not asking anyone to accept Christianity if his best reasoning tells him that the weight of the evidence is against it."[52] Lewis realized that argument, in this sense, would only take us so far.[53] It is also an indication that "secular" reason, far from being unbiased, uncommitted, and neutral, is itself a theology or anti-theology "in disguise," and is committed to "religious" assumptions that are no more justifiable than Christian positions.[54] The secular must itself be "instituted or *imagined*, both in theory and in practice . . . [The 'secular' as an autonomous object] was not . . . simply 'uncovered.' The space of the secular had to be invented. . . . However, this invention was itself . . . a theological achievement . . ."[55] This "achievement" lies in the secular attempt to unhook the immanent from the transcendent, while at the same time appealing to an implicit transcendent *telos* or meaning.

Lewis noted that our moods change and our reason will often follow them, and "often a person's emotional issues must be addressed before the person can sustain commitment to Christ."[56] And this is just where the imagination can play an explicit role: narrative just might open us up for this commitment.[57] The relationship between reason and imagination cannot be separated so easily. The faculty of imagination was and is a "power that philosophy never quite succeeded in fully appropriating or domesticating. Drawing upon this power, putting it in service to the highest interests, philosophy was always compelled also to exclude imagination . . ."[58] Although, it has never succeeded in doing so. Imagination has always had a pull over philosophy, "countering it precisely in driving it on . . ."[59]

In a letter to Sheldon Vanauken, Lewis had this to say about "proofs of Christianity:

> I do not think there is a *demonstrative* proof (like Euclid) of Christianity, nor of the existence of matter, nor of the good will & honesty of my best & oldest friends. I think all three are (except perhaps the second) far more probable than the alternatives. The case for Xtianity in general is well given by Chesterton; and I tried to do something in my *Broadcast Talks*.[60]

Lewis acknowledged that honest and intelligent people can and do come to different, reasonable conclusions about Christianity, and that the "strong believers or disbelievers of course think they have very strong evidence" so there "is no need to suppose stark unreason on either side."[61] In discussing the moral law in his book *The Abolition of Man*, Lewis gives examples of the moral *Tao* from sources culled from around the world. Lewis maintains that he is making "no pretense of completeness," and that the collection of sources is not an attempt to prove the validity of the *Tao* by argument from common consent: "Its validity cannot be deduced. For those who do not perceive its rationality, even universal consent could not prove it."[62] There are reasons to believe and there are reasons not to believe.[63] However, Lewis is still more often than not considered to be a triumphalistic rationalist. It is true that Lewis used strong language sometimes when describing his opponents' views. For example, he stated that atheism is "too easy" or that it is a "boy's philosophy."[64] Lewis was arguing against contrary viewpoints that used just as strong language (if not more so) to denigrate Christianity and its followers. However, Lewis was

> not infrequently accused of lacking charity, or of giving in to the temptation to bang those stupid unbelievers over the head, or of a lack of sympathy and compassion for his opponents, or of smug self-righteousness about his own viewpoint. Part of that tendency must be seen in the light of his deliberate forensic effort to puncture the balloon of non-Christian pomposity and deflate the superiority complex of contemporary naturalism.[65]

A closer look at his work reveals a man who was immensely interested in matters of reason and argument, but who was by no means a strict rationalist who thought that his arguments (let alone arguments in general) could be said to have the last and final word or be said to be universally recognized, unbiased, or uncommitted. In an essay entitled "Rejoinder to Dr. Pittenger," where Lewis is dealing with attacks against multiple works of his, he freely admits some of his mistakes.[66] But he also defends his viewpoints. At the end of this essay he wrote that when he began his defense of the Christian faith

> Christianity came before the great mass of my unbelieving fellow-countrymen either in the highly emotional form offered by revivalists or in the unintelligible language of highly cultured clergymen. Most men were reached by neither. My task was

therefore simply that of a *translator*—one turning Christian doctrine, or what he believed to be such, into the vernacular, into the language that unscholarly people would attend to and understand . . . I may have made theological errors. My manner may have been defective. Others may do better hereafter. I am ready, if young enough, to learn.[67]

Lewis was willing to admit his limitations, but he also thought that Christianity could and should be defended—even if its absolute rational certainty could not be established for all. We might say that Lewis "perhaps realized the truth of Charles Williams's maxim, 'No-one can possibly do more than decide what to believe.'"[68] That is, we must find which rationality is compelling for us.

Which Rationality?

Lewis understood the problems of argument and its limitations—as well as problems with notions of "pure reason." Lewis' position might be compared to critical rationalism, where a philosophical position can be a defendable one even if the argument is not convincing to everyone. Critical rationalism "does not require that an argument be convincing to everyone to hold that it provides justificatory evidence."[69] Victor Reppert, in *C. S. Lewis' Dangerous Idea*, argues just such a case; he directly compares Lewis' views to that of critical rationalism.

In the text *Reason and Religious Belief*, Peterson, Hasker, Reichenbach, and Basinger distinguish three modes of relationship between faith and reason. They are strong rationalism, fideism, and critical rationalism. Strong rationalism is "the position which holds that *in order for a religious belief-system to be properly and rationally accepted, it must be possible to prove that the belief-system is true*."[70] It is the position that relies upon a rationalist paradigm to decide matters of beliefs and actions. Fideists can be said to hold the view that *"religious belief-systems are not subject to rational evaluation."*[71] In this view we do not rely on reasoning or evidence to inform us about our religious beliefs. The third view put forward, critical rationalism, is the view that *"religious belief-systems can and must be rationally criticized and evaluated although conclusive proof of such a system is impossible."*[72] So, like strong rationalism, critical rationalism impels us to use our reasoning faculties, "to the greatest extent possible, in assessing religious beliefs."[73] We must make the best case we can for our beliefs, and we might then compare this with other belief systems. We can also engage in the objections that are brought against our belief systems (and we might also engage in elements of religious belief that do not involve argument). We can do all of these things, but we must not become overconfident in our assessments and conclusions. This view does not mean, however, that there is no such thing as truth, or that we can never find truth. In this view one attempts to avoid the quagmire of relativism by adhering to the notion that we do not *create* truth for ourselves, but instead we all must *seek* the truth for ourselves. Furthermore, critical rationalism does not hinder the commitment of faith as truth. And while it may be true that people who evaluate faith through arguments might go on forever in this way, they do not necessarily need to do so. It is perfectly reasonable in the critical rationalist view to have this open-ended inquiry alongside the commitment of faith.

Critical rationalism holds that there are different standards of rationality in different groups. This view is similar to Alisdair MacIntyre's notion of competing rationalities, and his account of rationality adds to my discussion of rationalistic argument and supposed rational certainty. MacIntyre notes that when we attempt to discover standards of rationality we will find conflicting accounts. What one group or theory counts as true, or rational, another group or theory will see as flawed. We see this demonstrated clearly in arguments of significance—for example, utilitarians will find a rationality that deontologists will see as deeply flawed.[74] There is a false sense of consensus that becomes exposed when a complex issue shatters the illusion of a common practical rationality: "... the expression of radical disagreement is institutionalized in such a way as to abstract that single issue from those background contexts of different and incompatible beliefs from which such disagreements arise."[75] The fundamental disagreements we find ourselves embroiled in are extremely difficult to solve because not only do we disagree about the problem at hand, but we also disagree about questions of framing.

MacIntyre asks us to consider rationality as abstracted from our particularities:

> Rationality requires, so it has been argued ... that we first divest ourselves of allegiance to any one of the contending theories and also abstract ourselves from all those particularities of social relationship in terms of which we have been accustomed to understand our responsibilities and interests. Only by so doing, it has

been suggested, shall we arrive at a genuinely neutral, impartial, and, in this way, universal point of view, freed from the partisanship and the partiality and onesidedness that otherwise affect us. And only by so doing shall we be able to evaluate the contending accounts of justice rationally.[76]

But what we find when we attempt to do this is more disagreement. First, there will be disagreement about which conception of justice is to be accounted as rationally acceptable. Second, there is the fundamental disagreement about framing: there is an implicit requirement to be disinterested, and this disinterestedness is itself an account of justice; this account, then, ignores the historically and socially conditioned context of its (and any other account's) character.[77] When we decide to approach a problem one way as opposed to another we are tacitly biasing the answers of the question of how to proceed.[78] Additionally, the laws of logic may be necessary to rationality, but they are not a sufficient condition for rationality: if, as Aristotle argued, "no one who understands the laws of logic can remain rational while rejecting them," it still remains to be seen what has been "added to observance of the laws of logic to justify ascriptions."[79] These resources may help to redefine and refine disagreements, but they "do not themselves seem to resolve the problems of those confronting the rival claims upon their allegiance . . ."[80]

This state of affairs may incline us towards fideism. The cynicism of Western culture towards the power of rational argument has created a number of adherents, if not always an explicit group of adherents.[81] This predisposition may be "because of a strong and sometimes justified suspicion" that those who wield arguments are not so much convinced of their positions on the grounds of their rationality, but "because by appealing to argument they are able to exercise a kind of power which favors their own interests and privileges . . ."[82] Arguments in this sense are seen as "weapons," not "expressions of rationality."[83]

MacIntyre claims that our current state of affairs (namely, the "inability to arrive at agreed justifiable conclusions on the nature of justice and practical rationality" and the coexistent "appeals by contending social groups to sets of rival and conflicting convictions unsupported by rational justification") arose chiefly as a result of the Enlightenment.[84] This can be seen in two ways: first, in the aspiration to set up standard public methods and practices of rational discourse and enquiry. Thus, reason could "displace authority and tradition."[85] Appealing to rational justification was seen, in essence, as appealing to undeniable principles (as a result, social and cultural particulars could be seen as "accidental clothing" of pure reason)—undeniable principles set up by the very people judging what could be considered as such (viz., the educated peoples of post-Enlightenment cultural and social institutions). However, the Enlightenment did not provide an agreed definition of said undeniable rational principles: Rousseau said one thing, Bentham another, Kant yet another. That is, the Enlightenment project, the attempt to set up agreed-upon rational principles, could not be achieved by its own adherents.

The second way in which the Enlightenment contributed to the current state of affairs is in its exclusion of other resources. However, it is important not to fall into a set-trap, "by, perhaps inadvertently, continuing to accept the standards of the Enlightenment."[86] The adherents themselves could not accomplish their own task, so we must not expect that those standards can be met.[87] Any competing view will be seen as just one more view unable to prove itself against its own principles, and will be seen as rationally unacceptable from an Enlightenment vantage point. The Enlightenment has thus deprived us of a rational enquiry based in tradition. It deprived us of a means by which we might judge the standards of rationality in terms of a tradition's history, as well as a means for conceptualizing standards of rational justification by means of a tradition's ability to "transcend the limitation of and provide remedies for the defects of their predecessors within the history of that same tradition."[88] However, not all traditions have an internal notion of rational justification inherent in their makeup, and, as such, MacIntyre argues that Enlightenment thinkers were right to dismiss certain traditions that rejected this internal rational justification.

MacIntyre insists that the idea of rational inquiry which is inseparable from intellectual and social tradition is likely to be misunderstood. He gives four ways of combating possible misunderstandings. First, tradition-constituted enquiry is essentially historical. That is, we justify by narrating "how the argument has gone so far. . . . [What] justifies the first principles themselves, or rather the whole structure of theory of which they are a part, is the rational superiority of that particular structure to all previous attempts within that particular tradition . . ."[89] There is to be no question that the argument is somehow to appeal to "all rational persons." Second, the way in which rational justification is conceived in traditions is very different from an Enlightenment paradigm.

An Enlightenment paradigm sees contending viewpoints as somehow ahistorical: that is, they are "rival doctrines, doctrines which may as a matter of fact have been elaborated in particular times and places, but whose content and whose truth or falsity, whose possession or lack of rational justification, is quite independent of their historical origin."[90] Contrary to this, tradition-constituted enquiry would hold that doctrinal claims are evaluated upon precise articulations of formation: e.g., its linguistic, historical, and spatial particularities. In a real sense, then, cultural-historical context is key: the arguments may appear again in different times and places, and the claims of truth being made may in fact be of a timeless nature, but the claims are being made in a time period—and even "the concept of timelessness is itself a concept with a history."[91]

The concept of rationality itself has a history, and "since there are a diversity of traditions of enquiry, with histories, there are . . . rationalities rather than rationality . . ."[92] This brings us to our third possible misunderstanding. An Enlightenment paradigm will undoubtedly have at its core an argument to combat notions of tradition-constituted rational enquiry. That is, Enlightenment thinkers will most likely say,

> You reproach us . . . with an inability to resolve the disagreements between rival claims concerning principles to which any rational person must assent. But you are instead going to confront us with a diversity of traditions, each with its own specific mode of rational justification. And surely the consequence must be a like inability to resolve radical disagreement.[93]

MacIntyre notes we might reply that an understanding of the diversity of traditions and an explanation of the diversity of standpoints arises as a result of tradition-constituted enquiry, and the tradition-based explanation is a better one than the Enlightenment can provide. For even though the diversity of answers is not immediately solved, tradition-constituted enquiry is more amenable to possible solutions—more so than the Enlightenment paradigm, which seeks to suppress other viewpoints through a once-for-all account of what it is to be rational; it stifles the possibility for compromise, deliberation and mutual understanding.[94] The mere fact that there are different answers does not mean that these differences cannot be resolved in rational ways. The possibility remains open for resolution.

However, MacIntyre's last caveat warns that tradition-constituted rational enquiry cannot be explained without reference to their specific exemplifications. That is, even though some traditions may have interpenetrated each other they each exhibit a unique account (e.g., of justice, relationships), and each displays different patterns of development which must be discerned.[95]

This Enlightenment program of rational enquiry laid out by MacIntyre (i.e., unbiased, universally accepted rational principles) is clearly at odds with Lewis' own notions of reason: it is seen not least in Lewis' perception that our answers to questions and our framing of questions will depend upon what philosophy we bring with us. What remains to be seen is Lewis' own specific program in his imaginative and explicitly argumentative works. Far from trying to set up irrefutable, universally accepted arguments, Lewis' position might be best seen in light of Platonic persuasion. Lewis was steeped in the Platonic corpus, and it is no secrete that his debt to Plato is immense. From Lewis' line in *The Last Battle* that "It's all in Plato,"[96] it is no fanciful leap to see that Lewis' approach to reason would undoubtedly be influenced by Plato's works.

Plato and Persuasion

In the *Phaedrus*, Plato places Socrates out in the country, away from his familiar city, alone with his friend Phaedrus. In this dialogue, Socrates attempts to inspire Phaedrus into a love of truth. In order to understand truth we must exercise attention and patience. We construct our arguments and our words carefully, but with the ever-present understanding that the words are resemblances of the Real, suggesting and pointing to Reality. The whole of rhetorical art, then, is a way of "directing the soul by means of speech . . ." and through this rhetorical process one can lead others on to truth (or untruth): "And won't whoever does this artfully make the same thing appear to the same people sometimes just and sometimes, when he prefers, unjust?"[97] We select our words to appeal to certain souls, so as to draw them on towards the truth:

> Since the nature of speech is in fact to direct the soul, whoever intends to be a rhetorician must know how many kinds of souls there are. . . . Those distinctions established, there are, in turn, so-and-so many kinds of speech, each of such-and-such a sort. People

> of such-and-such a character are easy to persuade by speeches of such-and-such a sort in connection with such-and-such an issue for this particular reason, while people of such-and-such another sort are difficult to persuade for those particular reasons.[98]

The orator, or as it were the writer, must learn this art, develop his or her ability to communicate through various means in order to persuade others to the life of truth. The task of finding out which speeches will persuade which people is a very difficult one indeed, nearly impossible.[99] But this is why we must "turn all our arguments every which way and try to find some easier and shorter route to the art . . ."[100] It is not difficult to see Lewis' varied writing activities—his argumentative works, literature, children's fiction, science fiction, literary criticism, theology, philosophy, etc.—in light of Platonic persuasion: as his attempt to "turn our arguments every which way." But what makes a good writer and what makes an inept one? Plato begins by having Socrates enumerate the shortcomings of writing: writing is lifeless and has no means by which to defend itself. There is no lack of Socratic irony occurring here: for here we have, written in words, Socrates warning us that writing, like painting, is not alive—contrary to what is happening to us as we read this dialogue—"You'd think they were speaking as if they had some understanding, but if you question anything that has been said because you want to learn more, it continues to signify just that very same thing forever."[101] Once we have written something down, we lose the ability to control its influence and audience:

> . . . every discourse roams about everywhere, reaching indiscriminately those with understanding no less than those who have no business with it, and it doesn't know to whom it should speak and to whom it should not. And when it is faulted and attacked unfairly, it always needs its father's support; alone, it can neither defend itself nor come to its own support.[102]

We seemingly have here a kind of apologetic for Plato's own dialogues: we presume that these risks are worth taking simply because we see Plato has undertaken the task himself. But of course we find in our reading of *Phaedrus*, and our reading in general, that not all of this is so: there are a variety of meanings that come out of repeating readings and out of various corners of thought—not to mention the thought of others. Plato offers a resolution:

> Socrates: Now tell me, can we discern another kind of discourse, a legitimate brother of this one? . . . It is a discourse that is written down, with knowledge, in the soul of the listener; it can defend itself, and it knows for whom it should speak and for whom it should remain silent.
>
> Phaedrus: You mean the living, breathing discourse of the man who knows, of which the written one can be fairly called an image.
>
> Socrates: Absolutely right.[103]

The writer sows his seeds, seeking to plant gardens for amusement, for reminding, and for those who want to follow in the writer's footsteps. The dialectician "chooses a proper soul and plants and sows within it discourse accompanied by knowledge—discourse capable of helping itself as well as the man who planted it, which is not barren but produces a seed from which more discourse grows in the character of others."[104] We use our writing artfully (ideally once we have learned sufficiently to communicate both in method and content) in order to teach or to persuade: "This is the whole point of the argument we have been making."[105]

Lewis' program falls clearly into Plato's notion of persuasion: there is not a sense that arguments are to appeal to "all rational people." Rather, we must discern the soul of our readers, patiently persuading, turning our arguments every which way, drawing them on towards the truth. However, to be drawn on towards the truth, and then to understanding, requires a belief that seeks understanding, such as St. Augustine proposed. But this proposed uniting of reason and faith is contrary to notions of faith as "imaginary" (i.e., believing in unreal things) and reason as universally accepted knowledge. For Augustine, this implies a priority to faith: that is, reason works on what is delivered; there is a faith upon which reason works, so that the two are always intertwined, and likewise, there is always an imagination upon which and through which reason works.

Augustine and Faith

It is not difficult to see that Augustine's concept of rationality differs significantly from the Enlightenment paradigm. The Enlightenment paradigm would have us map out a separate, uncommitted, unbiased sphere where "pure reason" could guide us. As Alasdair MacIntyre has noted, and as we have highlighted in the previous section on MacIntyre, this program has failed to produce such a universally accepted rationality. Instead what we find are many rationalities—not a monolithic Rationality. Knowing for Augustine is a combination of reason and faith—a unification of reason and revelation. Nothing is known without the mediation of God's revelation. Rowan Williams notes that for Augustine even our self-knowledge is impossible without God's revelation: "There is nothing that can be said of the mind's relation to itself without the mediation of the revelation of God as its creator and lover."[106] And Lewis echoed Augustine when he wrote, "I believe in Christianity as I believe that the sun has risen. Not only because I see it, but because by it I see everything else."[107] It is only by God's revelation that we can come to see all things: there is transcendent funding to all areas of life, including reason.

Augustine defined true wisdom as piety.[108] Augustine insisted "on the need for rational appropriation of faith.... The goal of faith is to move beyond belief to sight or vision; faith 'endeavors by purity of life to attain unto sight, where the pure and perfect of heart know that unspeakable beauty, the full vision of which is supreme happiness.'"[109] We trust in our reliable source (God), our indispensable source of knowledge. We must believe to understand: "Unbelievers indeed may lack the power to contemplate God's image in them.... Then they had best believe what the holy Books contain concerning the supreme Trinity that is God, instead of demanding for themselves a perfectly clear and rational account such as weak and sluggish human minds cannot take in."[110] It is only after we have gained an "unshakable belief" in the authority of scriptural witness that we then can "go on by prayer and enquiry and right living to the pursuit of understanding—which means the seeing with the mind (so far as is possible) of what is firmly held by faith."[111]

It is faith alone that can assure us of "our capacity for immortality ... and this faith rests upon the Incarnation, Cross, and Resurrection of Christ."[112] This is a rescue from despair that is most fitting—it is the assurance of God's love, "the love for sinners who can have no merits that are not his gifts."[113] This assurance, this faith, rests on the historic incarnation and atonement and thus falls "within the sphere of knowledge rather than wisdom. But in the Word made flesh are the 'treasures of wisdom' as well as of 'knowledge': in Christ we move through the latter to the former."[114] There is thus a "trinity of faith": things are believed and held in the memory, are recalled to thought by the act of will, and are accepted and loved.[115] Once again, true wisdom is found in the worship of God.[116] True wisdom's object is the eternal and divine, "while knowledge is of the temporal and human."[117] However, faith has been treated as belonging to the sphere of knowledge, "so that the image of the Trinity to be discerned in faith must needs be a transient thing. The true image of God in the human mind must be permanent and unchanging, even though it be temporarily defaced."[118]

Love is "the motive of seeking."[119] We must be patient as we enquire, and such an enquiry "deserves no censure, provided that our search for what must baffle knowledge and expression be made in unshaken faith."[120] We seek God always and we shall find. As St. Paul writes, we are known of God—we do not know God. We are called to reach out to the "things which are before" and "forget the things which are behind": "By perfection in this life [St. Paul] understands nothing but to forget the things which are behind, and to reach out intently after the things which are before.... The intent is rightly directed only if it set out from faith."[121] Our surest route to the beginning of knowledge is to secure a firm faith. However, sure knowledge will not be found in this life, not "till after this life when we shall see face to face."[122] The idea that we must first believe before we can see is not just for the religiously faithful. We must always create the space, imagine the world we see.

Augustine's inclusion of faith in knowledge is decidedly against the bifurcation of reason and faith given to us by the Enlightenment. It might be said that the oft-used Augustinian maxim "believe so that you might understand" is turned on its head: that is, faith is based on reason, not reason based on faith. The turn of the phrase is also often used to separate (and elevate) other theologians from Augustine. For example, it is often the case that Augustine's unification of faith and reason is seen in stark contrast to Aquinas' separation of faith and reason. But is this the case? Can we not see Aquinas in the light of this Augustinian tradition?

Aquinas and Reason

Of course, in general, there have been numerous critiques given against the general use of rational argument in Christian theology. Pascal's famous caveat comes directly to mind: the heart has reasons of which reason knows not.[123] In this tradition, Christian theology should affirm as equal—if not as primary—the role of other human faculties than just "pure" intellect.[124] We must keep in check our common penchant to subvert everything to the intellect and thus to give it a special privilege. That is, we must affirm other modes of knowing, especially the senses and the imagination.[125] Lewis might also be compared to Thomas Aquinas in his insistence that reason has its limitations and is given as divine illumination. To see Lewis as constructing a "reasoning beyond reason," it will be helpful also to follow Aquinas' lead (who follows Augustine's lead on epistemology[126]) on the role of reason and revelation in theology.

Aquinas was critical of the "doctrines and promises of the philosophers" and viewed their doctrines as

> severely constrained by the weakness of human reason. Before general audiences, Aquinas is reported to have said such things as that all the efforts of the philosophers were inadequate to understand the essence of a fly. In academic writings, whenever Aquinas argues for the appropriateness of God's revealing what might have been demonstrated, he insists on the weakness and fallibility of unaided human reason. He notes the same feelings in distinguishing the philosophical and theological bodies of knowledge about God.[127]

Of course, Aquinas did regard human reason as extremely valuable and necessary. However, the *sacra doctrina* is not deficient; our *understanding* of it is deficient and we need help in sorting out the *sacra doctrina*. We take comfort in reason, we work easily (as we are conditioned in this work) in the realm of reasoning and so our understanding of *sacra doctrina* needs assistance.[128] However, "God destines us for an end beyond the grasp of reason.... Now we have to recognize an end before we can stretch out and exert ourselves for it. Hence the necessity for our welfare that divine truths surpassing reason should be signified to us through divine revelation."[129]

Furthermore, there is to be no contradiction between faith and reason as a result of the assistance of reason to faith. Reason acts as a clarifying mechanism for our minds. However, where matters of reason can give adequate understanding we still need, even then, divine revelation to inform our understanding. So, "In this way, reason may be deployed 'for greater clarification of the things it [*sacra doctrina*] conveys.' So just as nature is at its most natural when perfected by grace, so human reason is *at its most rational* when it is engaged in clarifying and making manifest the implications of the message of *sacra doctrina*."[130] Rational truth about God can only be reached by a few and even then it can be riddled with mistakes.[131] Aquinas is not to be seen as a

> modern rationalist: he understood good reason to be an attentive reception, via the mediation of the senses and discursive operations, of the divine light of the *Logos*, in fundamental keeping (despite many scholarly denials) with the view of St Augustine. Finally, for Aquinas, good reason can only be such if implicitly it desires, and therefore mysteriously intimates in advance that which can only be received as a gift: namely the supernatural light of faith.[132]

The limits of reason are clearly articulated by Aquinas in his discussion of the comprehension of God's essence. Aquinas stated that "no created mind can attain the perfect sort of understanding that is intrinsically possible of God's essence."[133] A being like God (i.e., fully realized) cannot be known completely by a finite being, for God is infinite and thus can be infinitely understood.[134] It would also seem that God could not be comprehended, for to comprehend something means to contain that something, and something infinite cannot be contained in the finite.[135] However, Aquinas noted two different connotations for the word *comprehend*. The first sense is "to contain," which he rejected as inadequate. The second and broader connotation is to understand the term to mean "the opposite of letting something slip." Thus, we can hold onto God, preventing us from slipping away.[136] There is an intrinsic divide between our comprehension and understanding of God due to our finite natures. The problems of reaching God through reason are subject to this limitation (so are our other modes of understanding). Furthermore, our ultimate happiness cannot depend on our abilities to reason something out; it must rest in the knowledge of God, which is supernatural.[137] The human desire to know is not satisfied by theoretical knowledge alone; it must be assisted. For anything to be known it must be grounded in the divine: it must participate in the divine, or, rather, the divine must hold it up, suspend it, by participation. Our natural knowledge, for Aquinas, has its source in our senses, and our senses can extend only so far as they allow—namely, through the apprehension of sensible things.[138] It is thus that we can never really reach the knowledge of God's essence. We are *effects* of God (the primary cause), and the effects are not necessarily typical of their cause, and so knowing the cause of the effects does not lead one to knowing the causes in their entirety. The effects depend on a cause, and so we can know *that* something exists and that it belongs to the first cause. So, we can know about God as a first cause, as the primary cause of all things which is beyond all causes. Thus, we can know that creatures are related to God (i.e., God is the cause of them all) and that God is different from them (i.e., God is not created, not deficient, and is transcendent).[139] The undergirding principle is divine illumination and participation.

We can know through our reason "*that* a simple form is, even though [we] cannot attain to understanding *what* it is."[140] Furthermore, our reason can give us knowledge of God through images and effects. But knowledge of God's essence can be known only through the gift of grace, and thus belongs only to "the good."[141] Reason, however, belongs to all. Aquinas saw the knowledge of grace as giving us a deeper knowledge of God than the merely rational.[142] Our reason is deficient because it depends upon "images derived from the sensible world and the natural intellectual light by which we make abstract intelligible concepts from these images."[143] Human reason is helped by revelation in three ways: (1) "The light of grace strengthens the intellectual light"; (2) prophetic visions give us God-given images, which are preferable to human-made images, to express the divine; and (3) ". . . God has given us sensible signs and spoken words to show us something of the divine, as at the baptism of Christ when the Holy Spirit appeared in the form of a dove and the voice of the Father was heard saying, *This is my beloved Son*."[144] The images, signs, and words given by God are preferable those derived merely by the intellect of humankind, but they are all grounded in divine illumination and participation.[145]

Lewis and Aquinas share a sense of the limits, powers, and foundation of reason: reason, too, is a divine gift.[146] God "is the source from which all your reasoning power comes . . ."[147] Revelation can present to our "imagination something that has always baffled the intellect . . ."[148] Aquinas, too, stated,

> Although in this life revelation does not tell us what God is, and thus joins us to him as to an unknown, nevertheless it helps us to know him better in that we are shown more and greater works of his and are taught certain things about him that we could never have known through natural reason . . . The stronger our intellectual light the deeper the understanding we derive from images, whether these be received in a natural way from the senses or formed in the imagination by divine power . . .[149]

The immense power of the imagination also lies in its ability to deepen our understanding. The imagination can often, as Lewis would say, "steal past watchful dragons." In addition, the faculty of the imagination is a receiver of revelation and a motivational (and "gap-filling") foundation upon which our reasons are built. The recognition of a threshold between matter and spirit gives rise to the "mysterious alchemical point at which mind, in order to think at all, must produce its own shadowy sensations that must always be 'returned to' in order to complete a thought (*conversion ad phantasmata*)."[150] These "phantasms" are always at work, however secretly, in the way we "not only sense the world and all it includes, but necessarily and 'fantastically' sense it 'as something.'"[151] Both Lewis and Aquinas saw the power of reason as part of a whole—and it is thus that they might both say "that the intellect is [*one*] of the powers of the human soul."[152]

Notes

1. Lewis, "*De Descriptione Temporum*," 7.
2. Ibid., 9.
3. Zogby, "Triadic Patterns," 20. Tolkien, too, noted (after Lewis' death) this schism in Lewis. In a letter to Walter Hooper in 1966 Tolkien wrote, "I noticed, for the first time consciously, how dualistic Lewis' mind and imagination [were], though as a philosopher his reason entirely rejected this" (Tolkien, *Letters*, 371). Owen Barfield, for his part, thought that Lewis' shift in emphasis occurred during the 1930s and 40s, and that this shift was not necessarily connected with his conversion: ". . . . 'the great change that took place in [Lewis] between the years 1930 and 1940—a change that roughly coincided with his conversion . . . but which did not appear, and does not appear in retrospect, to be inevitably or even naturally connected with it'" (ibid., 451). It is true that Lewis' interest and struggle with imagination precedes his conversion, but this by no means divorces his conversion experience from this shift.
4. See Barfield, "On C. S. Lewis," 2.
5. Duriez, *Field Guide to Narnia*, 140.

Colin Duriez also notes that while some "have supposed that Lewis turned to writing children's stories because he had lost confidence in writing books that argued, often philosophically, for the Christian faith," this could not be "further from the truth. Writing for children is one of the most demanding of an author's tasks. The Narnian tales built on skills that Lewis had honed in writing earlier stories for grownups. . . . Therefore, in reading the stories we are reading not an author who has lost his way but one who has become so convinced of the way that he can effectively point its direction to a very large readership that unselfishly enjoys storytelling" (ibid., 11–12).

6. See Lewis, *Of Other Worlds*, 37. Lewis did focus on reasoning in his apologetic career, but he by no means abandoned the imaginative side of faith (as clearly evidenced by his poetry and fiction, such as the Space Trilogy). Furthermore, Lewis' imaginative

side shows up in his non-fiction work—as seen in his use of imagery, metaphor, analogy, and story in his more argumentative works. In 1946, in his essay "Modern Man and his Categories of Thought," Lewis speaks to this issue (while addressing evangelism) and notes that the "limitation of my own gifts has compelled me always to use a predominately intellectual approach. But I have also been present when an appeal of a much more emotional and also more 'pneumatic', kind has worked wonders on a modern audience. . . . But best of all is a team of two: one to deliver the preliminary intellectual barrage, and the other to follow up with a direct attack on the heart" (*Present Concerns*, 66). We can see here a major concern for Lewis and a possible explanation to his "dual" personality: i.e., his reasoning side and his imaginative side. Lewis saw the importance of both the head and the heart—and perhaps he found a way to be that "team of two" of which he spoke, by getting us to *look at* and to *look along* (to experience and participate) through the art of story.

7. Wilson, *C. S. Lewis*, 220.

8. Ibid., 214.

9. Ibid., 225

10. This statement was made by Derek Brewer, a friend of Lewis'; see "The Tutor: A Portrait," in Como, *C. S. Lewis*.

11. Carpenter, *Inklings*, 217.

12. According to John Beversluis, a Lewis critic, ". . . the myth that Lewis abandoned Christian apologetics overlooks several post-Anscombe articles, among these 'Is Theism Important?' (1952)—a discussion of Christianity and theism which touches on philosophical proofs for God's existence—and 'Obstinacy of Belief'—in which Lewis defends the rationality of belief in God in the face of apparently contrary evidence (*the* issue in philosophical theology during the late 1950s and early 1960s). It is rhetorically effective to announce that the post-Anscombe Lewis wrote no further books on Christian apologetics, but it is pure fiction. Even if it were true, what would this Argument from Abandoned Subjects prove? He wrote no further books on *Paradise Lost* or courtly love either" (quoted in Reppert, *C. S. Lewis' Dangerous Idea*, 18).

13. However, it should not be supposed that Lewis' imaginative works are to be seen as *formal* philosophical arguments for the Christian faith. Richard Purtill notes that ". . . those who think Lewis intended his fictional works as *arguments* for Christianity obviously have little idea of what argument is" (Purtill, *Lord of the Elves*, 137). But his fictive works do give their own imaginative case (yes, argument) for Christianity. They may not be "formal" arguments but they are imaginative arguments nonetheless. This is a form of reasoning that must be recognized as a special "imaginative reasoning." While Lewis' fictive works are not rationalistic syllogisms or proofs, they are reasoned work. In addition, even though proofs are not a part of imaginative writing in a formal sense, strict argument can and does appear in imaginative writing, "because an argument in real life, in a work of fantasy, or in a dream, can in each case be judged simply on its merits as an argument. Thus it is possible that a work of imagination should contain [formal] arguments worth considering" (ibid., 168).

14. Duriez, *Field Guide to Narnia*, 140. Additionally, in the final chapter of his thesis, "The Son and the Other Stars," now his popular book *Planet Narnia*, Michael Ward argues against Wilson's "retreat thesis" by suggesting that Lewis' turn to writing children's literature is an essential part of his response to Anscombe's criticisms of chapter 3 of his *Miracles*.

15. Much like the economist E. F. Schumacher, one might say Lewis saw, and even lived, the three stages of human development: "first was primitive religiosity, and then scientific realism. The third stage, which we are now entering, is the realization that there is something beyond fact and science. The problem, [Schumacher] explained, is that stage one and stage three look the same to those in stage two. Consequently, those in stage three are seen as having relapsed into magical thinking when, in reality, they have actually seen through the limitations of rationalism" (Inchausti, *Subversive Orthodoxy*, 113).

16. Lewis, *Miracles*, 6.

17. Ibid., 12.

18. For example, "Now it is important to see what is missing in this discussion: any treatment of what the arguments of Lewis and Anscombe actually were. Apparently Carpenter thinks he can draw the conclusion that Anscombe had shown Lewis's argument to be 'severely faulty' without analyzing the arguments themselves, simply based on biographical considerations.... In A.N. Wilson's biography, the Anscombe legend is pushed to extreme lengths: the incident's psychological impact explains Lewis's 'retreat' into children's fantasy (Narnia), the fact that a female witch offers skeptical arguments in the *Silver Chair* that nearly beguile the protagonists of that story, and the fact that Lewis enjoyed corresponding with American women . . ." (Reppert, *C. S. Lewis' Dangerous Idea*, 17).

19. It seems clear that Lewis did feel some emotion of the supposed defeat, for in "writing to Miss Aldwinkle in June 1950, he proposed a list of potential speakers for the next term's Socratic Club. Number four on the list was Miss Anscombe. 'I [should] press hard for no. 4,' he said, 'The lady is quite right to refute what she thinks bad theistic arguments, but does this not almost oblige her as a Christian to find good ones in their place: having obliterated me as an apologist, ought she not to succeed me?'" (Mitchell, "University Battles," 343–44).

20. Mitchell, "University Battles" (2007), 8.

21. Beversluis writes, "First, the Anscombe debate was by no means Lewis's first exposure to a professional philosopher: he lived among them all his adult life, read the Greats, and even taught philosophy. Second, it is simply untrue that the post-Anscombe Lewis abandoned Christian apologetics. In 1960 he published a second edition of *Miracles* in which he revised the third chapter and thereby replied to Anscombe. Third, most printed discussions of the debate, mine included, fail to mention that Anscombe herself complimented Lewis's revised argument on the grounds that it is deeper and far more serious than the original version. Finally, the myth that Lewis abandoned Christian apologetics overlooks several post-Anscombe articles . . . in which Lewis defends the rationality of belief in God in the face of apparently contrary evidence (*the* issue in philosophical theology during the late 1950s and early 1960s). It is rhetorically effective to announce that the post-Anscombe Lewis wrote no further books on Christian apologetics, but it is pure fiction" (quoted in Reppert, *C. S. Lewis' Dangerous Idea*, 18).

22. Starting on page 21 of *C. S. Lewis' Dangerous Idea*, Reppert gives an analysis of *A Grief Observed* to bolster this position.

23. Anscombe, *Metaphysics*, x.

24. "Part of the job of a professional philosopher is to be responsive to the major philosophical movements of one's time. When Lewis received his philosophical training, the philosophy of absolute idealism was a major player in the philosophical debate,

and anyone who wanted to do philosophy in that time would have to come to terms with absolute idealism. In a philosophy department today one can go through an entire Ph.D. program without ever having to come to terms with absolute idealism, except as part of a historical survey..." (Reppert, *C. S. Lewis' Dangerous Idea*, 19).

25. Ibid., 20.

26. Often, Lewis is criticized simply for not being a "professional" philosopher or theologian. However, it should go without saying that numerous influential ideas within these disciplines have not necessarily come from professional philosophers and theologians. Moreover, we do not even expect the professional philosophers to be able to anticipate, or even deal with, *every* criticism that may come against their views. This is one reason why there are modern philosophers who carry on developing or defending a philosopher's ideas against present concerns.

27. Downing, *Into the Wardrobe*, xvi.

28. Ward, *Planet Narnia*, 219.

29. See particularly ibid., 216–17.

30. Ibid., 215.

31. For one, Reppert cites J. R. Lucas: "'The received version should be treated with some caution: Professor Mitchell, who attended all the meetings of the Socratic Club at that time, has no memory of the encounter. Oxford legends often owe more to the attitudes of those who report them than to the facts which allegedly they report'" (Reppert, *C. S. Lewis' Dangerous Idea*, 16). Furthermore, Reppert recounts a story about Anscombe's husband, Peter Geach: "Ironically, Geach was married to the late Elizabeth Anscombe, who is famous for her critique of Lewis's version of the Argument from Reason. Interestingly enough, a well-known Anglo-American philosopher... once told me that he thought Geach agreed with Lewis, not his wife, in this controversy" (ibid., 45). Reppert also uses a quote from Geach that supports this claim: "'When we hear of some new attempt to explain reasoning or language or choice naturalistically, we ought to react as if we were told that someone had squared the circle or proved the square root of 2 to be rational. Only the mildest curiosity is in order—how well has the fallacy been concealed?'" (ibid., 45).

32. "'... I think it would be generally agreed, Lucas succeeded in sustaining Lewis' side of the argument. If one were to think in terms of winners or losers, I think maybe that Lucas was the winner on points.... Elizabeth and John agreed as to what the original Lewis-Anscombe debate had been about, and Lucas simply maintained that on the substantial issue Lewis was right and that, for the sort of reasons Lewis had put forward, a thoroughly naturalistic philosophy was logically incoherent. And the outcome of that debate was to make it perfectly clear that, at the very least, Lewis' original thesis was an entirely arguable philosophical thesis and as defensible as most philosophical theses are. So there was no warrant for supposing that in the original debate Lewis had been shown to be just hopelessly wrong'" (Walker and Patrick, eds., *Christian for all Christians*, 9–10).

33. Furthermore, to "say that this argument is open to objection, and those objections to answers, is simply to say that it is a philosophical argument. As Austin Farrer says, 'Philosophy is an evershifting, never-ending, public discussion'" (Purtill, *Lord of the Elves*, 175).

34. "James Jordan, 'Determinism's Dilemma,' *Review of Metaphysics* 23 (1969–1970): 48–66; William Hasker, 'The Transcendental Refutation of Determinism,' *Southern*

Journal of Philosophy 11 (1973): 175–83; *Metaphysics* . . . ; and 'Why the Physical Isn't Closed,' chapter 3 of *The Emergent Self* . . . " and also "Richard Purtill, *Reason to Believe* . . . pp. 44–46; J.P. Moreland, 'God and the Argument from Mind,' in *Scaling the Secular City* . . . pp. 77–105" and "Alvin Plantinga, *Warrant and Proper Function* . . . pp. 216–37. Plantinga acknowledges the similarity between his argument and Lewis's in the book's final footnote" (Reppert, *C. S. Lewis' Dangerous Idea*, 46).

35. While there are no doubt lines of defense a naturalist or materialist might take to defend against Lewis' argument, Reppert demonstrates how Lewis' argument might be defended, and he also demonstrates that Lewis' argument is not so easily dismissed as is commonly thought.

36. For example, Conor Cunningham notes that "Dostoyevsky writes in *The Brothers Karamazov* that if God does not exist *anything* is permitted. This certainly appears to be true. For it seems one cannot even register suffering without an appeal to transcendence; when it is said that there cannot be a God because there is suffering in the world, it might be argued that such a sentiment, although understandable, is incoherent. For without God there would not *be* any suffering. That is to say, it would be impossible to cognize such significance" (Cunningham, *Genealogy of Nihilism*, 248–49).

37. Smith, *Introducing Radical Orthodoxy*, 102.

38. Ibid., 103.

39. Ward, *Planet Narnia*, 217.

40. Ibid., 218.

41. Or, conversely, Lewis is often charged with being simplistic to a fault—e.g., his knowledge of the history and problems of theology as "compared to Barth . . . was slight, even simplistic" (Dorrien, "'Postmodern' Barth?" 5). It may be true that Lewis was not a professional theologian like Barth, but is it fair to say that his knowledge of these things is merely simplistic? Or that his knowledge of the history and problems of theology was slight? This may be due to a fundamental difference in purpose: Lewis thought that if one could not translate one's ideas into the vernacular, then one did not really understand the ideas one was trying to communicate. Furthermore, is simplicity (which can be quite beautiful) necessarily to be equated with dismissible, undemanding, or effortless? This seems a rather harsh statement, especially given that Lewis is often considered one of the most well-read persons of his time and is reported to have had a photographic memory of the books he had read. There are stories told that he would even play a sort of parlor trick in which he would ask students to pick random books from random shelves and read random lines, then he would continue quoting the paragraph from memory. He is also reported to have said to American Rhodes Scholar Robert Selig, "'The difficulty is that I remember everything I've ever read and bits pop up uninvited.' [Selig remarked] 'Surely not everything you've ever read, Mr. Lewis?' 'Yes, everything, Selig, even the most boring texts'" (Lindsley, *C. S. Lewis's Case for Christ*, 19–20).

42. Ibid., 83.

43. Ibid., 86.

44. Ibid., 83.

45. Beversluis, *Lewis and the Search*, 42.

46. Lewis, *Collected Letters*, 2:670–71.

47. Sadhu Sundar Singh's story "The Scholar" highlights this idea (i.e., the limitations of rationalistic reasoning) as well: "After his death, the soul of a German scholar

entered into the world of spirits. From a distance he saw the indescribable glory of heaven and the unending joy of those who dwell there. He was overwhelmed by what he saw, but his intellect and skepticism stood in his way and blocked his entrance to the realm of bliss. So he began to argue with himself: 'There can be no doubt that I see all this, but how can I be sure that it is real and not just a subconscious illusion? Let me apply the critical tests of science, logic, and philosophy; then we will see whether this apparent heaven really exists.' Now, the angels who dwelt in that place knew his thoughts and approached him, and one addressed him: 'Your intellect has warped your entire being. If you want to see the world of the spirit, you must look with spiritual eyes. You must apply spiritual insight, not the rational exercise of logic. Your science deals with material reality. In this realm, however, you can only apply the wisdom that arises from love and reverence. It is a pity that you do not take to heart the words of the Master: "Unless you change completely and become like a little child, you shall not enter the heavenly realm." Clearly you long to see spiritual truth. If you didn't—if your thoughts were only evil—you would not even see heaven from afar, as you do now. But until you tire of your folly and turn around, you will continue to wander the world, banging your philosophical head against reality. Only then will you gain true insight and be able to turn with joy to the light of God'" (Singh, *Essential Writings*, 111–12).

48. Ward, *Theology and Contemporary Critical Theory*, 121.

49. For example, as seen in Plato's *Meno* and *Phaedrus* dialogues. In *Meno* Plato attempts to demonstrate that learning is remembering. While discussing the matter with Menon, Socrates counters Menon's argument that humans cannot really attempt to find something out when they have no notion of what it is they are searching for—nor will they search for something they already know: "'Will you lay out before us a thing you don't know, and then try to find it? Or . . . how will you know this that which you did not know?'" (Plato, *Great Dialogues*, 41).

50. Lewis, *Collected Letters*, 2:671.

51. Lewis, *Mere Christianity*, vi.

52. Ibid., 108.

53. Even the Lewis critic John Beversluis notes that "although no one is likely to be argued into accepting Christianity, philosophical arguments can force people to face certain facts that prepare the way for accepting it. These arguments cannot establish religious conclusions, but they can establish conclusions that are relevant to religious belief and that make Christianity more plausible" (Beversluis, *Lewis and the Search*, 7). However, we must balance this statement with the assertion that the "secular" position is just as prerationally committed—i.e., no more justifiable or rational on the surface than the Christian positions.

54. Milbank, *Theology and Social Theory*, 3.

55. Ibid., 9–13.

56. Lindsley, *C. S. Lewis's Case for Christ*, 87.

57. As the writer Flannery O'Conner once wrote, the problem of getting people to accept imagination and mystery may be caused by the habituation of the "elimination of mystery" in teaching: "Not long ago a teacher told me that her best students feel that it is no longer necessary to write anything. She said they think that everything can be done with figures now, and that what can't be done with figures isn't worth doing. I think this is a natural belief for a generation that has been made to feel that the aim of learning is to eliminate mystery. For such people, fiction can be very disturbing, for the fiction

writer is concerned with mystery that is lived. He's concerned with ultimate mystery as we find it embodied in the concrete world of sense experience" (O'Conner, *Mystery and Manners*, 124–25).

58. Sallis, *Force of Imagination*, 43.

59. Ibid.

60. Quoted in Vanauken, *Severe Mercy*, 89. Pascal notes that the "metaphysical proofs of God are so far removed from man's reasoning, and so complicated, that they have little force. When they do help some people it is only at the moment when they see the demonstration. An hour later they are afraid of having made a mistake" (Pascal, *Pensees*, 63). Pascal highlights the transient nature of our moods in regards to proofs and also gives a clue to the gift of faith content and the conditional ground for it—the divine presence (gift) must be within the receiver to grasp it.

61. Lewis, *World's Last Night*, 20–21.

62. Lewis, *Abolition of Man*, 95.

63. Lewis stated, "As to *why* God doesn't make it demonstratively clear: are we sure that He is even interested in the kind of Theism which wd. be a compelled logical assent to a conclusive argument? Are *we* interested in it in personal matters? I demand from my friend a trust in my good faith which is *certain* without demonstrative proof. It wouldn't be confidence at all if he waited for rigorous proof" (quoted in Vanauken, *Severe Mercy*, 89).

64. Lewis, *Mere Christianity*, 32. In addition, he felt the need to defend Christianity strongly against reductionism. For example, we can see this type of attack in Bertrand Russell's essay "The Value of Free Thought," where he (reductionistically) claims that anyone's belief in God might be said to stem from three basic fears: fear of death, fear of going to hell, and fear of meaninglessness.

65. Cunningham, *C. S. Lewis*, 180. Lewis has been often accused of being a bully. But as George Sayer—a former pupil, friend and later biographer of Lewis—stated, "Although he enjoyed lively hammer-and-tongs argument, and in the heat of argument could be insensitive to the feelings of others, I never knew him to bully. He would often refrain from attacking a man whom he thought could not stand up to him" (Sayer, *Jack*, 415).

66. See particularly Lewis, *God in the Dock*, 177.

67. Ibid., 183.

68. Carpenter, *Inklings*, 217. Similarly, Lewis could be said to see clearly and fully Austin Farrer's point about philosophical argument: "It is commonly said that if rational argument is so seldom the cause of conviction, philosophical apologists must largely be wasting their shot. The premise is true, but the conclusion does not follow. For though argument does not create conviction, the lack of it destroys belief. What seems to be proved may not be embraced; but what no one shows the ability to defend is quickly abandoned. Rational argument does not create belief, but it maintains a climate in which belief may flourish. So the apologist who does nothing but defend may play a useful, though preparatory, part" (Gibb, *Light on C. S. Lewis*, 26).

69. Peterson et al., *Reason and Religious Belief*, 29.

70. Ibid., 41.

71. Ibid., 45.

72. Ibid., 49.

73. Ibid., 49.

74. That is, "To be practically rational, so one contending part holds, is to act on the basis of calculations of costs and benefits.... To be practically rational, affirms a rival party, is to act under those constraints which any rational person... would agree should be imposed. To be practically rational, so a third party contends, is to act in such a way as to achieve the ultimate and true good of human beings" (MacIntyre, *Whose Justice?* 2).

75. Ibid., 2–3.

76. Ibid., 3.

77. For example, "... it can be argued and it has been argued that this account of rationality is itself contentious in two related ways: its requirement of disinterestedness in fact covertly presupposes one particular partisan type of account of justice, that of liberal individualism, which it is later to be used to justify, so that its apparent neutrality is no more than an appearance, while its conception of ideal rationality as consisting in the principles which a socially disembodied being would arrive at illegitimately ignores the inescapably historically and socially context-bound character which any substantive set of principles of rationality, whether theoretical or practical, is bound to have" (ibid., 3–4).

78. Ibid., 4.

79. Ibid.

80. Ibid., 4.

81. Ibid., 5.

82. Ibid.

83. Ibid.

84. Ibid., 6.

85. Ibid.

86. Ibid., 7.

87. In MacIntyre's words, "we already have the best of reasons for supposing that those standards cannot be met, and we know in advance, therefore, that from the standpoint of the Enlightenment and its successors any account of an alternative mode of understanding will inescapably be treated as one more contending view, unable to vindicate itself conclusively against its Enlightenment rivals. Any attempt to provide a radically different alternative standpoint is bound to be found rationally unsatisfactory in a variety of ways from the standpoint of the Enlightenment itself. Hence it is inevitable that such an attempt should be unacceptable to and rejected by those whose allegiance is to the dominant intellectual and cultural modes of the present order" (ibid.).

88. Ibid.

89. Ibid., 8.

90. Ibid., 8–9.

91. Ibid., 9.

92. Ibid.

93. Ibid.

94. Ibid., 10.

95. Ibid.

96. See Lewis, *Last Battle*, 212.

97. Plato, *Complete Works*, 537–38.

98. Ibid., 548.

99. "He will now not only be able to say which kind of person is convinced by what kind of speech; on meeting someone he will be able to discern what he is like and make clear . . . that the person . . . in front of him is of just his particular sort of character . . . that he must now apply speeches of such-and-such a kind in this particular way in order to secure conviction about such-and-such an issue" (ibid.).

100. Ibid., 549.
101. Ibid., 552.
102. Ibid.
103. Ibid., 552–53.
104. Ibid., 553.
105. Ibid., 554.
106. Williams, "Sapientia and the Trinity," 323.
107. Lewis, *Weight of Glory*, 92.
108. "The true wisdom of man is piety" (Augustine, *Enchiridion*, 2).
109. Hibbs, "Introduction," viii.
110. Augustine, *Later Works*, 177.
111. Ibid., 177.
112. Ibid., 95.
113. Ibid.
114. Ibid., 96.
115. Ibid.
116. "True wisdom in men is the worship of God" (Ibid., 97).
117. Ibid.
118. Ibid.
119. Ibid., 57.
120. Ibid.
121. Ibid.
122. Ibid.
123. For example, in his *Pensees*, Pascal warned us that we know the truth through our reason and our heart: ". . . the heart has its reasons which reason itself does not know: we know that through countless things" (*Pensees*, 158). Through our hearts we know "first principles, such as space, time, movement, numbers [and these are] as certain as any that our reason can give us, and it is on this knowledge by means of the heart and instinct that reason has to rely, and must base all its argument. . . . The principles are felt, and the propositions are proved, both conclusively, although by different ways, and it is useless and stupid for the heart to demand of reason a feeling of all the propositions it proves, before accepting them" (ibid., 36). Despite the inability of reason to prove our "first principles," Pascal stated that this demonstrates nothing except the weakness of our reason: "So this powerlessness ought to be used only to humble reason, which would like to be the judge of everything, and not attach our certainty. As if argument alone were able to instruct us" (ibid.). Reason should be humbled in the face of this impossible task. We can learn from more than just our "rational" mind. Furthermore, the first step we can take in this task is to recognize that our reason is one thing among an infinite number of things beyond it—our reason cannot be expected to grasp the natural things beyond it, let alone the supernatural. However, Pascal was by no means

condemning human reason; he was issuing a warning about exalting the human mind over the human heart.

124. As James K. A. Smith notes, "Rather than a Platonic subordination of affective and imaginative *aesthesis* to intellectual *noesis* . . . a Christian epistemology in the Augustinian and Pascalian tradition affirms the priority of 'reasons of the heart of which reason knows nothing'" (Smith, *Introducing Radical Orthodoxy*, 224).

125. Again, as Smith notes, "Of interest from a Christian perspective is the way in which art is an embodied, incarnate means by which truth is communicated. Given a Christian anthropology that affirms the integrity of the embodied self (in contrast to a Platonic privileging of the soul), a Christian epistemology must resist the Western temptation to reduce knowing to only one of its modes—the cognitive—and rather appreciate the multiple modes of knowing (affective, tactile, sensible, etc.). Or to put it in terms of classic discussions of the faculties, rather than privileging the intellect, a Christian epistemology accords equal status, if not primacy, to the senses and imagination" (ibid.).

126. See, for example, Aquinas, *Summa Theologiae* (2008), 1:207, where Aquinas inquires about truth. There he explicitly follows Augustine's lead and asserts Augustine's epistemology: that what is true is that which *is*.

127. Jordan, "Theology and Philosophy," 234.

128. That is, "Human reasoning, which does not constitute a separate trajectory to the grace which comes through *sacra doctrina*, 'should assist faith as the natural loving bent of the will yields to charity'. This 'assistance' is not, however, due to any weakness in the science of *sacra doctrina* itself; rather, it arises because our understanding is wanting and is more conditioned to operate through natural reason" (S. Oliver, *Philosophy, God and Motion*, 86).

129. Aquinas, *Summa Theologiae* (1969), 1:42.

130. Oliver, *Philosophy, God and Motion*, 86.

131. Aquinas, *Summa Theologiae* (1969), 1:42.

132. Milbank, "Faith, Reason and Imagination," 11–12.

133. Aquinas, *Summa Theologiae* (1969), 1:181.

134. Ibid.

135. Ibid.

136. For example, ". . . anyone who attains anything, when he lays hold on it could be said to comprehend it. It is in this sense that God is comprehended by the blessed; *I held him and will not let him go*. . . . When we say that God is not comprehended we do not mean there is something about him that is not seen, but that he cannot be seen as perfectly as intrinsically he is visible. . . . Thus Augustine, defining comprehension, says something *is totally comprehended when it is so seen that no part of it is hidden, or so that all its limits can be seen* . . . our way of knowing does not measure up to this. Whoever sees God in his essence sees something that exists infinitely and sees it to be infinitely intelligible, but he does not understand it infinitely" (ibid., 1:182–83).

137. "Aquinas argues that our perfect happiness, the fulfillment of our natural desire, can consist only in the contemplation of God's essence, in the vision of God (*visio Dei*), in which we see the answer to the question *what* he is. From this he draws the conclusion (ST IaIIae.3.6) that 'our complete happiness cannot consist in theoretical knowledge,' that is, in philosophy, broadly conceived. The vision of God surpasses our natural powers and capacities. This end of ours is literally supernatural" (Aertsen, "Aquinas's Philosophy," 32).

138. Aquinas, *Summa Theologiae* (1969), 1:191.

139. Ibid., 1:191–92.

140. Ibid., 1:192.

141. Ibid.

142. Ibid., 1:193.

143. Ibid.

144. Ibid.

145. As a related aside, David Brown, in his book *Tradition and Imagination*, attempts to show how tradition is a primary sustainer of revelation and Scripture. "My aim is to show that tradition, so far from being something secondary or reactionary, is the motor that sustains revelation both within Scripture and beyond" (p. 1). He sees the imagination as primary to religious life. "The word 'imagination' occurs in the title of . . . this work. . . . This is not because I do not take doctrinal issues seriously, but because I regard them as secondary and parasitic on the stories and images that give religious belief its shape and vitality. The form of these stories and images change as a result of complex interactions between existing communitarian assumptions, new cultural contexts and the continuing work of God. Present-day Christianity, it seems to me, will go badly wrong, if it attempts an unmediated dialogue with the biblical text rather than recognizing also the intervening history that has helped shape its present perception of the text's meaning" (pp. 1–2). Brown suggests that Western religion is dependent upon imagination and has, in fact, worked mainly through the imagination by building upon existing narratives (p. 9).

146. For Lewis, the revelation of God is present in "all truth," and "God has revealed himself in various ways in different places. Through the conscience, dreams, myths, the moral law, the election of Israel, the creation of immortal longings . . . a divine pressure has been exerted on the mind of man" (Cunningham, *C. S. Lewis*, 87).

147. Lewis, *Mere Christianity*, 38.

148. Lewis, *Of Other Worlds*, 15.

149. Aquinas, *Summa Theologiae* (1969), 1:194.

150. Milbank, "Faith, Reason and Imagination," 22.

151. Ibid.

152. Gilson, *Philosophy of St. Thomas*, 189. One might also add Carl Becker's observation about eighteenth-century rationalists along with this: "It is possible to ask, with Carl Becker, whether the 'heavenly city' of these eighteenth-century philosophers was, in the faith on which its basic premises of the perfectibility of man, illimitable human progress, and their corollaries, rested, as unmedieval as its exponents chose to believe. Does the eighteenth-century outlook reflect, as Becker suggests, an age of faith based on reason as contrasted with a medieval age of reason based on faith?" (Ross and McLaughlin, eds., *Portable Medieval Reader*, 6).

two

The Function of the Imagination

WHEN MANY OF US think about the faculty of imagination, some general, key ideas typically spring to mind: it is the fanciful faculty, dealing in supposals and what-ifs and pure fiction.[1] The metaphysic of modernity does not allow for much else: it is broadly strung and becomes thin by denying the depth of things; and it is, as a result, highly skeptical of anything resembling transcendence or supernaturalism. Our modern epistemology is such that we believe in only those things that can be scientifically, empirically verified, things that are repeatable and demonstrable to all. Consequently, the imagination has been pushed back into the murky depths of the mind (viewed not as a proper mystery but mostly as nonsense), denigrated and passed over as a faculty saturated with falsehood and wishful thinking. It should come as no surprise that the imagination would be thought as such in this brand of epistemology. How else would the imagination be viewed in such a construction? It is relegated to the (material) unconscious mind. But is this necessarily so? Do we then merely mimic techniques? Is the faculty of reason a purely mechanical one devoid of any connections to imagination? Is it a step-by-step process, one in which truth and meaning are references to logical principles alone? Or is there more than just a mechanistic, deductive process at work? At the very least, it appears, there must be some account of what gets reason going in the first place. Is there or was there a conception that did not separate reason and imagination in such a harsh fashion? The answer lies in an examination of non-Enlightenment responses. In order to find out what the faculty of imagination does (including all of its fanciful elements), one must look to the idea of cognition in general. There, one will find that reason is working on what is already delivered—one will find reason is always intertwined with imagination. In order to look at cognition in this light, I will first examine Aquinas' epistemology to lead us to a conception that does not separate reason and imagination as radically as does the Enlightenment program. I will then look to build upon this by showing other non-Enlightenment conceptions (namely, through John Milbank's important recent contribution to our understanding of the theological imagination, through Lewis' mentor George MacDonald, and through Lewis' contemporaries and friends Austin Farrar and Dorothy Sayers) of imagination that bolster the idea of a deep connection between reason and imagination.

In the *Summa Theologiae* Aquinas inquires about truth. Following Augustine, Aquinas begins by refuting what could be seen as a common modern notion of truth: "'That is true which is seen.'"[2] But this is clearly false because, "it would follow that stones hidden in the bosom of the earth would not be true stones, as they are not seen."[3] Aquinas, again following Augustine, refuted the idea that truth is that "which is as it appears to the knower who is willing and able to know" because "it would follow that nothing would be true, unless someone could know it."[4] So, our Augustinian definition of truth arises: "'That is true which is.'"[5] It follows for Aquinas that

> As the good denotes that towards which the appetite tends, so the true denotes that towards which the intellect tends. Now there is a difference between the appetite and the intellect, or any knowledge whatsoever, that knowledge is according as the thing known is in the knower, whilst appetite is according as the desirer tends towards the thing desired. Thus, the term appetite, namely good, is in the object desirable, and the term of the intellect, namely true, is in the intellect itself. Now as a good exists in a thing so far as that thing is related to the appetite—and hence the aspect of goodness passes on from the desirable thing to the appetite, in so far as the appetite is called good if its object is good; so, since the true is in the intellect in so far as it is conformed to the object understood, the aspect of the true must needs pass from the intellect to the object understood, so that also the thing understood is said to be true in so far as it has some relation to the intellect.[6]

For Aquinas, then, there is a metaphysical permeating of the thing known and the knower, so that both are united in our intellect in such a way that they become one. This has far-reaching implications. If this is so, then all cognition is a process of participation—the knower and the known become united, the spirit passes between them and all things. Every knowing event has at its core this oneness. There is present then a preconceptual notion, a rationality that resides beyond reason. The spirit leads the intellect to where the intellect goes. When we cut off the spirit we are left with merely the appetitive lead. The appetitive drive will lead us not where the spirit would but where the desires would, whether good or bad. The notion of reason as the head of the desires and the spirit is turned on its head (unlike in Plato's *Phaedrus*[7])—no longer do we have control (as we like to assume our reason heads off our desires), for we have lost the spirit (we do not, in our modern notion, recognize any transcendence) and now the appetitive is our new leader (unbeknownst to us). This can be seen, as John Milbank notes, through the shadowy, secret mental work that goes on behind the scenes. For the imagination is "the threshold between matter and spirit: it is the mysterious alchemical point at which mind, in order to think at all, must produce its own shadowy sensations that must always be 'returned to' in order to complete a thought (*conversio ad phantasmata*)."[8] The alchemy of the imagination suggests the magical and unexpected elements of our thoughts: our imagination is formed from the phantasmata, but it is also mysteriously more than these impressions; it is provoked by the phenomenologically given but is more than the merely phenomenologically given. We stumble upon the "dumb immediacy" of our perception and normally "see 'right through' these phantasms in order to re-establish contact, via our senses, with the physical world outside us," but the shadowy alchemical points of our thoughts are "always secretly at work and this is exhibited in the way we not only sense the world and all it includes, but necessarily and 'fantastically' sense it 'as something.'"[9]

Of course, as the mysterious alchemical point, it is difficult to define in some more explicit fashion. It is there in the inferences we make and in the reasons for which we argue; it is there in the intuitive and creative mechanisms of the rational mind. It is there in "those fictions that we do not inhabit, or not fully, or which we know that we could never inhabit," and it is there in the pictures "of what has never been; symbols of the intrinsically absent and ineffably secret; stories that are simply 'made up' and may never be fully enacted. This is the realm of literature, where the secondary imagination absolutely rules."[10] So it is that the imagination functions on the two levels of reason and the senses: as the "mediating twilight threshold between spirit and matter," and it is both active and passive—we can direct our imagination to some end, "control . . . where we direct our gaze," but images also "flood into our mind when our eyes are shut, often unprovoked."[11] Even when we are conjuring "images at will . . . to shape the precise form which they take . . . at the point of seemingly most control, when we are being 'creative,' it is more as if we must find the trick of 'summonsing' in to the chamber of our mind elusive hidden realities that are seemingly in some sense 'already there.'"[12] The secondary imagination, the domain of art, is also "the very point at which reason and faith become conjoined," and it is because "the theological necessarily links rational reflection with the contemplative regard of historical events and visualised pictures or symbols."[13] Once again, this shadowy in-between is the exclusive realm of the imaginative, and "it is by exercise of the secondary imagination that we have to try to connect historical becoming (including the Incarnation and the emergence of the Church) with the descending emanation of all of nature and culture from the perfect Godhead."[14] There is a connection here between Aquinas' inquiries on truth and his conclusion about truth being that which is, and the notion of a fountain source of ideas, of images, of knowledge, that is grounded in the Godhead, in Being itself. The knowledge of our cognition resides in the source of all being. We work on realities that are in some sense already there—the faculty of imagination then leads the rational mind; it runs ahead of the rational mind delivering a reason beyond an Enlightenment notion of rationality, a reason beyond the step-by-step deductionism that works purely on the material.

In Lewis' corpus of work, the function of the imagination is not explicitly or definitively laid out for us in one specific essay or book on the subject. He treats the subject, like he treats many subjects, here and there—to be gleaned and pieced together from various sources: "Lewis nowhere defines imagination explicitly, and he uses the term in a number of ways," for example, "as the image-making power . . . the creative or inventive power . . . the power to make up things . . . the power to create fiction . . . the mysteriousness and adventurousness of romance . . . and imagination in some high Coleridgean sense."[15] However, it is in this high Coleridgean sense that we get a sense of Lewis' epistemology and his views of the function of the imagination. In *Biographia Literaria*, Coleridge distinguishes between the primary imagination and the secondary imagination (with a third distinction of Fancy). The primary imagination is the communication and participation of the divine in the human mind: "The primary imagination I hold to be the living Power and prime Agent of all human Perception, and as a repetition in the finite mind of the eternal act of creation in the infinite I AM."[16] The secondary imagination is the "echo" of the primary imagination, and in this sense it is the same in kind but not in degree. That is, the secondary imagination is an

> echo of the former, co-existing with the conscious will, yet still as identical with the primary in the *kind* of its agency, and differing only in *degree*, and in the *mode* of its operation. It dissolves, diffuses, dissipates, in order to re-create; or where this process is rendered impossible, yet still at all events it struggles to idealize and to unify. It is essentially *vital*, even as all objects (*as* objects) are essentially fixed and dead.[17]

Coleridge's distinctions lay out an epistemology that connects sensation, thought, and imagination. There is a "fusion of sensation and thought which imagination, and not reason alone, brings about."[18] The work of the secondary imagination is added "when the mind, in the absence of present physical realities, is capable of projecting its shadowy sensations back out into the sensorily perceived world in order to modify it."[19] It is, then, a faculty that gives form to thought. This implies a need to re-present reason in light of the work of the imagination: it implies a new (old) sourcing of the image supply. The images presented or created by the imagination must be through transposition: it is the higher, divine life communicated to the lower, so-called mundane life. It is in this process that the lower life is saved by being brought up into the higher life. As a result, the imagination is also the organ of meaning: it is the means through which we gain a *telos* and significance. It is the idea that the visionary world is preferred over the merely visible; that is, there is more to the world than what can be seen (rationalistically, empirically) and the imagination presents us with this "more." The imagination is the divinely gifted precursor to thought. The images produced are divinely formed and made. The imagination is the human faculty of receiving this divine inspiration. When we use this faculty we are implicitly referencing something other—a metaphysical reality that the images signify.

The attempt to rationalize, to pull the images to pieces and strip them down, is a limiting of the reality they signify—it is a (failed) surreptitious attempt to strip the images of their transcendent funding. The light of reason and revelation are, in essence, God's. The source of the images can then reveal something about the created world and the Creator.

As Dorothy Sayers noted, the characteristic common to God and humankind is apparently "the desire and ability to make things."[20] This is a key component to understanding the imagination: it is the *yetzer* (a chief Hebrew term for imagination), which is rooted in *yzr* and is related to *yetsirah* ("creation"), *yotzer* ("creator") and *yatsar* ("create"), and it is such that it "is of no little consequence that this word derives from the same root *yzr* as the terms for 'creation' (*yetsirah*), 'creator' (*yotser*) and 'create' (*yatsar*)."[21] There is a relation here between the created world, those beings who can create, and the Creator. However, we must freely admit that this commonality between God and humankind is also a metaphor, like any other statement about God. All language about God is, by necessity, analogical. "We need not be surprised at this, still less suppose that because it is analogical it is therefore valueless or without any relation to the truth. The fact is, that all language about everything is analogical; we think in a series of metaphors."[22] Nothing is spoken of in terms of itself; it is spoken of only in terms of something else. For even in matters of mathematics, it "can express itself" only "in terms of itself" and "only so long as it deals with an ideal system of pure numbers; the moment it begins to deal with numbers of *things* it is forced back into the language of analogy."[23] And when we speak of something of which we have no direct access, "we must think by analogy or refrain from thought."[24] We are compelled to speak by analogy because we have no other means of speaking.

However, the word "creation," or "creative," as used to describe the function of the imagination in humankind is still, according to George MacDonald, preferable to use in describing the "calling out of nothing which is the imagination of God."[25] For, although there is a "necessary unlikeness between the creator and the created" there is also an "equally necessary likeness of the thing made to him who makes it, and so of the work of the made to the work of the maker."[26] It is in God's image that we are made, and so, if the imagination of humankind is "made in the image of the imagination of God," then all "must have been of God first; and it will help much towards our understanding of the imagination and its functions in man if we first succeed in regarding aright the imagination of God, in which the imagination of man lives and moves and has its being."[27] We must admit that our similarity is far off and remote, and this difference shows in our creative efforts: we discover that where we would create a machine, picture, or book, "God makes the man that makes the book, or the picture, or the machine. Would God give us a drama? He makes a Shakespeare. Or would he construct a drama more immediately his own? He begins with the building of the stage itself, and that stage is a world—a universe of worlds."[28] The universe is God's poetry and science: "As the thoughts move in the mind of a man, so move the worlds of men and women in the mind of God, and make no confusion there, for there they had their birth, the offspring of his imagination. Man is but a thought of God."[29] Humans are then "rather *being thought* than *thinking*, when a new thought arises" in our minds—and we did not know it until we found it there, and, therefore, we "could not even have sent for it."[30] But we may, by some rare instance, come to "foresee that something is coming, and make ready the place for its birth . . ."[31] We do not create the forms that reveal our thoughts: the forms by which we reveal our thoughts are those forms which are already made. The forms are there to be recognized, and we must "light the lamp within the form," for our "imagination is the light, it is not the form. Straightway the shining thought makes the form visible, and becomes itself visible through the form."[32]

Modern Imagination

Lewis, Sayers, and MacDonald are clearly following a premodern trajectory: the imagination has a role in the process of cognition. And if all cognition is a process of participation—the knower and the known become united, the spirit passes between them and all things—then every knowing event has at its core this oneness. There is a preconceptual notion, a rationality that resides beyond the supposed step-by-step reason of modernity. The way in which reason and imagination are displayed as intimately connected betrays this premodern conceptuality.

It is not difficult to see the distinctions between the modern and the premodern. As Richard Kearney notes, one of the most common distinctions to be made between a modern view of imagination and a premodern view is the former's almost unchecked affirmation of the human side of the imagination equation: it is

> a marked *affirmation* of the creative power of [humankind]. The *mimetic* paradigm of imagining is replaced by the *productive* paradigm. No longer viewed as an intermediary agency—at best imitating some truth beyond [humankind]—the imagination becomes, in modern times, the immediate source of its own truth.[33]

But the mimetic quality still remains. For human resources are all that remain and, therefore, only recreated or reimaged phenomena derived purely and exclusively from the world of the senses, with no meaning (other than that prescribed by human assumption and fancy), truly remains. The transcendent function of the imagination is now at best relegated to the (Kantian) transcendental functions of the human mind.[34]

A basic Enlightenment framework (where reason is seen as unbiased, uncommitted and universal) attempts to separate knowledge and imagination—it positions truth as reference to logical principles alone.

As Alison Milbank notes, we are so used to this state of affairs that it is difficult for us to recognize possible alternatives. We do not see that "originally *aletheia* (truth) was the efficacious speech of the diviner, poet or king whose memory gave being to that which he spoke," and it is only "through the rise of an alternative social order of the warrior caste" that "the concept of truth moves towards the demonstrable, in the context of persuasion to action of a group of equals, later in the political context of the city. The effect on poetry of the secularising of truth in the development of Greek democracy and philosophy is to divorce it from its origin in *aletheia*."[35] The premodern idea that truth and imagination are connected was essentially "torn apart in the eighteenth-century Enlightenment" because of the radically empirical nature of the dominant philosophy: ". . . we cannot know anything super-sensible, like the soul or God. All we have is the world of the senses, and in that too we cannot know things in themselves. We only know things as they appear to us, as phenomena; not their noumenal character."[36] In a real sense, Lewis is to be seen (along with his fellow Inklings) as revaluing mythos "as a mode of truth-telling" and affirming that, "paradoxically, it is through fiction that we shall gain access to the real."[37] The mythopoeic is not meant to "take us away to an impossible fantasy world that we do not take seriously but aims to liberate our alienated consciousness and enable a reunion with the world beyond the self, which is allowed its own freedom."[38] Alison Milbank also gives us J. R. R. Tolkien's aims of fantasy (namely, escape, recovery, and consolation) as our path to liberate the alienated consciousness. It is through fantasy that we are able "to escape our imprisonment in our own perceptions" and this "allows us to encounter other beings such as dragons. We can fly; we can understand the speech of the animal world; we can be immortal."[39] Once we have escaped our own perceptions we can return "to a clear view, refreshed by the imaginative holiday," and this is another place where Lewis' views counter the dominant Enlightenment framework: we can escape into the "other" and bring back something of it. There is a restoration of knowing in a premodern sense: the mythopoeic "seeks to restore our ability to know, acknowledge and participate in the world beyond the self, not just the world of other people but that of birds, plants and inanimate objects."[40]

This premodern view of imagination and reason certainly flies in the face of cherished Enlightenment values and beliefs. The modern, rationalistic paradigm may see imagination as a faculty that uses the material world as its base and basis, but as such it is only reworked (often nonsensical waste) material that may have practical use—that is, if or when the rational mind can properly harness this "waste" material. When it is useful, it is because the material unconscious mind has seen something that the conscious, directed mind has not, and, as a result, the unconscious mind can widen out to view what the directed mind may have missed. But not only this, for this modernist notion limits the conversation to what is rational; only certain types of reasoning (mainly empirical) are legitimized. It views the faculty of reason as a purely mechanical one, influenced, no doubt, by an extreme empirical focus (due chiefly to its debt to a contemporary technical approach). The influence of experimental science and its fierce empiricism often pushes the idea of reason "as something mechanical, a step-by-step deduction or logic," and the Enlightenment descendents have taken up the idea with substantial vigor.[41] But there is more than just a mechanistic, deductive process at work. There must be, at least, an account of what gets reason (including reason of an empirical, technical sense) going in the first place. There is something that undergirds the faculty and pushes it along (e.g., through the inspiration of ideas, the jump to inferences that signal a reasoning beyond the mere step-by-step movements of rationalism).

The Enlightenment program has stretched across the disciplines, and theology too has taken up this program. As John Milbank notes, this was a gradual process,

> stretching from Scotus to Banez, theology started to conclude that human beings have two separate final ends, a natural and a supernatural one, and that the first remains substantially independent of the former. If previously the notion of a purely rational philosophy was shadowed by a sense of something pagan and unredeemed, now this is seen as an entirely legitimate exercise, within the bounds of "pure nature." A fully autonomous rational philosophy had at last arrived.[42]

This is the Reason by which all humanity can agree will lead to truth. The truth is now set in its empirical bonds (although, unrecognized or unacknowledged metaphysics undergirds it). As Pope Benedict has noted, we may believe we have found a

> philosophy that is universally valid and completely scientific, a philosophy in which the reason common to all [humanity] finds expression.... These philosophies are characterized by their positivist—and therefore anti-metaphysical—character.... They are based on a self-limitation of the positive reason that is adequate in the technological sphere but entails a mutilation of [humanity] if it is generalized.... It is true that the positivist philosophies contain important elements of truth; but these are based on a self-limitation of reason that is typical of one determined cultural situation, that of the modern West, and, as such, certainly cannot be considered the last word of reason.... They, too, have their cultural ties, since they are linked to the situation in the West today.[43]

The Enlightenment program, which has largely become the modern program, attempts to set up a rationality that is independent of people, of time and space, as if all rational beings should (and will?) come to the conclusion that it contains all of truth.[44] In this attempt, the program fails to recognize that it too has its own historical roots, its own ties with the past—that it too builds upon what has come before. It also fails to recognize that it too is asserting a metaphysical argument—one that surreptitiously tries to smuggle in meaning and purpose through the back door—a bias, a starting point, its own (subliminal) faith seeking understanding.

Notes

1. I am implicitly maintaining throughout this book that there is such a thing as the imagination, and that it is a faculty of the human mind. This faculty opens up other faculties: it gets reason going, opens up a space and time for thought to occur. This faculty is the creative faculty, and, as such, the "desire and ability to make things" is a "characteristic common to God and [humanity]" (Sayers, *Mind of the Maker*, 17). This faculty represents seen and absent things as present to the mind (and in the rendering it can present heretofore unseen, unknown possibilities). This faculty functions through image-like representation, and this faculty, in its image-like representational function, does mirror the phenomenal world—but it does so through analogy, relating the "more than" to the "less than" through transposition. Thought (even materialistic, naturalistic reasoning) is characterized by the use of analogy, but even when the imagination represents the "more than" through the "less than," there is an epiphenomenon that occurs—a significance is imparted, an infusion of meaning, a special sense of the "more than" is communicated. Eva Brann, in her sizeable tome *The World of Imagination*, argues for a particular interpretation of the imagination. Her thesis is stated explicitly: there "is an imagination; it is a faculty or a power; specifically it is a faculty for internal representations; these representations are image-like; therefore they share a certain character with external images; in particular, like material images, they represent absent objects as present; they do so by means of resemblance" (p. 5). Brann is aware of the controversial nature of her statements—each one of these statements has been (and will be) challenged. Brann notes the difficulty of definitions of imagination: "Mere definitions, ripped from the background of thought and opinion of which they are distillations, are hardly helpful" (p. 23). But there can be a sense in which these preliminaries might be helpful—"to get a first handle on the subject matter" (p. 23). So our primary concern should be with "articulating" the "nature" of the imagination (p. 23). In this chapter, I am heeding Brann's warning and attempting to avoid giving an easy starting definition, in effect ripping a definition from its background and context, and instead am trying to present the nature and function of the imagination somewhere within Lewis' tradition.

2. Aquinas, *Summa Theologiae*, Volume I, 207.
3. Aquinas, *Summa Theologiae*, Volume I, 207.
4. Aquinas, *Summa Theologiae*, Volume I, 207.
5. Aquinas, *Summa Theologiae*, Volume I, 207.
6. Aquinas, *Summa Theologiae*, Volume I, 208.
7. See *Phaedrus* in Plato, *Complete Works*, 524–31. In chapter 7, I again explore Plato's metaphor of the charioteer and his two horses.
8. Milbank, "Faith, Reason and Imagination," 22.
9. Ibid.
10. Ibid., 23.
11. Ibid.
12. Ibid.
13. Ibid.
14. Ibid., 24.
15. Schakel, *Reason and Imagination*, 183.
16. Coleridge, *Biographia Literaria*, 304. Coleridge's distinctions, and their relation to Lewis' thought, will be taken up again in the last chapter of this book.

17. Ibid.
18. Milbank, "Faith, Reason and Imagination," 22.
19. Ibid., 22.
20. Sayers, *Mind of the Maker*, 17.
21. Kearney, *Wake of Imagination*, 39.
22. Sayers, *Mind of the Maker*, 17.
23. Ibid., 17.
24. Ibid., 17–18.
25. MacDonald, "Imagination," 1.
26. Ibid., 1–2.
27. Ibid., 2.
28. Ibid.
29. Ibid.
30. Ibid.
31. Ibid.
32. Ibid.
33. Kearney, *Wake of Imagination*, 155.
34. The Kantian notion of the imagination as merely fancy or play (or what Paul Ricoeur labeled "free-flight of fancy") is drawn back from his original "discovery." As Richard Kearney notes, "In the first edition of his *Critique of Pure Reason*...[Kant] startled his contemporaries by announcing that imagination was the common 'unknown root' of the two stems of human cognition—understanding and sensation . . . declaring it to be the primary and indispensible precondition of all knowledge. . . . [However] he quickly became aware that such a declaration of independence on behalf of imagination meant nothing less than dismantling the traditional edifice of metaphysics and, by implication, the ultimate basis of philosophical rationalism. Indeed, so alarmed was Kant by his own arguments that he went to considerable lengths in the second edition of the *Critique of Pure Reason* . . . to take most of the harm out of his initial claims . . ." (ibid., 156–57). Kearney goes on to quote Heidegger's assessment of Kant's "discovery": "'Does not everything fall into confusion if the lower is put in place of the higher? What is to happen to the honorable tradition according to which, in the long history of metaphysics, *ratio* and *logos* have laid claim to the central role? Can the primacy of logic disappear? Can the architectonic of the laying of the foundation of metaphysics, i.e., its division into transcendental aesthetic and logic, be preserved if the theme of the latter is basically the transcendental imagination? Does not the *Critique of Pure Reason* deprive itself of its own theme if pure reason is transformed into transcendental imagination? Does not this laying of the foundation lead to an abyss? By his radical interrogation, Kant brought the 'possibility' of metaphysics before the abyss. He saw the unknown; he had to draw back'" (ibid., 195).
35. A. Milbank, "Knowledge and Truth," 1.
36. Ibid., 2.
37. Ibid.
38. Ibid.
39. Ibid.
40. Ibid.

41. Engell, *Creative Imagination*, 17.

42. Milbank, "Faith, Reason and Imagination," 13.

43. Benedict XVI, *Christianity and the Crisis of Cultures*, 39–41.

44. This is certainly not to say that the Enlightenment or modernity has not given us truth or good things. As Pope Benedict correctly notes, modernity is not simply to be rejected: "We must begin by replying that we have undoubtedly made important gains . . ." (ibid., 39). We must be careful with our assessment and admit the important contributions of Enlightenment thinking whenever possible; we are not merely jettisoning the Enlightenment. Again, as Pope Benedict remarks, "Does this amount to a simple rejection of the Enlightenment? Certainly not!" (ibid., 47).

three

The Imaginative Drive

The idea that the meaning and inspiration of Lewis' imaginative works can be understood without reference to the spiritual or transcendent (e.g., in terms of psychology) has gained some popularity over the years. It is not surprising that such an account would arise, given the general thrust of rationalistic Enlightenment modernity—of course imaginative works can be explained merely in terms of their references to the material world; this is all that exists, after all. If the imagination is merely reworked material, then its source is to be found in the murky waters of the psychology and biography of the author. This is not to say, of course, that psychology and biography have no merits or usefulness in criticism, but it can be a dangerous task to undertake (as Lewis argued) and should not be taken on lightly.

Lewis' rejection of such attempts lies at the heart of his premodern notions of imagination and reason: the work of the author does not just communicate his or her biography or psychology (if it does at all); it is instead an imperfect expression of the divine, which no doubt our finitude mutates in its own peculiar way. To this end, in this short chapter I will continue to bolster the position (against the specifically Wilsonian thesis) that Lewis' move into fiction should be seen as a deepening of his intellectual powers: it is the older more operative (premodern) man coming to light. This will be done, first, by examining the psychological critique brought against Lewis' fiction (specifically his children's fiction) and, second, by an exploration of Lewis' own literary criticism. Following this, I will consider Lewis' own reason for writing his children's fiction. Lastly, I will look at Lewis' own ideas about his personal make-up—namely, through an exploration of his older imaginative self coming to fruition. All of this will be done to oppose the idea that Lewis' turn to writing children's fiction is to be seen primarily in terms of outside influence (e.g., the Anscombe debate) or a sublimated psychological problem (e.g., a projection of fear).

Psychoanalyzing Lewis

It is interesting that The Chronicles of Narnia have been specifically attacked in a way Lewis devoted much time arguing against. The process of criticizing a work by psychologizing the author was one Lewis found particularly abhorrent. The subject is the foundation for a book penned by Lewis and E. M. W. Tillyard, published under the title *The Personal Heresy*. In his biography of Lewis, A. N. Wilson uses a version of the method that Lewis criticized. As mentioned earlier, Wilson cites the confrontation with Elizabeth Anscombe as the "greatest single factor which drove him into the form of literature for which he is today most popular: children's stories," with little evidence except his own insistence that this is so.[1] Wilson also states[2] that the witch in the book *The Silver Chair*—who traps the protagonist children underground and argues that there is no real world above them, only the darkness they currently see—is supposed to be a nightmare rendition of Lewis' encounter with Anscombe.[3] It seems clear that this interpretation is amateur psychological speculation. The only real evidence for it is Wilson's own insistence that it is the case. As Lewis wrote, the critic

> who speculates about the genesis of your book is the amateur psychologist. He has a Freudian theory of literature and claims to know all about your inhibitions. He knows what unacknowledged wishes you were gratifying. And here of course one cannot . . . claim to start by knowing all the facts. By definition you are unconscious of things he professes to discover. Therefore the more loudly you disclaim them, the more right he must be: though, oddly enough, if you admitted them, that would prove him right too. And there is a further difficulty: one is not here so free from bias, for this procedure is almost entirely confined

to hostile reviewers. And now that I come to think of it, I have seldom seen it practiced on a dead author except by a scholar who intended, in some measure, to debunk him. That in itself is perhaps significant.[4]

This amateur psychologist also has not had the benefit of having the author "on his or her couch" to analyze experiences and dreams, to go over the "whole case-history."[5] And the amateur psychologist will more often than not overlook the (obvious to the author) conscious reasons for the genesis of books in favor of the sublimated, hidden ones.[6] It is clear that Wilson suggests at times in his biography that Lewis' work might be explained in terms of a Freudian psychological analysis.[7] Lewis specifically attacked this type of criticism and biography and was deeply opposed to the idea that "literature is an expression of the writer's personality."[8] Lewis "distinguished the genuinely critical question, 'why and how should I read this?' from the purely historical question, 'why did he write it.'"[9] He also insisted that criticism should be primarily confined to the books themselves: "Your *first* job is simply the *reception* of all this work with your imagination and emotions. Each book is to be read for the purpose the author meant it to be read for: the story *as* a story, the joke *as* a joke."[10] And it is here that the spiritual light might be awakened in the reader. The opening up of space—of something beyond one's control, of an uncontrollable, spontaneous response—in narrative experience can release possibilities for spiritual awakening.

In Lewis' own literary criticism he was inclined towards textual criticism. Lewis was concerned with a reader's involvement with an author's work. Thus, the role of the critic is mainly, in Lewis' view, to illuminate and inform our own reading.[11] Lewis emphasized the importance of learning what the author meant and what the actual words used by the author meant. Coupled with his focus on textual matters is an interest in a certain kind of history of the text: namely, its "worldview, including the model of reality and the universe it embodied . . ."[12] As such, the *weltanschauung* and *zeitgeist* of the author can play an important role in criticism—by helping us to enter into, as fully as we can, the world of the author in order to understand his or her intentions.[13] Lewis was interested in finding the worldview of the author in order to uncover more meaning, but, taken too far, source criticism can be dangerous. When this is done, Lewis warned, we tend to create our own invented histories to replace the author's narrative sources (not to mention ideas, meanings, and intentions). Lewis' interest in the sources of an author's work was not necessarily to decipher the "real" or "hidden" meanings and purposes that lay behind the poem or story, but rather to see the historical-cultural context and imagination out of which the author was writing.[14] Ultimately, Lewis found that one of the most important features of a text was not merely the sources an author may have used but what the author did with these sources—the new patterns and combinations that may have been created from the old patterns and combinations.

There is also an added danger of seeing worldviews or world models as representations of literal reality—in that we tend to see our own worldview as a true representation and begin to see the worldviews of others (especially those of the past) as false or erroneous: "[Lewis] argues that our world model will eventually change, like others before it. This change in mentality will shape questions asked of nature, and thus what is considered evidence in support of a world model."[15] Lewis argued that the change of world models should not be seen as a progression from erroneous world models to true world models. For Lewis, no one view is a literal translation of reality. But neither are these views merely fantasies. They are collective attempts of eras to uncover the phenomena of the universe. Lewis further argued that each world model succeeded at grasping a great many things; and, conversely, each misses a great many things.[16] World models, as such, represent the prevailing psychology of their respective eras, by embodying and reflecting the outlook of what the era considers as knowledge. In addition, the use of world models to spark the imagination is something Lewis saw as a worthy task, and he freely did so in his own fiction (particularly in the Space Trilogy and the Chronicles where he used a medieval world model for its imaginative power).[17] The medieval worldview was especially important to Lewis because unlike a purely rationalistic, materialistic worldview it had at its core an explicit, built-in significance: "There was no question of waking [the universe] into beauty or life. . . . The achieved perfection was already there. The only difficulty was to make an adequate response."[18]

Lewis recognized that how one viewed the world depended upon the philosophy one brought to bear upon it. Lewis argued that the habituation of children in the right type of stories might do much to bring about the acceptance of the divine and the miraculous.[19] In Lewis' Narnia tales and his Space Trilogy he attempted to bring a sense of the *possibility* and the reality of the supernatural into the lives of his readers. There is a chance to "steal past the watchful dragons" of our *a priori* assumptions in story. For one, our suspension of disbelief may be in effect when we are reading. We might be more willing to accept something as true in a story if it is coherent, consistent, and flows naturally from the narrative. If we are educated in and experience the possibility of such acts and events (e.g., by the reading and rereading of fairy stories in our youth to our adulthood), the divine and miraculous may appear possible. There is also the possibility for participation of the divine in our lives: the divine just might permeate (and re-enchant) our world. The medieval worldview can be said, generally, to see the miraculous as intrinsically tied up with the natural world: "Events called *miracula* permeated life at every level, but they were so closely woven into the texture of Christian experience that there was no incentive to examine or explain the presuppositions that lay behind."[20] The medieval experience of *miracula* followed along the lines of Augustinian thought, and implicit in this medieval experience of *miracula* is that ideas of *natura* and *miracula* were not opposed in the medieval mind.[21] We can clearly see Lewis' attempts (in his fiction and nonfiction) to habituate the modern reader into this notion as well. At the very least, Lewis was trying to counteract (and if at all possible to eliminate) the common presupposition of the modern age that the miraculous is impossible, separate, and not real. Lewis' attempts at story and myth-making are in some sense attempts to regain the enchantment of the world. It is through his stories and myth-making that Lewis is attempting to get us involved in a meaning that lies behind the world—to see that there may in fact be fairies in the garden.

Knowing something about an author's biography (or possibly even his or her psychology) might be extremely appealing and interesting, and may even be fruitful in placing certain contexts. However, Lewis felt that if taken to the extreme it was a dangerous practice and was most often better left alone. We are doing more guess work in this vein of criticism and cannot be sure that what we say about supposed motivations and psychological symptoms are in fact the real cause or of an author's works.[22] An interesting parallel here between Paul Ricoeur and Lewis can be especially seen in their insistence on reader participation. Ricoeur insists that reading is a dynamic activity. As such it "is not confined to repeating significations fixed forever, but . . . takes place as a prolonging of the itineraries of meaning opened up by the work of interpretation. Through this . . . the act of reading accords with the idea of a norm-governed productivity to the extent that it may be said to be guided by a productive imagination at work in the text itself."[23] Lewis prefigures this notion when he insisted that the interpretation of a text involves actively participating in the author's intentions. Lewis and Ricoeur, however, might disagree as to how the meanings are opened up by an active imagination. Where Ricoeur wants to see in the "reading of a text such as the Bible a creative operation unceasingly employed in decontextualizing its meaning and recontexualizing it in today's *Sitz-im-Leben*," Lewis wanted a focus on the work itself, in order to understand and participate in the author's vantage point.

However, Lewis also encouraged the reader to use his or her imagination in order to find meanings applicable to life. Lewis understood that the author (as separate from the Divine author) is not the only judge, and often not the best judge, of his or her wrok's meaning, and we can have full range on meaning—we may "range without fear of contradiction from the author's superior knowledge."[24] The trouble comes when we insist that our interpretation is the only one that is right or fits properly, or when we purposefully and clearly contradict the author's intended meaning. We can very rarely (if at all) get behind the author's intention through historical-critical means to some other "real" intention: ". . . one is after all sailing by dead reckoning; the results cannot be checked by fact."[25] Ricoeur claimed his method is neither "positive or negative, concerning the currently dominant method of historical-critical exegesis."[26] Lewis' view of employing a productive imagination within the text can be made to correspond (to a degree) with Ricoeur's views when we take into account Lewis' view of the intention of the Divine: "If every good and perfect gift comes from the Father of Lights then all true and edifying writings, whether in Scripture or not, must be *in some sense* inspired."[27]

We can search texts for the meanings of the author and for the meanings of the Divine author—for allegorical, tropological, literal, and anagogical meaning and applicability. For Lewis the critic's job was "'to show others the work they claim to admire or despise as it really is; to describe, almost to define, its character, and then leave them to their own (now better informed) reactions.' . . . All is aimed at enhancing the reader's encounter with the work of art, with 'the object itself.'"[28] In finding the author's intention, we are attempting to come into contact with the text. As Hans Frei noted,

> ... the author's intention is not a separable mental entity or action from the consecutive activity of working out his writing. ... Especially in narrative, novelistic, or history-like form, where meaning is most nearly inseparable from the words—from the descriptive shape of the story as a pattern of enactment, there is neither need for or use in looking for meaning in a more profound stratum underneath the structure ... or in a separable author's 'intention' ... [29]

In attempting a kind of literary psychoanalyzing, or literary sleuthing, one is concurrently attempting an almost impossible task of searching and postulating "what vanished documents each author used, when and where he wrote, with what purposes, under what influences—the whole *Sitz im Leben* of the text."[30] And in the case of using psychological means to evaluate and criticize a text, we come across more dangerous territory: for we may not have much evidence other than a critic's idea of, say, Freudian imagery or psychological motivation. Flannery O'Conner was in agreement with Lewis here, and she even went so far as to describe this type of literary criticism as a way to avoid teaching literature:

> ... I found that another popular way to avoid teaching literature was to be concerned exclusively with the author and his psychology. Why was Hawthorne melancholy and what made Poe drink liquor and why did Henry James like England better than America? These ruminations can take up endless time and postpone indefinitely any consideration of the work itself. Actually, a work of art exists without its author from the moment the words are on paper, and the more complete the work, the less important it is who wrote it or why. If you're studying literature, the intentions of the writer have to be found in the work itself, and not in his life.[31]

The idea that works of literature can be explained in terms of the supposed psychology of an author is often thought to be highly suspect simply because of its speculative nature.[32] It can often be done with "immense erudition and great ingenuity."[33] However, we cannot be sure that what we have postulated as the case is in fact actually the case. Lewis wanted, as much as is possible, a reading to lead out of the text and to avoid a reading into the text (exegesis not eisigesis). It is often the case that the purveyors of these critical methods are the doubters, but Lewis turned the tables and freely encouraged the doubting of the doubters' assured methods. However, the methods can be extremely convincing.

Lewis admitted he might have been greatly influenced by such methods if he had not had personal experience that guarded him against accepting them outright. Lewis himself had been the subject of critical review. He found that reviews of his work contained more talk about "imaginary histories" than they did evaluation, praise. or censure of the work itself: "The very terms which the reviewers use in praising or dispraising often imply such a history. They praise a passage as 'spontaneous' and censure another as 'laboured'; that is, they think they know that you wrote the one *currente calamo* and the other *invita Minerva*."[34] In one case Lewis published a book that was praised by one reviewer for all the essays it contained except one—and this essay was, so thought the critic, the one written with the least amount of interest, effort, and inspiration. But Lewis knew that this particular essay was the one he felt most passionate about—the one he put the most effort into and felt the most inspiration in writing (consequently, he freely admitted that the critic was right to call it the worst essay in the book). Where the critic went wrong was in ascribing an imagined history to its composition. Lewis also saw this with other books written by other friends (where he knew the personal histories). One such example was of Tolkien's *The Lord of the Rings*. Some reviewers postulated that "the Ring in [the books] was suggested by the atom bomb. What could be more plausible? Here is a book published when everyone was preoccupied by that sinister invention; here in the centre of the book is a weapon which it seems madness to throw away yet fatal to use. Yet in fact, the chronology of the book's composition makes the theory impossible."[35] Lewis gained from this experience the impression that the reviewers nearly always get their "imagined histories" wrong. In his experience, he had not witnessed an instance where a reviewer got such a history right. Of course, Lewis conceded that he did not keep any records, so his impression might be mistaken: "What I think I can say with certainty is that they are usually wrong."[36] But this ought to give us pause, wrote Lewis. The reconstruction of a text by scholars often sounds very convincing:

> But one is after all sailing by dead reckoning; the results cannot be checked by fact. In order to decide how reliable the method is, what more could you ask for than to be shown an instance where the same method is at work and we have facts to check it by? Well, that is what I have done. And we find, that when this check is available, the results are either always, or else nearly always, wrong. The "assured results of modern scholarship," as to

the way in which an old book was written, are "assured," we may conclude, only because the men who knew the facts are dead and can't blow the gaff.[37]

In Lewis' case, he did give his own account of the reasons he composed his Narnia books, and a history different from a purely psychological account of those compositions can be reconstructed. This history and these reasons fly in the face of the claims of purely psychological motivations.

Reasons for Writing the Chronicles

It is clear that Lewis' ideas for the first book of Narnia, *The Lion, the Witch, and the Wardrobe*, came about much earlier than his encounter with Anscombe in 1948. The instance of inspiration can be found within his own life story. When bombs began falling on London in 1940, Lewis opened up his household to evacuated children from the vulnerable coastal cities. One particular child may have sparked Lewis' imagination: ". . . one of the children asked Lewis if she could climb inside a freestanding wooden wardrobe he had in the house. She also asked him whether there was anything behind it."[38] It is clear that Lewis had started composing *The Lion, the Witch, and the Wardrobe* in the Fall of 1939, with small periods of writing continuing throughout parts of 1940, and then eventually he left off in the Winter of 1940. He resumed writing in earnest in the Summer of 1948, finishing the book in the Spring of 1949. The book was published in the Fall of 1950. While the Anscombe debate took place in February of 1948, and the writing for the book began in earnest the summer after their debate, it is clear that Lewis had begun thinking about (and even writing) his children's story well before his encounter with her.[39]

In Lewis' own account of the formation of the book and the reasons behind it, he claimed that all of the Chronicles of Narnia, and also the Space Trilogy, began with seeing pictures in his head.[40] They were not stories in and of themselves, but only images. The particular image that came to Lewis for *The Lion, the Witch, and the Wardrobe* was of a faun carrying parcels in the snow by a lamppost. This image had been in his head since he was sixteen, and it was not until he was older that he said, "Let's try to make a story out of it."[41] Lewis claimed that the story was at first ambiguous to him, and it was only when Aslan came bounding into it that it all came together. Aslan then "pulled the six other Narnian stories in after Him."[42] Lewis' inspiration for Aslan, he claimed, came mainly from dreams of lions he was having at the time.[43] According to Lewis, the reason for writing the Chronicles of Narnia was two-fold: what he deemed as the "Author's" reason and the "Man's" reason. On the Author's side, Lewis found that mental images would "bubble up" from time to time (e.g., his images of a faun carrying an umbrella, a queen on a sledge, a lion). He contradicts the notion that when he first composed his Narnian tales he specially thought out how he could say something about Christianity to children.[44] But, of course, these mental images would come to nothing unless a form was present to "pour" these images into.[45] And Lewis saw that the fairy tale was the perfect form for what he had to say.[46] After the Author had his turn, the Man in Lewis had his turn. Lewis saw how these stories might "steal past watchful dragons"—might make the ability to feel and understand love and respect for God become not obligatory but truly potent.[47] The Man in Lewis could get across points through the mode of story and image. However, Lewis personally disliked the mechanical implantation of morals in writings. That one could somehow write a good story specifically for the purpose of having a moral told was a disastrous task according to Lewis. The question "What do children need?" is dangerous because asking the question will not get us a good moral.[48] The moral should arise inevitably, from the author's being, as a direct result of the story and as a result of the imagination pushing its own moral lessons into the story. Neither should the morals or lessons be demarcated or singled out: they are understood within the context of the images and of the narrative. A good story is one in which we continually derive different lessons and morals and meanings, not one where we are *told* (didactically) the meaning and moral. It may be true that sometimes stories or myths have morals that are purposefully placed, and they may be sufficient (i.e., if they have been placed there by the author through a deep-seated awareness). But it is invariably the morals or lessons that arise of their own accord that give us the deepest, most varied and complex meanings.

The motivation for Lewis' imaginative fiction writing was to present images that bubbled up in his mind and compelled him to pour these images into a form in a meaningful way. It was this part of Lewis, the deepest aspect of Lewis, that pushed him into his writing of children's fiction and fiction in general. The older, more continuously operative man in Lewis is the imaginative man, the mythmaker, the storyteller. Of course, these images that bubbled up can still be relegated (by those who wish to do so) to their merely phenomenal, material aspects—so the "bubbling up" is just psychological repression—of sublimated wishes and fancies. And Lewis himself, before he became a Christian, had taken this account to be true. So how was it that Lewis came to change his mind?

The Older and More Continuously Operative

Lewis' primary problem in reconciling reason and imagination was a direct result of Enlightenment assumptions about rationality: that imagination is mere "fancy," human-created illusion; that a certain kind of rationality is king—unfettered, recognized by all, uncommitted, ahistorical, and unbiased. After his conversion Lewis' views on reason and imagination are to be seen primarily in terms of growth—of the older imaginative man (the premodern man) expressing himself explicitly.[49] Shifts in emphasis from book to book are clear (where a more formal reasoning takes a front seat or an explicitly image-laden depiction dominates), but they are to be seen in light of the purpose of the book and the "turning of our argument every which way," persuading an audience through different means.[50] It seems apparent that as a result of his conversion Lewis felt freedom to explore the imaginative realms (they were no longer mere fancy but a divine gleam falling upon the human mind) and to see more clearly that the imaginative realms are reasoned work.[51]

Lewis' allegory *The Pilgrim's Regress*, his first book written after his conversion, also expresses a rejection of "19th century rationalism." Our protagonist, John, meets Mr. Enlightenment after leaving his home, Purtania. Mr. Enlightenment attempts to convince John of an absolute certainty:

> "Purtania! Why, I suppose you have been brought up to be afraid of the Landlord. . . . You may make your mind at ease, my boy. There is no such person."
> "There is no Landlord?"
> "There is absolutely no such thing—I might even say no such *entity*—in existence. There never has been and never will be."
> "And this is absolutely certain?" cried John . . .
> "Absolutely certain. Look at me, young man, I ask you—do I look as if I was easily taken in?"[52]

The only rational position permitted, for Mr. Enlightenment, is the one he puts forward, viz., rejection of the Landlord. However, John eventually rejects Mr. Enlightenment's philosophy. The last expression of this comes in Plato's allegory of the cave (which Lewis quotes before the chapter begins): having escaped the cave, into reality, John realizes the real shape of the world.

Lewis' premodern influences find expression with his conversion to Christianity. His love of myth is clearly prior to his conversion, but it is after his conversion that we see these sources used unabashedly. The rationalist Lewis, the pre-Christian Lewis, would have rejected (not without difficulty and contradictions within himself—as is seen in his writing of this period) such sources as "beautiful lies breathed through silver." Lewis labels himself a lifelong lover of romance in his autobiography, and in his early letters to his friend Arthur Greeves we see clearly that Lewis was "bent . . . toward all that stimulated the imagination artfully . . ."[53] Lewis "made both the form and the content [of his fiction] work in harness," and from an early age he "had thought, analyzed, and responded to fiction . . ."[54] Lewis' venture into children's fiction can also be seen, as Colin Duriez notes, as a culmination of Lewis' skills—suggesting that Lewis needed to live and learn more before he could express himself effectively in fairy stories.[55] Lewis did see his predominately intellectual approach as a limitation of his mythopoeic skills.[56] However, Lewis did use a "team of two" in his imaginative writing—assailing the head and the heart through the use of story. Lewis asserted that the imaginative side of him was the "older" aspect of his personality. It was the clear driver in his efforts to become an author and to become a Christian:

> [The] imaginative man in me is older, more continuously operative, and in that sense more basic than either the religious writer or the critic. It was he who made me first attempt (with little success) to be a poet. It was he who, in response to the poetry of others, made me a critic, and, in defense of that response, sometimes a critical controversialist. It was he who, after my conversion led me to embody my religious belief in symbolical or mythopoeic forms, ranging from *Screwtape* to a kind of theological science-fiction. And it was, of course, he who has brought me, in the last few years to write the series of Narnian stories for children; not asking what children want and then endeavoring to adapt myself (this was not needed) but because the fairy-tale was the *genre* best fitted for what I wanted to say.[57]

Lewis saw his own development in terms of internal growth—where the more imaginative man led him to embody his religious belief in mythopoeic fiction—and his conversion was the deepening point of this process. When Lewis was an atheist, he felt a "contradiction between his reason and his imagination. That which he passionately loved in the realm of imagination—aspirations to meaning, dignity, immortality, beauty and contact with the supernatural—were what drew him into the writings of poets, philosophers and saints."[58] The denial of the meaning in myth, narrative, and poetic language (indeed, imagination) was a direct result of his rationalistic assumptions. However, when Lewis became a Christian the dilemma of reason versus imagination was to a large extent ameliorated—through a rejection of rationalistic, Enlightenment presuppositions about imagination and rationality and a flourishing of his premodern influences. There is also room here for a valuation of Lewis' continued growth as a writer and person, a deepening of understanding and effectiveness. Lewis found a marriage of sorts where the reasoned work of the imagination could be seen as a pointer to something real, meaningful, and true.

Notes

1. Wilson, *C. S. Lewis*, 211.
2. See ibid., 226.
3. This seems a particularly puzzling parallel for Wilson to draw, for the Queen of Underland in *The Silver Chair* uses, unambiguously, a materialist and even Freudian ideology. In the story, the Queen of Underland attempts to convince the children, Rilian, and Puddleglum that there is no Overland, no sun, and no Aslan; there is only her Underworld. Lewis, in part, used this scene to undermine "modernist ideas about myth and meaning.... What the Witch says assumes that only things we can see and touch are real. She tells the children, Rilian, and Puddleglum that the sun and Aslan are only myths. Having seen a lamp lighting a room, they projected a greater 'lamp' that lights the world and called it *sun*, and having seen cats, they imagined a greater cat and called it a *lion*. 'The lamp is the real thing; the *sun* is but a tale.' Such materialism leads to a 'bottom up' theory of myth which says that the 'higher' conceptions in myths are generated from the lower. It is, in fact, a modernist means of explaining away that which is regarded as 'mythological'" (Schakel, *Way into Narnia*, 78).
4. Lewis, *Of Other Worlds*, 50.
5. Ibid., 51.
6. Ibid.
7. One might want to see Kathryn Lindskoog's essay "A.N. Wilson Errata" for an account of some areas where Wilson does such psychoanalyzing of Lewis. In George Sayer's biography, *Jack*, he also speaks to Wilson's tendency to psychoanalyze Lewis through Freudian means (see particularly the "Afterword," pages 413–23). One might also look at Walter Hooper's essay "Narnia: The Author, the Critics, and the Tale," in Schakel, ed., *Longing for a Form*. In this essay, Hooper deals with David Holbrook's

essay "The Problem of C. S. Lewis." Hooper writes that Lewis found arguing with Freudians to be particularly exasperating. For anything one was likely to say would be used as evidence against oneself: "The difficulty, [Lewis] said, about arguing with such Freud-ridden sheep is that *whatever* you say to the contrary, no matter how clear and obvious to a sensible man, the Freudian uses it to support what he's already decided to believe. Or, as Lewis says elsewhere, they argue in the same manner as a man who should say, 'If there were an invisible cat in the chair, the chair would look empty; but the chair does look empty; therefore there is an invisible cat in it. A belief in invisible cats cannot be logically disproved, but it tells us a good deal about those who hold it'" (Schakel, ed., *Longing for a Form*, 108).

8. Sayer, *Jack*, 261.
9. Plank, "Some Psychological Aspects", 26.
10. Lewis, *Collected Letters*, 2:644.
11. Duriez and Porter, *Inklings Handbook*, 144.
12. Ibid.
13. Ibid. Lewis himself was and is often accused of using too many literary allusions in his own work, particularly in the Chronicles of Narnia. Some see Lewis' "borrowing" as something that is used at the "expense of his own originality" (Ford, *Companion to Narnia*, 272). However, others see this process of using allusions as a natural one for authors of all kinds. One of Lewis' friends, Roger Lancelyn Green, takes this latter view: "This background of thought is apparent throughout the Narnia stories, and for this reason it is of little importance to look for 'sources' and 'originals.' Such research might tell us what books Lewis had read, and where some of his ideas came from: but pure invention is almost impossible, and all authors receive their inspiration with the aid of suggestions or trains of thought induced by the odd word, line, sentence or even idea in another man's book—or in the general background of myth from which as often as not the previous writer himself had drawn. What matters is the use made of these hints, ideas and inspirations" (Green, *C. S. Lewis*, 34).
14. "Lewis generally disliked source criticism, the interpretive approach that assumes major characters and images in a story can usually be traced to something in an author's life or reading habits.... Lewis also warned that source critics may expend so much ingenuity in 'getting behind the text' that they lose sight of the text itself; however, even though 'Lewis distrusted source criticism, he did not try to argue that creative ideas appear out of nowhere'" (Downing, *Into the Wardrobe*, 32).
15. Duriez and Porter, *Inklings Handbook*, 94.
16. For example, Lewis spoke to the vices and virtues of medieval literary devices: "[Medieval literature's] typical vice, as we all know, is dullness; sheer, unabashed, prolonged dullness, where the author does not seem to be even trying to interest us.... One sees how the belief in a world of built-in significance encourages this. The writer feels everything to be so interesting in itself that there is no need for him to make it so. The story, however badly told, will still be worth telling; the truths, however badly stated, still worth stating.... And yet, I believe, it is also connected with the characteristic virtue of good medieval work. What this is, anyone can feel if he turns from the narrative verse of, say, Chapman or Keats to the best parts of Marie de France or Gower. What will strike him at once is the absence of strain. In the Elizabethan or Romantic examples we feel that the poet has done a great deal of work; in the medieval, we are at first hardly aware of a poet at all. The writing is so limpid and effortless that the

story seems to be telling itself. . . . The telling is for the sake of the tale; in Chapman or Keats we feel that the tale is valued only as an opportunity for lavish and highly individual treatment" (*Discarded Image*, 204–5). In Lewis' writing of children's stories he enjoyed the "strictness" of the prose—that it was there for the sake of the story and not for the sake of the storyteller: ". . . the Model universe of our ancestors had a built in significance. And that in two senses; as having 'significant form' (it is an admirable design) and as a manifestation of the wisdom and goodness that created it. There was no question of waking it into beauty or life. . . . The achieved perfection was already there. The only difficulty was to make an adequate response" (ibid., 204). This built-in significance to the medieval worldview was just what Lewis attempted to put to work in the Chronicles: all that was left, presumably, was the opportunity for the proper and adequate response to the story from the reader.

17. It is claimed that in using the medieval worldview in his fiction, "Lewis's task was not to argue for the intellectual vitality of the medieval worldview but rather to show its imaginative beauty" (Downing, *Into the Wardrobe*, 111). However, doesn't intellectual vitality equal imaginative beauty? Lewis' use of the medieval worldview makes just such a case: it is a valued response to the universe, beautiful, powerful, affective, and effective. For a look at some authors who delve into this aspect of Lewis' Chronicles, one might want to examine Don King's essay "Narnia and the Seven Deadly Sins." King there argues that Lewis, being a medieval scholar, had an intimate knowledge of the seven deadly sins and either consciously or unconsciously used the seven chronicles to highlight each sin: "He has taken the seven deadly sins into Narnia, shown their destructive power, and set before us examples to avoid." Another scholar who deals with Lewis' medieval influences is Michael Ward. Ward argues that in the medieval understanding of the universe there were seven planets, and each planet reflected certain images and emotions to medieval peoples. Lewis was familiar with these notions and may have composed each volume of the Chronicles according to the planetary evocations. So *The Lion, the Witch, and the Wardrobe* relates to Jupiter, *Prince Caspian* to Mars, *The Voyage of the Dawn Treader* to the sun, *The Silver Chair* to the moon, *The Horse and His Boy* to Mercury, *The Magician's Nephew* to Venus, and *The Last Battle* to Saturn. See Ward's thesis, "The Son and the Other Stars," or his book *Planet Narnia*.

18. Lewis, *Discarded Image*, 204. As an aside, James Bruce Ross and Mary Martin McLaughlin noted that the "whole Christian revelation, the drama of medieval religion, is made manifest in tangible forms with . . . symbolical meanings. . . . Very little that medieval men built or painted or wrote can be fully comprehended without some understanding of that mode of observation and thought which expressed itself by means of symbolism and allegory. In this way of looking at things and thinking about them, the visible object is clothed with supernatural significance, and the abstract conception given concrete form in an image. . . . To the medieval mind symbolism explained the observed facts of nature in terms of the Christian and eternal facts of life. It exalted and justified both image and concept, supporting them with the weight of tradition and of divine authority" (Ross and McLaughlin, eds., *Portable Medieval Reader*, 19).

19. Plato also thought that stories could be of similar use when teaching children. The virtues could be demonstrated and responded to through the use of story. The use of games was also an important tool in the moral education of children: "We should try to use the children's games to channel their pleasures and desires towards the activities in which they will have to engage when they are adult" (Plato, *Great Dialogues*, 72). It is in fairytales that we first hear about the gods, and it is here that we should take care: "'As

regards the gods then,' said I, 'these are the sorts of things, as it seems, which ought and ought not to be heard from childhood, by those who are to honour God and honour their parents, and to hold dear the friendship among themselves'" (Plato, *Laws*, 182). Plato could be seen as urging the writers of fairytales to tell tales that encourage belief in the good, the true, and the beautiful.

20. B. Ward, *Miracles*, 1–2.

21. Ibid., 2.

22. Lewis told us that an author is rarely if ever a good judge (and definitely not a perfect judge) of his or her book's meaning (*Of Other Worlds*, 57). The trouble with this is when the critic insists on a strict allegorical interpretation, where the allegory the critic finds is interpreted to be the final word on the subject—or in other words, where the critic confuses applicability with a single interpretation or single allegory. Of course, every story can be interpreted allegorically, but the problem arises when the critic thinks that his or her allegory is all that the story means or intends or that the author intended the story to be an allegory when it was not.

23. Ricoeur, *Figuring the Sacred*, 145.

24. Lewis, *Of Other Worlds*, 57.

25. Lewis, *Christian Reflections*, 160.

26. Ricoeur, *Figuring the Sacred*, 148.

27. Lewis, *Letters* (1993), 480.

28. Oury, "'Thing Itself,'" 10. Additionally, in a very limited sense, Lewis could also be compared to the literary movement known as reception theory. In very general terms, reception theory refers to the "general shift in concern from the author and the work to the text and the reader" (Holub, *Reception Theory*, xii). Hans Robert Jauss, a major theorist of the movement, attempted to "overcome the Marxist-Formalist dichotomy" by "viewing literature from the perspective of the reader or consumer. The 'aesthetics of reception' . . . maintains that the historical essence of an artwork cannot be elucidated by examining its production or by simply describing it. Rather, literature should be treated as a dialectical process of production *and reception*" (ibid., 57). Jauss observed that a sense of pleasure was needed in evaluating literature. For example, two movements can be detected in aesthetic pleasure: "In the first, which is also applicable to all pleasure, there occurs an unmediated surrender . . . of the ego to the object. The second moment, which is peculiar to aesthetic pleasure, consists of 'taking up of a position that brackets the existence of the object and thereby makes it an aesthetic one'" (ibid., 74). Wolfgang Iser, another major theorist in the movement, also attempted to find the conditions of meaning for a reader (ibid., 83). He contrasted with traditional interpretation, "which . . . sought to elucidate a hidden meaning in the text," by locating meaning in the "interaction between text and reader, as 'an effect to be experienced,' not an 'object to be defined'" (ibid.). It is clear that Lewis has something in common with these responses. Lewis found that the critic's job was to understand and deal with the text (as much as is possible) as the author intended. And Lewis valued aesthetic pleasure highly and appreciated its role. However, Lewis has some serious distinction from the movement. Lewis would have a very difficult time with Iser's insistence that a text is to be experienced but not become an object to be defined (depending upon the exact meaning of such an idea). For Lewis saw one of the main jobs of the critic as finding the object's form—for the form of the story or text is also important to its intents and purposes. The fairytale is chosen by an author for a specific purpose and intent: it

allows him or her to say best what he or she needs to say. But Lewis would most likely agree that we must not simply adhere to formalism. The experience of the text (including the participation of the reader and the divine) and the form are both very important components making up a literary encounter.

29. Frei, *Eclipse of Biblical Narrative*, 281.
30. Lewis, *Christian Reflections*, 158.
31. O'Connor, *Mystery and Manners*, 126.
32. For an extremely brief, general explanation of this method, see in Cuddon's *Dictionary of Literary Terms* the entry on "Freudian criticism/psychoanalytic criticism": "Broadly speaking, so-called Freudian criticism or classical psychoanalytic criticism—which is often speculative—is concerned with the quest for and discovery of (and the subsequent analysis of) connections between the artists . . . themselves and what they actually create . . ." (p. 356).
33. Lewis, *Christian Reflections*, 158.
34. Ibid., 159.
35. Ibid., 160.
36. Ibid.
37. Ibid., 160–61.
38. Duncan, *Magic Never Ends*, 106.
39. See Paul Ford's book *Companion to Narnia*, particularly appendix 1, p. 451, for an account of the dates of composition of all the Narnia books.
40. Lewis, *Of Other Worlds*, 42.
41. Ibid.
42. Ibid.
43. Ibid.
44. "Some people seem to think that I began by asking myself how I could say something about Christianity to children; then fixed on the fairy tale as an instrument; then collected information about child-psychology and decided what age group I'd write for; then drew up a list of basic Christian truths and hammered out 'allegories' to embody them. This is pure moonshine. I couldn't write in that way at all. Everything began with images. . . . At first there wasn't even anything Christian about them; that element pushed itself in of its own accord. It was part of the bubbling" (Ibid., 36).
45. We can see a distinct similarity here with the writer Flannery O'Conner: "In the act of writing, one sees that the way a thing is made controls and is inseparable from the whole meaning of it. The form of a story gives it meaning which any other form would change, and unless the student is able, in some degree, to apprehend the form, he will never apprehend anything else about the work, except what is extrinsic to it as literature. The result of the proper study of a novel should be contemplation of the mystery embodied in it, but this is a contemplation of the mystery in the whole work and not of some proposition or paraphrase" (O'Conner, *Mystery and Manners*, 129).
46. "As these images sorted themselves into events (i.e., became a story) they seemed to demand no love interest and no close psychology. But the Form which excludes these things is the fairy tale. And the moment I thought of that I fell in love with the Form itself: its brevity, its severe restraints on description, its flexible traditionalism, its inflexible hostility to all analysis, digression, reflections and 'gas'. . . . On that side (as Author) I wrote fairy tales because the Fairy Tale seemed the ideal Form for the stuff I had to say" (Lewis, *Of Other Worlds*, 36–37).

47. "Why did one find it so hard to feel as one was told one ought to feel about God or about the sufferings of Christ? I thought the chief reason was that one was told one ought to. An obligation to feel can freeze feelings. And reverence itself did harm. The whole subject was associated with lowered voices; almost as if it were something medical. But supposing that by casting all these things into an imaginary world, striping them of their stained-glass and Sunday school associations, one could make them for the first time appear in their real potency? Could one not thus steal past those watchful dragons? I thought one could" (Ibid., 37).

48. "If we ask that question we are assuming too superior an attitude. It would be better to ask 'What moral do I need?' for I think we can be sure that what does not concern us deeply will not deeply interest our readers. . . . But it is better not to ask the question at all. Let the pictures tell you their own moral. For the moral inherent in them will rise from whatever spiritual roots you have succeeded in striking during the whole course of your life. But if they don't show you any moral, don't put one in. For the moral you put in is likely to be a platitude, or even a falsehood, skimmed from the surface of your consciousness. It is impertinent to offer the children that. For we have been told on high authority that in the moral sphere they are probably at least as wise as we. . . . The only moral that is of any value is that which arises inevitably from the whole cast of the author's mind" (Lewis, *Of Other Worlds*, 33).

49. In Peter Schakel's *Reason and Imagination in C. S. Lewis*, he argues that reason and imagination are juxtaposed in Lewis' thought and work. He insists that a shift in emphasis occurred in the late 1940s and early 50s, not at the time of Lewis' conversion. Schakel notes that before the shift in emphasis, Lewis relied primarily upon reason, allowing the imagination to play an ancillary role. It is not until later in Lewis' life that we see a reconciliation and uniting of reason and imagination in his work. Schakel argues that while Lewis initially struggled with his dual interest in imagination and reason, his conversion to Christianity did not immediately unite the two. Instead, for Schakel, we see the critic and the storyteller of the 30s (where imagination is a servant); the apologist of the 40s (where reason is master); the autobiographer of the 50s (where reason and imagination are reconciled); and the personal writer of the 60s (where reason and imagination are united). Schakel's assessment is fine when it is viewed as a description of Lewis' growth as a person and writer. However, his view unnecessarily bifurcates the Christian Lewis into an Enlightenment rationalist and imaginative poet by using watershed moments in Lewis life—namely, the Anscombe debate, the influence of Tolkien and Barfield, and the acknowledgement of an element of subjectivity in perception. As a result Lewis' use of reason and focus on imagination does not really seem to be a culmination of his old, inner self coming to fruition (nor does the view recognize the reasoned elements of the imagination—to see it as a foundational, motivating function). The problem is that we lose the importance of Lewis' premodern roots and the importance of his Christian conversion: i.e., Lewis' adherence to his premodern influences, and the role of his conversion experience in the reinvigoration of those premodern sources, is marginalized. Scott Burton and Jerry Walls also have a noteworthy critique of Schakel's argument: "We do . . . question one of Schakel's apparent assumptions, namely, the impropriety of elevating reason above the imagination. Schakel seems to suggest that such an arrangement is flawed and imbalanced. Any work not entirely synthesized is somehow less than it ought to be. But this assumption is highly questionable, for some projects inherently require disparity. If one is presenting a rational case for the Christian faith, it is not surprising to find reason taking center stage, with imagination filling out the supporting cast with illustrative metaphors. Surely there is a place in

apologetics for predominately rational works, just as there is a place in apologetics for predominately imaginative works. The work should not be evaluated in light of its rational and imaginative balance but rather in light of its inherent purpose.... [We] simply highlight Lewis's remarkable balance and dexterity in utilizing both direct and indirect appeals.... Quite simply, it seems good writing [for Lewis] is both rational and imaginative. Lewis's advice reveals a balanced integration" (Burton and Walls, *C. S. Lewis and Francis Schaeffer*, 168–69). The "reasoning-man" of the 40s looks more like a man who is positioning the Christian faith as a reasonable, rational option (through Platonic persuasion)—not as a proposition for "secular" certainty and/or rationalistic assent to proofs. This is a fundamental misunderstanding of Lewis in terms of Enlightenment ideas about rationality. The purpose of the work needs to be evaluated as well: some work is inherently going to be explicitly reason-centered and some explicitly image-centered: the two are different expressions of the same divine truth.

50. We must "turn all our arguments every which way and try to find some easier and shorter route to the art..." (Plato, *Complete Works*, 549).

51. As an aside, another argument against the Wilsonian thesis is presented by Marvin Hinton, who suggests that Lewis found the writing of apologetics to be a dangerous task and knew the limits of such work: "Some writers have suggested that a difficult philosophical debate at the Socratic Club with Oxford philosopher Elizabeth Anscombe may have moved him away from apologetics and toward fantasy.... Or it may be that, having written *The Problem of Pain*, *Mere Christianity*, and *Miracles* within the past decade, Lewis simply felt he had carried philosophical apologetics as far as he needed to, or possibly even as far as was good for him. In an August 2, 1946, letter to Dorothy Sayers, he remarked that apologetic writing was 'dangerous to one's own faith'..." (Hinten, *Keys to the Chronicles*, 2). However, we must be clear and take into account Lewis' publishing record, which shows he did not simply stop writing such work altogether.

52. Lewis, *Pilgrim's Regress*, 20.

53. Glover, *C. S. Lewis*, 8.

54. Ibid., 2–3.

55. As noted earlier, "Writing for children is one of the most demanding of an author's tasks. The Narnian tales built on skills that Lewis had honed in writing earlier stories for grownups.... Therefore, in reading the stories we are reading not an author who has lost his way but one who has become so convinced of the way that he can effectively point its direction to a very large readership that unselfishly enjoys storytelling" (Duriez, *Field Guide*, 11–12).

56. As noted earlier, in 1946 Lewis wrote, the "limitation of my own gifts has compelled me always to use a predominately intellectual approach. But I have also been present when an appeal of a much more emotional and also more 'pneumatic', kind has worked wonders on a modern audience.... But best of all is a team of two: one to deliver the preliminary intellectual barrage, and the other to follow up with a direct attack on the heart" (*Present Concerns*, 66).

57. Lewis, *Letters* (1993), 444.

58. Lindsley, *C. S. Lewis's Case for Christ*, 93.

four

Desire and Longing in Lewis, Plato, and Augustine

L̲EWIS' DEBT TO PLATO is deep, and from his statement in *The Last Battle* it is plain to see: "It's all in Plato."¹ Lewis essentially pulls back the veil on his Narnia tales here: Narnia is swallowed up into New Narnia. There is a Platonic-Augustinian ontology that has been playing out in the back ground, and he has, at the last book, revealed explicitly to his audience what has been going on all along. This is clearly revealed in Narnia being pulled up into New Narnia: it is the lower, or mundane life that is brought up into the higher, divine life; it participates and gains its meaning and *telos* from transcendent funding. In this chapter I continue the thread of a reasoning beyond reason by examining the role of desire or longing within the work of Lewis, Plato, and Augustine. This is done in an effort to place Lewis firmly within a premodern framework, particularly the Platonic-Augustinian tradition, as well as to demonstrate the connection between imagination and Platonic-Augustinian desire. There is also a further connection between Plato and Lewis on the idea of the moral imagination: namely, in the inculcation of children in the virtues through game or story. This, in turn, places a focus on the role and function of art: that is, art gains its *telos* and meaning when it reverts back to (participates in) its higher, divine source.

Joy

Lewis argued that there is in each one of us a sense of longing or desire for joy (what he calls, technically, *Sehnsucht*[2]). Lewis' experiences of joy or longing "are recognizably one with the Platonic-Augustinian 'ascent of the soul,' in which the human heart, incited by the limited goods and beauties of creation, discovers within itself a restless, piercing desire for the unlimited source of all reality and perfection."[3] This deep-seated desire indicates a real presence of the divine in human hearts—and, for Lewis, was an indicator that a relationship with the creator was the ultimate aim of this desire. Lewis thought that normally our desires correspond to actual objects in experience. For example, if we are hungry then there is such a thing as food to satisfy this desire. If we have sexual desire, then there is something such as sex. While Lewis was intrigued with the line from Matthew Arnold, "Nor does the being hungry prove that we have bread," he took issue with it on one account: "But surely, tho' it doesn't prove that one particular man will *get* food, it *does* prove that there is such a thing as food!"[4] Lewis also took this argument a step further. He asked, "If you are really a product of the materialist universe, how is it you don't feel at home there?"[5] Lewis concluded that there is a desire or longing for joy present in us, though it often is mistaken for something else.[6] Furthermore, this desire present in humankind has no direct corresponding element in the world.[7] This desire is special and secret to each person. Lewis spoke to this in his sermon "The Weight of Glory":

> I am almost committing an indecency. I am trying to rip open the inconsolable secret in each one of you—the secret which hurts so much that you take your revenge on it by calling it names like Nostalgia and Romanticism and Adolescence; the secret which pierces with such sweetness that when, in very intimate conversation, the mention of it becomes imminent, we grow awkward and affect to laugh at ourselves; the secret we cannot hide and cannot tell, though we desire to do both. We cannot tell it because it is a desire for something that has never actually appeared in our experience. We cannot hide it because our experience is constantly suggesting it, and we betray ourselves like lovers at the mention of a name.[8]

This particular joy is not to be confused with other forms of longing. Lewis warned us of treating these moments of longing as mere memories of the past or mere recognition of beauty. The beauty we find in other things (e.g., a good book, a nice piece of music) is something through which the experience of joy communicates: it is *through* them and not *in* them that we find this real sense of longing. These things point beyond themselves to reveal a more essential or real beauty. In the Platonic-Augustinian tradition it is crucial that only the Good—or God—is wholly and solely desirable. To desire for its own sake that which mediates God, as if the mediator of desire were the ultimate end, is idolatry. Anything that is created is to be viewed in this light: in other words, it is dangerous to view created things as ends in themselves, even if one does not espouse an ultimate teleology.

Moreover, this sense of joy can be distinguished from pleasure and happiness. It is neither of these, but happiness and pleasure do have something in common with our deep-seated longing, namely, the fact that we will want it again. Lewis' sense of longing can be distinguished from other types of longings in two ways. First, though this special desire may communicate a type of pain or aching, it is still felt as an enjoyment—joy is marked by the sense of an inconsolable feeling that stabs and comes with pangs, but it is more desirable than any other satisfaction.[9] Second, this joy is experienced as enchantment, as mystery; it is experienced as an unknown quantity—there is no corresponding object in the material world to which the desire directly points.[10]

Lewis first experienced this sense of joy in his life at a young age. In his autobiography, *Surprised by Joy*, he recounted a story of his older brother bringing him a garden created out of moss and twigs and flowers. The garden sparked something within Lewis' imagination. The toy garden did something for Lewis that no real garden had ever done: "It made me aware of nature—not, indeed, as a storehouse of forms and colors but as something cool, dewy, fresh, exuberant."[11] This experience of his brother's toy garden stayed with Lewis, and even the memory of it aroused a special sense of longing:

> It is difficult to find words strong enough for the sensation which came over me; Milton's "enormous bliss" of Eden . . . comes somewhere near it. It was a sensation, of course, of desire; but desire for what? not, certainly, for a biscuit tin filled with moss, nor even (though that came into it) for my own past . . . and before I knew what I desired, the desire itself was gone, the whole glimpse withdrawn, the world turned commonplace again, or only stirred by a longing for the longing that had just ceased. It had taken

only a moment of time; and in a certain sense everything else that had ever happened to me was insignificant in comparison.[12]

This sense of longing occurred throughout Lewis' life. He described these instances of joy as the clearest moments in his consciousness. However, Lewis came to see these moments of joy as not being important in and of themselves, but rather as pointers to something more, to something other: "I believe . . . that the old stab, the old bitter-sweet, has come to me as often and as sharply since my conversion as at any other time of my life whatever. But I now know that the experience, considered as a state of my own mind, had never had the kind of importance I once gave it. It was valuable only as a pointer to something other and outer."[13] However, the phenomenal world does not become meaningless: the transcendence of the experience suspends the material through which it communicates; it brings the experience (or that through which the divine communicates) up into the divine life. But without the divine the mere experience terminates on itself and loses its meaning and *telos*. These moments of joy for Lewis were the "secret signature of each soul": "[Lewis] saw this unquenchable longing as a sure sign that no part of the created world, and thus no human experience, is capable of fulfilling fallen humankind."[14] Though, of course, the created world can mediate this longing. For the proper end of desire we must look beyond the mere experience of joy (or the object through which joy communicates) to the "Something" which triggers it and fulfills it.[15] It is only here, in this bringing up of the material into the divine life, that we can then "save" the appearances.

Plato and Longing

The influence of Plato's work upon Lewis is extensive. It is clear not least from Lewis' declaration in *The Last Battle* that "It's all in Plato."[16] Plato was indeed diffused in quite a lot, though clearly not all, of Lewis' work. Lewis' idea of longing, or *Sehnsucht*, has clear parallels with Plato's works, such as *Meno* and the *Phaedrus*, which deal with Plato's theory of recollection. In addition, Lewis also has many shared views with Plato on education and moral instruction: they both saw the importance of education in the receptivity of longing. Plato saw education starting in childhood by the acquisition of virtue: "I call 'education' the initial acquisition of virtue by the child. . . . Then when he does understand, his reason and his emotions agree in telling him that he has been properly trained by inculcation of appropriate habits."[17] Virtue must be cultivated, but it is understood only after the habit of moral action has been formed. Lewis shared a similar vision in regards to the moral education of children. He came to believe that the best way to teach children about morality and God was to teach them through story, and particularly through the fairy story. We see a clear resemblance here with Plato's ideas about the education of children: ". . . what we have in mind is education from childhood in *virtue*, a training which produces a keen desire to become a perfect citizen who knows how to rule and be ruled as justice demands."[18] Plato also suggested using children's games as a means of teaching: "We should try to use the children's games to channel their pleasures and desires towards the activities in which they will have to engage when they are adult."[19] Lewis took this idea through another channel—by teaching through the "game" of fairy story. Fairy was also important to Plato. He stated in *The Laws* that if

> only they [those who do not believe in the gods] believed the stories which they had as babes and sucklings from their nurses and mothers! These almost literally "charming" stories were told partly for amusement, partly in full earnest. . . . When some people contemptuously brush aside all this evidence without a single good reason to support them . . . and oblige us to deliver this address— well, how could one possibly admonish them and at the same time teach them the basic fact about gods, their existence . . . ?[20]

Both Plato and Lewis focused on the experience of and participation in the divine as being of the utmost importance: for real experiencing and participation offers more, not less, than the process of a flat rationalism. The idea of the importance of experience can be seen in Plato's *Republic*, where proper reasoning is something that must come after the experience of the reality of the Forms.[21] We must first take in the reality of the experience before we can discuss it—though we must be keenly aware that the reality of the Forms is not something that we experience in the same way as we might experience a table or a sunset. The Good, in particular, is not something we can directly experience in itself, or know in itself. Such experience and knowledge is always mediated.

In *The Republic* Plato noted that education begins in the nursery. We first hear about the gods in our nursery tales, and it is here that one must take care. Plato urged the writers of tales to keep a high moral tone for the benefit of children and to portray the divine in a virtuous light, as the author of ultimate Good: "'As regards the gods then,' said I, 'these are the sorts of things, as it seems, which ought and ought not to be heard from childhood, by those who are to honour God and honour their parents, and to hold dear the friendship among themselves.'"[22]

It has often been suggested that Plato's Forms and his image of the cave be used to suggest that one should abandon or neglect this life in favor of the true life we might find outside the cave—that immanence, in fact, should be abandoned because it is merely shadow. However, we must also keep in mind that Plato noted, in *The Republic*, the pity we are to feel for those who do not see the brilliance of reality.[23] This is at least one sense in which this life is not to be deserted—we are compelled to help others—but we can also see that the shadows are beautiful too because they are able to lead us (however indirectly and dimly) to what is plain if we can only turn our heads around in the cave. The shadows do not therefore lose all meaning and purpose because they are divinely gifted; they can be saved because they can be suspended by transcendence. That is, immanence is brought up into the divine life, is saved from nihilism, and gains importance, meaning and purpose. What is also often overlooked in Plato's metaphor of the cave is the continuing dialogue in the *Republic* that follows the metaphor of the cave. Plato's inclusion of two other metaphors to illustrate his line of reasoning strongly suggests that it is best to read all three metaphors together because no one metaphor on its own does full justice to Plato's view. There is, consequently, another avenue for Plato that will draw us to make the ascent: it is through the "*summoners*," through the things that summon our thoughts toward being. Plato declares that it is calculation, as a subject of knowledge, that does this: "It leads the soul forcibly upward and compels it to discuss the numbers themselves, never permitting anyone to propose for discussion numbers attached to visible or tangible bodies."[24] But the metaphor of the sun tells us that the world of becoming is to be valued as well, placing a bit more worth on the realm of becoming than is often credited to Plato. We are not surprised that when someone has seen the Good that his or her "sight is dim, and . . . hasn't yet become accustomed to the darkness . . ."[25] This one will often behave "awkwardly" and appear "completely ridiculous."[26] However, anyone with "understanding would remember that the eyes may be confused in two ways": first, by coming from the light to the darkness, and, second, by coming from the darkness to the light.[27] So it is with the soul: when one sees another soul that is disturbed and not able to perceive, one will not "laugh mindlessly, but [will] take into consideration whether it has come from a brighter life and is dimmed through not having yet become accustomed to the dark or whether it has come from greater ignorance into greater light and is dazzled by the increased brilliance."[28] The power to learn, then, is present in everyone and this power is "like an eye that cannot be turned around from darkness to light without turning the whole body. This instrument cannot be turned around from that which is coming into being without turning the whole soul..."[29] So, to stay in the light and refuse to go down to the prisoners of the cave is the incorrect path: the "founders," those who have seen the light, are obligated to compel the best natures to make the ascent.

Interestingly, Lewis' children's stories have also been accused of being escapist fantasies, of abandoning the realm of becoming (in addition to being labeled as retreats away from hard reason).[30] Lewis (and Tolkien) argued for something quite the opposite of escapism. Despite fantasies simply taking one away to another world, they also have the function of re-enchanting the world we inhabit. The pertinent question is whether fairy tales teach children to "retreat into a world of [mere] wish-fulfillment":

> There is no doubt that [the fairy tale and the "school story"] both arouse, and imaginatively satisfy, wishes. We long to go through the looking-glass, to reach fairy land. We also long to be the immensely popular and successful schoolboy or schoolgirl.... But the two longings are very different. The second, especially when directed on something so close as school life, is ravenous and deadly serious. Its fulfillment on the level of imagination is in very truth compensatory: we run to it from the disappointments and humiliations of the real world: it sends us back to the real world undivinely discontented.... The other longing... is very different. ... [F]airy land arouses a longing for he knows not what. It stirs and troubles him (to his life-long enrichment) with the dim sense of something beyond his reach and, far from dulling or emptying the actual world, gives it a new dimension of depth. He does not despise real woods because he has read of enchanted woods: the reading makes all real woods a little enchanted.[31]

By reading fantasy or fairy tales (as well as taking in other forms of art, such as music or films) one may, in fact, reorient oneself to the world and its problems—by possibly seeing more than we could see before or finding courage to tackle difficult problems. In a fictionally created world, one might see events and actions played out that can be cultivated and embodied (or, conversely, avoided) within the immanent world.

The idea of forcing someone to learn moral and divine reality is unappealing for both Plato and Lewis. As noted earlier in the first chapter, we are not in the game of having people assent to the divine life through coercion or rationalistic assent to proofs. In the manner of Platonic persuasion, we must discern the bent of the soul, guiding when we can, turning our argument every which way, suggesting and pointing the way. Lewis commented that he had difficulty when he was young dealing with the compulsion of religious instruction. This is something Lewis tried to get around when he wrote the Chronicles of Narnia.[32] He wanted the feeling of compulsion to disappear in the story of Aslan's dealings with humanity and Narnian creatures. Plato echoes this sentiment in *The Republic*: "'. . . no compulsory learning can remain in the soul' . . . 'No compulsion then, my good friend,' said I, 'in teaching children; train them by a kind of game, and you will be able to see more clearly the natural bent of each.'"[33] We do not inculcate in proper moral behavior by formal instruction: we habituate, and "remember," the proper stock moral responses that are present through less formal inculcation, e.g., through a game. Plato's (via the character of Socrates) hypothesis about virtue being knowledge in *Meno* suggests that virtue can be taught.[34] However, Plato also has Socrates consider counter-arguments against his own—so that it might seem that virtue is gifted and therefore not teachable.[35] Plato and Lewis shared the idea that humanity is born with knowledge of the Good; as Plato has Socrates say in *Meno*, the desire to do good is "in all, and in this respect one man is no better than another."[36] Even though Lewis argued, like Aristotle, that all people want to know, he was very much aware of Plato's warning that people often have an equal desire not to know, that they will enforce a self-imposed blindness: "The famous Aristotelian dictum that 'all men want to know' (in the opening line of his *Metaphysics*) must always be balanced by Plato's dialogues. All people, says Plato, also have a desire *not* to know, a tendency to resist truth, a tendency toward self-deception."[37] We can often resist the truth—we will, like Plato's prisoners in the cave, prefer to face the shadows and not turn to see the fullness of the world.

Plato has knowledge coming from the remembrance of the Forms in our former life.[38] In one instance in the *Meno* dialogue, Plato attempts to demonstrate that learning is remembering.[39] While discussing the matter with Menon, Socrates counters Menon's argument that humans cannot really attempt to find something out when they have no notion of what it is they are searching for, and nor will they search for something they already know: "'Will you lay out before us a thing you don't know, and then try to find it? Or . . . how will you know this that which you did not know?'"[40] Socrates replies to Menon that obviously one does not attempt to find what one already knows: for one already knows it and hence no search is necessary. Furthermore, one cannot attempt to find that which one does not know because one does not know what to attempt to find. Socrates offers the solution of anamnesis: if one is remembering what one already knows but has forgotten, then the attempt to retrieve it becomes a way to untangle the problems of discovering what we already know and attempting to find that which we do not know. The search is propelled by desire. If there is no love for what is unknown, we cannot search for knowledge of ourselves or the divine, unless, in some sense, the divine has made itself known.

The idea of desire ties in with the imagination, the manifestation of this longing. The desire for the divine gives us freedom from self-serving desires or self-serving images. As in Aristotle, we build character through habit. This is Lewis' view as well. The Chronicles of Narnia, for example, attempt to build character, they do not inculcate children in proper moral behavior by formal instruction—Lewis admonished those who would write children's stories with set morals to get across to let the images of the story tell their own morals.[41] Instead, Lewis attempted to engage children's moral imaginations: by showing good and bad characters doing good and bad things, he shows how most children will, when presented with characters and situations in a story, cheer for the good characters and the good actions and hold the bad characters and the bad actions in contempt. We are placed in a narrative framework where the virtues (or even moral duties and 'rules) have a context of meaning and purpose: ethics, morality is located in its context, given a proper *telos*.

There is also the added Aristotlelian concept of influence—namely, the failure of direct argument. As Aristotle noted, arguments sometimes "have the power to stimulate and encourage those of the young who are liberal-minded, and although they can render a generous and truly idealistic character susceptible of virtue, they are incapable of impelling the masses towards human perfection."[42] This is often the case because we are ruled by fear (not by shame), so it is that we refrain from evil on the basis of eluding punishment and not from a sense of disgrace.[43] Ruled by feelings and the pursuit of pleasure, we are susceptible to mistaking these things as good, while being ignorant of that which is truly pleasurable.[44] Aristotle asks us what kind of argument would sway such people. Can we "dislodge" them from their habits with arguments? No, for to "dislodge by argument habits long embedded in the character is a difficult if not impossible task."[45] We are "lucky" to come to some sense of the Good and should be content if "the combination of all the means that are supposed to make us good enables us to attain some portion of goodness," since it may come from nature (which we have no control over), from habit, or from instruction.[46] Argument and instruction are not effective in all cases, and "just as a piece of land has to be prepared beforehand if it is to nourish the seed, so the mind of the pupil has to be prepared in its habits if it is to enjoy and dislike the right things."[47] Those who are bound to their feelings will not listen to argument; they are, in fact, unable to understand because they cannot be persuaded otherwise. In that case, feeling will only yield to force. We must have, therefore, "a character to work on that has some affinity to virtue: one that appreciates what is noble and objects to what is base."[48]

With Lewis' fiction, we see something similar to the above: namely, that we attempt to show, to persuade through story and character, what would otherwise be lost by direct argument. Furthermore, knowledge of the Good predominates Lewis' thinking, and he claimed we long for the Good. However, we may also desire not to know, as Aristotle demonstrated in our discussion above, because we can be living under the sway of our emotions, and pursuing our feelings at the cost of "true pleasures." So, it may take some persuasion or a letting down of our guard to see through these feelings. For Lewis, this is just what story, at its best, can do. It can often make us see that we desire the Good when we are presented with characters who must choose between two opposing actions or events that depict either terrible dealings or surprisingly wonderful ones. The story puts the virtues into a context which gives meaning and purpose. Lewis argued, along the same lines as Plato, that though the longing for the Good is held by all, not everyone accepts the Good—there can be a willful rejection of the Good despite the longing that is present in us, and, clearly, all are not persuaded to see the reality of the Forms. There must be free choice to accept or reject this reality.

Nevertheless, Lewis clearly believed that "even the cave-dwellers have some longings, dreams, intimations of immortality for a world beyond the shadows."[49] For Lewis, our sense of longing comes from an intimate relationship with a participatory Creator. The longings we experience are not the rememberings of things forgotten in a life no longer lived, but instead are the gift of a loving Creator who continues to use such means to draw us nearer.

Plato and Poetry

Plato's theory of art is well known. His "devaluing" (mainly, the reluctance to give art an autonomous value) of art is commonly noted. His cultural setting is telling: Plato was arguing for a reasoned theory of art in a world where rhetoricians and sophists and playwrights and others frequently advocated the value of art without an understanding of the good, true, and beautiful. Plato clearly saw some use in poetry—evidenced by his literary and poetic dialogues; he is arguably one of the most poetic philosophers. He did give a positive role to the arts, for instance, in *The Republic*, where he noted the role of the arts in education:

> It is, then, only poets we have to supervise, compelling them to make an image of a good character in their poems or else not to compose them among us? . . . Or must we rather seek out craftsmen who are by nature able to pursue what is fine and graceful in their work, so that our young people will live in a healthy place and be benefited on all sides, and so that something of those fine works will strike their eyes and ears like a breeze that brings health from a good place, leading them unwittingly, from childhood on, to resemblance, friendship, and harmony with the beauty of reason?[50]

We must habituate our children into the virtues; we must encourage their natural proclivities towards the good, the true, and the beautiful. Poetry can be a help in this regard. Plato also recognized that the role of poetry in the education of children was an inevitable one. In *Protagoras*, Plato noted, through Socrates, that in education children are given and will continue to be given "the works of still good poets" to instruct them.[51]

Plato's most sustained attack against the arts is in *The Republic*. There are two main charges laid against art and poetry. The first is that poetry is merely mimesis. Poets create false images and this allows the writer to hide behind the characters and settings of his work.⁵² Furthermore, the creation of something that is not real is far removed from truth.⁵³ So, if we have a craftsman who makes a bed we can see that the bed is an imitation of the Form bed. But when a writer or painter makes an image of a bed (either through word or line) we see that this is a further imitation of the craftsmen's bed. It is a copy of a copy in a sense, and much the poorer for it, for it is not even a real thing which the poet or artist makes but merely an image of an image.⁵⁴ The second charge against poetry is the impact it has on the psyche of the receiver:

> [The poet] produces work that is inferior with respect to truth and that appeals to a part of the soul that is similarly inferior rather than to the best part. So we were right not to admit him into a city that is to be well-governed, for he arouses, nourishes, and strengthens this part of the soul and so destroys the rational, in just the way that some one destroys the better sort of citizens when he strengthens the vicious ones and surrenders the city to them. Similarly, we'll say that an imitative poet puts a bad constitution in the soul of each individual by making images that are far removed from the truth . . .⁵⁵

In the ideal city there is no need for imitation of reality, for we would then have real and proper law regulated by reason: "If you admit the pleasure-giving Muse, whether in lyric or epic poetry, pleasure and pain will be kings in your city instead of law or the thing that everyone has always believed to be best, namely, reason."⁵⁶ It initially appears unclear if Plato means to exclude all forms of poetry from his ideal city. However, he does allow for some forms to remain.⁵⁷ Plato's insistence is that poetry that aims merely at imitation or pleasure is to be banned. Poetry that exults and praises is allowed to remain. Liturgical poetry is allowed because it "does not involve self-division."⁵⁸ That is, even though these liturgical forms "engage in a certain amount of mimetic representation . . . [to] give praise to what is praise-worthy by definition involves participation in it . . ."⁵⁹ There is an implicit combining of the function of art with the Forms: that is, the proper function of art and artist is to aim at Reality—suggesting, participating in, the eternal Forms. Poetry that reverts back to Reality is allowed to remain. Plato's view is also a rational one, whereby true philosophical understanding is seen as superior to a merely responsive view (the emotional, pleasurable, aesthetic view).

There is an obvious devaluation that might be deduced from his statements. However, Plato makes his own myths, and even though on occasion "*mythos* . . . is opposed to *logos*, 'made-up myth' to 'genuine account' . . . his Socrates actually does not care much for his contemporaries' rationalistic exposures of the old myths."[60] Plato saw his role differently: it is to tell myths, using them, revising them, correcting them, and superseding them.[61] But also, Plato's specific use of myth displays a sense that the merely rationalistic account is incomplete "and often inexpedient, especially when Socrates wants his interlocutor to make a dialectical leap . . ."[62] Plato's (and Augustine's) real concern about art and drama, notes John Milbank, lies in the distinction between *fiction* and *poiesis*. That is, Plato and Augustine "worry about *fiction*, not about *poiesis* as such, and part of this worry is that whereas the liturgical image *does* revert to the highest source . . . the fictional 'image of an image' is simply cancelled out in favor of an illusory abstract message or private delusory consolation."[63] All art is to be viewed liturgically. If not it sinks into mere fancy, "mere fiction and spectacle and can become a drug, a distraction, or an incitement to sadistic violence."[64] The protection offered by reverting back to the divine is present: the merely self-serving is subverted. The materialist, rationalist view takes the depth of the world and flattens it: the imagination is only used to find "useful" material ends—allows us to view the world as a measured object, merely a means for our own ends—and loses the revolutionary possibility of divine love through the revelations of imagination. The separation of the material from the divine allows for an opportunity of violence: we allow the world to be merely material, to be used, and the revelations become mere means to ends of our own.

Comparatively, Lewis would also see the imitative and merely pleasurable as ultimately superfluous once we have reached that for which we are striving. The value in art as art is in the leading pleasure to be found through the senses. We can also admire the craft of the artist and the form of the art—divine gifts that they are. Plato's assessment in *The Republic* that poets put "bad constitutions" in the souls of others must be tempered with his insistence that proper poetry can help lead one on to, and participate in, Reality. Additionally, Plato did see the poet's gifts as a possible tool for the instruction of children, and also—it seems obvious because of his poetic proclivities (seen in his dialogues and myth-making)—adults. Like Augustine, Lewis can be seen as linking the imagination with Plato's theory of anamnesis. Art functions as a means to re-enchant the world—there are signs everywhere; the world is full of signs. For Lewis, art may be pleasing and entertaining, but it gains its deeper value from participating in the Reality it suggests. The image is (ultimately) valuable only in so far as it participates in and brings us closer to this Reality.[65]

Augustine and Longing

We can see in his *Confessions* how Augustine begins his quest for God after he has come to terms with the reasonableness of the Christian faith. Augustine initially came to consider the faith through an examination of reasoned judgments. It was not the reasoned judgments that made Augustine take the final leap of faith, but it was only after he had found that Christianity could be defended (that it was reasonable) that he then had his conversion experience. Lewis' and Augustine's conversion experiences share a similarity: Augustine in the garden at Milan "deeply disturbed" in his spirit; and Lewis in his room troubled in his soul, the self-proclaimed most reluctant convert in all of England. It was after hearing Bishop Ambrose preach that Augustine began to see that "what he said began to seem defensible," and that he "did not now think it impudent to assert the Catholic faith, which [he] had thought defenseless against Manichee critics."[66] There is no doubt that Augustine's quest for God does begin with his search for wisdom—where he searches the philosophers to find truth.[67] However, Augustine clearly found no rest from the philosophers; they could not truly satisfy and fulfill him. He ultimately found wisdom and rest in God and Christ; only by believing could he be healed.[68] Furthermore, he found no problem believing by the authority of the church what could not necessarily be demonstrated by a strict "rational proof."[69]

Augustine saw that in his own experience he came to believe many things based on the authority of others. He noted numerous things in life that he believed to be true and did not see for himself, "such as many incidents in the history of the nations, many facts concerning places and cities which I have never seen, many things accepted on the word of friends, many from physicians, many from other people."[70] We must often believe many things we are told, such as the identity of our parents.[71] Augustine saw no necessary fault in believing on authority. Additionally, he saw that questions of doubt regarding the authority of the church or Scripture had to do with matters of belief and not necessarily provable "bare" facts.[72] The weakness of so-called pure reasoning necessitated, for Augustine, the need for authoritative Scriptures that can help reveal (not solve) the mystery of God: we must recognize the mystery that is God. Augustine was, in his early quest for truth, quite "troubled by the Skeptics' arguments that one can be certain of nothing, and that careful thinking in no way provides a reliable guide to a wiser life."[73] But by turning inward, as the Platonists suggested, he discovered an immutable truth far removed from the variability of the world. He also came to see that sense experience can give reliable knowledge.[74] Augustine listed "sample knowledge" that he found certain (which he somewhat dared the skeptic to refute), and

> these sample knowledge claims fall naturally into three groups: *logical truths* (for example, "There is one world or there is not"), *mathematical truths* ("Three times three is nine"), and *reports of immediate experience* ("This tastes pleasant to me"). . . . In response to the skeptic's taunt that one might be asleep and dreaming, Augustine claims that truths in each of these three groups are unassailable, whether one is awake or dreaming.[75]

Augustine's response to the skeptics seems strikingly similar to Descartes' refutation of complete skepticism: by turning inward, "I find that I am, and that I delight in that being and that knowing. This knowledge I cannot doubt; for if I doubt, then I am, I know that I am, and I delight in that. At least, then, I know one truth: that I doubt, and that in doubting I am. And so knowing *a* truth, I cannot doubt Truth."[76] However, this is not to make a link backwards from Descartes to Augustine. For one, there is too severe a separation between the body and soul in Descartes' formulation. Where Descartes' "account of the human person [is] essentially a 'thinking thing' that only accidentally 'occupies' a body," Augustine's account could not tolerate such strict dualism: the body and soul are more intimately connected; ". . . the material and the bodily [are seen] as a site of both revelation and redemption: God both appears in the flesh and seeks to redeem it."[77] Furthermore, there is a vast distinction between reason as understood by Descartes and as understood by Augustine. For Descartes, the task of reason is worked out from utter skepticism, utter doubt. He has reason getting from nowhere to somewhere—that is, Descartes' ultimate skepticism has him doubting everything and admitting nothing. It is supposedly from this starting place of nothing that he then demonstrates the solid nature of the knowledge of his own existence (as well as the existence of God), from the simple fact that he is thinking. For Augustine, however, there is no such prior state before faith. Reason always works on what is already given. There is faith, upon which reason works, so that the two are always intertwined.

In addition, Augustine's experience could be seen as a discovery of humility.[78] The merely intellectual might seek to dominate, unfairly: it may seek to solve the mystery, but failing to solve the mystery would then be ignoring it or pushing it aside. But part of surrendering to the mystery of God requires a childlike nature. Augustine wrote that we must become like children.[79] We must be childlike, not childish: the childish nature insists on its own way, looks merely for the pleasures or immediate answers of the temporary; but the childlike nature, seated in humility and wonder, looks to the re-enchantment of the world—it will see the world through the lens of possibility and future understanding; it will see the physical world containing only a small portion of what is contained in the whole; and it will ultimately gain its meaning and *telos* from transcendence. The signs of the things made point beyond themselves to the things that are unseen. We often attempt to rely on supposed immediate or raw observation of nature to tell us everything there is to know about the universe at the expense of ignoring other key elements.[80] The things that are made and seen gain importance, meaning, and purpose from the reality of God.[81]

The theme of longing for God permeates the *Confessions*.[82] The longing displayed in the *Confessions* demonstrates an extension of our prayers and our self; it deepens our understanding by urging us to quest for God constantly. The longing of this life cannot be terminated. The search is ongoing, continuous. It is through this longing for God that we learn about the inexhaustible nature of God, the God who cannot be limited—let alone limited by human reason. For God is not completely discoverable (God is not a definable figure but the invisible power within and without) and certainly not reducible to mere bare physical facts: "So too let him rejoice and delight in finding you who are beyond discovery rather than fail to find you by supposing you to be discoverable."[83] Humanity is alienated from God: "How long will your flowing current carry the sons of Eve into the great and fearful ocean which can be crossed, with difficulty, only by those who have embarked on the Wood of the cross (Wisd. 14:7)?"[84] There is a wholeness to which we strive that has been lost, and "Augustine seems to have wholeheartedly adopted the idea that the human soul had somehow fallen away from its primordial condition of wholeness . . . And it is again to this state of oneness or integrity of soul that it would, in this life, continually strive."[85] But it is a profound paradox of Augustine's *Confessions* that God is very far from us, yet so utterly near: "You are so high among the highest, and I am low among the lowest, a mean thing. You never go away from us. Yet we have difficulty in returning to you."[86] As one consequence of this alienation we might only experience the happiness of God in short intervals, in flash-points: ". . . I was not stable in the enjoyment of my God. I was caught up to you by your beauty and quickly torn away from you by my weight."[87] We might experience the reality of God in short, unsustainable moments. The satisfaction in these moments comes in glorious spurts; the finitude of our being wilts at the touch of eternity. "That is how it was when at that moment we extended our reach and in a flash of mental energy attained the eternal wisdom which abides beyond all things. If only it could last, and other visions of a vastly inferior kind could be withdrawn."[88]

Our longing is not to be completely satisfied in this life, but it is not a drain upon our energies either. Our longing for God has no end because God has no limits. God (and thus our longing for God) is completely inexhaustible, and yet we are never exhausted in our longing for God. But, conversely, the search for temporal things merely wearies us and wastes our energies: "In desiring to find their delight in externals, they easily become empty and expend their energies on 'the things which are seen and temporal' (2 Cor. 4:18). With starving minds they can only lick the images of these things."[89] The longing for God, however, is an energizer. The search for and the journey towards God is a renewing and revitalizing one. And yet, we may ask, why is this the case? There may be a sense in which the desire for God (or the Good) could be thought of as some kind of an addiction. We might then wonder why desire is good in Augustine's sense and not the other. The distinction of these kinds of desires lies in the nature of their repetition. Addiction is the desire for the same thing over and over again; it is a form of identical repetition. Because of this desire for the same thing in endless repetition, it reduces us to a state in which there is no motion, no development. This is what causes the addict's desire to be exhausting: it is because the attempted fulfillment of this desire is merely the renewal of that same desire; it is the attempt to fulfill that same desire to the exclusion of all other desires.

We then desire only that one thing (whatever it may be) in a spiraling, endless repetition. This desire is to be viewed, then, as a properly idolatrous desire. This desire is idolatrous precisely because it makes one material thing, for example a drug, the thing that contains the whole of the Good. For Augustine, however, the true desire for God leads us to an infinite variety, and it does so because the mediation of God can never be exhausted. This drives us forward, as opposed to stagnating us, in non-identical repetition. We are drawn into participation with the Holy Trinity and all that this relationship implies. It is by participation in the eternal desire of the Trinity that we are called to the non-identical, non-repetitious, never-exhausting praise of God.

Both Lewis and Augustine keyed in on the importance of longing and also the importance of experiencing pain—often great pain that will be overcome in the long run by great pleasure in the kingdom of God. Lewis noted that our longing could almost be considered somewhat painful.[90] Augustine noted some confusion at the way God chooses to reveal pleasure in this way: "In every case the joy is greater, the worse the pain which has preceded it. Why is this, Lord my God?"[91] He mused that the reason this is so is because God, being most high, necessarily imposes limits on the created order. Augustine exposed a major theme in the way God often reveals: there is often a dark descent before the dawn, crucifixion and death before resurrection and glory. Augustine noted that humans experience this in life's pleasures, for "after discomforts" come the "pleasures of human life."[92] Ultimately, for Augustine and Lewis, the great pain of this world is overcome by the coming pleasure of the kingdom of God.

Augustine used the "happy life" as a common image in the *Confessions*. Augustine said the "desire for happiness is not in myself alone or in a few friends, but is found in everybody."[93] Augustine further claimed that this joy is not to be found externally but internally: "Even if one person pursues [happiness] in one way, and another in a different way, yet there is one goal which all are striving to attain, namely to experience joy. Since no one can say that this is a matter outside experience, the happy life is found in the memory and is recognized when the words are uttered."[94] It may be that if we ask two people what will make them happy we might get two opposing views. But if we truly turn inward to find God, claimed Augustine, then we get no opposing senses of joy or happiness. We will find there the unity of joy or happiness in the being of

God. The multiplicity of happiness we see in the temporal world, in the finite world, is a mere signal of the one true joy found in God. It is the "desire for happiness" that is "certainly universal," but "the great variety of beliefs as to what constitutes happiness proves that the knowledge of it is by no means equally so."[95] There is also beauty to be found in the physical world. The beauty of the physical world is not the ultimate resting place for our longing,[96] but these temporal things can trigger our sense of longing (they cannot in and of themselves satisfy our longing, for they are not the real source of that longing). One may then find that what is experienced in life points beyond the finite things and finds its larger purpose in a higher order. The life of immanence, then, is brought up into the divine—it is saved, redeemed.

Imagination, Freedom, and Memory

In Augustine's theory of imagination, we see a distinction between two types of images. There is phantasia, which is the image of our memories in the mind. There is also phantasma, which is the mind's work of self-created image. For Augustine, the imagination is, then, both positive and negative. It is positive in that it provides a storehouse for the divine, a divine method of transposition. However, while there can be a semblance of truth reflected in the imagination, there can also be false images which need to be guarded against. As such, the imagination is negative in that it can deceive the mind, through its close relation with sense experience, by orienting it towards the phenomenologically given rather than towards God. The danger in the images of mere fancy, of the work of the finite mind, is that they terminate on the merely material—whereas the image from the divine life reinvigorates the merely material, bringing it up into the divine, deepening and enriching the material world. So, we must be careful of the images we receive through the imagination.[97] Images that do not ultimately revert back to the unchangeable, single, and invariable divine are not to be trusted. But just as we have senses to apprehend things of the material world, so too do we have a kind of supra-sense of the divine. The imagination is our supra-sense to apprehend (through a glass, darkly) that other reality. Augustine noted that one way of seeing the imagination is to reflect upon the art of remembering.[98] Lewis too believed that people could recognize truth through images presented in fictional form. Just as Augustine insisted that we might rediscover something through authority (the act of trusting someone who tells us), Lewis' notions of discovering joy through art forms can be seen as an attempt to accomplish something similar. Augustine also stated that the act of remembering can be seen as a rekindling of sorts.[99] Lewis thought that our initial response to joy was the ache of Platonic remembrance and that being misled or deceived through this God-gifted capacity took a decidedly self-serving effort on the part of the receiver. The way to guard against the false images or desires is through the attempt to revert back (in the vein of Platonic and Augustinian desire) to the divine source.

In this fashion, there is a protection against merely self-serving images and desires. According to Augustine, we are led around by our desires; we are slaves to them: "The choice of the will, then, is genuinely free only when it is not subservient to faults and sins."[100] Freedom for Augustine lies in the absence of sin. Augustine noted that the primary condition of the world is rooted in goodness—for evil is only a corruption of the good; it does not have primary order. One can only be free when the desire to sin is controlled. Otherwise we are merely being lead around by our desires. God first gives the gift of free will and then the gift of sinlessness (to come in the hereafter), and this is what allows true freedom: "The first freedom of will, given to man when he was created . . . was an ability not to sin, combined with the possibility of sinning. But this last freedom will be more potent, for it will bring the impossibility of sinning; yet this also will be the result of God's gift, not some inherent quality of nature."[101] We can partake of God's nature (namely, in God's inability to sin) but we cannot, of course, be God. We receive the gift of sinlessness as a gift. The first gift of free will is designed for acquiring merit, and the second gift (sinlessness) is designed for reward. For in the kingdom of heaven "there will be freedom of will. It will be one and the same freedom in all, and indivisible in the separate individuals. It will be freed from all evil and filled with all good."[102] So, we find a connection between imagination and memory—the storehouse of all our images from beyond (and of all our thoughts and experiences) —and freedom. Desire for God is the one desire that leads to freedom. This desire comes to us in our (Platonic) memory, our imaginings and longings.

For Augustine the memory (*memoria*) has connections not regularly given to it by our common notions. Memories are "fields and vast palaces . . . where are the treasuries of innumerable images of all kinds of objects brought in by sense-perception."[103] But not only this, memory contains whatever we think about, "a process which may increase or diminish or in some way alter the deliverance of the senses and whatever else has been deposited and placed on reserve and has not been swallowed up and buried in oblivion."[104] Augustine linked memory with anamnesis,[105] and at the same time he linked memory with the unconscious. These are the hidden, vast storage rooms of the mind—a natural endowment from God, of infinite profundity, a means to understanding through self-awareness. The link between memory, understanding, and will lies within Augustine's insistence that they are contained within each other.[106] Augustine's notion of love as a search is present here: we cannot love that which is unknown. But in our pursuits of knowledge, for example, there is great love. So, the "student . . . already knows the value of . . . knowledge in general: his love is directed to an ideal present to his mind. He seeks to know the unknown for the sake of something that he already knows."[107] Once again, the search is propelled by desire: if there is no love for what is unknown, we cannot search for knowledge of ourselves or the divine, unless, in some sense, the divine has made itself known. For Augustine we know ourselves intrinsically, and this knowledge has mostly been submerged in us by our involvement in the world. In a sense we have forgotten ourselves, but our memory of ourselves lies under the surface of our conscious selves. The recall of our memory is of course the all-important activity—we can recover the divine, ourselves, and all our knowledge through our memory. Augustine's Neo-Platonism is clearly evidenced here: the act of learning is one of recalling. Lewis, too, as has been mentioned, advocated a similar act of recall in his work. The act of calling up images is akin to Augustine's connections between memory and anamnesis. If memories are "fields and vast palaces . . . where are the treasuries of innumerable images of all kinds of objects . . . brought in by sense-perception," then the images we receive through creating and reading myth are to be viewed in the same fashion.[108] These images are the vast palaces that hold keys to ourselves and, ultimately, to God.

We can clearly see the effects of this within Lewis' fiction. For example, the children in *The Lion, the Witch, and the Wardrobe* are deliverers of imagination. They enter a frozen world (the metaphor cannot be by accident) and are ushered in to revitalize the world of Narnia. The old stories of Narnia are forgotten, except by a chosen few, and the remembrance of the stories of old rekindles the spark of spring, of hope and wonder and possibility. Not only this, but Aslan himself enters at this moment of recollection. The imagination is fired once again, and the Platonic idea of anamnesis is lurking in the shadows. The imagination must have meaning for Lewis, otherwise it degenerates into mere fancy—that is, it spirals into nihilism. The imagination fires the mind to want to seek, to know. What is present if the imagination is not theological? If we choose to view the rationalist account as demarcating off the whole of the universe, what role is there for the imagination? We cannot even envision this world without the imagination: it is itself a deliverance of imagination, full of an implicit meaning. What would fire the mind, in this "untheological" world, to know something? Imagination cannot ultimately survive the harsh winter of pure, cold rationalism. In this model there can be no ultimate meaning or foundation behind our discoveries, no ultimate force behind our reasons, ideas, and ideals, no ultimately meaningful life for our images—and, eventually, no images at all.[109]

Notes

1. Lewis, *Last Battle*, 212.

2. As an aside, Freud also argued that there was a deep-seated desire (he even used the same technical term Lewis did to refer to it, *Sehnsucht*) present in humanity. In the first pages of *Civilization and Its Discontents*, Freud speaks to the "oceanic" sense of "eternity" that occurs in human beings (p. 11). However, his ultimate conclusion about the source of such feelings was an "early phase of ego-feeling" (p. 19). Freud settled upon the notion of religion as wish-fulfillment as the answer to this problem of "ubiquitous" religious feeling. For an account of how Lewis answered these objections, one would want to look at Armand Nicholi's *The Question of God*.

3. Ford, *Companion to Narnia* (2005), 333.

4. Lewis, "Dates of Letters," 93. As a related aside, in *God and the Reach of Reason*, Erik Wielenberg puts these three thinkers into a dialogue. Wielenberg argues that Lewis has been dismissed unfairly by professional philosophers, but also takes issue with many of Lewis' arguments. For example, as relates here specifically, Wielenberg takes issue with Lewis' "argument from desire." Steve Lovell's review of Wielenberg's book lays things out clearly: "The argument runs thus: 1. All normal human beings have an innate, natural desire (Joy) that is for some thing x, where x lies beyond the natural world. 2. Every desire that is innate and natural to all normal human beings can be satisfied. 3. Sp: Joy can be satisfied (from 1 and 2). 4. If Joy can be satisfied, then there is something that lies beyond the natural world. 5. Therefore, there is something that lies beyond the natural world (from 3 and 4) (p. 110) Wielenberg grants premise (1) and looks for support for (2). This support he finds lacking, and I am inclined to agree" (Lovell, "Steve Lovell Reviews Erik," 2). Whatever one concludes from these statements it is not as if the question Lewis raised is now solved for the ages: Is this sense of longing simply a natural desire gone awry (Freud) or a desire that requires something completely other to satiate or explain it (Augustine, Plato)? But this is the nature of philosophical discussion—arguments are given, objections are made, counter-arguments are given,

counter objections are made, ad infinitum. There is a danger in putting Lewis' arguments into this formal manner: we find a rationalist debate being held, placing Lewis within Enlightenment views of rationality—i.e., in general, searching for arguments, or proofs, somehow to be universally accepted by all rational beings. While presenting a fair case for Lewis' arguments in light of this debate, it is still operating under the assumption of an unbiased, uncommitted rationalist guise—that there is such a thing as pure reason and that if we would get on the train (the argument) it will take all of us to the same destination (truth). Might we not see the discussion as a practice of Platonic persuasion and as something other than rationalist assent to proofs? Lovell hints at this in his review when he states that "I'll admit that, in that formulation it is unlikely to persuade the hardened atheist, but what about the agnostic?" (ibid., 3). We bring with us to our arguments pre-rational commitments, or better, rational pre-commitments. As Lewis warned, what we find and what counts as evidence will depend on the philosophy we bring with us.

5. Lewis, "Dates of Letters," 93.

6. Lewis' idea of Joy could also be compared to a similar phenomenon observed in the area of comparative religions. While Lewis associated this experience with the Christian God, comparative religious studies uses it as indicator of a general type of religious experience. Comparative religious studies discusses gods "not for their intrinsic qualities as distinct, supernatural beings but as instances of a form of religious language and behavior" (Paden, *Religious Worlds*, 121). We can also see something similar in F. D. E. Schleiermacher, where religion is the feeling of absolute dependence: "The only remedy is for each . . . to allow himself . . . to be affected by the infinite. In every species of religious feeling he will then become conscious of all that lies beyond . . ." (Schleiermacher, *Pioneer of Modern Theology*, 95). The source of true religion for Schleiermacher is the "taste" and the "sense" of the Infinite (ibid., 36). Schleiermacher's insistence on feeling was a direct response to the rationalism and post-Christian romanticism of his time. The nature of religion, according to Schleiermacher, should be defended as an "indelible aspect of human existence, not an antique and superfluous adornment," and furthermore should not be wrongly entered into competition with "natural science. . . . But the 'feeling' or 'sense' of God as the Infinite in which all finite things exist, does not subsist in isolation as some self-contained element of the human consciousness" (ibid., 36). Comparatively, William James also wrote that "feeling is the deeper source of religion . . ." (James, *Varieties of Religious Experience*, 470). Religion is for James the "*feelings, acts, and experiences of individual men in their solitude, so far as they apprehend themselves to stand in relation to whatever they may consider the divine*" (James, *Varieties of Religious Experience* (2002), 36). Thus, religion is an individualistic matter, a matter that relies on so-called pure or raw religious experience. Lewis can be seen to differ from Schleiermacher in his insistence that some aspects of this experience might be grasped by explicit reason (and reasoning that cannot be limited to rationalistic conceptualizations). Specifically, Lewis believed that religion could not be reduced to mere feeling; it must include theological reflection, reasoning, and church community as well (See Lewis, *Mere Christianity*, 120). Lewis also cited Rudolf Otto as an influence upon his thought. Otto recognized the experience of the numinous and saw that it manifested in three different types of senses. First, we might experience a sense of dependence upon this greater reality: we are all mere creatures, finite and fragile, and we find ourselves overwhelmed by the experience of our own "nothingness in contrast to that which is supreme above all creatures" (Otto, *Idea of the Holy*, 1). Second, we might experience a sense of religious dread or awe—the *mysterium tremendum*—at

the presence of this Other. Third, we might experience a sense of longing that fascinates us—*mysterium fascinans*.

7. Lewis continued on in this line of reasoning: "Do fish complain of the sea for being wet? Or if they did, would the fact itself not strongly suggest that they had not always been, or [would] not always be, purely aquatic creatures? Notice how we are perpetually *surprised* at Time. . . . why? Unless, indeed, there is something in us which is *not* temporal" (Lewis, "Dates of Letters," 93).

8. Lewis, *Weight of Glory*, 6–7.

9. For example, ". . . [Joy is] an unsatisfied desire which is itself more desirable than any other satisfaction. I call it Joy, which is here a technical term and must be sharply distinguished both from Happiness and Pleasure. Joy . . . has indeed one characteristic, and only one, in common with them; the fact that anyone who has experienced it will want it again. Apart from that, and considered only in its quality, it might almost equally well be called a particular kind of unhappiness or grief. But then it is a kind we want. I doubt whether anyone who has tasted it would ever, if both were in his power, exchange it for all the pleasures in the world. But then Joy is never in our power and pleasure often is" (Lewis, *Surprised by Joy*, 17–18).

10. Ibid., 72.

11. Ibid., 7.

12. Ibid., 16.

13. Ibid., 238.

14. Duriez and Porter, *Inklings Handbook*, 132.

15. As a related aside, an intriguing account of religious experience lies in Nicholas Lash's book *Easter in Ordinary*. In this book Lash criticizes William James' notions of so-called pure or raw human experience: ". . . there is no such thing as pure or raw experience, any more than there is any such thing as pure or raw size or quantity or color" (p. 12). He also takes issue with James' individualistic slant with religious experience (i.e., by emphasizing the element or quality of religious experience we do not meet anywhere else, James is assuming an unmitigated, undifferentiated and universal religious experience). Lash admits that this seems sensible at first glance, for it does seem that if there was no quality or element that could be separated, then religious experience could not be differentiated from political, sexual, moral, or philosophical experience (p. 38). However, he claims that we all have differing accounts of religion, which makes isolating that religious element extremely difficult. Lash suggests defining experience in a grammatical rather than an empirical fashion, getting away from the Cartesian dualism that has as its task the separation of the mind from the body (p. 39). This dualism also has the result of separating the body from the community and tends to make us believe that we can somehow stand above or outside the world when we examine it. It also has the effect of making the material and the spirit separate *things*, as if there is some clear-cut differentiated reality that contains spirit and matter.

16. Lewis, *Chronicles of Narnia*, 759.

17. Plato, *Great Dialogue*, 86.

18. Ibid., 73.

19. Ibid., 72.

20. Plato, *Laws*, 414. It is also interesting to note that Lewis' own nurse, Lizzie Endicott, told him Irish tales and lore in his childhood. She can be seen as an impetus for Lewis' interest in fairy-tales and his own writing of them.

21. For instance, "'Suppose, now,' said I, 'that someone should drag him thence by force, up the rough ascent, the steep way up . . . would he not be distressed and furious at being dragged. . . . 'He would have to get used to it, surely . . . if he is to see the things above. First he would most easily look at shadows, after that images of mankind and the rest in water, lastly the things themselves. After this he would find it easier to survey by night the heavens themselves and all that is in them. . . . 'Last of all, I suppose, the sun; he could look on the sun itself by itself in its own place, and see what it is like, not reflections of it in water or as it appears in some alien setting. . . . 'And only after all this he might reason about it, how this is he who provides seasons and years, and is set over all there is in the visible region . . ." (Plato, *Great Dialogues*, 314–15).

22. Ibid., 182.

23. For example, see ibid., 315.

24. Plato, *Complete Works*, 1142.

25. Ibid., 1135.

26. Ibid.

27. Ibid.

28. Ibid.

29. Ibid.

30. Lewis noted that "[Fantasy] is accused of giving children a false impression of the world they live in. But I think no literature that children could read gives them less of a false impression. I think what profess to be realistic stories for children are far more likely to deceive them. I never expect the real world to be like the fairy tales. I think that I did expect school to be like the school stories. The fantasies did not deceive me: the school stories did. All stories in which children have adventures and successes which are possible, in the sense that they do not break the laws of nature, but almost infinitely improbable, are in more danger than fairy tales of raising false expectations. Almost the same answer serves for the popular charge of escapism . . ." (*Of Other Worlds*, 28–29).

31. Ibid., 29–30.

32. See ibid., 37.

33. Plato, *Great Dialogues*, 336.

34. See Plato, *Complete Works*, 887.

35. See ibid., 896.

36. Plato, *Great Dialogues*, 38.

37. Ford, *Companion to Narnia*, 341.

38. See Plato, *Great Dialogues*, 42.

39. See ibid., 41–50.

40. Ibid., 41.

41. For example, see Lewis, *Of Other Worlds*, 33.

42. Aristotle, *Nicomachean Ethics*, 277.

43. For example, "For it is the nature of the many to be ruled by fear rather than by shame, and to refrain from evil not because of the disgrace but because of the punishments" (ibid.).

44. That is, "Living under the sway of their feelings, they pursue their own pleasures and the means of obtaining them, and shun the pains that are their opposites; but of that which is fine and truly pleasurable they have not even a conception, since they have never had a taste of it" (ibid.).

45. Ibid.
46. Ibid.
47. Ibid.
48. Ibid., 278.
49. Johnson and Houtman, "Platonic Shadows," 81.
50. Plato, *Complete Works*, 1038.
51. Ibid., 760.
52. Ibid., 1031.
53. Ibid., 1202.
54. Ibid., 1202–3.
55. Ibid., 1209–10.
56. Ibid., 1211.
57. For example, "But you should also know that hymns to the gods and eulogies to good people are the only poetry we can admit into our city . . ." (ibid.). Furthermore, Plato notes that if art can give a fair argument it might yet be included in a well-governed city: "Then let this be our defense—now that we've returned to the topic of poetry—that, in view of its nature, we had reason to banish it from the city earlier, for our argument compelled us to do so. But in case we are charged with a certain harshness and lack of sophistication, let's also tell poetry that there is an ancient quarrel between it and philosophy. . . . Nonetheless, if the poetry that aims at pleasure and imitation has any argument to bring forward that proves it ought to have a place in a well-governed city, we at least would be glad to admit it . . ." (Ibid., 1211).
58. Pickstock, *After Writing*, 39.
59. Ibid.
60. Brann, *World of Imagination*, 554.
61. Ibid.
62. Ibid.
63. Milbank, "Foreword," 16.
64. Ibid., 16.
65. As Peter Kreeft notes, ". . . in a work of fiction, such as *The Lord of the Rings*, the characters and creatures and landscapes and histories can seem either 'fake' . . . or 'real' . . . not by conforming to the physical world (except in purely realistic or naturalistic fiction) but by conforming to Platonic Ideas. . . . Tolkien's Elves are more real, more elvish than any other writer's elves have ever been. We can't help believing in them. Now, why is that? There are no physical Elves in the world. . . . So how do we know Tolkien's Elves are more real? We must know the Platonic Idea of Elves, or Elvishness, to be able to use it to compare Tolkien with Shakespeare, for example, and find Shakespeare 'elvishly challenged'. . . . In *The Lord of the Rings* everything seems to be more itself, more Platonic. The earth is more earthy, nature is more natural, the history more historical. . . . [In this way the] eye of the poet sees less clearly, but sees farther than the eye of the scientist. . . . In *The Allegory of Love*, C. S. Lewis explained the connection between Platonism and Symbolism: 'Symbolism comes to us from Greece. It makes its first effective appearance in European thought with the dialogues of Plato. The Sun is the copy of the Good. Time is the moving image of eternity. All visible things exist just in so far as they succeed in imitating the Forms. [A Platonic myth] reminds you of something you can't quite place. I think the something is 'the whole *quality* of life as we actually experience it.' . . . I've

never met Orcs or Ents or Elves—but [I have met] the feel of it, the sense of a huge past, of lowering danger, of heroic feats achieved by the most apparently unheroic people.' The most striking example of this Platonic symbolism in Lewis's own writings, I think, comes at the end of *The Last Battle*, when the whole world of Narnia dies and is swallowed up into its Heavenly Platonic archetype . . ." (Kreeft, *Philosophy of Tolkien*, 44–47).

66. Augustine, *Confessions*, 88.

67. For example, "They used to say 'Truth, truth,' and they had a lot to tell me about it; but there was never any truth in them. They uttered false statements not only about you who are the Truth, but also about the elements of the world, your creation. On that subject the philosophers have said things which are true, but even them I would think to be no final authority for love of you, my supremely good Father, beauty of all things beautiful" (ibid., 41).

68. Ibid., 95.

69. "I thought it more modest and not the least misleading to be told by the Church to believe what could not be demonstrated—whether that was because a demonstration existed but could not be understood by all or whether the matter was not one open to rational proof—rather than from the Manichees to have a rash promise of knowledge with mockery of mere belief, and then afterwards to be ordered to believe many fabulous and absurd myths impossible to prove true" (ibid., 95).

70. Ibid.

71. Ibid.

72. "'How do you know that these books were provided for the human race by the Spirit of the one true and utterly truthful God?' That very thing was a matter in which belief was of the greatest importance; for no attacks based on caviling questions of the kind of which I had read so much in the mutually contradictory philosophers could ever force me not to believe that you are (though what you are I could not know) or that you exercise a providential care over human affairs" (ibid., 96).

73. Gilkey, "Ordering the Soul," 426–30.

74. For example, "Augustine never loses confidence that there is 'truth'; the problem, as he sees it, lies with human capacity. The example of sense-knowledge suggests that first-hand experience is a possible route to knowledge, but there is a huge range of possible knowledge neither 'subjective' nor mathematical nor logical; religious claims fall outside these limits . . ." (Rist, "Faith and Reason," 28).

75. Matthews, "Knowledge and Illumination," 172. Lewis also gave a 'refutation' of 'Descartes' demon' in his essay "Is Theology Poetry?": "This is how I distinguish dreaming and waking. When I am awake I can, in some degree, account for and study my dream. The dragon that pursued me last night can be fitted into my waking world. I know that there are such things as dreams; I know that I had eaten an indigestible dinner; I know that a man of my reading might be expected to dream of dragons. But while in the nightmare I could not have fitted in my waking experience. The waking world is judged more real because it can thus contain the dreaming world; the dreaming world is judged less real because it cannot contain the waking one" (Lewis, *Weight of Glory*, 92).

76. Gilkey, "Ordering the Soul," 427–28.

77. Smith, *Introducing Radical Orthodoxy*, 76.

78. "Augustine's experience may . . . amount to a discovery of humility. Errors of understanding are bound up with the corruption of the heart through pride, and man

only finds the truth which brings happiness by subjecting his intellect to faith and his will to grace, in humility" (Gilson, *Christian Philosophy*, 227).

79. "For you have hidden these things from the wise and revealed them to babes. . . . They disdain to learn from him, for 'he is meek and humble of heart'. 'For you have concealed these things from the wise and prudent and have revealed them to babes' (Matt. 11:25)" (Augustine, *Confessions*, 122–31).

80. "About the creation they say many things that are true; but the truth, the artificer of creation, they do not seek in a devout spirit and so they fail to find him . . . surely the person with a scientific knowledge of nature is not pleasing to you on that ground alone. The person who knows all those matters but is ignorant of you is unhappy. The person who knows you, even if ignorant of natural science, is happy. . . . You have said to man: 'See, piety is wisdom' (Job 28:28)" (ibid., 75–76).

81. "At that time, after reading the books of the Platonists and learning from them to seek for immaterial truth, I turned my attention to your 'invisible nature understood through the things which are made' (Rom. 1:20)" (ibid., 129–30).

82. "I took them to be you, I ate—not indeed with much of an appetite, for the taste in my mouth was not that of yourself. You were not those empty fictions, and I derived no nourishment from them but was left more exhausted than before" (ibid., 41).

83. Ibid., 8.

84. Ibid., 18.

85. Schrodt, "Augustine in Recent Research," 171.

86. Augustine, *Confessions*, 138.

87. Ibid., 127.

88. Ibid. 172.

89. Ibid., 161.

90. See Lewis, *Surprised by Joy*, 18.

91. Augustine, *Confessions*, 138.

92. Ibid., 146.

93. Ibid., 198.

94. Ibid.

95. Augustine, *Later Works*, 95.

96. Augustine stated, "It is not physical beauty nor temporal glory nor the brightness of light dear to earthly eyes, nor the sweet melodies of all kinds of songs, nor the gentle odour of flowers and ointments and perfumes, nor manna or honey, nor limbs welcoming the embraces of the flesh; it is not these I love when I love my God. . . . And what is the object of my love? I asked the earth and it said: 'It is not I.' I asked all that is in it; they made the same confession (Job 28: 12 f.). I asked the sea, the deeps, the living creatures that creep, and they responded: 'We are not your God, look beyond us.'" (Augustine, *Confessions*, 183).

97. ". . . from these arts some false colors and forms pour, as it were, into the mirror of thought, and often mislead those who make inquiries, and deceive those who think that what they know or inquire about is all there is. Such imaginations are to be avoided with great caution. Their deceit is detected when they change with what we called the changing mirror of thought, while the face of truth remains single and invariable" (Augustine, *Soliloquies*, 94).

98. For example, "Briefly explain the difference between a true shape which is

contained in the intellect, and the kind which contemplation makes for itself and which is called in Greek phantasia or phantasm. *Reason*: What you seek is something which only the purest can see. . . . We have gone through these wanderings for no other reason than for your training, so that you might be fit to see it. But perhaps I can briefly make it clear to you . . . that there is a great difference. Suppose that you have forgotten something, and others want to recover it in some way for your memory. Therefore they say, 'Is it this or that?' citing different things as though they were similar to it. You do not see what you wish to remember, but you do see that it is not among the things mentioned to you. When this happens, does it seem to you that that memory has been completely obliterated? For that discernment which keeps you from accepting the false reminders is itself a part of remembering. *Augustine*: So it seems. *Reason*: Such people do not yet see the true thing, but nonetheless cannot be misled or deceived, and they know what they are seeking well enough. But if someone were to say to you that you laughed a few days after you were born, you would not dare say that it is false; and if the one who said that were someone you trusted, you would not remember it, but would believe it, because that entire time is hidden from you in the deepest oblivion" (Augustine, *Soliloquies*, 91–92).

99. For instance, ". . . there is another kind which is more similar and nearer to remembering and receiving the truth. An example of this is when we see something, think for certain that we have seen it before, and even say that we know it, but as for where or when or how or in whose presence it came to our notice, we are hard pressed to recollect and remember. For example, if this happens to us with a person, we ask him where we met him; and when he tells us, suddenly the whole event floods back into our memory like a light and it is no longer a chore for us to remember. Those who are well educated in the liberal arts are like this. While learning, they uncover and in some way dig up things which were undoubtedly buried in forgetfulness. Nevertheless, they are not satisfied and will not stop until they gaze fully and completely at the face of truth, whose splendor shines faintly in those arts" (ibid., 94).

100. Augustine, *City of God*, 569.

101. Ibid., 1089.

102. Augustine, *City of God*, 1089.

103. Augustine, *Confessions*, 185.

104. Ibid.

105. "On this theme of notions where we do not draw images through our senses, but discern them inwardly . . . we find that the process of learning is simply this: by thinking we, as it were, gather together ideas which the memory contains . . . and . . . we arrange them in order as if ready to hand, stored in the very memory where previously they lay hidden, scattered, and neglected" (ibid., 189).

106. ". . . in fact they are covered, not only each by each but all by each. I remember that I possess memory and understanding and will: I understand that I understand and will and remember: I will my own willing and remembering and understanding. And I remember at the same time the whole of my memory and understanding and will. Whatever I do not remember as part of my memory, is not in my memory; and nothing can be more fully in my memory than the memory itself. Therefore I remember the whole of it. Again, whatever I understand, I know that I understand, and I know that I will whatever I will; but whatever I know, I remember. Therefore I remember the whole of my understanding and the whole of my will. Similarly, when I understand these three, I understand all three in whole. For there is nothing open to understanding that I

do not understand except that of which I am ignorant; and that of which I am ignorant I neither remember nor will. It follows that anything open to understanding that I do not understand, I neither remember nor will, whereas anything open to understanding that I remember and will, I understand" (Augustine, *Later Works*, 88–89).

107. Augustine, *Confessions*, 72. Augustine resembles Plato here. For example, in the *Meno*, Plato attempts to demonstrate that learning is remembering. While discussing the matter with Menon, Socrates counters Menon's argument that humans cannot really attempt to find something out when they have no notion of what it is they are searching for—nor will they search for something they already know: "'Will you lay out before us a thing you don't know, and then try to find it? Or . . . how will you know this that which you did not know?'" (Plato, *Great Dialogues*, 41). Socrates replies to Menon that obviously one does not attempt to find what one already knows: for one already knows it and hence no search is necessary. Furthermore, one cannot attempt to find that which one does not know because one does not know what to attempt to find. Socrates offers the solution of remembering: if one is remembering what one already knows but has forgotten, then the attempt to retrieve it becomes a way to avoid the dilemma of discovering what we already know or attempting to find that which we do not know.

108. Augustine, *Confessions*, 185.

109. In Robert Inchausti's book *Subversive Orthodoxy*, he draws a similar parallel with the work of William Blake: "If one were to seek the great archetypal precursor for prophetic Christian thinkers championing the soul's return from the spiritual exile of Enlightenment rationalism, then William Blake comes very close to casting the mold. . . . [He] was one of the first to point out exactly how the new sciences were distorting the role of the imagination in human affairs and putting the soul to sleep. . . . England, Blake argued, was losing its connection to the transcendent realm, replacing a scandalous, revolutionary faith in Christ with the respectable idol of pure reason. . . . Blake remarks that 'Reality is forgot & the Vanities of Time & Space only remembered & called Reality,' [and] he is speaking specifically of the spiritual state of Enlightenment England, not the primordial state of man. . . . Blake explained the fall of the imagination from direct revelation to its recovery via the Gospels. . . . For him, the Hebrew Bible and the Greek Gospels expressed the 'true' eschatological meaning of existence in the liberation of the human imagination from the blinders of doubt and materialism. . . . Blake's problem with Sir Francis Bacon, John Locke, Rene Descartes, and Sir Isaac Newton lay in their misappropriation of human reason. Rather than heal the growing disassociation of thought and feeling, they drove a truck through it. . . . The new sciences stripped reason of its role as the natural ally of visionary experience—directing the imagination down certain useful materialist paths, rather than allowing it to give birth to unforeseen revelations of divine love. . . . In other words, Blake understood that when the spirit loses confidence in itself, the mind falls into the objective world and beings [sic] to see creation as something independent. It stops participating with life, stops perceiving beauty and possibility, and, instead, stands in judgment of everything, measuring differences, contrasts, and oppositions. This false objectivity can only be transcended through a return to visionary experience, which alone can restore us to our true, imaginative selves" (pp. 19–25).

five

The Ethics of Fairyland

LEWIS' ETHICS TAKE SHAPE in a unique way. He often argued for a general sense of morality, as seen in *Mere Christianity* and *The Abolition of Man*. But this general sense of morality that Lewis often advocated is not necessarily, despite various surface examinations, a straightforwardly universal or rationalist ethical agenda. It is no doubt a rational ethic for Lewis: for he was moral realist, that is, he believed that there is a real Good independent of our particularity and traditions, but it is always mediated through our particular tradition. But his arguments in service of moral law are often used as evidence of Lewis' rationalistic side: Lewis is thought to argue for a universal morality that is accepted by all humans at all times and places. But is this the case? Is Lewis arguing for a universal morality or merely a particular Christian interpretation of morality? Is he arguing for a particular Christian position that he sees as reasonable—against the idea of irrational Christian morality? Lewis' arguments for a general sense of moral sensibilities must be tempered by his other statements and a fuller understanding of his idea of the moral Tao as evidenced through his narrative work. The answer is not so clear-cut as one might expect. Lewis gives varying descriptions of his ethical views, both in explicitly philosophical form and in explicitly narrative form. But his reliance upon Plato and Aristotle remain his main touchstones.

In this chapter, I argue that Lewis rejected a purely rationalist ethical paradigm. This is particularly evident in Lewis' views of storytelling and of rationalist ethics (seen primarily in the commitment to "universal rational consent" and because of the reliance upon a more fundamental, unspoken reasoning beyond rationalistic conceptions of reason). Lewis advocated a relational ethic—which can be specifically seen against a Kantian paradigm—which develops explicitly in his narrative work. This narrative framework implicitly indicates that we are all part of a narrative framework (whether a Christian narrative, a scientific narrative, or otherwise) and that we find our ethic when we first recognize the narrative in which we find ourselves a part. In this chapter, therefore, I will first examine Kant's views of reason and his accompanying moral formula (the categorical imperative) in order to place Lewis' position in counterdistinction to an attempted universal rationalist account of morality. I will then explore Lewis' position on the moral Tao and what it is—and how we might navigate it. Lastly, I will place Lewis' ethical agenda in the context of his fiction in order to show that his ethics develop most clearly through narrative.

Kant and Reason

As a mode of drawing parallels and counterdistinguishing Lewis' view, and to reinforce the role of the imagination in reason, it will be beneficial to follow Kant's line of thought and the idea of reason as the central human faculty. Kant believed that we could not know things in themselves; we can only know the appearances of the things as they are presented to the senses.[1] As such, we cannot even know ourselves as we are: humans come to know about themselves through empirical evidences and not *a priori* evidences.[2] Humans have a distinctive quality—namely, reason.[3] Thus, we see a definite break from Aquinas and Lewis here: for Kant rationality is primary and autonomous; revelation and imagination are secondary. Whereas with Aquinas and Lewis, reason and imagination are not so harshly separated: it is not as if revelation and imagination are first in such a way that reason is relegated; it is rather that reason and imagination are always intertwined, working together in an intimate way.

For Lewis this can be seen especially well in his fictive works. In a scene in *The Voyage of the Dawn Treader*, the characters Edmund, Lucy, Caspian, Reepicheep, and Eustace encounter a "retired" star, Ramandu.

Lucy asks if Ramandu is still a star, and Ramandu proceeds to tell the travelers his mythology:

> "I am a star at rest, my daughter. . . . When I set for the last time, decrepit and old beyond all that you can reckon, I was carried to this island. I am not so old now as I was then. Every morning a bird brings me a fire-berry from the valleys in the Sun, and each fire-berry takes away a little of my age. And when I have become as young as the child that was born yesterday, then I shall take my rising again (for we are at earth's eastern rim) and once more tread the great dance."[4]

After Ramandu recounts his narrative, Eustace remarks, "In our world . . . a star is a huge ball of flaming gas," and Ramandu rejoins, "Even in your world, my son, that is not what a star is but only what it is made of."[5] Here we see a presentation of the intertwining of imagination and reason: there is an imagination already present upon which reason works. Eustace's observation betrays his rationalistic, reductionistic imagination, which attempts to limit the world to the merely phenomenologically given. There is, then, already an imaginative framework upon which his reason has worked—that is, if material is all there is, then whatever this star is made of is *all* of what the star is. Eustace's imagination sees the star as merely "flaming gas." Ramandu offers a deeper account that invokes a star's *is*-ness (its being, meaning, and story) not just its bare materiality—although his account also takes this into consideration, never leaving the material behind.

Kant saw reason as the distinguishing faculty of humanity (consequently, describing the imagination as rule-governed fancy). Lewis and Aquinas (and Aristotle) also saw reason as the distinguishing characteristic of humanity, but this distinguishing characteristic is not the Enlightenment notion of "pure" reason (such as Kant is trying to put forward), but an intertwined reason and imagination—which gives this distinguishing characteristic an added weight. Paul Ricoeur remarks that Kant saw the imagination as a "free play" game in which the power of creation involved in using the imagination had no other end than itself: ". . . imagination can be described as a rule-governed form of invention or, in other terms, as a norm-governed productivity. This is how Kant conceived imagination in his *Critique of Judgment* by coordinating the free play of the imagination and the form of understanding in a teleology that had no goal beyond itself."[6] Furthermore, it seems clear that Kant's priority was the higher faculty of reason "alone."[7] Kant distinguished between the productive imagination and the reproductive imagination. The productive imagination is the transcendental and spontaneous power that holds sensibility and thinking together.[8] The reproductive imagination is the ordinary empirical imagination.[9] But this implies that the imagination is to be seen as a means to mediate between concepts and precepts, and as a consequence the imagination should, in actuality, be seen as the absolute fundamental faculty of Kant's system.[10] In order to have any kind of meaningful and connected experience the imagination must be in operation, simply by way of its creating a timelessness within time, an ordering and connecting of our experience.[11] Kant recognized a shared meaning outside of conceptual and propositional content, and as such recognized "a preconceptual activity of imagination that is not merely subjective.... That is, he sees that there is a rationality without rules, which is subject to criticism and so is not arbitrary. He sees that there are structures of imagination that can be shared by communities of people."[12] The suggestion here is that Kant is wrestling with the idea that the imagination is, in fact, intertwined with reason, but his rationalist commitments will not allow a rationality that goes beyond an Enlightenment framework (i.e., a framework that has construed rationality as strictly rule governed).

Lewis, on the other hand, saw the imagination as a primary faculty —the way in which the divine can touch upon the finite human mind and the way in which the finite mind in its limited capacity can grasp the infinite world in an imperfect and incomplete manner. It is also the way in which ideas find their way into consciousness. Supposed pure reason cannot account for all of reason: there are gaps, or what John Sallis calls "metaphysical spacings," which the imagination fills in. Of course, these metaphysical spacings can be found in Kant too.[13] In Kant we see an attempt to suppress these spacings, and they are the most rigorous form of suppression because they are texts in which "even metaphysics itself comes to be regarded as having been only an errant roaming, a spacing that must still be secured, that is to be replaced by a pure space of truth."[14] But what we find instead are "outbreaks of spacing that would disrupt the tranquil space of reason."[15] The role for the imagination in reason is all too important: it not only is the source for our original ideas and concepts but is also the primary connector between ideas, the gap filler that moves us from idea to idea and delivers real insight.[16]

The term "reason" as Kant used it seems to cover quite a bit of ground—for example, the discursive reasoning faculties and the metaphysical nature of understanding.[17] However, in striking such a rigid view of reason there arise difficulties, such as problems of holding thought together (i.e., of space and time) and the problems of "metaphysical spacings," that so-called pure reason alone cannot account for—as well as problems of creating a sort of dualism between the head and the heart. Too often we unnecessarily oppose the head and the heart.[18] The head and the heart are not so easily separated, despite the claims to the contrary of "secular" reason. Lewis, too, has often (unfairly) been accused of drawing too distinct a line between the head and the heart, vaulting rationalistic proofs above all things. But did Lewis simply present a rationalistic proof for his ethics? Is there any evidence of Lewis' rejection of such a task? I believe evidence can be found in his criticism of ethics that place one ethical concern over and above other ethical concerns.[19]

Kant and Moral Reason

To get a clearer picture of Lewis' relational, participatory ethics—the ethics of fairyland—it will be beneficial first to follow a more rationally based ethic as a counterdistinction. Kant's ethic will serve such a purpose. Kant saw moral conceptions as deriving from *a priori* reasons, and as such "they cannot be obtained by abstraction from any empirical and therefore merely contingent knowledge; that it is just this purity of their origin that makes them worthy to serve as our supreme practical principle . . ."[20] Lewis saw the moral Tao as based upon *a priori* (spiritually gifted) knowledge: that is, there is always something given upon which reason and imagination work. No rationalistic deductions can prove that such a thing exists; it is recognized as common, revealed knowledge.[21] In the *Fundamental Principles of the Metaphysics of Morals*, Kant attempted to establish "*the supreme principle of morality.*"[22] For Kant, the only thing that is truly good is a good will. The person who possesses a good will is one who has a certain determination to make decisions based on the moral law. Furthermore, the good will is separate from any consequences.[23] The consequences of our actions become truly irrelevant. It seems very counterintuitive to say, however, that moral consequences do not matter, and, of course, this aspect of Kant's theory has received much negative attention. Many have argued that we do not think less of actions that are done from a sense of emotional commitment—for instance, those actions done for the love of a friend or neighbor, or from sympathy.

For Kant a person with a good will sees his or her moral actions in terms of duties, and the moral law is seen as a constraint upon his or her desires. One follows the maxim and follows it to the detriment of all one's desires.[24] In this sense, one cannot be really free without certain rules or duties, otherwise one is ruled by the desires and instincts and not really free to move otherwise. The sense of duty takes precedence over "feeling," or inclinations. However, added to this is the notion that it is the desire, for Kant, for the fulfillment of the moral law that is primary: this defines the good will. But to feel a sense of worth or happiness in performing a moral action is not something of strictly moral worth to Kant. One must not merely or simply feel a sense of duty—for then duty and moral actions depend upon the agent's mood. Finding pleasure in an act of kindness is not enough for Kant.[25] A real sense of duty comes from a bare sense of respect for the moral law: "*Duty is the necessity of acting from respect for the law.*"[26] Real respect comes from giving no thought of consequences or effects, or of seeing means to ends.

If we are motivated by anything other than a sense of duty, we might fall into danger: (1) by basing our moral actions on transitive moods that easily be otherwise, and (2) by using certain feelings of altruism for ends we desire. For Kant, to be motivated by true duty is the only way out of this means-to-ends quagmire. It may be true that we can opt out of our sense of duty to laws, but usually this is because we have found another law that we respect more than the one we have rejected. Kant's sense of duty to the moral law is different in that no one can opt out of it due to the moral law's requirement of rational assent. As such, we cannot ignore our sense of duty: it is obligatory because it has universal rational validity. Our moral actions must be coherent and consistent to be vaulted into the realm of universality. The categorical imperative is, according to Kant, just such a universally valid axiom upon which we can base our moral actions: "*Act only on that maxim whereby thou canst at the same time will that it should become a universal law.*"[27] Kant also gave a second formulation of the categorical imperative: "*So act as to treat humanity, whether in thine own person or in that of any other, in every case as an end withal, never as means only.*"[28] We can see the moral reasoning that might occur by applying the categorical imperative to our actions. We would first form a maxim that would function as our reason for doing some particular act. Then we would make our maxim into a universal law, a law that all rational beings must follow. Next, we would consider whether our maxim could be held coherent and consistent if it did have universal status: could we will that it become a universal law for all to follow? If it does hold up, we can then act upon it. If it does not hold up as a universal law, then we must reject it as being part of the universal moral law.

So, for example, we might want to break a promise to our friend because it interferes with some other activity to which we would like to attend. Our first maxim might be, "I will break a promise to my friend." We could then make this into a universal law: "It is permissible to break promises." Now, could we will that this becomes a universal law? In a world where it is universally permissible to break promises, promises lose their meaning altogether: promises become meaningless because they can be broken, and this is antithetical to their definition (namely, promises are meant to be kept). So it would seem that we cannot make this maxim into a valid universal law because of its inherent inconsistency and incoherency.

It is fruitful to examine Elizabeth Anscombe's response to this. If we take as an example Kant's insistence that it is always wrong to lie (as prohibited by the categorical imperative), we see that Kant's reason for thinking it is always wrong stems from the notion that to lie is self-defeating if put into a universal maxim for all to follow. So, if a murderous person is at our doorstep, insisting that we tell him or her if a particular innocent child is present, our intuition seems to tell us that a lie in this situation would be permissible—that is, our intuition tells us that it is reasonable to lie to send the murderer away and thus save the life of an innocent person. In Kant's theory, however, there is no room for such a consideration (we might still, however, stand in between the murderer and his intended victim). Kant's reasoning might be laid out as follows:

> (1) You should do only those actions that conform to rules that you could will to be adopted universally. (2) If you were to lie, you would be following the rule "It is permissible to lie." (3) This rule could not be adopted universally, because it would be self-defeating: People would stop believing one another, and then it would do no good to lie. (4) Therefore, you should not lie.[29]

Elizabeth Anscombe suggested that such "rigoristic convictions" are not necessarily applicable to all types of lies. There might be exceptions, and these exceptions might be coherent and universally valid:

> [Kant's] own rigoristic convictions on the subject of lying were so intense that it never occurred to him that a lie could be relevantly described as anything but just a lie (e.g., as "a lie in such-and-such circumstances"). His rule about universalizable maxims is useless without stipulations as to what shall count as a relevant description of an action with a view to constructing a maxim about it.[30]

Anscombe highlighted the problems of the second and third steps in Kant's argument: first, by noting the debatable issue that we are following the maxim "It is permissible to lie"; and second, by noting the problem with the notion that we cannot universalize this maxim. Anscombe observes that both of these aforementioned problems hinge upon how we formulate our maxim. In other words, why must we formulate it in the way Kant does? If we change our maxim from the general "It is permissible to lie" to the more specific "It is permissible to lie to a known murderer who is going to kill an innocent child" our maxim becomes universalizable, that is, not self-defeating.[31] Anscombe's position here can be seen as stressing the problem of Kant's insistence on a universal (unbiased, uncommitted) position—in other words, "What counts as universally rational?" or "Whose rational position are we going to start with?"

Anscombe ultimately suggested that we return to virtue ethics and abandon notions of strict deontology: "The concepts of obligation, and duty—*moral* obligation and *moral* duty, that is to say—and of what is *morally* right and wrong, and of the *moral* sense of 'ought,' ought to be jettisoned . . . It would be a great improvement if, instead of 'morally wrong,' one always named a genus such as 'untruthful,' 'unchaste,' 'unjust.'"[32] Lewis, too, insisted on the virtues as primary elements that make up what we consider to be moral acts or moral persons, and he sets up his "good" fictional characters in an attempt to embody these virtues. Lewis did speak of ethics in terms of duty: e.g., duty to one's neighbor, child, parents, elders, and "tribe," and to humanity. However, these duties are ultimately translated into character traits (trustworthiness, truthfulness, and courageousness) in participation and relation.[33] Lewis' ultimate focus was on love. The duties we must practice are only a substitution for love, a crutch for the imperfect human creature:

> A *perfect* man [would] never act from a sense of duty; he'd always *want* the right thing more than the wrong one. Duty is only a substitute for love (of God and of other people) like a crutch which is a substitute for a leg. Most of us need the crutch at times; but of course it is idiotic to use the crutch when our own legs (our own loves, tastes, habits etc.) can do the journey on their own.[34]

Like Anscombe, Lewis disagreed with Kant's insistence on some kind of formal rational ethical theory, namely, the categorical imperative. Lewis claimed that any such attempt to treat ethics in this sense fails because, for one, it singles out one aspect of the moral Tao and sets it up as the one rule we ought to follow at all costs. So, for example, Kant may use the duty to veracity as his overriding law in one instance (which is *part* of moral Tao) to set the criterion of an ethical behavior, but one chief problem Lewis saw with a deontological formulation of ethics is that it is dangerous to set one part of moral Tao up as the criterion by which to judge acts; it must always be checked and balanced against the whole.

Navigating the Tao

Lewis did not see vast, wholesale differences between the ethics of different cultures and societies. As such, on some issues we are apt to find agreement (e.g., protecting children, prohibitions against murder), although cultural differences still dictate variations.[35] But additionally we may ask if "morality" can be Christian. John Milbank asks just such a question, and his answer is "no". It is not "'no' there cannot be a specifically Christian morality. But no, morality cannot be Christian."[36] For "Christian morality is a thing *so* strange, that it must be declared immoral or amoral according to all other human norms and codes of morality."[37]

So it is that Milbank concludes that Christians are not moral women and men, but are instead persons of good confidence; they are not persons of "good *conscience*, who [act] *with* what [they know] of death, scarcity and duty to totalities."[38] The Christian has "given up" on being "good" in this sense and attends to the other, ceasing to be "self-sufficient in the face of scarcity . . . receiving from the all-sufficiency of God, and acting excessively out of this excess."[39] Milbank's project, then, is to avoid the reduction of Christian theology to simply moral philosophy, and to articulate what is unique or exceptional in Christianity. Milbank is here looking for the proper *theological* response. The philosophical response to ethics is a fundamentally *reactive* one. That is, in philosophical systems, we act out of a need in the other that prompts a charitable response from us. However, the Christian response is different: we don't rely on the need of others to have an occasion to be good. We do not act out of categorical imperatives, notions of the greatest good for the greatest number, social contracts, or protection of individual rights. This is not, theologically speaking, the proper disposition. In essence, we must simply *be* good. So, for example, as Christians we do not need a special lack or need to respond in a generous fashion. We are to be generous all the time, acting out from the love of God—through the love of God we are to be kind and loving and giving to everyone, and through the plenitude of creation we are to acknowledge that God has provided sufficiently for our needs. Our actions are not then parasitic upon a prior lack or need—they are properly responsive to the love of God.

Lewis also argued that Christianity should be seen as ethically "unoriginal." That is, Christianity does not demand ethical conversion in a strict sense:

> Did Christian Ethics really enter the world as a novelty, a new, peculiar set of commands, to which a man could be in the strict sense *converted*? . . . The convert accepted forgiveness of sins. But of sins against what Law? Some new law promulgated by the Christians? But that is nonsensical. It would be the mockery of a tyrant to forgive a man for doing what had never been forbidden until the very moment at which the forgiveness was announced. The idea . . . that Christianity brought a new ethical code into the world is a grave error. If it had done so, then we should have to conclude that all who first preached it wholly misunderstood their own message: for all of them, its Founder, His precursor, His apostles, came demanding repentance and offering forgiveness, a demand and an offer both meaningless except on the assumption of a moral law already known and already broken.[40]

This does not mean, however, that Christianity does not deepen or focus or emphasize or reorient us to certain aspects of morality. But it is not the promulgation, strictly speaking, of moral discovery: it is addressed to penitents who acknowledge their falling away; it offers forgiveness to those who have fallen away; it offers (supernatural) help to return; and it reaffirms the law by doing so.[41] But does this not take away the particular narrative of Christian virtues? No. Christianity is not to be seen as constituting a *wholly* new moral code or law—because if it was *wholly* new how would we recognize it? And how would this play on the goodness God bestows upon creation? This would appear to reject the view that in some sense creation always already anticipated what was more fully and completely revealed in Christ. Christ is to be seen, in Lewis' view, not as a completely unexpected, completely foreign, invading knowledge that has nothing to do with the world. Rather, Christ is to be viewed as the (unique) fulfillment of the law.

However, the questions may still remain in our minds, "Does Lewis' account constitute a rationalist universal morality?" Or does he recognize the particularity of his position in a postlapsarian, pluralistic world? Lewis certainly can be said to be a moral realist, that is, he believed that there is a real Good independent of our particularity. However, this Good is always mediated through our particularity. So it is that Lewis recognized an underlying current to the "surface fluctuations."[42] And this is the moral Tao: through his study of various ethical systems and statements throughout different times and cultures he claimed to have recognized certain elements that seemed "steady." While it is true that certain moral differences, for example the rights of women, are not minor discrepancies, there might still be an undercurrent that can be detected even in such actions. But how can Lewis say that there is no difference between a culture that treats women as subservient, slave-like, second-class citizens, and one that treats women as important, equal partners? Obviously, there have been and are still vast differences in the treatment of women (not to mention other groups) throughout cultures and times. Lewis would, of course, agree that these are not insignificant differences. But Lewis insisted that these types of differences stem from the emphasis put on certain aspects of the moral Tao at the expense of others. So, one culture that treats women dreadfully still has the notions of general beneficence (i.e., principles referring to our general duty of respect of life and betterment of humanity in general) and special beneficence (i.e., principles referring to our duties towards specific individuals and to our tribe or group). However, what some cultures may have done is to assert the principle of special beneficence (say, that men are the exceptional group who should have special rights) over and above the principle of general beneficence (that humanity in general, which includes all sexes, should be treated with respect and honor). Lewis divided the moral Tao into specific groups, with two main overarching classifications: that of special beneficence and general beneficence. Under the law of general beneficence, we have notions of respect for life and betterment of humanity. Under the law of special beneficence, we have notions of respect for specific individuals and for our tribe or group. So within these two groups we have values of respect towards parents, elders and ancestors, and respect for children and posterity. We have the law of justice, which refers to our values of justice—for example, retribution for actions such as murder and stealing. We have the law of good faith and veracity, referring to our ideas of truthfulness, faithfulness, and trustworthiness. We have the law of mercy, referring to our values of treating humankind well and helping the sick and the poor. We have the law of magnanimity, referring to our values of courage and of fighting for what is right (correcting injustices).

It is clear that Lewis thought natural law to be rational and universal,[43] but it is in the vein of Aquinas that we see the nature of this universality. The recognition of a moral law does not necessitate the acceptance of a rationalist, universal ethic that will be recognized by all beings in all times and places. As Aquinas noted, natural law "is nothing other than the light of understanding placed in us by God; through it we know what we must do and what we must avoid. God has given this light or law at creation."[44] The light of understanding is placed in us at creation, but the finite world is a fallen world. As such, as St. Paul warned, the law cannot be kept and thus we need divine help. This is why Lewis noted the same regarding natural law: "But can one just leave out the whole endless Pauline reiteration of the doctrine that law, as such, cannot be kept and serves in fact to make sin exceedingly sinful?"[45] There is a recognition that this law cannot be kept and may not be understood in a postlapsarian world. In essence, then, Lewis' position is maintaining that there is the Good, the True, and the Beautiful. The fluctuations seen in morality are a result of the way in which the Tao is mediated and revealed. So it is that, through a Christian perspective, certain traditions may mediate the Good in particular but inadequate ways. For Christianity, the perfect mediation is Christ, but the mediation itself is also the Good. Christ is, then, not just one way among many possibilities for mediating the truths of God. Additionally, we have more explicit evidence that Lewis was not producing a rationalist ethical system. He did temper his advocacy of the moral Tao with statements that pulled him back from just such a rationalistic position—for example, Lewis did not maintain that the Tao will "provide an answer to every particular moral problem with which we may be confronted."[46] Nor is it to be viewed as a rationalistic proof, because its "validity cannot be deduced. For those who do not perceive its rationality, even universal consent could not prove it."[47] The Tao for Lewis constitutes a recognition of (God created) human similarities; it does not replace moral tradition or give us an infallible guide to right or wrong actions. In other words, it is not an Enlightenment ethical program in the vein of the categorical imperative. In Lewis' view, in order to navigate this code one must order his or her love correctly, which implies a particular Christian narrative framework and context. Lewis implied that the moral Tao should be used in a harmonizing balance (as opposed to, say, Kant's view of taking one law or duty and elevating it above the others). Much like Anscombe, Lewis saw the importance of recognizing the circumstances of ethics: duty—either to veracity, one's self, one's tribe, or one's fellow humans—must be tempered by other moral responsibilities, such as mercy, justice, magnanimity, honor, and courage.

For Lewis, to balance the Tao would be to follow the will of God—but even this gives us no definite and guaranteed way to navigate successfully. For humans are finite, tarnished, and corruptible, and even if we know what is right we often cannot do it.[48] But this begs the further questions "How do we really know God's will?" and "Don't people have different views as to what God's will is?" As Austin Farrer noted, if there is a God,

> how can we doubt that he desires to make not merely human animals but noble souls, enriched with knowledge, active in kindness, strong in achievement? Men do not become so by bodily constitution alone; they become so by careful training, by strenuous effort, by generous action, both on their own part and on the part of others. If, then, it is the aim of God to make them what he would have them, it is an aim he will not in fact achieve except through what they do themselves by will and by choice.[49]

Farrer insisted that it is possible for humans to fall in line with the will of God. Farrer also recognized the objection that it may be we merely claim to do God's will without really knowing what it is. He noted that objectors may say we merely

> wish to claim that our doing of God's will has an experimental value in showing that there is a God and that he actually wills. But all it comes down to is that we guess God's will and act for

ourselves in accordance with our guesses. I may say that I am doing the will of my great-aunt in Australia by keeping up a subscription in her name to the Putney dogs' home, but maybe I have no great aunt in Australia (she died last year) and maybe her last act was to call down the curse of heaven on the Putney dogs' home and all its inmates. You talk as though when we do someone's will, that person's will is a mysterious something which gets inside us and directs us, in the way in which our own will directs us; but that's nonsense, surely.[50]

Farrer observed that while it may be true that this is nonsense when we speak it of great-aunts, it is not so with God. This is because great-aunts, like all other persons, are outside of us and outside of others. But with God we are not mutually external in this fashion: "Is not the whole hypothesis we are considering precisely this, that the will of God takes actual effect in what his creatures do of their own motion?"[51] As such, the problem of our knowing God, and knowing God's will, "is never a problem of his being made present, but always of our being able to apprehend his presence."[52] This participation of God in the finite world clears the way for a moral Tao, which is not merely abstract and distant but is present and alive within the community of believers.

Notions of irrationality and closedmindedness also raise their heads here. For many, "listening to the will of God" amounts to an abdication of rationality (or of sanity) and does not in any way resemble "reason delivered." One sees the religious perspective as fundamentally mistaken or as nonsense. It is in essence a non-starter in dialogue. However, to borrow Alasdair MacIntyre's inference,

> there is no other way to engage in the formulation, elaboration, rational justification, and criticism of accounts of practical rationality and justice except from within some one particular tradition. . . . There is no standing ground, no place for enquiry, no way to engage in the practices of advancing, evaluating, accepting, and rejecting reasoned argument apart from that which is provided by some particular tradition or other.[53]

We are all part of a tradition, a narrative framework. Questions about the fundamental nature of reality will be determined by the tradition, the narrative, in which we find ourselves. But we must also heed the voices of those outside our traditions. It is important always to recognize that we must hear the voices of outsiders, for we might fail to recognize our own fallenness.

The idea of a moral Tao also raises questions about the nature of God: whether God is merely an enforcer of an antecedent law or just an arbitrary lawgiver. Lewis' view here can be seen to deal with this dilemma. In Plato's dialogue *Euthyphro*, a discussion arises in which the problem of moral rightness is disputed. It is contended that "right" might be defined as that which the gods command.[54] However, Socrates raises a skeptical question: he asks if conduct is right because the gods command it or if the gods command it because it is right.[55] Either way we answer seems to get us into trouble. First, if we say that conduct is right because God commands it, then we make God's commands seem arbitrary, for this would mean that God could have given other commands—for instance, a command for lying that would make lying right. Second, if we say that God commands right conduct simply because it is right, then we are setting up a standard of right and wrong that is independent of God's will: God somehow recognizes that right conduct is right and then commands it, making the rightness independent and even prior to God's command. Lewis attempted to overcome this dilemma by asserting that the goodness of God is part of God's essential being, and as such morality is not greater than God (i.e., God does not simply recognize the good and then command it) and God is not greater than morality (i.e., God does not just arbitrarily command conduct and then call it "good").[56] Lewis claimed that when

> we attempt to think of a person and a law, we are compelled to think of this person either as obeying the law or as making it. And when we think of [God] as making it we are compelled to think of [God] either as making it in conformity to some yet more ultimate pattern of goodness (in which case that pattern, and not He, would be supreme) or else as making it arbitrarily. . . . [But] God neither *obeys* nor *creates* the moral law. The good is uncreated; it could never have been otherwise; it has no shadow of contingency; it lies, as Plato said, on the other side of existence. . . . God is not merely good, but goodness; goodness is not merely divine, but God. These may seem like fine-spun speculations: yet I believe that nothing short of this can save us. A Christianity which does not see moral and religious experience converging to meet at infinity . . . has nothing, in the long run, to divide it from devil worship.[57]

Lewis' view here has similarities with the divine simplicity doctrine: viz., that God is identical to God's attributes. God is a necessary being and thus morality is a necessary corollary. When we recognize the good, it is because we recognize that God is good. God's commands are ultimately good because God is good. If the good is uncreated then the good is simply a descriptive attribute of God and not necessarily a prescriptive set of rules. The key idea here is that God is not a moral agent, hence, God's commands are ultimately good because God is good. We see this played out clearly in Lewis' Chronicles. Here we see the God-symbol Aslan as the ultimate Good, and as such Aslan is not merely an arbitrary lawgiver or an impassive enforcer of some preformed law; rather, Aslan is a character—to be related to as the supreme Person. This can be seen, for example, in a key scene in *The Voyage of the Dawn Treader*. The character Eustace, after being turned back into a boy from his spell as a dragon, explains his situation to Edmund, and Edmund, in turn, speaks to their curious relationship to Aslan by an inversion of Eustace's question:

> "I think you've seen Aslan," said Edmund.
> "Aslan!" said Eustace. "I've heard that name mentioned several times since we joined the *Dawn Treader*. And I felt—I don't know what—I hated it. But I was hating everything then. And by the way, I'd like to apologize. I'm afraid I've been pretty beastly."
> "That's all right," said Edmund. "Between ourselves, you haven't been as bad as I was on my first trip to Narnia. You were only an ass, but I was a traitor."
> "Well, don't tell about it, then," said Eustace. "But who is Aslan? Do you know Him?"
> "Well—he knows me," said Edmund.[58]

The characters, as such, are forgiven their trespasses and, in turn, they forgive each other. The relational aspect of the law is present here. Aslan has effected a change in both of them—Eustace, here, on the Dawn Treader, and Edmund during his first encounter with Narnia—not by exacting some distant (uncontextualized and thus arbitrary) abstraction upon the boys or by impassively enforcing some preformed rule. Rather, Aslan has effected the change by being Good—by relating to the boys and *knowing* them.

Additionally, Lewis insisted that in a special sense the moral law might be "transcended." The idea of transcending the moral Tao becomes apparent when we begin to see that we cannot obey by ourselves—we need God's grace to help us. It is only when we finally see that we cannot ultimately succeed on our own that we make any real progress. The transcendence comes from the top to the bottom, suspending the bottom and bringing it up into the divine: God covers the ground for our deficiencies, and God forgives our transgressions. Lewis' idea of transcending the moral law might be compared, in a special sense, to the Kierkegaardian idea that the ethical might be transcended (i.e., the teleological suspension of the ethical).[59] Lewis is attempting to show us that our sense of duty is a crutch in the place of love. He did not talk explicitly about a "suspension of the ethical" in the way Kierkegaard formulated it, however, the chief idea is that one is not following an abstract set of propositions: one is following, participating in, the character and will of God. The point of Kirkegaard's focus on the story of God asking Abraham to sacrifice his son, Isaac, is that our understanding of the Good may need to be suspended in the face of the divine. Abraham cannot comprehend the received command because it is a command that defies the existing categories of morality, and, in fact, he does not even discuss it with Sarah before he leaves. There is the sense of a proper *telos*, a proper aim or target to which we must direct ourselves.

Similarly, we might see an echo here of Aquinas' insistence that we must "order love":

> Love cannot be rightly ordered unless the proper goal of our hope is established; nor can there be any hope if knowledge of the truth is lacking. Therefore, the first thing necessary is faith, by which you may come to a knowledge of the truth. Secondly, hope is necessary, that your intention may be fixed on the right end. Thirdly, love is necessary, that your affections may be perfectly put in order.[60]

Lewis argued in a similar vein when he wrote, "by valuing too highly a real, but subordinate good, we have come near to losing that good itself. . . . You can't get second things by putting them first; you can get second things only by putting first things first."[61] Additionally, Alasdair MacIntyre notes that without this concept of a "final *telos*" we cannot begin to navigate our moral life-quest.[62] We need some conception of the good, and it "is in looking for a conception of *the* good which will order other goods . . ."[63] It is in this search or quest for the good that we extend our understanding and discover that the quest "is not a search for something already adequately characterized, as miners search for gold or geologists for oil. It is in the course of the quest that the goal is finally to be understood."[64] We navigate our moral lives through a direct relation and participation with God, the proper aim and goal of our love. We come to this special knowledge through faith. It is a deliverance of divine reason. The Supreme Will and the moral Tao, then, are not two separate entities: the Tao is not merely inanimate laws but the Living Will alive and participating in the finite. We cannot necessarily demarcate certain actions to follow at all times or in all cases.[65] Humans are finite, imperfect, but if we order our love properly, we do not then bother with duties: for we might then act in accordance with the will of God.[66] Kierkegaard also fixed upon the personal relationship between God and humanity and its unique place within the Christian tradition: "Here is evident the necessity of a new category if one would understand Abraham. Such a relationship to the deity paganism did not know. The tragic hero does not enter into any private relationship with the deity . . ."[67] This is where Lewis and Kierkegaard can be seen to coincide. The key for Lewis is the relationship between God and humanity. Morality is to be understood through this special relationship, not through the fragmented rules that a rationalistic ethic may champion.

It is just such a rationalistic formulation of ethics that has caused, according to Alasdair MacIntyre, our modern situation, which requires a sort of choice between two prevailing moral views: the Aristotelian and the Nietzschean. His thesis is that morality has survived only through a continuation of fragmented Aristotelian ethics.[68] The rejection of the Aristotelian tradition "was a rejection of a quite distinctive kind of morality in which rules, so predominant in modern conceptions of morality, find their place in a larger scheme in which the virtues have the central place."[69] Additionally, can we completely escape, as Nietzsche suggested, the categories of good and evil? For then the good in this view becomes the will to power, and evil is the failure to recognize this and act. It is an attempt to set up a "new" meta-ethic in place of the "old" one. What we also find is that we are now implicitly referencing a transcendent meaning or purpose within our "new" meta-moral category. Why *ultimately* bother to grasp onto the will to power if it too has no real meaning? By the simple grasping of the idea of the will to power we latch on to something other than the will to power—an implied, unspoken meaning and *telos* has entered by the backdoor.

Lewis can be seen as striving for something similar to MacIntyre's vision in his insistence on morality not being strictly "rule governed." The rules or duties find their larger place within the virtues. Unlike Kant with his notion of duty, his universal rational principle, Lewis held that our duties are to God and to persons; they not merely abstract principles.

Yet this is not an abandoning of reason: it is a fresh reason, a divine reason, revealed, gifted, to humanity. This relational characteristic extends to humans on all levels. We might also see and learn from human exemplars. And for Lewis, the best way to understand the virtues and duties is to see them. In other words, if you want to see what courage is go find a courageous person and observe. As Aristotle noted, goodness is induced in a perceptive character: ". . . just as a piece of land has to be prepared beforehand if it is to nourish the seed, so the mind of the pupil has to be prepared in its habits. . . . Therefore, we must have a character to work on that has some affinity to virtue . . ."[70] We have exemplars and we are to be trained from an early age in the right habits: ". . . it would seem to be right for each individual to help his own children and friends on that way to goodness."[71] Lewis' help can be found in his works of fiction, where he attempts to show us the liveliness of the Tao through character and relation.

Relation and Story

Lewis' fictional characters embody virtues we should be exemplifying or, conversely, demonstrate the failure to exemplify the virtues. Lewis' essentially bad characters each represent one or more flawed relationships to the Tao—for example, they are in self-imposed ignorance of the moral law (e.g., the character of Mark, and the scientists at Belbury, in *That Hideous Strength*), attempt to create a new morality (e.g., the White Witch in the Chronicles), or focus on one aspect of the Tao at the expense of all others (e.g., Weston in *Out of the Silent Planet*, who sees the continuation of the human species as the most important duty). In the Chronicles of Narnia all of the essentially good characters display one common and important characteristic: they all have the propensity to follow the will of Aslan. By following the will of Aslan, the characters teach us to relate to the Good in a personal fashion (not merely through abstract principles)—for in a perfect world we would not need to follow duties; duty is only a substitute for love.[72] Lewis recognized the fact that most times we can only try (however imperfectly) to follow God's will. Ultimately, we navigate our lives through relational, participatory ethics. We must discern the correct action through a severe and serious attention to the will of the One who is the embodiment of them. In the vein of the Hebrew Prophets and of Jesus, the idea that morality can simply be reduced to a set of rules—or that a relationship with God can be reduced merely to theological statements—is to be resisted.[73] Often religion can become merely what tradition and custom dictate, the rational element of duty displacing the reasoning of love. But Lewis advocated a genuine relationship with God and God's creation (which, of course, can and should acknowledge tradition). Instead of purely focusing on the outward forms of morality, Lewis advocated a real sense of presence within moral considerations. We are relating to a Someone, and to our fellow beings, not a mere set of abstract propositions. The ethics of fairyland for Lewis are the ethics of relation and participation.

Much like Plato, Lewis saw the idea of moral training as "inculcation through habituation."[74] Moral education involves preparing the reader for life with training in the stock responses:

> Moral education... does not look much like teaching. One cannot have classes in it. It involves the inculcation of proper emotional responses and is as much a "knowing how" as a "knowing that." ... The picture we get when we think of "knowing how" is the apprentice working with the master. And the inculcation of right emotional responses will take place only if the youth has around him examples of men and women for whom such responses have become natural. ... Lewis, like Aristotle, believes that moral principles are learned indirectly from others around us, who serve as exemplars. ... This is also the clue to understanding the place of the *Chronicles of Narnia* within Lewis's thought. They are not just good stories. Neither are they primarily Christian allegories (in fact, they are not allegories at all). Rather, they serve to enhance moral education, to build character. ... To overlook the function of the *Chronicles of Narnia* in communicating images of proper emotional responses is to miss their connection to Lewis's moral thought.[75]

Lewis saw the impossibility of "pure"—uncommitted, recognized by all—ethical reasoning and teaching, and his fictive works tend to inspire the moral imagination[76] (by placing us in a narrative context) rather than analyze abstract, rational moral principles.[77] But in Lewis' fiction there is an attempt, as seen in the mediaeval worldview, to "exalt and justify both image and concept, supporting them with the weight of tradition and of divine authority."[78] In the vein of Aristotle,[79] Lewis suggested, if you want to see what a good person looks like, or if you want to see what courage looks like, go and look at a good or courageous person—Lewis and Aristotle do not make an exact moral inventory of how to be a good or courageous person.[80]

Specifically as Christians, we are a part of a community, living out a distinctively Christian narrative. And clearly, the connection between ethics and narrative should not be missed. As Stanley Hauerwas notes, narratives and metaphors "suggest how we should see and describe the world—that is, how we should 'look-on' ourselves, others, and the world—in ways that rules and principles taken in themselves do not."[81] Additionally, as Alasdair MacIntyre notes, "In understanding what someone is doing we place a particular episode in the context of a set of narrative histories, histories both of the individuals and of the settings in which they act. Action has a basically historical character."[82] Essentially, we live our lives through the context of narratives and understand them as such. Humans are storytelling animals, and we can "only answer the question 'What am I to do?' if [we] can answer the prior question 'Of what stories do I find myself a part?'"[83] Furthermore, we learn, we are educated in the virtues through narrative:

> It is through stories about wicked stepmothers, lost children, good but misguided kings, and eldest sons who waste their inheritance, that children learn what a child and what a parent is, what the cast of characters may be and what the ways of the world are. Deprive children of stories and you leave them unscripted, anxious stutterers in their actions as in their words.[84]

In his fiction, Lewis attempted to demonstrate the virtues by *showing* what a good person looks like (and showing how attractive this person is to us).[85] It is in his fictionalized characters that we get a real sense of what goodness is or of what courage is for Lewis.[86] Learning from exemplars in story can help us to embody the virtues. By embodying the virtues we are attempting, in our small and finite way, to imitate God, to attempt to participate in the Good.

Coupled with this is Lewis' attempt to show us our common values, which unfortunately he might be said to fail to uphold at times.[87] And, of course, it must be noted that the Chronicles are not for everybody, as they obviously do not appeal to everyone's taste or imagination.[88] While Lewis fails at a few points he also greatly succeeds in many areas, and the general thrust of a shared moral sense can still find its way through the failings.[89] Furthermore, the demonstration of moral law within story does not trump the particularity of the mediation; it does not give us solutions for every moral problem.⁹⁰ There are not easy answers to navigating the Tao. For Lewis, the best way we can understand how to navigate the Tao is through experiencing it ourselves. It is a reason gifted, a special knowledge gained, by the imagination that transcends what we typically term the merely "rational," and transcends the merely phenomenologically given. In Lewis' fictive works, he might also be seen as showing us, through story, some shared moral values—not by merely analyzing them, or looking *at* them, but by having us experience them, or look *along* them.

Notes

1. For instance, "... all the 'ideas' that come to us involuntarily (as those of the sense) do not enable us to know objects otherwise than as they affect us; so what they may be in themselves remains unknown to us ... we can by them only attain to the knowledge of *appearances*, never to that of *things in themselves*" (Kant, *Basic Writings*, 208).

2. Ibid.

3. Additionally, Kant valued the faculty of Reason above the faculty of Understanding: "the latter is a spontaneity and does not, like sense, merely contain intuitions that arise when we are affected by things (and are therefore passive), yet it cannot produce from its activity any other conceptions than those which merely serve *to bring the intuitions of sense under rules*, and thereby to unite them in one consciousness, and without this use of the sensibility it could not think at all; whereas, on the contrary, Reason shows so pure a spontaneity in the case of what I call Ideas [Ideal Conceptions] that it thereby far transcends everything that the sensibility can give it, and exhibits its most important function in distinguishing the world of sense from that of understanding, and thereby prescribing the limits of the understanding itself" (ibid., 209).

4. Lewis, *Voyage of the Dawn Treader*, 226.

5. Ibid.

6. Ricoeur, *Figuring the Sacred*, 144.

7. One way to see this is to look at the structure of *The Critique of Pure Reason*: "The *Critique of Pure Reason* begins ... with the discussion of the 'lower faculties of knowledge,' sensibility and understanding.... [I]n its last and longest section ... Kant turn[s] to questions about reason, the 'higher faculty of knowledge'" (O'Neil, "Vindicating Reason," 282).

8. For example, "The objective unity of all empirical consciousness in one consciousness, that of original apperception, is thus the necessary condition of all possible perception; and [this being recognized we can prove that] the affinity of all appearances, near or remote, is a necessary consequence of a synthesis in imagination which is grounded *a priori* on rules. Since the imagination is itself a faculty of *a priori* synthesis, we assign to it the title, productive imagination" (Kant, *Critique of Pure Reason*, 145). Furthermore, Kant's definition of imagination is "traditional," in that it is the "'faculty for representing an object even *without its presence* in the intuition,'" (Brann, *World of Imagination*, 95). So, the imagination belongs to sensibility, since the intuition is sensible.

9. For example, Kant noted that "The concept 'dog' signifies a rule according to which my imagination can delineate the figure of a four-footed animal in a general manner, without limitation to any single determinate figure such as experience, or any possible image that I can represent *in concreto*, actually presents. This schematism of our understanding, in its application to appearances and their mere form, is an art concealed in the depths of the human soul, whose real modes of activity nature is hardly likely ever to allow us to discover, and to have open to our gaze. This much only we can assert: the *image* is a product of the empirical faculty of reproductive imagination; the *schema* of sensible concepts, such as of figures in space, is a product and as it were, a monogram, of pure *a priori* imagination, through which, and in accordance with which, images themselves first become possible" (Kant, *Critique of Pure Reason*, 182–83).

10. As noted in chapter 2, Richard Kearney remarks that Kant "pulled back" from his "discovery" that imagination and reason are intimately connected: so it was that in the "first edition of his *Critique of Pure Reason* . . . [Kant] startled his contemporaries by announcing that imagination was the common 'unknown root' of the two stems of human cognition—understanding and sensation . . . declaring it to be the primary and indispensible precondition of all knowledge. . . . [However] he quickly became aware that such a declaration of independence on behalf of imagination meant nothing less than dismantling the traditional edifice of metaphysics and, by implication, the ultimate basis of philosophical rationalism. Indeed, so alarmed was Kant by his own arguments that he went to considerable lengths in the second edition of the *Critique of Pure Reason* . . . to take most of the harm out of his initial claims . . ." (Kearney, *Wake of Imagination*, 156–57).

11. That is, ". . . all meaningful experience and all understanding involves the activity of imagination which orders our representations (the reproductive function) and constitutes the temporal unity of our consciousness (the productive function). If imagination were not always at work, we could never have any coherent and unified experience or understanding" (Johnson, "The Body in the Mind," 1).

12. Johnson, "Body in the Mind."

13. See Sallis, *Spacings*, especially chapters 1 and 3. The release of spacings is "stationed at the threshold. . . . That threshold is spaced out in certain Kantian and 'post-Kantian' texts . . . [and what] makes such texts the threshold of occlusion is their duplicity" (Sallis, *Spacings*, xv).

14. Ibid.

15. Ibid.

16. To add to this discussion, it is important to keep before our mind common modern notions of a split between reason and imagination and a pre-modern concept that does not split the two. As David Brown notes, "It is still common to find the Enlightenment as a whole depicted as hostile to religion, with deism as merely a superficial veneer. . . . In fact, imagination and reason were not at all perceived as necessarily in opposition. The dominance of classical models of philosophy ensured that writers could not possibly suppose that philosophy required of them the abandonment of narrative. Far from it. Plato's use of story and myth in his dialogues or Seneca's working out of his Stoicism through his plays suggested a very different answer" (Brown, *Tradition and Imagination*, 12–16). Brown also notes that though other philosophers have attempted to combine the imagination and reason (most notably Plato and Kierkegaard), there is still a common assumption that the two modes of thought are necessarily opposed. In

fact, Brown notes that theologians are so used "to engaging with the written word that it is all too easy for them to forget that for most of Christian history, with the great mass of the population illiterate, most Christians' primary experience of their faith will have been visual and, though probably to a lesser degree, aural" (ibid., 322).

17. For example, "This must furnish a distinction, however crude, between a *world of sense* and the *world of understanding*, of which the former may be different according to the difference of the sensuous impressions in various observers, while the second which is its basis always remains the same" (Kant, *Basic Writings*, 208). Furthermore, Kant's view of the "logical use of reason" also "requires some transcendental backing" (Wartenberg, "Reason and the Practice of Science," 230).

18. As Marshall McLuhan noted, "Neither mode is more important except in transitional forms of awareness. It is culture that makes one or the other dominant and exclusive. A culture builds itself on a preference for one or the other . . . instead of basing itself on both" (McLuhan, *Medium and the Light*, 53).

19. Kant's views of rationality label it as the defining marker of humanity. For example, Kant noted, "Now man really finds in himself a faculty by which he distinguishes himself from everything else, even from himself as affected by objects, and that is *Reason*" (Kant, *Basic Writings*, 209). However, Kant is described by Allen Wood as never attempting "to provide a systematic answer to" the question 'What is the human being?': "Kant even thinks it is *impossible* to define what is peculiar to the human species. For this species is only one possible variant of rational nature, yet we are acquainted with no other variants with which to compare it and arrive at specific differentia" (Wood, *Kant's Ethical Thought*, 198). It may be that there is the possibility for other types of rationality in Kant's view, but it is still rationality that is at the forefront. Wood's interpretation seems to close the door for Kant on animal rationality, since Kant saw "no other variants with which to compare" our rationality.

20. Kant, *Basic Writings*, 169.

21. "[The moral Tao's] validity cannot be deduced. For those who do not perceive its rationality, even universal consent could not prove it" (Lewis, *Abolition of Man*, 95).

22. Kant, *Basic Writings*, 150.

23. "A good will is good not because of what it performs or effects, not by its aptness for the attainment of some proposed end, but simply by virtue of the volition, that is, it is good in itself, and considered by itself is to be esteemed much higher than all that can be brought about by it in favor of any inclination, nay, even the sum total of all inclinations" (ibid., 152).

24. Ibid., 159.

25. Kant "maintains that in such a case an action of this kind, however proper, however amiable it may be, has nevertheless no true moral worth, but is on a level with other inclinations, *e.g.* the inclination to honour, which, if it is happily directed to that which is in fact of public utility and accordant with duty, and consequently honourable, deserves praise and encouragement, but not esteem. For the maxim lacks the moral import, namely, that such actions be done *from duty*, not from inclination" (ibid., 156).

26. Ibid. 158.

27. Ibid., 178.

28. Ibid., 186.

29. Rachels, *Elements of Moral Philosophy*, 126.

30. Anscombe, "Modern Moral Philosophy," 2.

31. Anscombe criticized John Stuart Mill on similar grounds. She stated that "Mill also, like Kant, fails to realize the necessity for stipulation as to relevant descriptions, if his theory is to have content. It did not occur to him that acts of murder and theft could be otherwise described. He holds that where a proposed action is of such a kind as to fall under some one principle established on grounds of utility, one must go by that; where it falls under none or several, the several suggesting contrary views of the action, the thing to do is to calculate particular consequences. But pretty well any action can be so described as to make it fall under a variety of principles of utility (as I shall say for short) if it falls under any" (ibid., 2).

32. Ibid., 1–6. This is not to say that virtue theory as an ethical system is somehow problem free or does not have its detractors. There are problems in naming the virtues—i.e., what virtues one is to include on the list. There is the problem of decision: e.g., "The first problem, once one realizes how varied and sometimes controversial the virtue lists can be, is deciding whether one has chosen the right virtues for one's list" (Veatch, *Basics of Biomedical Ethics*, 189). Furthermore, the problem of how one is to embody the various virtues in a given situation also arises. There is the additional problem of determining why the virtues are important in the first place: some claim they are intrinsically valued and others claim that they are to be instrumentally valued (ibid., 189). The problem of incompleteness also raises its head here. For example, we may say that a person who is tempted to lie should not do so because lying is dishonest and dishonesty is not a desirable character trait. But what then does honesty mean? Does it mean following rules, such as "Do not lie?": ". . . [we] cannot avoid asking why such rules are important. Why shouldn't a person lie, especially when there is some advantage to be gained from it? Plainly we need an answer that goes beyond simple observation that doing so would be incompatible with having a particular character trait; we need an explanation of why it is better to have this trait than its opposite. Possible answers [tend to look like other ethical theories, and in] any case, giving any explanation at all seems to take us beyond the limits of unsupplemented virtue theory" (Rachels, *Elements of Moral Philosophy*, 191).

33. This is not to confuse the virtues with character actions. Virtue theory typically refers to the character of the people who engage in the actions—to avoid strict consequentialism: "*Benevolence* and *beneficence* should be contrasted. *Benevolence* is a virtue, the virtue of willing to do good. *Beneficence* is a principle of actions, the principle of actually acting in such a way that good consequences result." (Veatch, *Basics of Biomedical Ethics*, 6–7).

34. Lewis, *Of Other Worlds*, 277.

35. Philosopher James Rachels also brings up an argument for moral similarity in his book *Elements of Moral Philosophy*. Rachels maintains that it is common to see values shared by different cultures (e.g., valuing truth telling and protecting children). His general point is that "*there are some moral rules that all societies will have in common, because those rules are necessary for society to exist*" (p. 30). Rachels is emphasizing the coherence of some ethical norms (e.g., truth telling and prohibitions on murder). Rachels notes the inherent contradiction of a society that does not respect honesty or value life: for one, the society would not have much to say to one another if everyone valued lying—for then nothing could be trusted; and secondly, one could never feel or be secure in a society where murder was permissible—and society itself might not be tenable because no one would want to associate with others for fear of being murdered.

Some rules we do find enforced and valued in all viable cultures: "Cultures may differ in what they regard as legitimate exceptions to the rules, but this disagreement exists against a background of agreement on the larger issues. Therefore, it is a mistake to overestimate the amount of difference between cultures. Not every moral rule can vary from society to society" (ibid.). However, exactly what this agreement means is certainly still open to debate—e.g., is it an agreement for the sake of protection and societal safety, or is it because there is some special sense in which we are participating in a grander reality that happens to be written in our hearts?

36. Milbank, *Word Made Strange*, 219.
37. Ibid.
38. Ibid., 231.
39. Ibid.
40. Lewis, *Christian Reflections*, 46.
41. Lewis, *Christian Reflections*, 46–47.
42. As an example, Lewis noted that cultures may "have differed as regards what people you ought to be unselfish to—whether it was only your own family, or your fellow countrymen, or everyone. But they have always agreed that you ought not to put yourself first. Selfishness has never been admired" (Lewis, *Mere Christianity*, 5).
43. For example, "We are absolutely at one about the universality of the Nat. Law, and its objectivity, and its Divine origin" (Lewis, *Collected Letters*, 3:23).
44. Aquinas, *Catechism*, 528.
45. Lewis, *Collected Letters*, 3:23.
46. Lewis, *Christian Reflections*, 56.
47. Lewis, *Abolition of Man*, 95.
48. As St. Paul noted, "We know that the law is spiritual; but I am unspiritual, sold as a slave to sin. I do not understand what I do. For what I want to do I do not do, but what I hate I do. And if I do what I do not want to do, I agree that the law is good. As it is, it is no longer I myself who do it, but it is sin living in me. I know nothing good lives in me, that is, in my sinful nature. For I have the desire to do what is good, but I cannot carry it out. For what I do is not the good that I want to do; no, the evil I do not want to do—this I keep on doing. Now if I do what I do not want to do, it is no longer I who do it, but it is sin living in me that does it" (Rom 7:14–20).
49. Farrer, *God Is Not Dead*, 98.
50. Ibid., 99.
51. Ibid.
52. Ibid., 86.
53. MacIntyre, "Virtue Ethics," 350.
54. See Plato, *Complete Works*, 6.
55. See ibid., 9.
56. Lovell, "C. S. Lewis and the Euthyphro Dilemma," 15.
57. Lewis, *Christian Reflections*, 107–8.
58. Lewis, *Chronicles of Narnia*, 475.
59. However, it should also be noted that Lewis found no interest in Kierkegaard. For example, in a letter of 1958, he remarked, "Kierkegaard still means almost nothing to me" (*Collected Letters*, 3:979). Kierkegaard's paradigm case for demonstrating a teleological

suspension of the ethical is the biblical story of Abraham and Isaac: "Now the story of Abraham contains such a teleological suspension of the ethical.... Abraham's relation to Isaac, ethically speaking, is quite simply expressed by saying that a father shall love his son more dearly than himself" (Kierkegaard, "Is There Such a Thing," 15). Kierkegaard highlighted the fact that Abraham, in doing such a deed, is following a higher *telos* than the universal ethical imperatives: "As the individual he became higher than the universal: this is the paradox which does not permit of meditation" (ibid., 16). Kierkegaard concluded that God tested Abraham for proof of faith: "Why then did Abraham do it? For God's sake, and (in complete identity with this) for his own sake. He did it for God's sake because God required this proof of his faith; for his own sake he did it in order that he might furnish the proof" (Kierkegaard, "Teleological Suspension of the Ethical" 16). And this raises a set of objections and problems for modern peoples. For example, how do we know that we are hearing the will of God? What if we heard of a man who killed (or attempted to kill) his son all on the premise that God told him to do so? Would we today accept someone's account of a story similar to that of Abraham's? It seems fair to say, no. Furthermore, we must consider that Abraham did not actually kill his son, as he was stopped by God's servant. Traditionally this story is seen as a test of Abraham's character and not a demonstration of God's willingness to change moral imperatives. This traditional interpretation is located, obviously, where the original Hebrew describes the binding of Isaac, where the Hebrew verb "to test" is used. Although, many would still question a God who is willing to test humanity in such a way, and many still express uncertainty over other seemingly questionable actions attributed to God in the biblical narratives, e.g., in 1 Samuel, God's command to Saul (through Samuel) to kill all of the Amalakites, including the women and children—thus, seemingly, asking Saul to commit genocide.

60. Aquinas, *Aquinas's Shorter Summa*, 4. There is also a clear echo of Aristotle here, namely, in Aristotle's ordering: the material cause, the efficient cause, the formal cause, and the final cause (*telos* or purpose). According to Aristotle, everything has a function and purpose. All living things have the potential to become something. Thus, the goal of life is to fulfill this potentiality (see Aristotle, *New Aristotle Reader*, 363). Furthermore, "Aristotle's metaphysics is ... teleological, in the sense that everything in the universe has its own form, or end, or purpose ... to fulfill. Aristotle's ethics ... follows from this teleological view of reality. The good, he says, is whatever the nature of a thing aims at as its formal cause. What is good for man? It is what man by his nature seeks: happiness.... There are two kinds of virtue for man: moral and intellectual. Moral virtue ... consists in the rational control of irrational desires and appetites of the soul.... In distinction from the moral virtues, the intellectual virtues consist in the contemplation of truth—the truths of science, art, philosophy, intuitive reason, and ethics. Since happiness lies in fulfilling our nature, the greatest happiness lies in fulfilling the best and noblest aspect of our nature: the activity of contemplating truth. The life of contemplation is man's ultimate good and his greatest happiness" (Lavine, *Socrates to Sartre*, 74–75).

61. Lewis, *God in the Dock*, 280.

62. MacIntyre, "Virtue Ethics," 255.

63. Ibid.

64. Ibid.

65. Additionally, Lewis argued that "Christianity has not, and does not profess to have, a detailed political programme for applying 'Do as you would be done by' to a

particular society at a particular moment. It could not have. It is meant for all men at all times and the particular programme which suited one place or time would not suit another. And, anyhow, that is not how Christianity works. When it tells you to feed the hungry it does not give you lessons in cookery. When it tells you to read the Scriptures it does not give you lessons in Hebrew and Greek, or even English grammar. It was never intended to replace or supersede the ordinary human arts and sciences: it is rather a director which will set them all to the right jobs, and a source of energy which will give them all new life, if only they will put themselves at its disposal. People say, 'The Church ought to give us a lead.' That is true if they mean it in the right way, but false if they mean it in the wrong way. By the Church they ought to mean the whole body of practicing Christians. And when they say that the Church should give us a lead, they ought to mean that some Christians—those who happen to have the right talents—should be economists and statesmen . . . and that all economists and statesmen should be directed to putting 'Do as you would be done by' into action. . . . The job is really on us, on the laymen. The application of Christian principles, say, to trade unionism or education, must come from Christian trade unionists and Christian schoolmasters . . ." (*Christian Reflections*, 316).

66. Lewis also noted that a "Christian society is not going to arrive until most of us really want it: and we are not going to want it until we become fully Christian. I may repeat 'Do as you would be done by' till I am black in the face, but I cannot really carry it out till I love my neighbor as myself: and I cannot learn to love my neighbor as myself till I learn to love God: and I cannot learn to love God except by learning to obey Him. And so . . . we are driven on to something more inward—driven on from social matters to religious matters. For the longest way round is the shortest way home" (ibid., 318).

67. Kierkegaard, "Is There Such a Thing," 16.

68. See MacIntyre, *Dependent Rational Animals*, 257.

69. Ibid.

70. Aristotle, *Nicomachean Ethics*, 278.

71. Ibid., 280.

72. See Lewis, *Christian Reflections*, 277.

73. As just one example, one can see this insistence in the story of Jesus' healing of the man with the shriveled hand: ". . . [Jesus] went into the synagogue, and a man with a shriveled hand was there. Some of them were looking for a reason to accuse Jesus, so they watched him closely to see if he would heal him on the Sabbath. Jesus said to the man with the shriveled hand, 'Stand up in front of everyone.' Then Jesus asked them, 'Which is lawful on the Sabbath: to do good or to do evil, to save life or to kill?' But they remained silent. He looked around at them in anger and, deeply distressed at their stubborn hearts, said to the man, 'Stretch out your hand.' He stretched it out, and his hand was completely restored" (Mark 3:1–5).

74. Again, as an example, Plato noted, "I call 'education' the initial acquisition of virtue by the child. . . . Then when he does understand, his reason and his emotions agree in telling him that he has been properly trained by inculcation of appropriate habits" (Plato, *Great Dialogues*, 86). And again: ". . . what we have in mind is education from childhood in *virtue*, a training which produces a keen desire to become a perfect citizen who knows how to rule and be ruled as justice demands" (ibid., 73). Plato also saw the use of tales as a means to habituate the stock responses and to teach about 'otherness': ". . . [if] only they [i.e., those who do not believe in the gods] believed the

stories which they had as babes and sucklings from their nurses and mothers! These almost literally 'charming' stories were told partly for amusement, partly in full earnest. . . . When some people contemptuously brush aside all this evidence without a single good reason to support them . . . and oblige us to deliver this address—well, how could one possibly admonish them and at the same time teach them the basic fact about gods, their existence . . ." (ibid., 414).

75. Meilaender, *Taste for the Other*, 212-13. Lewis' interest in the medieval age is present here too—the medieval worldview was such that all education was in some sense a moral education: "In the middle ages, someone has said, almost everyone was always trying to educate or to advise everyone else . . . in a sense all education was a school of service. For in the medieval view, education was moral training, a preparation for the 'good life,' and, since the real business of life was salvation, for eternity" (Ross and McLaughlin, eds., *Portable Medieval Reader*, 21).

76. Gayne J. Anacker notes that the term "moral imagination" refers to the "ability to consider our decisions, our values, and our lives from fresh and different moral perspectives. These perspectives make it easier to make important choices and changes that we might not have made if we had remained fixed in our old mental ruts" (Anacker, "Narnia," 130).

77. As an interesting connection, in Steven Fesmire's *John Dewey and Moral Imagination*, he suggests that "Debates about moral conduct remain at an impasse," and that this impasse has inspired "numerous moral philosophers in the past two decades" to challenge and reject the "Janus faces of absolutism and relativism . . . the Enlightenment foundations of mainstream twentieth-century moral theory" (p. 1). Fesmire uses Dewey's pragmatic ethic (which Fesmire suggests has been ignored by current moral philosophers) to find the imaginative help we need in assessing moral dilemmas: "According to Dewey's theory of the psychology of deliberation, imagination arises as the hunting phase of any situation involving perplexity. We probe optional futures and envision participating in them before acting overtly. A complete deliberation forecasts altered conditions that would ensue if this or that route were opted for, until an option is hit upon that can be trusted to integrate conflicting factors and restore equilibrium. In contrast with an emotive outburst, imaginative rehearsal is guided by exigencies of a situation along with a vast array of internalized social habits. Conventional metaphors are crucial in this respect. . . . [It] matters what order we throw realities into. Since there is no single correct way to take things, moral philosophers must ask about the effects of conceptual frames. Research on metaphor bears profoundly on pragmatist ethics since it advances Dewey's project of 'intellectual disrobing,' enabling us to critically inspect intellectual habits to see 'what they are made of and what wearing them does to us'. . . . Habits form characters, so ignorance of them leaves characters to haphazard development. If we do not own metaphors imaginatively, they own us mechanically" (pp. 90-91).

78. Ross and McLaughlin, eds., *Portable Medieval Reader*, 19.

79. Lewis once remarked, "You will find people who say I am much influenced by Thomism. I do (now) *use* the *Summa* a good deal, mainly as a sort of dictionary of medieval belief. But the appearance of influence is really due to the fact that I am often (especially on ethics) following Aristotle where Aquinas is also following Aristotle; Aquinas and I were, in fact, at the same school—I don't say in the same class! And I had read [*Nicomachean*] *Ethics* long before I ever looked at the *Summa*" (Lewis, *Collected Letters*, 3:980).

80. For example, in the *Nicomachean Ethics* Aristotle noted, "Since, then, the present inquiry does not aim at theoretical knowledge like the others (for we are inquiring not in order to know what excellence is, but in order to become good, since otherwise our inquiry would have been of no use), we must examine the nature of actions, namely how we ought to do them . . . the whole account of matters of conduct must be given in outline and not precisely. . . . [M]atters concerned with conduct and questions of what is good for us have no fixity, any more than matters of health. The general account being of this nature, the account of particular cases is yet more lacking in exactness; for they do not fall under any art or set of precepts, but the agents themselves must in each case consider what is appropriate to the occasion, as happens also in the art of medicine or of navigation" (Aristotle, *New Aristotle Reader*, 377).

81. Hauerwas, *Hauerwas Reader*, 167. To see an example of Hauerwas' construal of how narrative and ethics are intertwined and how this might be articulated and accomplished through a specific narrative, one would also want to look at his essay "A Story-Formed Community: Reflections on *Watership Down*" in the above.

82. MacIntyre, "Virtue Ethics," 253–54.

83. Ibid., 254.

84. Ibid.

85. Additionally, as David Brown notes, the ability to innovate is integral to the Christian tradition; the Christian tradition has drawn its primary strength from this ability to innovate and its "capacity to transmit the biblical story in ways which at times could speak more powerfully to contemporaries than the original deposit" (Brown, *Tradition and Imagination*, 324). A powerful means of innovation can be had by recognizing the ways in which we can identify with God and the Christian story: "We may identify with Christ by imitating him. We may identify through identifying with those who in turn identified with him, as for instance Mary rejoicing in the child to whom she has given birth or weeping over her dead son. Finally, God can identify with us in Christ" (ibid., 358). Lewis was on a similar path with his Space Trilogy and Chronicles of Narnia: he was attempting to communicate with a contemporary audience through the use of narrative; he was attempting to get them to relate to the religious through identifying imitation, both through Christlike symbols and representations and characters who are Christ imitators; and he was attempting to have them realize God's relation to humanity.

86. We might also get, as Northrop Frye noted, a sense of our conventions. Frye stated that literature or story gets us to notice our conventions (conventions of life we have grown so accustomed to that we think of them as natural) because when they are dipped into a story we are not used to them: "These conventions seem to have something to do with making literature as unlike life as possible. . . . Almost every story we read demands that we accept as fact something that we know to be nonsense: that good people always win, especially in love; that murders are complicated and ingenious puzzles to be solved by logic and so on" (Frye, *Educated Imagination*, 35). But where Frye sees the poet as a "bad guide," there is a sense in which these conventions from story reflect a "true home," a "true way," a "search," and a "stretching out." The poet may sometimes be a "bad guide"—as Frye stated, "[The reader's] life may imitate literature in a way that may warp or even destroy his social personality"—but the poet is most certainly not always in such a state (ibid., 36). The poet might lead us to these "ideals" (not mere conventions) through his or her imaginative faculties. And the nonsense of story can be both representative of life as well as directional to life, i.e., pointing beyond itself.

87. For example, many claim that Lewis' sexist views present themselves in the Chronicles from time to time. It is interesting to note, especially in regards to Susan's character, the debate over Lewis's treatment of women in the Chronicles. With the character of Susan, it is often claimed that Lewis sends her to hell. But this is blatantly false. Lewis leaves Susan alive at the end of the Chronicles and even leaves room for her possible salvation. In a letter to Martin on January 22, 1957, Lewis remarked, "The books don't tell us what happened to Susan. She is left alive in this world at the end, having by then turned into a rather silly, conceited young woman. But there is plenty of time for her to mend, and perhaps she will get to Aslan's country in the end—in her own way" (Lewis, *Letters to Children*, 67). Lewis' Chronicles have been charged with, among other things, being racist and sexist. For a look at the issues dealing with women in Lewis' work, one might want to look at Candice Fredrick and Sam MacBride, *Women among the Inklings*, as well as the following articles: Carnell, "Meaning of Masculine and Feminine"; Hannay, "'Surprised by Joy'"; Linskoog, "C. S. Lewis"; Leyland, "Lewis and the Schoolgirls"; and Fry, "No Longer a Friend." For a more general treatment of the charges of racism and sexism (and a defense of Lewis against these charges), one might want to look at Easterbrook, "In Defense of C. S. Lewis." One might also want to look at Ford's *Companion to Narnia*, under the headings "Sexism" and "Susan," and in the revised edition's short section on "Racism and Ethnocentrism."

88. Especially in regards to morality: many claim that the Chronicles are too didactic. Furthermore, even Lewis' close friend Tolkien found the Chronicles disagreeable: "It is sad that 'Narnia' and all that part of C. S.L.'s work should remain outside the range of my sympathy . . ." (Tolkien, *Letters*, 352).

89. For example, using Lewis' own categories, we might see where he made the mistake of asserting a special beneficence (that of putting masculine attributes over feminine attributes) above a general beneficence (that of recognizing the inherent worthiness of masculine and feminine attributes).

90. Again, as an example, Lewis stated that ". . . I am not of course maintaining that [the Tao] will provide an answer to every particular moral problem with which we may be confronted" (*Christian Reflections*, 56).

six

Poetic Labors

IN THE PREVIOUS CHAPTER I maintained that Lewis rejected a purely rationalistic ethic and that he advocated a relational ethic, which was expressed most clearly in his narrative work: we find ourselves part of a narrative framework, and find our ethic when we first recognize the narrative in which we find ourselves a part. Finding ourselves intrinsically bound to a narrative, it is a natural step to want to see how a narrative framework might play out through specific undertakings. It is in the practice of making, specifically for Lewis and MacDonald of creating a narrative through fairy story, that we get a glimpse of the theological imagination: the practice of art becomes a means to a sense of the other. It is for this reason that, in this chapter, I first describe the role of phantasm and fairy as explicated by George MacDonald—to which Lewis' line of thought is indebted. Lewis' idea of the work of phantasm and fairy is inherited from his admitted "master" George MacDonald. MacDonald provided Lewis with a special sense of the numinous, through his fairy tale *Phantastes*. The sense of the other that Lewis gained from reading MacDonald's fairy tale resulted in his own attempts to communicate and provide this experience. I then attempt to present Lewis' focus on story (and its revealing of his chief ideas): for Lewis' focus on story demonstrates a looking *along* and a looking *at*, in that we both experience and contemplate in narrative activities. Mythopoeic works communicate the numinous especially well according to Lewis, for myth can communicate special knowledge because of its ability to go beyond the expression of things already known. We sense this numinous quality through our (Augustinian-Platonic) sense of joy or desire, and we gain this special knowledge through our participation in the work and in the attempt at authorial discernment. But we must be, as St. Augustine noted, in the right place spiritually to receive the spiritual gifts: it is divinely gifted and is not only the condition for the reception but the content as well.

Ultimately, Lewis found that through narrative he could communicate his chief ideas as experiences and as ideas. His focus on story demonstrates this dual function of narrative. Lewis thought that stories afforded him the chance to put into concrete form what was normally conveyed only in abstractions. Narrative discloses reasoning beyond reason—reasoned work that acts as a fountain source for "rational" thought; it goes beyond reason in its more restricted, modern sense. The meaning-filled nature of narrative allows for the mysterious sense of the other—an epiphenomenon of the work. Mythopoeia can communicate special knowledge in its ability to go beyond the expression of things already known. The connection between imagination and myth here is readily apparent and cannot be missed: in the overt image-making work of narrative, the imagination plays an explicit role; and the imagination is also connected with myth through the epiphenomenon of the other—that is, through Augustinian-Platonic joy or desire. The Augustinian-Platonic sense of joy or desire excites the human soul through the mediation of creation's beauty. It is through the pangs of this excitement that the human soul recognizes a sense of the other—a "God-shaped hole" that cannot be filled by any other than God. This applies, for Lewis, to Scripture as well as to literature. As already mentioned, one must have the spiritual light already present for understanding. Understanding comes through the language of myth (through analogy). By the same token, Lewis saw Scripture as unique revelation that demands a response from the reader.

Moving from Lewis' sense of narrative and Scripture, I then examine Owen Barfield's notion of poetic diction: his view of language as essentially poetic. This implies a deep connection between thought and imagination. The imagination can then be seen as the deeper level of consciousness: so-called pre-rational commitments we bring with us are, in fact, what gets reason going. And, for Lewis, language is poetic diction. It is in seeing language as essentially poetic that we see the deep connection between thought and imagination. The imagination is a fountain source and motivational faculty because of its divine funding—only the theological (explicitly or implicitly) can give meaning and purpose to the narrative. However, the concessions of poetic language must be recognized, for the finite cannot fully express the infinite; transcendence cannot be reduced to immanence. But if there is a relationship between God and humanity, it must be apprehended somehow, must have a point of connection—and analogy is just such a connection. Analogies are ultimately inadequate to express the divine. However, the transposition of the "higher" life must be communicated to the "lower" through the lower forms: the images and language from the phenomenal world communicate analogously, poetically, because the lower cannot receive the higher in any other fashion. This is how the mysterious sense of the numinous can break through the phenomenal world of narrative and image making to deliver an awareness of the supernatural. Lewis' view is an expansive one, for it opens up the works of all art by revealing their divinely gifted nature, but, like Plato, the art that is allowed in this "republic," so to speak, must be liturgical (i.e., it must, in its ultimate sense, be an attempt to lead one back to its source), otherwise it loses its grounding for meaning and purpose and devolves into nothingness.

Phantasm and Fairy in McDonald

The role of fairy is essential to Lewis' thought, and George MacDonald was an important influence upon Lewis in this regard. We can see this clearly in *The Great Divorce*, where Lewis makes MacDonald his adviser and guide. Lewis once wrote, "I have never concealed the fact that I regarded him as my master; indeed I fancy I have never written a book in which I did not quote from him."[1] MacDonald viewed the imagination as a gift originating from the Creator. This general view also became the "foundation of [Lewis'] thinking and imagining."[2] Lewis claimed that MacDonald "baptized" his imagination. When Lewis first picked up a copy of MacDonald's book *Phantastes* he had, without consciously knowing it, engaged with a sense of holiness.[3] The story did not at first change Lewis' intellect or his conscience—all of that came later. What it did do was set him upon a path, and once he was on that path he found that MacDonald was there with him—telling him much that he could not have told him before, but, oddly enough, telling him much the same things as he had when he first began.

Lewis' entrance into children's fiction can also be seen in these terms: to set others on a path; to place readers in a narrative context of meaning; to show a "spiritual light" that precedes understanding; to deliver a reason beyond the categories of mere rationalism; to impart a sense of wonder, a sense that myth is a source of meaning and truth, a sense that he too could baptize imaginations. In a letter to Sister Penelope, Lewis picked up on the importance of symbolical narratives for children and the "uninitiated." Sister Penelope was concerned about the communication of symbols to children in her religious play *The Holy Seed*. Lewis stated that it may be

> true that many of the children will not understand the symbolism. But (a.) All the symbolical passages are quite capable of standing on their own feet as probable and affecting detail for the Isaac story considered in itself. (b.) What they do not understand at the time will go into their semi-conscious mind and help them to understand the Cross years later—will perhaps all the more if they don't remember it. Symbolism exists precisely for the purpose of conveying to the imagination what the intellect is not ready for.[4]

Lewis emphasized that one may baptize the imagination in preparation of future understanding; the imagination grasps what the merely rationalistic mind is not ready for and could not receive in any other fashion.

This further emphasizes the need for divine gift, even in reason and intellect: "To come to know the truth, the learner (disciple) must receive from the Teacher (God) not only the *content* of the truth but also the very *condition* for receiving it. The dispensation of the condition is an act of grace by the work of the Holy Spirit."[5] And the implications of the MacDonald-Lewisian view (namely, that the creative act of making is a divinely gifted one) are far reaching. For one, the fruits of the imagination, then, are to be brought up into the divine life. The Creator has given us the gift of the ability to make, which by being given imparts meaning into the exercise of this ability. It is not a leap to see that the value within the practice, within the gift, gives it its ultimate worth, which is then worthy of being saved if it is valued by the Creator. As such, poesis is then rescued from being mere fiction and swallowed up into the divine by being saved through transcendence. The act of making, which is divinely gifted, rescues the practice of art from being mere "fancy"—that is, a merely material act or a retreating from the world. But this view also allows art to be viewed liturgically. When art is viewed thus it is in reversion: it refers back to the divine life by which it was gifted. Conversely, if art is merely fictional, it terminates on its mere materiality—it is, then, merely material processes valorized by human minds, and is ultimately nihilistic.

It is through MacDonald's work that Lewis first came to a sense of the other, and it is through this experience of the other that Lewis came to see MacDonald as a master maker of fairy. The fairy world of MacDonald's *Phantastes* awakened within Lewis the excitement of the soul—the sense that his desires would lead him beyond the merely phenomenologically given. And in MacDonald's essay "The Fantastic Imagination," we see the precursor to Lewis' view of the imagination. First, Macdonald insisted that the desire to create new beings and forms is not to be confused with a desire to escape the domain of law: "Nothing lawless can show the least reason why it should exist, or could at best have more than the appearance of life."[6] Just as the natural world has its laws, so too must the fantasy world have its laws.[7] The human fantasy creation reflects the divine creation; the fantasist is a sub-creator. The human mind, according to MacDonald, lives in the realm of law. It is by obeying the law that we come to resemble our Creator. If we do not obey law, we make ourselves fools: for not to follow the internal law of our own story makes that story tedious and dull and ultimately incredible and unbelievable.[8]

Life in the moral world is not significantly different from life in the fairy world. In the fairy tale, a writer may be inventive, but must not then break the rules of his or her own making—nor could he or she make new moral rules. With the moral law a writer may

> clothe in new forms, and for this employ his imagination freely, but he must invent nothing. He may not, for any purpose, turn its laws upside down. He must not meddle with the relations of live souls. The laws of the spirit of man must hold, alike, in this world and in any world he may invent. It were no offence to suppose a world in which everything repelled instead of attracted the things around it; it would be wicked to write a tale representing a man it called good as always doing bad things, or a man it called bad as always doing good things: the notion itself is absolutely lawless. In physical things a man may invent; in moral things he

must obey—and take their laws with him into his invented world as well.[9]

The parallel with Lewis' idea of the moral Tao cannot be missed. We do not invent moral law: one draws from the basic law—the Tao.[10] We may even find ourselves more willing to see the good character or action as good and the bad character or action as bad in a story which projects us into not just the character's actions but the generalized human consequences and ramifications of such good or bad actions, events, or characters. We are given a context for meaning. A good story does not *tell* us (through didacticism) who is good or who is bad—it *shows* us by actions and consequences. The reader's conscience, then, may be awakened.

A good story for MacDonald is one that does not have merely one meaning put into it by the author. A good story is one in which various people will derive various meanings and values from it—and often ones that the author does not consciously intend: "Everyone, however, who feels the story, will read its meaning after his own nature and development: one man will read one meaning into it, another will read another."[11] However, this raises the question of how we are to know that we are not merely reading our own meaning into the story rather than taking a meaning from the story. MacDonald said that a "Genuine work of art must mean many things; the truer the art, the more things it will mean."[12] We cannot strictly teach meanings of stories. They are there to be recognized. The most a storyteller can hope to do is to awaken the reader to things previously unacknowledged.[13] We let our stories awake meanings in our readers: story can awaken a sense of wonder about the world, a sense of enchantment and longing.

Macdonald compared the fairy story to a sonata.[14] He insisted that we might discern a sonata's meaning. However, if we ask a group of people to write down what that meaning is we will most likely get a set of related feelings but no common thought.[15] This is partially because, according to MacDonald, words are not necessarily meant just to carry precise meanings—they very seldom carry the exact meaning the user of them intends—and words do not simply denote but also connote, especially in a story.[16] Therefore, even if words do carry definite meanings, it does not follow, claimed MacDonald, that they must not carry anything else. Words do not merely describe, they also *impress*.[17] We can, in story, rouse the conscience of our reader—such as by presenting the reader with dilemmas, real choices, actions, consequences, and ramifications.

We show our readers things that they can contemplate and experience, and we can hope to give our readers awakenings.

However, if readers may get any meaning they please from a story, then, seemingly, they may get a meaning one never intended. A reader, then, may not draw from the story what the author pleases, but only what the reader can draw from the story:

> If he be not a true man, he will draw evil out of the best; we need not mind how he treats any work of art! If he be a true man, he will imagine true things; what matter whether I meant them or not? They are there none the less that I cannot claim putting them there! One difference between God's work and man's work is, that, while God's work cannot mean more than he meant, man's must mean more than he meant.[18]

The good comes of its own accord. We cannot worry about what others, who see no good, will see in our stories. The finite cannot grasp the full meaning. We are by nature limited. Only God can give the full and final meaning. The finite can only suggest the infinite, which also gives rise to longings for the infinite. The author's "object is to move by suggestion, to cause to imagine, then let him assail the soul of his reader as the wind assails an Aeolian harp. If there be music in my reader, I would gladly wake it. Let fairytale of mine go for a firefly that now flashes, now is dark, but may flash again."[19] Story may give truth in flashpoints of understanding—the finite touching the infinite. Such flashpoints are extremely useful to us while we are on our journey. To borrow an illustration from Lewis, to a person traveling on a dark road at night, a view of the few yards ahead of the precipice he or she is traversing might be more useful than a complete view of the mountain top toward which he or she is heading.

Finally, MacDonald implored us to become like children. We can spoil some things by being "intellectually greedy"—by expecting to grasp everything through a rationalist program: "He who will be a man, and will not be a child, must—he cannot help himself—become a little man, that is, a dwarf. He will, however, need no consolation, for he is sure to think himself a very large creature indeed."[20] If we become like children, we might avoid the dangers of grown-up-ness: the protected and protective ego; over-reaching rationalist propositions, forsaking the role of imagination; a loss of the depth of the world by a termination on immanence and the reduction of all things to material—in essence, the loss of wonder and enchantment about the world. Lewis, too, warned of the dangers of losing our childlikeness. In *The Silver Chair*, Lewis cautions that "Even in this world, of course, it is the stupidest children who are the most childish and the stupidest grown-ups who are most grown-up."[21] In fact, all throughout the Chronicles Lewis champions children as the "heroes and heroines . . . who are brought to Narnia time and again to clean up the messes made by adults."[22] Lewis felt that holding on to childlikeness was an all too important tool.[23] We are disadvantaged by not keeping it.[24] Lewis gave children very serious consideration.[25] Trying to be "grown-up" limits our abilities to access the mythical mode, and the mythical mode (which takes the childlike mind to comprehend) can open us up to reasons and experiences we might never otherwise have.[26] The mode of "Story" as a means of conveying meaning and truth was an important idea for Lewis, and this can be seen, not least, in the seriousness with which he undertook the process of making stories and the seriousness with which he came to define Story as a form of literature. And Lewis' view of Story also reveals, as we will see in the next section, a relation between reason and narrative.

Looking Along and Looking At

Lewis labeled "Story" as a special kind of literature. It is a form of literature that does not exist "merely as a means to something else—for example, the novel of manners where the story is there for the sake of the characters, or the criticism of social conditions . . ."[27] These forms have the story there for the purpose of something other than the story itself. The forms of literature that have everything else there for the sake of the story are what Lewis deemed "Story." And, according to Lewis, they have "been given little attention."[28] In a good story we are not merely looking for the excitement of the adventure or merely the escape from the ordinary. In a good story we are looking for something beyond our grasp—something that is eternal: "In life and art both, as it seems to me, we are always trying to catch in our net of successive moments something that is not successive. . . . I think it is sometimes done—or very, very nearly done—in stories. I believe the effort to be well worth making."[29] The adventure may certainly be there in a good story, but it "is the *quality* of unexpectedness, not the *fact* that delights us. It is even better the second time. Knowing that the 'surprise' is coming we can now fully relish the fact . . ."[30] The escape is certainly there, but the "whole story, paradoxically enough, strengthens our relish for real life. This excursion into the preposterous sends us back with renewed pleasure to the actual."[31]

Lewis attempted to build worlds through his own stories, and, as an example of his attempts, one need look no further than the Chronicles of Narnia. The Chronicles embody Lewis' key ideas—and, as noted earlier, a key idea that permeates Lewis' writing (especially his fiction) is longing. Narnia represents the search for a place perhaps once remembered, somehow known in the imagination. Lewis focused on a sense of a home. We experience longing—that blast of cool, fresh desire that tells us we belong somewhere Other. The ability to sense the numinous is divinely gifted but is often undeveloped and unrecognized. The longing presents itself as a search, often a search for something we have lost. As Tolkien once noted, the notion of the fall of humankind has possibly produced something in us that longs for the return to paradise.[32] Lewis was always, throughout his life, searching and "yearning for those 'lenton lands' beyond which something better and permanent awaited him."[33] He partly translated this longing into a created world, namely, Narnia.[34] It is a reflection of Lewis' vision of the numinous, and it is a representation of a home to which we long to return. Indeed, in the Chronicles Narnia is presented as the real place, as the real home of the characters.[35] Ultimately, Narnia is to be seen as a way to re-enchant this world: by envisioning it as a portal to "more" reality, our own world becomes soaked with enchantment. We might even find that such portals exist here and now. We might be brought into that reality (finding we are already a part in it) which participates in and informs our current reality.

Lewis demonstrated the experience of the numinous most notably through the character of Aslan:[36] "Aslan has all of the 'hidden power and majesty and awesomeness which Lewis associated with God, but also all his glory and tenderness and even the humor which he believed belonged to him, so that children could run up to him and throw their arms around him and kiss him.'"[37] Aslan demonstrates the characteristics of *mysterium fascinans* and *mysterium tremendum*. Even the White Witch of Narnia has a clear sense of fear of Aslan: "'Wow!' roared Aslan half rising from his throne; and his great mouth opened wider and wider and the roar grew louder and louder, and the Witch, after staring for a moment with her lips wide apart, picked up her skirts and fairly ran for her life."[38] In *The Lion, the Witch, and the Wardrobe*, we also see the representation of right relation to the numinous.[39] Aslan can be stern, through which his numinous qualities cause trembling; he can be magnificent and majestic, thus displaying *mysterium fascinans*: "When [the children] see him they know that they are face to face with one who is both good and terrible.... He is a figure of immense power and beauty. When, after his resurrection, 'he opened his mouth to roar his face became so terrible that they did not dare to look at It . . .'"[40] Lewis lets us know that Aslan is not a tame lion.

The sense of longing Lewis attempts to create in the Narnia stories also reflects the disparity between divine a-temporality and earthly chronology. In Narnia, time moves differently. One might be in Narnia for years, but upon coming back time might only have moved minutes or seconds. There is a real sense of the Greek distinction between *chronos* and *kairos*. *Chronos* can be defined as clock time or time as it is measured—the quantitative element. *Kairos* can be seen as qualitative time or the "fullness" of time. *Kairos* can break into the world, into *chronos*. We can often find in our own lives a sense of this. There may be times in our lives when an action is possible that was not possible before or after—when it is the right time to act, because we (and/or time) are mature enough. St. Paul and the early church also spoke of *kairos*, or the right time of the coming of the Christ. The coming of Christ to the world is seen as a fulfillment of vast preparation—that all of history has been leading up to this point, the moment of "full" time, where the Christ can enter, where *kairos* can break into or touch *chronos*. In Lewis' Chronicles, we can see the fullness of time, the qualitative element breaking into the world. In *The Lion, the Witch, and the Wardrobe*, we see the children's fortuitous entrance into Narnia, fulfilling prophecy.[41] Lewis also highlighted a common experience of childhood, namely, that as children we might have the most access to, or recognition of, *kairos*. However, *chronos* is still present—the school year begins, our friends must go home, death comes to someone close, the chores must be done, adults may put us to an unpleasant task. It may be that as children we deal primarily with *kairos*, and as we age we may deal more and more in *chronos*. Madeleine L'Engle also speaks to this. She suggests that *kairos* is the initial state of our being—we learn the chronological aspects of our world through our living.[42] Lewis was also teaching us to step back into childhood to find that quality which we may have lost—and the imagination can be seen as a key in this curious fact: it creates that sense of timelessness within time; it is the element which allows us to resist the push of time. It is also an interesting aspect of childhood that it often seems the longest period of our lives—it is a time that does not often seem to have a "pushing" quality. Lewis might say that this could give us a clue as to why the most interesting aspects of autobiographies tend to be the parts about the subjects' childhoods: "I never read an autobiography in which the parts devoted to the earlier years were not by far the most interesting."[43]

We can also see the limits of rationality as conceived in a modern sense in the Chronicles of Narnia. For example, in *The Lion, the Witch, and the Wardrobe* reason is one of Professor Kirke's main attributes, but also tied up with this is a real sense of the mysterious and numinous. The children at one point ask the professor to solve a dispute. The dispute is about whether Lucy's tale of going into Narnia is true or whether Edmund's claim that they were just making up the story is true. The professor attempts to resolve the dispute through argument: "Why don't they teach logic at these schools? There are only three possibilities. Either your sister is telling lies, or she is mad, or she is telling the truth. You know she doesn't tell lies and it is obvious that she is not mad. For the moment then and unless any further evidence turns up, we must assume that she is telling the truth."[44] Lewis emphasized, through this argument, reason coupled with the mysterious and unexplainable. The professor tells the children that nothing is more probable than the possibility that there are other worlds, unnoticed by many, right next to ours. And once the children have come back from their journey, they tell the professor their tale. Contrary to the common reactions children often get when they tell such tales to adults, the professor wholeheartedly believes their tale—he is practiced in the arts of discerning God. Within the Chronicles there is a real sense in which humanity can, "[against] any sort of ultimate skepticism or irrationality," understand "much of reality, make true judgments, and recognize objective values."[45] But the function of rationality in the Chronicles is also to show that it "is not only fragile and finite but fallen."[46] We can see this demonstrated in the above example of Lucy's tale. The truth of Lucy's story cannot be decided upon with complete rationalistic certainty: ". . . unless any further evidence turns up, we must assume that she is telling the truth."[47] So, we come to have trust in Lucy's character and person and not simply or merely in abstract, rationalist propositions. It is a relational, participatory trust of character that supplicates or realizes our knowledge. Lucy is, like the professor, adept at discerning the things of God. She has a character that allows her to see such things.

Many will undoubtedly see Lewis' famous "trilemma" argument in Lucy's story.[48] Lewis' central concern seems to be the issue posed to us by the Jesus of the Gospels: "Who do you say that I am?" The various modern accounts of the historical Jesus serve to highlight the difficulty of a universally accepted history of Jesus. Much like the nineteenth-century quest for Jesus' religious personality in the "Life of Jesus" movement, the various (and often vastly different) reconstructions of Jesus appear suspect simply because the accounts seem to betray the views of the authors of the Gospels—in that Jesus is seen to embody what each author finds worthy and redeemable about Jesus' character.[49] Lewis attempted to put us in the text, imaginatively: to move beyond (but never leaving behind) the phenomenologically given to the wonder and enchantment the texts generate when being read with the spiritual heart. We engage with the text first as a narrative that demands a response.[50] In this sense we can see something new, something overlooked, in Lewis' trilemma. We can see an apparent attempt to engage with the text in a literary-theological fashion. His trilemma can be seen to present a version of literary engagement with the New Testament, which might be otherwise missed if we simply stopped at the question of supposed universal or secular historical reliability and did not also imaginatively engage ourselves in the text. It is here that we get the relational question, "Who do you think I am?" presented to us. Lewis saw that literary engagement with the New Testament might allow a reader to enter the story, to relate and participate intimately with the character presented to us. By entering a story one might develop responses that plant the seeds for understanding, development, and growth. One might, as it were, have the ever-watchful dragons mystified for a time while this engagement occurred. Lewis' emphasis is that the Christian story is better served by meeting it on its own ground—one could then see the common quagmire of historical inquiry as a result of allowing the Christian story to meet the secular only in the secular's own terms.

In a letter, Lewis noted the primary function of the Gospels for the fresh reader: "The first real work of the Gospels on a fresh reader is, and ought to be, to raise [very] acutely the questions 'Who—or What—is this?' For there is a good deal in the character which, *unless* He really is what He says He is—is not lovable nor even tolerable."⁵¹ Lewis highlighted here the idea that relational, participatory concerns are at the forefront. In the case of Lucy, the professor is asking the others to trust in Lucy's *character*, to base their decisions upon knowing who she is (even though the reliability of her statements cannot be checked by supposedly bare facts). Her character reveals to us the nature of spiritual adeptness: Lucy is in relation with the divine and can see what we may not yet see. And it is here that we see the real value in the trilemma argument: it is to have the reader experience Christ as a real and living person, to trust in him, in his character, to relate to him and allow for Christ's entrance and participation.

The emphasis on relational knowledge and the limits of knowing with rationalistic certainty can also be seen in *The Voyage of the Dawn Treader*. On the Island of the Three Sleepers, Lucy, Edmund, Eustace, King Caspian, and Reepicheep encounter three former Lords of Narnia asleep at an impressively laid table of food. They assume that the three Lords have eaten this food and fallen under an enchantment. A most beautiful young woman appears at dawn and they ask her about the three Lords: whether the food has caused their enchantment and what their story is. The lady answers "No" to the question of enchantment and continues to tell them about the table's purpose and the plight of the three Lords. However, there are some intellectual doubts still present in some of the company, particularly Edmund:

> "Look here," he said, "I hope I am not a coward—about eating this food, I mean—and I'm sure I don't mean to be rude. But we have had a lot of queer adventures on this voyage of ours and things aren't always what they seem. When I look in your face I can't help believing all you say: but then that's just what might happen with a witch too. How are we to know you're a friend?"
>
> "You can't know," said the girl. "You can only believe—or not."
>
> After a moment's pause Reepicheep's small voice was heard.
>
> "Sire," he said to Caspian, "of your courtesy fill my cup with wine from the flagon: it is too big for me to lift. I will drink to the lady."⁵²

It is no accident that Lewis had Reepicheep, the bravest character in the Chronicles, take the first drink to prove his trust and courage. Here Lewis can be seen as pointing to the courage it takes to face the quagmire of ultimate skepticism. One must trust in character and in oneself even if no other evidence presents itself to overcome the ultimate doubt of skepticism. But facing skepticism with courage does not rule out the continued possibility for doubt. Doubts will arise. We must admit that even the permanent and certain psychological exclusion of doubt is (at the very least) extremely rare. Our moods change and our reason will often follow our moods—and even if we do not have faith, there will be times when our position seems very doubtful to us. We can will ourselves to continue in faith; it is the "art of holding onto the things your reason has once accepted, in spite of your changing moods."[53]

In the face of utter skepticism and pessimism the decision to remain faithful was championed by Lewis: there is a reason that cannot be communicated in any other fashion; it is faith preceding understanding; it is reason delivered. The trust in character is not merely a substitute for rational certainty—as if once we have rational proof we can forgo the knowledge of character. It is a reason all its own—or, better yet, it is an integral part of reason that is neglected by modernist, Enlightenment paradigms. In *The Silver Chair*, Lewis has Puddleglum (the most pessimistic character in the Chronicles) say, "I'm on Aslan's side even if there isn't any Aslan to lead it. I'm going to live as like a Narnian as I can even if there isn't any Narnia."[54] Rationalistic discourse may get us to certain destinations, but we stay the course even if at moments our moods change or because rationalistic argument cannot establish some kind of universal, absolute certainty. We may know, truly, our faith in our hearts and minds. There may be doubts, but we can hold fast to our faith despite the transient nature of our moods.

The Chronicles of Narnia also represent Lewis' view of God and Christ—again, most explicitly in the character of Aslan. The parallels of Aslan and Jesus within the *The Lion, the Witch, and the Wardrobe* alone are abundant. For a prime example, one need only look at Aslan's sacrifice for Edmund. Aslan's sacrifice can be seen to resemble the Christian notion of Jesus' sacrifice for humanity. Aslan's sacrifice overcomes the evil forces of Narnia. The evil forces—in this case the White Witch and her followers—of Narnia think they have conquered Aslan through securing his death, but we find that just the opposite has happened: it is a eucatastrophe.[55] Aslan has risen and conquered death, thus making what was thought evil into good. Aslan's sacrifice also repays and covers the sin that Edmund has committed—so that Edmund and the others can be reunited to Aslan and the Emperor Beyond the Sea. Another example of Aslan's parallels with Jesus is the taunting and beating Aslan receives while on his way to the Stone Table.[56] Of course, the similarity to the Gospel reports that Jesus was taunted and beaten on his way to be crucified cannot be missed.[57] Aslan is the Christ of Narnia. Lewis described this relation in a unique way, namely, in a set of supposals: suppose that there is a world of talking creatures; suppose this world needed to be saved; how would God go about such a process? Lewis' answer is Aslan the lion.

Additionally, Lewis' central representation of good in the Chronicles is Aslan.[58] Aslan has all the colorings of the Christian God: loving, fearsome, compassionate, merciful, alarming, just, fair, and righteous. The personal relationship between the children and good characters of Narnia are the primary way in which Lewis communicates the relationship of God to humanity. It is a key element of Lewis' writing that he focuses on the ability of story or myth to communicate a theosis.[59]

Furthermore, love and salvation, sin and damnation, are to be seen in a relational fashion. Sin is separation from God, and it is a free choice. For example, Eustace Scrubb, in *The Voyage of the Dawn Treader*, chooses not to see Narnia for what it is. However, his experience soon leads him to change his mind—to reorient himself and to put himself in right relation. In his adventure on Dragon Island, Eustace leaves the others behind on the ship in order to avoid helping with some work. Eustace travels down a cliff with no way back up. He begins to feel very lonely and to suspect that the others will leave him behind. He finds a dragon's lair with hoarded treasure and enters into it. Eventually he falls asleep and soon discovers that he has become a dragon himself. At first, Eustace feels relief, for there is now "nothing to be afraid of any more. He was a terror himself and nothing in the world but a knight (and not all of those) would dare to attack him. He could get even with Caspian and Edmund now—"[60] But soon enough Eustace feels regret: "He wanted to be friends [with Edmund and Caspian]. He wanted to get back among humans and talk and laugh and share things. He realized that he was a monster cut off from the whole human race. An appalling loneliness came over him."[61] Eustace realized that the desire to be on his own, to be his own person, had cost him dearly. Sin and hell become the gulf of despair, separating one from communion with the Creator of all that is good and true.

As discussed in the previous chapter, there is also the sense in the Chronicles of Narnia of the moral Tao: the good characters all follow the moral Tao.[62] Narnia shows a

> complete acceptance of the Tao, of the conventional and traditional moral code. Humanity, courage, loyalty, kindness, and unselfishness are virtues. Children who might perhaps object to the code if they were taught it in churches and schools accept it easily and naturally when they see it practiced by the characters they love. They are learning morality in the best and perhaps only effective way.[63]

In Narnia, Lewis created a particular narrative moral context. When a character tries to deceive, this becomes even more obvious. Lewis creates a world where the Tao reigns and the characters who betray the Tao are recognized for what they are. What Lewis wanted to do was to take the Tao and "put [it] into another context where we're not, where we don't bring the same prejudices, where we don't bring the same sort of dulled sensibilities. In those worlds, we open ourselves up in ways that we're not opened to in our daily life here..."[64] Lewis wanted our experience of Narnia to enhance and re-enchant this world. "Lewis is saying that if we looked at our own lives, we'd see that they are just as enchanted. A cup of tea here is just as enchanted as a cup of tea in Narnia. A tree here is just as enchanted as a tree in Narnia."[65] He responded to the problems of religious belief and relation to God by posing the question, "'Why should anyone desire to believe in God?' And the answer that [Lewis gives] is *because God is Attractive.*"[66] However, this sense of re-enchantment is not simply that things which once appeared normal are now suddenly strange or weird, or simply mysterious. This sense of re-enchantment is a basic understanding of the world that sees the meaning inherent in creation. The utter saturation of the world with this meaning gives it its enchantedness.

The Chronicles of Narnia embody Lewis' key ideas: the sense of longing and the sense of the numinous; the limits of modern rational discourse; the sense of the moral Tao; humanity's and nature's relation to God and Christ; and the function of myth and meaning and narrative and story. The supposed retreat into children's fiction seems in reality to be a continuation of Lewis' lifelong preoccupation with the imaginative world and his realization that the power of imagination (through myth-making and story) can not only be combined and harmonized with the intellect, but is reasoned work itself. When Lewis was an atheist, he first saw the imagination as giving us false impressions. Then, through his talks with Barfield, Tolkien, and Dyson, he came to see the imagination as the "'organ of meaning' or reality rather than of conceptual truth," but "[Lewis] and [Tolkien] as writers valued looking at reality in a symbolic way," and they came to believe that "we actually win truth by employing metaphor, including imaginative models."[67]

The focus on the imagination in no way suggests that rationality can be abandoned or marginalized. For one, what is received and created by the imagination must still be processed, interpreted, and ordered. Also, the imagination is not only the fountain source for our ideas and concepts but is also the primary connector between ideas, the gap filler that moves us from idea to idea, that delivers real insight, the timeless element that allows us to resist and experience the duration of moments. However, imagination can fail us: ". . . imaginations can go bad or interfere with reality. Uncle Andrew's vain imagination [in *The Magician's Nephew*] causes him to play down Jadis's fearsomeness, and to exaggerate his handsomeness. But when she bursts in on him and Letitia, her real presence dissipates all of his daydreaming."[68] As with anything imperfect and finite, imagination can be misused, mistaken, or faulty. Some checks and balances are needed to interpret and possibly to correct and refocus. There are always false, deceiving chimeras to guard against. We may be able to protect ourselves against some false imaginings by attending carefully to images (e.g., ambitious fantasies) that are strictly or merely self-regarding. Lewis suggests that an untempered concern for self-regarding imaginings and our own imaginative lives is dangerous, and this insight may in turn give us a possible protection against false dreams: "By the imaginative life I here mean only my life as concerned with Joy—including in the outer life much that would ordinarily be called imagination, as, for example, much of my reading, and all my erotic or ambitious fantasies; for these are self-regarding."[69] This desire is the childish one: the childish instinct insists on its own way, looks merely for the pleasures of the temporary; the childlike looks not to things temporal but to things eternal. By attending to the images that revert back to their source, we may protect against vain images.

With a narrative we attempt to marry two ways of knowing.[70] According to Lewis, we know about something commonly through two means: (1) through thinking about it and (2) through experiencing it.[71]

By concentrating on the story, on the narrative, we avoid the dilemma of abstracting "into nothing" by *experiencing*, but we utilize our rationality by *contemplating* the story. In abstract thinking one tends to *look at* rather than *look along*. Lewis wants us to *look along*, for one can

> reason about or *look at* another's experience all day and be able only to abstract about it; it is only when we *look along* that person's experience (if not actually, at least in imagination) that we can see, touch, taste what that person is experiencing. In this sense it can be said of theologians and many ordinary people that they contemplate Christianity but they do not enjoy it. In the *Chronicles of Narnia*, Lewis reverses this trend: he allows people, especially Children, to look along Christianity without, perhaps, knowing Christ explicitly. He wants people to experience the meaning of the Christian facts first, to have their own feelings spontaneously, and then to become aware that this meaning is fact.[72]

Lewis' sense of imagination and story, then, give both an experiential aspect and an intellectual aspect: they teach us to look along, to feel and experience the meaning of the story. We might also experience events and situations we might not otherwise have experienced through the means of story. And we might also experience events and situations in ways we could never experience them in our own lives. As an example, the reading experience and the actual experience of being in grave danger, say, in space—with the threat of slipping into that cold, dark nothingness—might evoke quite different mindsets. If we were actually in the situation, we might then be simply overwhelmed by the pure sense of imminent death. However, while we are reading we can still feel that threat of imminent death, but we can also find something else unusual: we might find that the sense of cold, dark nothingness gives a unique fear of which we know not: the quality of fear becomes more than the mere threat of death; it becomes that threat combined with some unknown experience.

Stories also teach us to contemplate the meaning they present.[73] The images presented, the meanings presented, are reasoned work.[74] Narrative work also presents experiences—ones we might live along and read as new, validating, authentic. The narrative form, indeed the imagination, is logocentric.[75] It is concretized abstraction; it is reasoned work. But it is also the mediator of experiences, both phenomenal and epiphenomenal. As I have noted earlier in this chapter, Lewis' sense of the other, of the excitement of desire or joy, is communicated through the means of imaginative works. We do not merely get facts or information (though information can be and sometimes is communicated through poetic work), but we also get, as Lewis noted, the mysterious, meaning-filled "information" of mythic wisdom. And it is to this mythic "information" that we now turn.

An Experiment in Myth

Myth has a value in itself for Lewis that is apart from the particular articulation of the myth: "The story of Orpheus strikes and strikes deep, of itself; the fact that Virgil and others have told it in good poetry is irrelevant. To think about it and be moved by it is not necessarily to think about those poets or to be moved by them."[76] It is true that myth has few ways to reach us but through words; however, if there were another way in which the myth could reach us (e.g., through silent film or music or pictures) the myth would still affect us in the same way.[77] Lewis wrote that the word "myth" may be misleading, for the Greek word *mythos* does not necessarily mean the particular thing Lewis is attempting to pinpoint, but rather any sort of story. The some stories classified as myths by anthropologists may not have the quality of which Lewis was speaking, and some modern stories that might not normally be classified as myths might have this quality.[78] Lewis listed the mythic qualities for which he was searching. First, it is an extra-literary quality: the myth comes through no matter who is telling it or how it is told; it is not dependent on the storyteller or the storyteller's particular words. Second, the pleasure of myth comes not from "narrative attractions," such as suspense or surprise. The story is felt to be inevitable. Even from the first hearing there is a sense of permanence—of something to be contemplated, and this something is not the mere narrative structure. The narrative story seems to be somewhat absent in a sense: "The idea that the gods, and all good men, live under the shadow of Ragnarok is hardly a story."[79] Third, sympathy and character projection are not really present. That is, we do not necessarily put ourselves into the place of a character: it is the pattern of the story that moves us and is seemingly relevant to our lives; there is not necessarily a transportation of ourselves into just *one* particular character. "The story of Orpheus makes us sad; but we are sorry for all men rather than vividly sympathetic with him . . ."[80] The idea is that we get a whole tract of experience rather than just one segment. Fourth, myth deals with the fantastic. Myth "deals with impossibles and preternaturals."[81] Fifth, myth is always grave: it may be sad or joyful but never strictly comic. Sixth, the experience of myth is grave but it is also awe inspiring. There is a numinous quality to the work: "It is as if something of great moment had been communicated to us. The recurrent efforts of the mind to grasp—we mean, chiefly, to conceptualize—this something, are seen in the persistent tendency of humanity to provide myths with allegorical explanations."[82] Yet, even after all the allegories have been produced, the myth still remains more important than the allegories.[83] Lewis further claimed that what may appear to be a myth to one person may not appear to be a myth to another. His aim was not to provide criteria by which we might decide what is mythical and what is non-mythical.[84] He was concerned with the ways of reading and the ways in which myth affects us as readers.

As stated above, the value of the myth for Lewis is not to be found in any particular writer's words but in the pattern of events recounted. However, one who is interested in such matters may come to appreciate the literary qualities of a particular telling. But the enjoyment of the myth is still separate from this literary enjoyment, "just as our pictorial enjoyment of Botticelli's Birth of Venus is distinct from our reactions, whatever they may be, to the myth it celebrates."[85] Again, the importance of myth lies in the pattern of events:

> If the story is anywhere embodied in words, that is almost an accident. What really delights and nourishes me is a particular pattern of events, which would equally delight and nourish if it had reached me by some medium which involved no words at all—say by a mime, or a film. And I find this to be true of all such stories. When I think of the story of the Argonauts and praise it, I am not praising Apollonius Rhodius . . . nor Kingsley . . . nor even Morris. . . . In this respect stories of the mythical type are at the opposite pole from lyrical poetry. If you try to take the "theme" of Keats's *Nightingale* apart from the very words in which he has embodied it, you find that you are talking about almost nothing. Form and content can there be separated only by a false abstraction. But in a myth—in a story where the mere pattern of events is all that matters—this is not so. Any means of communication whatever which succeeds in lodging those events in our imagination has, as we say, "done the trick."[86]

The words that convey the myth are secondary to the pattern. The myth gives us more than just things we are familiar with: these patterns suggest an otherness, a longing for something of which we know not.[87] The wisdom we learn from myth is just as lasting and just as strong and important for Lewis as the work of the great poets—and perhaps it is better because it gives us delight and wisdom and strength and goes beyond the expression of things already known.[88] It may be that "speech is invention about objects and ideas," but

> myth is invention about truth, transcending thought and transforming the objective into a quality rather than a quantity. Myth and language are part of one knowing process. Myth has the ability to make concrete what would otherwise remain abstract. In fact, without the shaping of our perception by myth, and other imaginative creations (such as metaphors and models), we would not know real things, only abstractions. There is therefore an intimate connection between myth and thought.[89]

Lewis' view flies in the face of common modern notions of myth and truth as diametrically opposed, where myth is falsity, mere fiction, and not in any way related to truth. This, in essence, is why it is thought that myths and legends and even Scripture must be "demythologized"—that is, we must remove the mythic (read false) elements to get at the reality or truth of the matter. This is also why modern biblical literalists also equate myth with falsity—they have accepted the modern notion that mythic equals false and as such myth is to be seen as a parasite on the truth or reality of the literal Word. If we remove the notion that myth and truth are diametrically opposed, however, we might find that myth can be seen, as Lewis might have it, as human imagination working on truth in order to present it in new forms or in a new light. We might then be able to read in a new way. We might then become good readers.

But how is it that we get the most out of myth or story, and how is it that we become good readers? In *An Experiment in Criticism*, Lewis stated that the "behaviour of the myth-lover is extra-literary.... He gets out of myths what myths have to give."[90] And this echoes MacDonald's notion that the best a storyteller can do is to suggest and awaken thoughts previously unknown, so that the reader gets out of the story what he or she can.[91] However, Lewis suggested that there are some things one can do to make him or herself a better reader. Of primary importance for Lewis was the belief in reader participation and in finding the intention of the author.[92] There is a spiritual sense to what we are reading, and though the author's intention remains important the ultimate intention we are searching for is the intention of the divine author.[93] And one must be in the right place spiritually to grasp fully what the texts are telling us—one must sense a spiritual principle.[94] The condition, not only the content, of truth must be divinely gifted. Similarly, Augustine told us that we must come to the text with an open and pure heart to find the intention of the divine author.[95] We must come with hope to the text—hope that we might find what we are looking for and what was intended; and we must come with faith to the text—to find what should be loved. This echoes the philosopher Boethius, too: "The way anything is received depends on how the receiver is fitted to receive it' . . . [and] Lewis restates the adage of Boethuis [in *The Magician's Nephew*]: 'For what you see and hear depends a good deal on where you are standing: it also depends on what sort of person you are.'"[96] We must be ready to receive the gifts of the divine if we are to be truly good readers.[97]

Austin Farrer also noted that a special kind of knowledge can be gained from mythic language, particularly scriptural language. There is a supernatural action which can occur in the mind:

> Such knowledge bestows an apprehension of divine mysteries, inaccessible to natural reason, reflection, intuition or wit. Christians suppose such mysteries to be communicated to them through the scriptures. In particular, we believe that in the New Testament we can as it were overhear men doing supernatural thinking of a privileged order, with pens in hand.[98]

Austin Farrer critiqued the efforts of demythologization in his own time and admitted that, as modern people, many think we cannot tolerate myth any longer because it is just too primitive, too unbelievable.[99] Farrer stated that there are four common refusals the modern mind might make regarding myth—the necessary, accidental, lamentable, and factitious. The necessary refusal comes in the guise of "established, or virtually established, positions of science and history . . . as when we refuse to believe that the world was created eight thousand years ago or that the sun stood physically still for Joshua."[100] Accidental refusals arise when modern people do not pay attention to certain aspects of mythic language, for example, "in the case . . . of industrial workers who have a blind eye for imagery based on the procedures of pre-scientific agriculture."[101] But "accidental refusals become lamentable refusals when they involve the atrophy of a spiritual function, for example, the sense for poetry."[102] Finally, factitious refusals are "those that arise from a philosophy or attitude which men either embrace or swallow, [such as] Communism, physical materialism, or economic utilitarianism."[103]

Farrer noted that if we cannot understand mythic language it is usually because we have adopted a dogmatic materialism—a factitious type of refusal. If one has lost his or her sense of poetic expression and metaphor (lamentable refusal) we therefore "ought to sustain and augment whatever rudiments of poetical sense remain. If because the Biblical images draw on unfamiliar fields of experience, it is accidental and must be met largely by the substitution of familiar images, not . . . by demythicization but by remythicization."[104] Farrer observed that there are two senses of understanding mythic language. In the first sense, one sees poetical symbol for literal fact. This is a view no one should accept. So, when we talk about angels "above us" and devils "below us," it is not to mean that some form of excavation or aeronautics will allow us to reach these entities or places. However, "How far symbol is to be taken for literal fact in the New Testament is a subtle question," and it is here that Farrer's second sense of understanding mythic language is found: how far are we to take symbols as literal facts?[105] Farrer thought that the task of demythologizing had (limited) merits, and he saw it as a task that could be continued to some degree, for "St. Augustine was aware of the importance of distinguishing the literal from the symbolic, and the School-men theorized the problem almost *ad nauseam*."[106]

However, Farrer believed there were more important problems. Two of those problems were the problem of miracle and the problem of transcendence. The problem of miracle for Farrer lies in the assumption of knowledge: are miracles to be viewed as examples of myth (in the sense of symbolic reality and not factual reality) or not?[107] Farrer saw the problem of transcendence in general terms: to what does a symbolical reality refer? "God cannot be described in literal terms, but only in analogies from the created world. To what sort of reality beyond the analogies do the analogies refer?"[108] Lewis saw this problem similarly. He maintained that one "cannot know that everything in the representation of a thing is symbolical unless [one has] independent access to the thing and can compare it with the representation."[109] The symbolical reality still refers to *something*, some reality beyond the analogies. In the case of Christianity, for Lewis, it remains a "Myth even when it becomes Fact. The story of

Christ demands from us, and repays, not only a religious and historical but also an imaginative response. It is directed to the child, the poet, and the savage in us as well as to the conscience and to the intellect. One of its functions is to break down dividing walls."[110] Accordingly, myth is also, in Lewis' view, not merely "misunderstood history (as Euhemerus thought) or diabolical illusion (as some of the Fathers thought) nor priestly lying (as the philosophers of the Enlightenment thought) but, at its best, a real though unfocused gleam of divine truth falling on human imagination."[111] Lewis saw the relationship between humanity and God as so unique that it cannot, in an ultimate sense, be adequately compared with other relationships.[112] However, this unique relationship must be apprehended somehow, must have a point of contact with the human. One such way is through analogies.

But how can we speak of God? It is not so readily apparent how we might go about it. On one hand, we use metaphorical language to talk of God being like something (e.g., a lion), but we know that literally it is not true—God is not in a literal sense a lion. However, there is something within the metaphor that delivers some sense of truth. But the use of the metaphor may not readily present to us the problem of speaking about God in an acute way, for we can see that it is not meant literally. But if God is beyond all human conception, how is it that we can talk about God using the language of the finite world? For St. Thomas Aquinas, there are distinctions to be made about how we speak of God which would allow for finite creatures to talk about God. We derive our "knowledge of God from creatures," that is, we can talk about God using the language of finite things because effects resemble their causes. We can see something (through a glass, darkly) in the thing created that resembles the Creator. Aquinas noted that when we talk about God we might appear to be speaking equivocally: it appears that when names are applied to God they "are synonymous names. For synonymous names are those which mean exactly the same. But these names applied to God mean entirely the same thing in God: for the goodness in God is His essence, and likewise it is his wisdom."[113] For Aquinas we do not speak equivocally when we speak of God. This is because our intellect, knowing God from creatures (effects resembling their causes), "forms concepts proportional to the perfections flowing from God to creatures, which perfections pre-exist in God unitedly and simply, whereas in creatures they are received and divided and multiplied."[114] There is thus one simple principle represented by different perfections of creatures in various manners, and this applies to our variously comprised intellects: "There corresponds one altogether simple principle, according to these conceptions, imperfectly understood. Therefore although names applied to God signify one thing, still because they signify that under many and different aspects, they are not synonymous."[115] Synonymous terms name one thing under one aspect, and terms that name multiple aspects of one thing do not "signify primarily and absolutely one thing; because the term only signifies the thing through the medium of the intellectual conception..."[116] So it is that when we speak of God as good and speak of our friend George as good, we are not using the same word in completely unrelated ways; we are not equivocating. There is a resemblance to be seen. However, it is not that God causes George's goodness—for God is goodness. George's goodness is given, attributed to George through his relation to God. George's goodness, then, is a sign of God's goodness. One may see, however dimly, through George's goodness, the goodness of God.

Aquinas also noted that when we talk about God we might be speaking univocally, that is, using the same term in an identical way. So, for example, when we talk about a loving God and a loving dog we might appear to be using the term "loving" in identical senses. But Aquinas rejects this as well. For creatures resemble but do not share in the identity of God: in Aquinas' language, "every effect which is not an adequate result of the power of the efficient cause, receives the similitude of the agent not in its full degree, but in a measure that falls short..."[117] To use our example, when we speak of a loving God and a loving dog, it should be clear that we do not mean the same exact things; what it means to be a loving God is quite different from what it means to be a loving dog. So, for Aquinas, when we speak of God we are neither equivocating nor speaking univocally. We are instead using analogy. Analogy is a mean between equivocation and univocation:

> ... in analogies the idea is not, as it is in univocals, one and the same, yet it is not totally diverse as in equivocals; but a term which is thus used in a multiple sense signifies various proportions to some one thing; thus "healthy" applied to urine signifies the sign of animal health, and applied to medicine signifies the cause of the same health.[118]

So, when we apply the term "healthly" to a person, we know that the person is, so to speak, healthy in him or herself. However, when we apply the term "healthy" to a type of food or drink, say a "health shake," we know that the shake is not healthy in itself, but is only healthy as it applies to the person who drinks it. Accordingly, through analogy we can see how the human approach can refer to something beyond itself by bringing us into a relationship with the object of reference. These analogies are clearly not to fence-in the infinite in any way. As James K. A. Smith notes, there must be a "certain 'humility' attentive to the play of signifiers and the elusiveness of transcendence."[119] We must avoid the temptation to claim possession of the divine: the attempt to analogize is not an attempt to demarcate the divine, but rather is an attempt to open us up to the Wholly Other. Analogies may be ultimately inadequate to express the divine, for the infinite cannot be reduced to the finite; God cannot be reduced to immanence. However, analogies are still essential. Far from reducing God to immanence, the use of analogy reveals to us divine presence. Analogy must be used if we are to receive any revelation at all—for how else could the infinite be received, revealed, or manifested? There must be some point of contact between the divine and the human. If we want to begin with a theology of revelation, we must understand that revelation needs first and foremost to be "*received*, and there are conditions for that reception: all reception is according to the mode of the perceiver. Thus any revelation must be *given* in terms that are in some sense commensurate with the conditions for its reception by the receiver—in this case, finite human beings."[120]

Lewis championed the idea that there is no real demythologizing when we attempt to "rationalize" the world: there is only remythologizing—and usually a poorer sort of abstract mythology is being substituted for a richer one. Lewis (and Farrer) argued that the ancient symbols and myths supplied by the biblical narratives give a deeper, multitudinous interpretation of that reality. Other forms of narrative, symbol, and myth may also do the same in a limited fashion. But mere abstraction tends to terminate on itself: the abstract gives a definitional quality that detrimentally captures one aspect of the reality at the sake of the whole. Mythic language gives more than itself, does not terminate on itself, and brings forth seemingly unending meanings and interpretations. Yet even the impoverished remythologizing is indeed relying on (heretical) transcendence. In other words, all diction is poetic. Lewis' friend Owen Barfield defined "poetic diction" in the following way: "When words are selected and arranged in such a way that their meaning either arouses, or is obviously intended to arouse, aesthetic imagination."[121] However, in general, the words we use are selected and arranged in ways meant to arouse our desires. It is not just an issue for the "aesthetic imagination"—as if only specifically poetic or "artsy" works are trying to convey a story of the world. All language, in some sense, participates in this narratival, poetic practice, whether it be that of scientific materialism or humanistic atheism or specifically religious traditions. And in Barfield's seminal work, *Poetic Diction*, we do see the inchoate emergence of just such a case.

Poetic Diction

Lewis and his friend Owen Barfield had what Lewis termed a "Great War," which began in the early 1920s and ended about 1931, after Lewis' conversion to Christianity.[122] It at first centered on the difference between Barfield's insistence that imagination could be a way to truth, and Lewis' rejection thereof (as well as Lewis' rejection of Barfield's anthroposophy and his idea of an "evolution of consciousness"). Over the course of their friendship, Lewis eventually found many of Barfield's ideas appealing and credited Barfield with delivering him from "Chronological Snobbery," "the twentieth-century intellectual's inability to consider seriously the ideas generated before the Enlightenment. This emotional barrier cast down, Lewis could entertain belief in the supernatural, hence ultimately Christianity, and embark on the imaginative recreation of the medieval and renaissance worlds for which he is renowned."[123] Lewis eventually found that truth could be found through the imagination and even that an "evolution of consciousness"[124] of sorts could be found—for example, as seen in Lewis' idea of pre-Christian myths as "preparation" or "pre-evangelism." However, Lewis still differed on many counts with Barfield's thoughts.[125] The Great War was beneficial to Barfield because of the way Lewis forced him to think "systematically and accurately," but Barfield helped Lewis to "think imaginatively . . . to combine his imagination with his formidable intellect. This was a 'slow business' however, according to [Barfield]."[126]

Barfield was a notable influence upon Lewis—Lewis said that Barfield changed him much more than he changed Barfield.[127] Barfield saw the poetic as a means to change our consciousness. We can be transported to another type of consciousness through poetic means—so that we see something through the eyes of the poet and not merely our own: we experience the poet's meaning, and we experience it quite often as something different from our own experience. However, the beauty we experience in poetry is not always merely foreign:

> ... wonder is our reaction to things which we are conscious of not quite understanding.... The element of strangeness in beauty has the contrary effect. It arises from contact with a different kind of *consciousness* from our own, different, yet so remote that we cannot partly share it, as indeed, in such a connection, the mere word "contact" implies. Strangeness, in fact, arouses wonder when we do not understand; aesthetic imagination when we do.[128]

The experience of this change of consciousness occurs, said Barfield, when we move from one plane of consciousness to another, and we do so by means of appreciation of the poetic. However, the pleasure of appreciation depends upon the rare and transitory change itself.[129] The "poetic mood" then operates in a circuitous manner: "... the poetic mood, which, like dreams to which it has so often been compared, is kindled by the passage from one plane of consciousness to another. It lives during that moment of transition and then dies, and if it is to be repeated, some means must be found of renewing the transition itself."[130] The poetic elements give us flashes of another consciousness, but these temporary flashes must be renewed and not merely repeated in order to be experienced again. Consequently, when we have truly experienced poetry, have "possessed" it, we can then do away with the specific diction of the poetic:

> ... when [poetry] has entered as deeply as that into our being, we no longer concern ourselves with its *diction*. At this stage the diction has served its end and may be forgotten. For if ever we go back to linger lovingly over the exquisite phrasing of some fragment of poesy whose essence has long been our own, and of which the spirit has become a part of our every waking moment, if we do this, is it not *for the very reason* that we want to renew the thrill which accompanied the first acquisition of the treasure?[131]

Like Barfield, Lewis also saw the deep experience of the mythic as the really important element: once the core of the myth has been communicated and grasped we might then do away with a specific mode by which it was received, though we will still need to have some mode of communication and reception, and we may still enjoy particular versions and elements of certain tellings for their literary qualities. However, the Christian myth would be different for Lewis, for it is both a myth and a Christian historical reality—and the elements of its communication (its combined unique and specific religious-liturgical-historical importance) would demand that the particular narrative embodiment in Scripture be preserved and supported. The Christian myth, for Lewis, would not be a telling that is separable from its mythic mode—and, of course, other traditions could lay the same claims.

Moreover, there is something to capture in the initial spark of our first encounter. The imagination works on the deeper level of consciousness, so that what we may normally call "deep" (say, strictly rationalistic thinking) is really the surface, and the deeper imaginative quality works subterraneously and is the real director of the intellect and surface levels of consciousness:

> Taste is formed in those moments when aesthetic emotion is massive and distinct preferences then grow conscious, judgements then put into words will reverberate through calmer hours; they will constitute prejudices, habits of appreciation, secret standards for all other beauties. . . . Thus the volume and intensity of some appreciations, especially when nothing of the kind has preceded, makes them authoritative over our subsequent judgements. On those warm moments hang all our cold systematic opinions; and while the latter fill our days and shape our careers it is only the former that are crucial and alive.[132]

The poetic and mythic fundamentally utilize the imagination, the deeper level of consciousness. The imagination is the force of the intellect, in that it directs our intellectual concerns. The act of reasoning through an argument may possibly make us change our minds about some particular issue, but it rarely seems to do so. It most often makes us re-evaluate our premises—to rework them to account for the supposed error or errors—and not our conclusions. Rational discourse may sometimes make people re-evaluate their conclusions, but the deep-seated preconceptions people harbor are often another matter. Who really knows why some arguments are convincing to some and not to others? Lewis and Barfield recognized the ineptitude of rationalistic arguments to establish absolute certainty either way: we might see the reasons for both sides of an argument (and still intuitively know one of them as "right for us"). That is, there is no uncommitted, universal reason that is secular or unbiased. We each bring to the table our commitments. We might argue for our case and make our case as coherently and consistently as we possibly can, but we are left with something else that motivates and drives our concerns, commitments, and intellects. In this sense, the imagination could be seen as that deeper force driving our concerns and intellects.[133] It might then be possible to utilize the imagination to "steal past these watchful dragons" too and really change the consciousness of the reader—first, to habituate the reader through image, symbol and emotion; and second, to set the reader on a path to reconsider their conclusions and not just their premises. One can then also see Lewis' stories clearly in light of "baptizing the imagination"— that is, to make the reader involved in story, in a particular narrative (other than the one held), and to awaken a sense of wonder and enchantment and longing. We might also awaken the conscience of our reader by introducing characters and situations and images that engage the moral imagination. Imagination is a prelude to action; it is a motivator not just a playful fancy. It seems clear that the impact of story, of myth, of literature, of art and music expressing authentic experience can make us re-evaluate ourselves and our world.

There is an added benefit of reinvigorating the immanent. The ontology of a strict rationalism is ultimately nihilistic and squeezes reality down to the merely phenomenologically given. Rationalism attempts to uphold the appearances, but fails to do so; it is supposedly devoid of meaning, reduced to mere material means or nothingness (yet even here it is relying on a heretical theological funding). The theological imagination, however, saves the appearances by being more than the merely immanent. Transcendence reinvigorates the immanent by placing it in a context of participatory ontology—that is, through transcendence a proper valuation of immanence can occur. We can see this most clearly from a Christian perspective through revelation and incarnation: God created the immanent; God reveals through the immanent (through creation, i.e., people, communities, things, works, etc.); God appeared in flesh and redeems flesh. In this we get the immanent thrown in with transcendence. Or, as Lewis stated, "Aim at heaven and you will get earth 'thrown in'; aim at earth and you get neither."[134] We then see the world as infused with the grace of the divine, with God "lurking around every corner."[135]

Lewis, too, saw the importance of the imagination as a means to awaken enchantment. Contrary to the belief that story, fantasy, and imagination tend to steer one away from the world into escapism, Lewis saw the importance of these things as a means to recovery.[136] Lewis, too, emphasized the importance of the negative, but he most often was guarding against the unwarranted privileging of abstraction, which he thought the "fatal" image: "Unless you sit to it tightly, continually murmuring 'Not thus, not thus, neither is this Thou', the abstraction is fatal. It will make the life of lives inanimate and the love of loves impersonal."[137] It is important to metaphorical language and analogical language that there is a real sense of similarity and participation. Lewis much more readily affirmed the positive side, the participatory side, of analogous language. However, Lewis affirmed the corrective nature of both analogical and dialectical language. Lewis recognized the concession of imaginative language.[138] But he allowed for a real imaginative similarity, a real essential knowledge (as might be understood by the finite and fallen) that cannot be expressed or grasped by us through any other means. Lewis saw the relationship between humanity and God as so unique that it cannot, in an ultimate sense, be adequately compared with other relationships. However, this unique relationship must be apprehended somehow, must have a point of contact with humanity, and this is through analogy. Accordingly, through analogy we can see how the human approach can refer to something beyond itself by bringing us into a relationship with the object of reference. For the Christian the special revelation of Scripture is just such an analogous point of contact: Scripture communicates the particular Christian mysteries.

Narrative and Scripture

Lewis saw Scripture as displaying some new form of literary genre: it is mythic, narrative history.[139] It is some strange new hybrid of narrative: he particularly keyed in on the extraordinary and peculiar combination of mythic, narrative elements with historical reportage found in Scripture. Lewis saw Scripture primarily through narrative terms, and as such he saw Scripture as relational, as participatory. He acknowledged that Scripture can give us historical data, though it is not necessarily the type of "facts" (viz., rational, unaided, and universal) some envision. Michael Christensen notes that "literary inspiration" is a useful term to denote

Lewis's view of Scripture.[140] The Bible is to be approached as specially inspired literature. Its literary elements—images, symbols, myths, and metaphors—are actual embodiments of spiritual reality and vehicles of divine revelation.[141] To view Scripture in this way is in no way to diminish its truth and its value. When Scripture is taken metaphorically, it is often concluded that it therefore need not be taken very seriously at all.[142] Lewis clearly recognized the danger of viewing Scripture *merely* as literature—that some readers might take less seriously the "metaphors" of the Bible. He also offered some approaches to Biblical exegetics.[143] His first warning was never to take the images of Scripture literally: that is, we must not devolve into a literalist approach to biblical exegesis.[144] But, as a protective corollary, we are to trust the images wholeheartedly: that is, when the meaning of the images (as they apply to our fears, hopes, wills, and affections) conflict with any theological abstractions, we must hold tight to the meaning of the images.[145] And although literary aspects of Scripture can be distinguished they must not be separated from the inspired message. Scripture requires us to be "good readers": to take, as much as is possible, the work as it was intended (from the perspective of the author, through the images the author communicates); to see the work as an artistic imitation of reality; and to see the work as communicating the universal reality, even though humans can only describe this reality imperfectly. The extent to which Lewis proposes an engagement with Scripture as literature is sometimes difficult to discern. But his main mode of criticism is that of his "day job"—a literary critic. As such, Lewis approaches Scripture just as we have laid here: we must be "good" (in Augustine's sense) readers, recognizing that the right disposition leads to the right reading, and we must enter into the text that the author presents and suspend disbelief and attempts to make the text conform to our understandings (eisegesis); we must understand that we approximate beauty through language and do not create it.[146] We show the realities of truth and beauty through our poesis; we recognize the role of the imagination in this process, as a delivered reason.

Additionally, some may see similarity with neoorthodoxy here in Lewis' view of divine inspiration. But when "Lewis comes close to a neoorthodox position when he says the Bible 'carries' the Word of God," it must be noted that he does not intend "carry" to

> mean what neoorthodox theologians mean when they say the Bible 'becomes' or 'contains' God's Word. . . . Lewis differs with

neoorthodoxy in recognizing that there are real spiritual truths being conveyed through the words of Scripture. The Bible is not simply a witness to God's Word but is, in a literary package, the special revelation of God. At the same time, Lewis would acknowledge that it is the ongoing revelation of God in Christ, not its embodiment in Scripture, which is infallible. It is the *message* of the living Word of God, not the *medium* of its expression, which is authoritative. Scripture, as the primary medium of divine revelation, conveys, presents, or as Lewis prefers, "carries" God's truth in finite human form.[147]

Lewis' view reveals the necessity for divine participation in Scripture. It also leaves the door open for the inspired status of other works of art: "If every good and perfect gift comes from the Father of Lights then all true and edifying writings, whether in Scripture or not, must be *in some sense* inspired."[148]

There is a serious overlap here between Lewis and the approach of narrative theology. For one, Lewis recognized that narrative is the main literary mode found within Scripture. In this sense, by approaching Scripture as narrative, we might be able to approach it more faithfully than by approaching it in a strictly theoretical fashion. Lewis emphasized that we must be "good readers," and this entails reading Scripture through the imagery of the author. Also, narrative theology can often avoid the pure abstract penchant of some academic forms of theology. As such, narrative theology "invites us to reflect upon a story—a vivid, memorable account of something that actually happened (such as the story of Jesus), or that may be treated as if it really happened (such as the parables of Jesus). There is an appeal to the imagination . . . a sense of realism, of personal involvement, which is often conspicuously absent from theology."[149] Where Lewis' view might be seen to part ways with a strict narrative theology approach is in his view of historical truth and its relation to Scripture. Lewis' approach to theology certainly has resonances with the narrative theologian Hans Frei. But Frei (and the narrative approach in general) has often been accused of ignoring natural human curiosity, especially regarding historical referents. However, Frei modified some of his views from *The Eclipse of Biblical Narrative* to account for this natural curiosity about historical referents: ". . . about certain events in the gospels we are almost bound to ask, Did they actually take place?"[150] Lewis' answer was to emphasize the mythic and narrative quality of Scripture as well as its historical referents. Thus, Lewis asserted that one of the most distinctive elements of the biblical narrative is its combination of (and movement from) myth to fact (i.e., a mythic story going from who knows where or when to being located in a particular place at a particular time with a particular person). However, this is not to say that the "facts" are unmediated or not interpreted—they are divinely conditioned, and must be received. Scripture, then, for Lewis, functions in all the same ways that a true myth functions in the world, with one definitive difference—for the Christian it actually happened: "To be truly Christian," suggested Lewis, "we must both assent to the historical fact and also receive the myth (fact though it has become) with the same imaginative embrace we accord to all myths."[151] Hans Frei's account of the rise of critical historical inquiry and the debate over miraculous accounts also moves to the forefront this particular theological dilemma:[152] namely, that, on one hand, the theologian would have to acknowledge the human origin of the writing and the unreliability of its factual elements; and on the other hand, the theologian would have to acknowledge that biblical writings are factually sound and reliable—infallible in fact.[153] Frei saw the hermeneutical issue (seen especially in German biblical scholarship) as "How do we cover the gap between history-like statements and the meaning of the other seemingly a-historical statements"?[154] Frei observed that the "mythophiles" who tried to interpret the biblical writings within this hermeneutic had difficulty making the biblical writings fit precisely into the category of myth.[155] He suggested that the biblical writings have—indeed, as does any narrative where story and meaning are intimately intertwined—its own special hermeneutics.[156] Where we find meaning is in fact within the text—we locate the meaning within "the narrative structure or sequence itself."[157] The structure of the narrative gives us our meaning, places us within a context. Scripture, then, combines myth, truth, and history in a unique fashion for Lewis, so that it is within this particular narrative structure itself that we are placed in a distinct context. So, unlike Lewis' conception of myth not having a value in a particular telling—for Lewis, myth comes through no matter who is telling it or how it is told; it is not dependent on the storyteller or the particular words—Scripture is intimately tied to its communal, historical, liturgical contexts, such that its meaning cannot be separated from its particular form of deliverance. To the outsider, the narratival context might seem strange or even just plain wrong, and this issue really goes back to our questions of myth and truth at the beginning of the section "An Experiment in Myth" above: to what extent is truth to be seen in myth—if at all? Lewis' notions of myth and truth certainly come into conflict with modern notions of myth as falsehood. In these modern conceptions, myth and truth are diametrically opposed; myth has noting to do with truth. Myth is the parasite that has latched on to truth and we must give our legends and past accounts a special treatment to rid it of this parasite. As we noted earlier, this is, in essence, why it is thought Scripture must be "demythologized"—it is the proper treatment for the parasite. We must remove the mythic (false) elements to get at the reality or truth of the matter. One sees this on both sides of the aisle, so to speak: modern biblical literalists also equate myth with falsity—in that they have accepted the modern notion that myth equals false, so they too prescribe a remedy—to rid it of the charge of falsehood they must hold fast to the utter truth or reality of the literal Word. And Frei highlighted just such a cognitive dissonance. Both Lewis and Frei advocated the removal of the notion that myth and truth are diametrically opposed. Once this notion is removed, then we might be able to see myth as the human imagination working on truth in order to present it in new forms or in a new light. We might then be able to read in a new (old) way. A premodern way of reading (without the dichotomy of myth vs. fact) might be the way towards a better understanding of the truths of Scripture. The right heart, then, becomes the most important tool. Again, as highlighted earlier, Augustine guides us here:

> when someone has learnt that the aim of the commandment is "love from a pure heart, and good conscience and genuine faith" [1 Tim 1:5], he will be ready to relate every interpretation of the holy scriptures to these three things and may approach the task of handling these books with confidence. For when the apostle said "love" he added "from a pure heart", so that nothing is loved except what should be loved. He added "good" to "conscience" because of hope; for a person with the incubus of a bad conscience despairs of reaching what he loves and believes. Thirdly, he said "with genuine faith": for if our faith is free of untruthfulness then we do not love what should not be loved, whereas by living aright it is impossible for our hope to be in any way misguided.[158]

The aim of the heart becomes of the most importance, for it is through the heart and the ordering of love that we might hit the right target. "Faith seeking understanding" becomes the chant. The heart awakens

Poetic Labors   173

an otherness, the (Platonic-Augustinian) desire—the excitement of the soul, the sense of a "God-shaped hole."

But also through this sense of the other there might come an awakening for the slumbering reader—and this is a common thread also between Lewis, Tolkien, MacDonald, and Chesterton. For these men, the human condition is grounded in a fundamental way in the making of art. One of the first things we know, Chesterton claimed, about our ancient ancestors is that they were artists. Chesterton saw humankind as a revolution within the world:

> ... I would ask my reader to make with me a sort of experiment in simplicity.... Man is not merely an evolution but rather a revolution. That he has a backbone or other parts upon a similar pattern to birds and fishes is an obvious fact.... But if we attempt to regard him, as it were, as a quadruped standing on his hind legs, we shall find what follows far more fantastic and subversive than if he were standing on his head.... [A] certain childish directness is needed to see the truth about the childhood of the world. It illustrates what I mean by saying that a mixture of popular science and journalistic jargon have confused the facts about first things, so that we cannot see which of them really comes first.[159]

A distinguishing aspect of the human animal is its ability to wonder, to imagine. Chesterton used the example of a priest and boy who enter a cave to find ancient drawings. What we find in the caves of our ancestors is not their clubs but their art. The image of the young boy may best suit us here: namely, through the wonder of childhood and the possible enchantment of finding and entering into a hitherto unknown cave. What Chesterton pointed out is that the artist in the cave may have felt the wonder of the boy and not the supposed distanced interest of a scientist studying the cave rationalistically. What the cave person drew on the walls was not only something that could be seen as pleasing and interesting (or that the lines drawn were marked with care and detail). It betrays a sense of wonder and amazement, of something other. The detail of the drawing was not that of the accurate, lifelike technique, but of a captured essence. Here the imagination is the key to understanding the motivations of our ancestors: the imagination is the key to uncovering the mystery, by presenting the bigger mystery.

Lewis' views on myth-making give us insight into a way of perceiving divine reality in (re)new(ed) and fascinating ways: by awakening deep-seated longings; by opening up the possibility for works of literature to be seen as God-given and thus divinely inspired; by "baptizing the imagination" of others, so that one can more readily accept the gifts of the divine; by imploring us to step back into childhood to move forward; by plumbing the depths of the imagination to find meaning that can lead to truth within myth, fairytale, symbol, and narrative; by trying to move beyond the process of mere rationalism into the realm of dialectical-analogical relationship (i.e., by getting us to look along as well as look at something in order to see the alluring, captivating and mesmerizing). Additionally, the seemingly unexpected move into children's literature can be seen more clearly through an examination of Lewis' preoccupation with the mythopoeic: that it was the best means to say what he had to say and as a way to get us further along, to move or point us towards the divine, to move beyond mere rationalist conceptions of reason might—and it is then that we might see the imagination as the deeper, motivating foundation, to see it as delivering knowledge that we could not receive in any other fashion, to see it as a reasoning beyond reason. In Lewis' fiction, we see a unique appeal to the childlike in us, an appeal to wonder, mystery, and enchantment. Lewis took Jesus' saying to heart, with a rare seriousness, and implored us to do the same: "Truly I tell you, unless you change and become like children, you will never enter the kingdom of heaven" (Matt 18:3).

Notes

1. Lewis, *George MacDonald*, xxxii.
2. Duriez and Porter, *Inklings Handbook*, 149. In Alison Milbank's *Chesterton and Tolkien as Theologians*, she highlights the separation between Tolkien and Chesterton's view of fairy and George MacDonald's. She notes that while MacDonald, Chesterton, and Tolkien are all aiming towards the same end, i.e., conceiving the artistic imagination as a mode of sub-creation, there is a marked difference in their approach that parts ways with MacDonald's Coleridgean conception of the secondary imagination: "The distinction between truth and its embodiment derives from MacDonald's mode of Platonism and is quite foreign to Chesterton and Tolkien's view of the work of art as a thing in itself, and a form in the scholastic sense, in which its radiance is inseparable from its formal qualities. . . . The difference for MacDonald lies in the wholly positive valence both writers give to the invented and constructed nature of the artwork. . . . To use Tolkien's terminology . . . the artist 'assists with the effoliation', and adds leaves to the tree of creation, as a response to the skill and imagination with which he or she has been gifted, whereas MacDonald's model is of the artist echoing at one remove an original idea of the true, the good and the beautiful" (Milbank, *Chesterton and Tolkien*, 143). The case might be made that Lewis would also hold to Milbank's version of Tolkien's and Chesterton's views in this regard: Lewis did not subscribe to the idea of "leaving the

appearances behind"—quite the contrary. Lewis wanted to "save the appearances." One can see this clearly in his Chronicles of Narnia, where all that is worthy and good and true in Narnia is brought up into New Narnia. But we must also temper this with Lewis' other words. For example, it appears that with a myth (but not just any story) Lewis believed that the mode of the myth's appearance did not so much matter if its content could be conveyed through other means: "The story of Orpheus strikes and strikes deep, of itself; the fact that Virgil and others have told it in good poetry is irrelevant. To think about it and be moved by it is not necessarily to think about those poets or to be moved by them" (Lewis, *Experiment in Criticism*, 41). It is true that myth has few ways to reach us but through words; however, if there were another way in which the myth could reach us (e.g., through silent film or music or pictures) the myth would still affect us in the same way (ibid.). And Lewis also warned that we must never believe that we "bring beauty or wisdom" into existence "which did not exist before," but we must see ourselves "simply and solely as trying to embody in terms of [our] own art some reflection of eternal Beauty and Wisdom" (Lewis, *Christian Reflections*, 7). These views might be troublesome to some: for then only God truly exists in himself. But if only God exists in himself, then all other creatures exist secondarily. It might appear to follow with certainty that, therefore, creation is not real or meaningful in any sense. But this is to miss Lewis' metaphysics of participation. God gifts the creation. Therefore, it is real, but only in so far as it participates in God's gift of being. This is, as we have mentioned, what is at stake in Lewis' view of Old Narnia being brought up into New Narnia: it is through the participation within the transcendent that the things of this world are given value and meaning. It is a transposition of the higher life to the lower life.

3. Once he had picked up this book, it was only a few hours later that he knew he had "Crossed a great frontier. . . . Nothing was at that time further from my thoughts than Christianity. . . . I was only aware that if this new world was strange, it was also homely and humble; that if this was a dream, it was a dream in which one at least felt strangely vigilant; that the whole book had about it a sort of cool, morning innocence, and also, quite unmistakably, a certain quality of Death, *good* Death. What it actually did to me was to convert, even to baptize . . . my imagination" (Lewis, *George MacDonald*, xxxiii). It is also interesting to note Lewis' use of the phrase "good Death." This echoes Tolkien's notions of the eucatastrophe, i.e., the idea of a happy or good catastrophe. This is something that is a unique marker of the fairy story: it has the unexpected twist of the perceived evil being turned to good. For Tolkien, the ultimate example of eucatastrophe is the death and resurrection of Jesus. For an example of this see Tolkien's essay "On Fairy Stories" in Lewis, *Essays Presented to Charles Williams*.

4. Lewis, *Collected Letters*, 2:565.

5. Smith, *Introducing Radical Orthodoxy*, 166.

6. MacDonald, "Fantastic Imagination," 1.

7. That is, ". . . man may, if he pleases, invent a little world of his own, with its own laws . . . which is the nearest, perhaps, he can come to creation. When such forms are new embodiments of old truths, we call them products of the Imagination; when they are mere inventions, however lovely, I should call them the work of Fancy: in either case, Law has been diligently at work. His world once invented, the highest law that comes next into play is, that there shall be harmony between the laws by which the new world has begun to exist; and in the process of his creation, the inventor must hold by these laws. The moment he forgets one of them, he makes the story, by its own postulates, incredible" (ibid.).

8. Lewis echoes this by saying that the "logic of fairy-tale is as strict as that of a realistic novel, though different. Does anyone believe that Kenneth Grahame made an arbitrary choice when he gave his principal character the form of a toad . . ." (*Of Other Worlds*, 13).

9. MacDonald, "Fantastic Imagination," 2.

10. In Paul Ricoeur's *Figuring the Sacred*, he too argues that the imagination should be highlighted for its impressive qualities (qualities normally misconceived by philosophy), which are (1) its rule-governed nature—which is more often seen as a free-flight of fancy—and (2) its ability and power to redefine or remake reality (p. 144).

11. MacDonald, "Fantastic Imagination," 2. Once again, we see that Lewis' view echoes MacDonald's. Lewis also felt that the best stories with the best morals were the ones where no moral had been "put in." The meaning arises from the images—it is inherent in the story or bubbling up naturally from the author's being (Lewis, *Of Other Worlds*, 33).

12. MacDonald, "Fantastic Imagination," 2.

13. For example, "If my drawing . . . is so far from being a work of art that it needs THIS IS A HORSE written under it, what can it matter that neither you nor your child should know what it means? It is there not so much to convey a meaning as to wake a meaning. If it do [sic] not even wake an interest, throw it aside. A meaning may be there, but it is not for you. If, again, you do not know a horse when you see it, the name written under it will not serve you much" (ibid.).

14. For example, "The true fairytale is, to my mind, very like the sonata. We all know that a sonata means something; and where there is the faculty of talking with suitable vagueness, and choosing metaphor sufficiently loose, mind may approach mind, in the interpretation of a sonata, with the result of a more or less contenting consciousness of sympathy" (ibid., 3).

15. For example, "But if two or three men sat down to write each what the sonata meant to him, what approximation to definite idea would be the result? Little enough—and that little more than needful. We should find it had roused related, if not identical, feelings, but probably not one common thought. Has the sonata therefore failed? Had it undertaken to convey, or ought it to be expected to impart anything defined, anything notionally recognizable?" (ibid.).

16. That is, "It is very seldom indeed that they carry the exact meaning of any user of them! And if they can be so used as to convey definite meaning, it does not follow that they ought never to carry anything else. Words are like things that may be variously employed to various ends. They can convey a scientific fact, or throw a shadow of her child's dream on the heart of a mother. They are things to put together like the pieces of a dissected map, or to arrange like the notes on a stave" (ibid.).

17. For example, "The cause of a child's tears may be altogether undefinable: has the mother therefore no antidote for his vague misery? . . . A fairytale, a sonata, a gathering storm, a limitless night, seizes you and sweeps you away: do you begin at once to wrestle with it and ask whence its power over you, whither it is carrying you? The law of each is in the mind of its composer; that law makes one man feel this way, another man feel that way. To one the sonata is a world of odour and beauty, to another of soothing only and sweetness. To one, the cloudy rendezvous is a wild dance, with a terror at its heart; to another, a majestic march of heavenly hosts, with Truth in their centre pointing their course, but as yet restraining her voice. The greatest forces lie in the region of the uncomprehended" (ibid.).

18. Ibid., 4.
19. Ibid.
20. Ibid.
21. Lewis, *Chronicles of Narnia*, 661.
22. Ford, *Companion to Narnia*, 105.
23. In Lewis' own life he was often considered by friends to have a childlike quality about him. Ruth Pitter, a poet and friend, once remarked that Lewis' "response to daily life reflected 'an almost uniquely persisting *child's* sense of glory and nightmare.'" Another friend, Kathleen Raines, said Lewis "had about him an aura of 'boyish greatness' . . . [Lewis] considered the willingness to become like a child a mark of maturity. 'When I became a man,' he explained, 'I put away childish things, including the fear of childishness and the desire to be very grown up'" (Downing, *Into the Wardrobe*, xiii–xvi).
24. A friend of Barfield's (and consequently a friend of Lewis'), A. C. Harwood, spoke to this issue as well. Harwood was an anthroposophist, like Barfield, and believed that a sense of repetition—similar to Lewis' conviction that children understand the thrill of the repetition of stories, that myths and good stories get better the more times we read them—"still lives in children, when the seasons brought round their customary festivals, songs and plays. They look forward to the return of the same events as the year comes around, the same carols and the same play at Christmas. . . . Until childhood has lost its own traditions there were always seasonal games . . ." (Harwood, "Recovery of Man," 301).
25. Indeed, "more serious, in fact, than . . . the grown-ups. Upon entering Narnia, children become subtly older and more mature, but they retain their childlike innocence, candor, and innate knowledge of right and wrong. . . . Lewis has not forgotten what it is like to be a child, and the stories are told from a child's point of view. Children are often much more intelligent than grown-ups think they are, and can use this to their advantage . . . Lewis tries to communicate through the *Chronicles* the importance of remaining child*like*—as opposed to child*ish*—in outlook. In Aslan's country, people are always and forever in the prime of life" (Ford, *Companion to Narnia*, 105–6).
26. Lewis spoke to the idea of "grown-up-ness" and its limitations when he wrote, ". . . it is certainly my opinion that a book worth reading only in childhood is not worth reading even then. The inhibitions which I hoped my stories would overcome in a child's mind may exist in a grown-up's mind too, and may perhaps be overcome by the same means. The Fantastic or Mythical is a Mode available at all ages for some readers; for others, at none. At all ages, if it is well used by the author and meets the right reader, it has the same power: to generalize while remaining concrete, to present in palpable form not concepts or even experiences but whole classes of experience, and to throw off irrelevancies. But at its best it can do more; it can give us experiences we never had and thus, instead of 'commenting on life', can add to it" (*Of Other Worlds*, 38).
27. Ibid., 3.
28. Ibid.
29. Ibid., 20–21.
30. Ibid., 17.
31. Ibid., 15.
32. See *Letters of J.R.R. Tolkien*, where Tolkien remarked that ". . . there was an Eden on this very unhappy earth. We all long for it, and are constantly glimpsing

it: our whole nature at its best and least corrupted, its gentlest and most humane, is still soaked with the sense of 'exile'. . . . As far as we can go back the nobler part of the human mind is filled with the thoughts of *sibb*, peace and goodwill, and with the thought of its *loss*" (p. 110). In addition, this idea can be found in Tolkien's view of sub-creation: "According to Tolkien, the fantasist 'proves a successful sub-creator.' He makes a Secondary World which your mind can enter. To enter it is to realize that one has been in prison, and 'why should a man be scorned, if, finding himself in prison, he tries to get out and go home?'" (Cox, "Epistemological Release," 168). Escaping "from a false reality to a truer view of reality is not an escape from reality but an escape to reality" (Lindsley, *C. S. Lewis's Case for Christ*, 97).

33. Hooper, *Past Watchful Dragons*, 136.

34. As an interesting aside, literary critic Northrop Frye postulated that all characters and all stories belong to a great interlocking family, and that the stories and characters might be traced back to a single myth: that of a golden age or garden of Eden where humankind, indeed the world, is lost. This myth might also show us how we could some day get it back again. See Frye, *Educated Imagination*, particularly pages 18–22.

35. "There is no question that Narnia is real. In fact, Narnia is more vivid, more substantial, more intensely real than the hours spent in the professor's house in the English countryside. Not that this world is *less* than real, but that Narnia is more! Narnia is reached by going 'further in'; 'further in' to reality, not an escape from it" (Shoemaker, "Beyond the Walls," 65).

36. Lewis was aware that people are often "reluctant . . . to move from the idea of an abstract and fuzzy deity to a living God who has a determinate character and makes demands upon us. He realized that fantasy and fairy story, like myth, have the remarkable power to make abstractions concrete and real. In the Chronicles the distinctiveness and particularity of God is demonstrated in the magical figure of Aslan, elusive but definite, wild, surprising and always shaping events providentially" (Duriez, *Field Guide*, 65).

37. M. Nelson, "'One Mythology among Many,'" 7.

38. Lewis, *The Lion, the Witch, and the Wardrobe*, 141.

39. For example, "'They say Aslan is on the move—perhaps has already landed.' And now a very curious thing happened. None of the children knew who Aslan was any more than you do; but the moment Beaver had spoken these words everyone felt quite different. Perhaps it has sometimes happened to you in a dream that someone says something which you don't understand but in the dream it feels as if it had some enormous meaning—either a terrifying one which turns the whole dream into a nightmare or else a lovely meaning too lovely to put into words, which makes the dream so beautiful that you remember it all your life and are always wishing you could get into that dream again. It was like that now. At the name of Aslan each one of the children felt something jump in his inside. Edmund felt a sensation of mysterious horror. Peter felt suddenly brave and adventurous. Susan felt as if some delicious smell or some delightful strain of music had just floated by her. And Lucy got the feeling you have when you wake up in the morning and realize that it is the beginning of the holidays or the beginning of summer" (ibid., 64–65).

40. Hooper, *Past Watchful Dragons*, 95.

41. It is interesting to note that in the Chronicles there are four prophecies (one in *The Voyage of the Dawn Treader* and three in *The Lion, the Witch, and the Wardrobe*). In *The Voyage*, the character Reepicheep is given a prophecy at birth—by a Dryad (creatures in Roman and Greek mythology, commonly known as wood nymphs, that are

intimately connected with—and indeed live in—trees) —that he will find what he seeks in the Utter East. In *The Lion*, Mr. and Mrs. Beaver tell the children of three prophecies: first, that Aslan's return will bring spring back to Narnia; second, that there are four thrones at Cair Paravel for two sons of Adam and two daughters of Eve; and third, that two sons of Adam and two daughters of Eve will bring about the destruction of evil when they sit on the thrones at Cair Paravel.

42. For example, "Chronology: the word about the measurable passage of time, although its duration varies: how long is a toothache? How long is standing in line at the supermarket? How long is a tramp through the fields with the dogs? Or dinner with friends, or a sunset, or the birth of a baby? Chronology, the time which changes things, makes them grow older, wears them out, and manages to dispose of them, chronologically, forever. Kairos is not measurable. Kairos is ontological. In kairos we *are*, we are fully in isness, not negatively, as Sartre saw the isness of the oak tree, but fully, wholly, positively. Kairos can sometimes enter, penetrate, break through chronos: the child at play, the painter at his easel, Serkin playing the *Appassionata* . . . [the] saint at prayer, friends around the dinner table, the mother reaching out her arms for her newborn baby, are in kairos. I sit in the rocking chair with a baby in my arms, and I am in both kairos and chronos. In chronos I may be nothing more than some cybernetic salad on the bottom left-hand corner of a check; or my social-security number; or my passport number. In kairos I am known by name: Madeleine. The baby doesn't know about chronos yet" (L'Engle, *Glimpses of Grace*, 222).

43. Lewis, *Surprised by Joy*, viii.

44. Lewis, *The Lion, the Witch, and the Wardrobe*, 45.

45. Ford, *Companion to Narnia*, 256–57.

46. Ibid., 258.

47. Lewis, *The Lion, the Witch, and the Wardrobe*, 45.

48. In Reppert's *C. S. Lewis' Dangerous Idea*, he presents Lewis' trilemma in the following fashion: "1. Jesus' claims in Scripture are best interpreted not merely as claims to be the Jews' Messiah but as claims to be God. 2. The Gospels are a reliable historical record of what Jesus said and did. 3. No sane person can form the false belief that he himself is God. 4. The claim 'Jesus is God' is more antecedently probable than the admittedly improbable claim that Jesus was a great moral teacher and either a liar or a madman" (p. 14). Reppert acknowledges that all of these assumptions have been debated and criticized, and acknowledges that Lewis did give some defense of each of these claims in his various works. In the vein of critical rationalism, if all of these assumptions are defensible, then, Reppert says, the argument is a good one.

49. Jack Miles has a related comment worthy of noting regarding the practice of historical criticism: "Modern historical criticism has labored diligently to bring the Bible to the 'normal' condition of clearly identified authors with consistent agendas and clearly identified audiences. Postmodern criticism can and should acknowledge the value, even the grandeur, of this enterprise of rationalization and yet not surrender its right to observe that historical criticism almost inevitably aborts certain highly stimulating and fruitful kinds of literary engagement" (Miles, *Christ*, 331).

50. Lewis' view might be compared to Ludolf of Saxony. In *Vita Christi*, Ludolf of Saxony noted the importance of engaging with the New Testament imaginatively, feeling, embodying, and living the gospel story: "If you want to draw fruit from these mysteries, you must offer yourself as present to what was said and done through our Lord Jesus

Christ with the whole affective power of your mind, with loving care, with lingering delight, thus laying aside all other worries and care. Hear and see these things being narrated, as though you were hearing with your own ears and seeing with your own eyes, for these things are most sweet to him who thinks on them with desire, and even more so to him who tastes them" (Ludolf, "Reading Scripture Imaginatively," 90–91).

51. Lewis, *Collected Letters*, 2:375.
52. Lewis, *Chronicles of Narnia*, 518.
53. Lewis, *Mere Christianity*, 125.
54. Lewis, *Chronicles of Narnia*, 633.
55. Aslan's sacrifice may be compared to Gregory of Nyssa's statement that God "was under the veil of our nature, so that, as with ravenous fish, the hook of the Deity might be gulped down along with the bait of flesh" (Gregory of Nyssa, "Oration on the Deity," 494). Augustine also echoed this when he said that the "cross of the Lord became a trap for the Devil; the death of the Lord was the food by which he was ensnared" (Augustine, *Sermons on the Liturgical Seasons*, 392). However, there is not a clear sense of Lewis putting forth the notion that God accomplished humanity's salvation through trickery. The perfect sacrifice of Jesus is seen as a way back to God—though "repayment" (as it is normally conceived) to evil is not really what God requires, for this might imply a too severe separation of the work of Christ and God and a misconception of the penalty, i.e., the idea that God specifically *owes* something to evil and is not "paying the cost" for our free wills and our reconciliation. Repentance "is simply a description of what going back to God is like: it is surrender, submission, dying, and receiving God into oneself" (Cunningham, *C. S. Lewis*, 111). Humanity cannot do this for itself, so God must effect humanity's salvation. Particularly in *The Lion, the Witch, and the Wardrobe*, evil (namely, the White Witch) is portrayed as being ignorant of the "Deeper Magic from before the dawn of time." Aslan effects salvation by being a perfect, pure sacrifice—standing in the stead of Edmund—to bring about new relational elements of Narnia. Salvation is to bring about a reorientation of the world—Narnia can now be in right relation with the Emperor Beyond the Sea despite the sin of Edmund. The White Witch claims that every traitor belongs to her and that Aslan knows this "deep magic." Aslan knows that for every treachery she has a right to kill. But this is the gift of freedom: that every creature has the ability to obey or disobey. The payment for freedom is the possibility of doing wrong. The repayment is not for God's necessity but for ours: *we* need to be re-established and re-oriented because of *our* separation from God. There is also a good defense of Lewis' position by Charles Taliaferro and Rachel Traugher in their essay "The Atonement in Narnia." They note the possible problems with the ransom theory of Christ's death, particularly J. R. Lucas' criticisms. Lucas criticizes the ransom theory on the grounds that it requires a literal belief in Satan, gives Satan the right to torture those in his power, requires God to make a deal with Satan (which is repugnant), and requires God to deceive Satan in the process.
56. See Lewis, *The Lion, the Witch, and the Wardrobe*, 149–52.
57. "Lewis goes on to accentuate the parallels between the passion of Christ and the passion of Aslan: both seek the comfort of a few close friends, both suffer ridicule and torture at the hands of their enemies, both are cruelly tied down and savagely executed, the bodies of both are ministered to by friends . . . and, rising out of sight of anyone (the empty table suggests the empty tomb), both must reassure their loved ones that they are indeed alive, and alive in a new way" (Ford, *Companion to Narnia*, 21).

58. "[Aslan is the] Lion King of the land of Narnia and of all its creatures, the son of the Emperor-beyond-the-sea, true beast and king of beasts, the highest king over all high kings, and the as-yet-unrecognized good and compassionate Lord of all . . . The beholding of his beautiful face sustains one all one's days; and the recognition of the face with love and awe at the end of time opens out onto an eternity of joy . . . [but] to be rebuked by him is an everlasting shame. Whom he praises with an earthshaking 'Well done' remains forever favored" (ibid., 17).

59. That is, ". . . the participation of [humankind] in the life of God. . . . In his presentation of the traditional Christian Myth, Lewis offers readers an important and accessible vision of [humankind's] salvation, one that is uniquely capable of satisfying [humankind's] deepest aspirations and longings. . . . As Lewis writes, 'The whole purpose for which we exist is to be thus taken into the life of God'. . . . For Lewis, the doctrine of *theosis* means the unity of God and all God's creation. People are brought into that unity through Christ, who comes to us through the Church, which is his Body. But Christ came to save the whole creation, not just the Church. As Lewis says, Christ came to save 'human nature; but, associated with it, all nature, the new universe.' Or, to put it another way, when all people are participating in God as new creatures in Christ, the distinction between Church and creation will not be evident. There is no Church on Malacandra, that unfallen planet. There is no Church in Narnia" (Knickerbocker, "Myth That Saves," 1–5).

60. Lewis, *Chronicles of Narnia*, 466.

61. Ibid.

62. ". . . C. S. Lewis's emphasis in his fantasy novels, in this world he made [i.e., Narnia], is on objective values, on decisions that make a real difference, on the actions that can be described as really good or really evil" (Shoemaker, "Beyond the Walls," 69). Lewis' presentation of the moral law within the Chronicles has been severely criticized by many. Still others see this criticism as unfair: "The Chronicles have been unfairly criticized for alleged didacticism. The stories do not talk down to readers, do not preach about correct behavior and values. Rather, the stories present proper behavior and values objectively, as something readers already know perfectly well. They do instruct, they remind, thus following a maxim of Samuel Johnson, the eighteenth-century moralist whom Lewis admired greatly: 'Men more frequently require to be reminded than informed'" (Schakel, *Way into Narnia*, 117).

63. Sayer, *Jack*, 317.

64. Duncan, *Magic Never Ends*, 167. As an aside of interest, Dale Nelsen notes the problems associated with communicating the Christian message to a modern world and the important role the imagination can take in the health of the soul: "When unhappy young people used to visit the St. Herman of Alaska skete in the hinterlands of northern California, the late priest-monk Seraphim Rose realized that they often had basic needs of the soul that had to be addressed, matters not specifically Christian. And so, rather than directing their attention to the ascetic-mystical texts and practices that some of them were interested in, he would have these adolescents watch an old Dickens film, listen to Bach, or read Dostoevsky. 'Dickens communicates an extremely warm feeling about human relationships, which is not given in school today. And this very feeling of warmth about human relationships might have more effect in keeping a boy pure than giving him the abstract standard of Orthodoxy,' he said. 'By contrast . . . the contemporary upbringing in schools emphasizes crudity, coldness, and inability to judge what

is better and what is worse—total relativity, which only confuses a person and helps fit him into the world of apostasy.' Rose's visitors needed to be fed, without haste, with wholesome imaginative fare to strengthen their anemic or poison-accustomed souls" (Nelson, "Imagination," 1).

65. Duncan, *Magic Never Ends*, 167.

66. Shoemaker, "Beyond the Walls," 95.

67. Duriez and Porter, *Inklings Handbook*, 38–39.

68. Ford, *Companion to Narnia*, 242.

69. Lewis, *Surprised by Joy*, 78–79.

70. Lewis used two terms to describe the theme and form of story: "*Poiema*: (something made) The words themselves, stacked upon each other and shaped by careful attention to techniques ranging from allegory and symbolism to the use of humor, sentiment, and irony. *Logos*: (something said) The meaning of those words which awakens the reader's sense of a longing or feeling never so clearly understood before. There is a skill required to link the form and content (*Poiema* and *Logos*) and make them so support and reinforce each other that readers scarcely realize that Lewis is consciously manipulating each to produce an effect" (Glover, *C. S. Lewis*, 4).

71. As Ford notes, "Thinking is incurably abstract; experiencing is always concrete. . . . The thinking and the experiencing come together in only one place: a good story. A good story gives a concrete experience of a universal. As a work of imagination, it helps people both to *contemplate* and to *enjoy* either an aspect of reality they already know or something that they don't know and that the author of the story thinks would be good for them to know" (Ford, *Companion to Narnia*, xxx).

72. Ibid., xxxi.

73. Story, by having a dual means of communication (i.e., intellectual and experiential), can also set the scene for a realization of "what the Swiss theologian Hans Urs von Balthasar describes as the 'theo-drama': a drama *enacted* by God the Son, *written* by God the Father, and *directed* by the Holy Spirit. Each of us is offered a role in this cosmic drama, a mission to perform in mythic space. In relation to Christ, 'each individual is given a personal commission; he is entrusted both with something unique to do and with the freedom to do it. Bound up with commission is his own, inalienable, personal name; here and only here role and person coincide'" (Caldecott, "Speaking the Truths," 5).

74. Robert Inchausti notes something similar: "Only in the context of a renewed appreciation for the power of myth does the contemporary religious imagination begin to revive" (Inchausti, *Subversive Orthodoxy*, 48).

75. Again, Robert Inchausti notes something similar: The reasoned work of literature is not the drifting back into primitive "irrationality" but is instead a moving "forward into an information-saturated, multidimensional, multidisciplinary mediated environment of the whole—into a world so dense with significance that only literature can penetrate it" (ibid., 49). The imaginative forms (myth, literature, art and poetry) are the "fastest and most information-laden methods of modern communication . . . the very best means by which existential existence and reason can be conjoined into a single, unified expression" (ibid.). In trying to squeeze out imaginative forms in their discourses the "theologians in their conversation with the scientists and philosophers have simply taken the wrong road home. How could they not have seen that the contents of the novel are the same as those of religion?" (ibid.). The imaginative nature of poetry stresses the "concrete over the abstract, the incarnational over the merely

theoretical, and the synthesis of character, thought, and action in the person rather than in a 'theory of man.' Narrative form, as it turns out, is inherently eschatological, logocentric, humanist, and humane" (ibid., 50).

76. Lewis, *Experiment in Criticism*, 41.
77. Ibid.
78. Ibid., 42.
79. Ibid., 43.
80. Ibid., 44.
81. Ibid.
82. Ibid.
83. Ibid.
84. Ibid., 45.
85. Ibid., 47.
86. Lewis, *George MacDonald*, xxvii.

87. "[Myth] arouses in us sensations we have never had before, never anticipated having, as though we had broken out of our normal mode of consciousness and 'possessed joys not promised to our birth.' It gets under our skin, hits us at a level deeper than our thoughts or even our passions, troubles oldest certainties till all questions are reopened, and in general shocks us more fully awake than we are for most of our lives" (ibid., xxviii).

88. Ibid.
89. Duriez, *Field Guide*, 89.
90. Lewis, *Experiment in Criticism*, 48.
91. See MacDonald, "Fantastic Imagination," 2.

92. "Lewis was deeply concerned to recover the author's intention: "'It is not enough to make sense' when we interpret, he writes in his introduction to *Studies in Words*; 'we want to find the sense the author intended' . . ." (Jeffrey, "C. S. Lewis," 3).

93. "[Lewis had a] strong belief in the continuous operation of the Holy Spirit in transmitting the intention of the Divine Author to the consciousness of all who attend well to it," and as regards Scriptural stories he "does not imagine that there is no relation between worldwide Creation myths and the early chapters of Genesis, nor, on the other hand, does he accept that Genesis is simply one among many such nebulous accounts. Rather, he sees that the Genesis account bears about it a sense of God's transcendence as Creator more clearly than any other, and he takes it that the clarity itself is a sign of the distinctive operation of the Holy Spirit" (ibid., 5).

94. ". . . even as it was in St. Augustine (On Christian Doctrine) . . . it suggests that in faithful reading a lack of critical distance may be the almost indispensable condition of getting things spiritually right" (ibid.).

95. For example, "when someone has learnt that the aim of the commandment is 'love from a pure heart, and good conscience and genuine faith' [1 Tim 1:5], he will be ready to relate every interpretation of the holy scriptures to these three things and may approach the task of handling these books with confidence. For when the apostle said 'love' he added 'from a pure heart', so that nothing is loved except what should be loved. He added 'good' to 'conscience' because of hope; for a person with the incubus of a bad conscience despairs of reaching what he loves and believes. Thirdly, he said 'with genuine faith': for if our faith is free of untruthfulness then we do not love what should

not be loved, whereas by living aright it is impossible for our hope to be in any way misguided" (Augustine, *On Christian Teaching*, 29).

96. Ford, *Companion to Narnia*, 261–62.

97. It is also fruitful to note the four medieval ways of interpreting Scripture—the *quadriga*: the literal, the allegorical, the tropological (or moral), and the anagogical: "The letter teaches events, allegory what you should believe, morality teaches what you should do, anagogy what mark you should be aiming for" (Lubac, *Medieval Exegesis*, 1). It is also important to key in on the traditional unifying factor of the four senses of Scripture. Henri de Lubac noted that the unity of the four senses of Scripture is found in eschatology, which stirs within us a desire for eternity: "It is in traditional eschatology that the doctrine of the four senses is achieved and finds its unity. For Christianity it is a fulfillment, but in this very fulfillment it is a promised hope. Mystical or doctrinal, taught or lived, true anagogy is therefore always eschatological. It stirs up the desire for eternity in us. This is why the fourth sense is forced to be the last. No more than it could really lack the three others could it be followed by a fifth. Neither is hope ever lacking nor, in our earthly condition, is it ever surpassed even if it already encroaches upon its term" (ibid., 197). Lewis was certainly extremely familiar with the *quadriga*, being a medieval and Renaissance scholar of literature. There may be a clue in the medieval interpretation of Scripture to Lewis' writing of the Chronicles. There is a clear sense in which the idea, coupled along with the general medieval worldview, that his stories should be read on the four levels of interpretation. The Chronicles can be read for literal stories (for the stories in themselves); for allegorical appreciation (we can see applicability to countless relevancies); for a moral sense (the Chronicles display characters and actions that one can either avoid emulating or model him or herself after); and for an anagogical sense (the main aim of the Chronicles is eschatological, i.e., to reach Aslan's country—to be in right relation, which requires participation in the divine and an intimate relationship with the Creator).

98. Farrer, *Glass of Vision*, 35.

99. "We are simply being called upon to acknowledge that one of the things the modern man cannot take is myth. To judge of Bultmann's argument by its conclusion, 'modern man' means for the purpose of the present question a being sufficiently sophisticated to appreciate the existentialist approach which is Bultmann's offered remedy . . ." (Farrer, "English Appreciation," 2).

100. Ibid.

101. Ibid.

102. Ibid.

103. Ibid.

104. Ibid., 3.

105. Ibid. For example, "On the whole it is truer to say that the relation of mythical expression to literal belief is left undecided, than to say that it is decided in the sense of literalism. There are undoubted cases of decision in both directions; for example, St. Luke did think that the Biblical genealogies gave a tolerable idea of the number of generations from the beginning of the world to his own day; St. John did not think that his description of the Heavenly Jerusalem would or could be executed by angelic hands in gold and precious stones. But the middle cases between the two are the more typical; if we ask with Bultmann, for example, whether spirits good and evil were really thought to be breaths of subtle and potent air physically invading the human person, we run into a mist of ambiguities" (ibid.).

106. Ibid.

107. For example, "Are alleged historical events like the virginal conception of our Savior in Mary's womb examples of myth in the sense we have just defined, or are they not? Bultmann appears to beg the question. He writes as though he knew that God never bends physical fact into special conformity with divine intention; the Word never becomes flesh by making physical fact as immediately pliable to his expression as spoken symbols are. Bultmann seems to be convinced that he knows this, but I am not convinced that I know it, and I cannot be made to agree by the authority of the truism that symbolism ought not to be mistaken for physical fact. For it still ought to be taken for physical fact, if and where God has made it into physical fact" (ibid.).

108. Ibid., 4. Farrar continued on this train of thought: "The only case which allows of a perfectly simple answer is one in which a non-symbolical description can be alliteratively supplied.... But when nothing at all of this kind can be done, philosophical difficulties arise, and they reach their maximum in the case of religious expressions. An angel may be talked of as though he were a luminous and filmy man, but when we have decided that such images are mere parables, then to what are we to refer the parables? Are they parables about a non-luminous and non-filmy not-man? About a conscious and voluntary finite being of indeterminate species? About an impression made in the senses of a visionary by God himself?" (ibid.).

109. Lewis, *Christian Reflections*, 165–66.

110. Lewis, *Miracles*, 134.

111. Ibid.

112. For example, see Lewis' *Problem of Pain*, where he talks about the use of analogies to speak about God, particularly pp. 42–50.

113. Aquinas, *Summa Theologiae* (2008), 1:142–43.

114. Ibid., 1:143.

115. Ibid., 1:144.

116. Ibid.

117. Ibid., 145.

118. Ibid., 1:146–47.

119. Smith, *Speech and Theology*, 169.

120. Ibid., 167. And as Northrop Frye noted, we may "find that analogy, or likeness to something else, is very tricky to handle... because the differences are as important as the resemblances" (Frye, *Educated Imagination*, 11).

121. Barfield, *Poetic Diction*, xxx.

122. For an account of the Great War, see Lionel Adey's excellent book *C. S. Lewis' "Great War" with Owen Barfield*. Also, in Lewis, *Collected Letters*, vol. 3, some of the Great War letters are reprinted (pp.1596–646).

123. Adey, *C. S. Lewis' "Great War"*, 3.

124. Barfield saw myths, and "myth-thinking," as representing the "earliest meanings," and as such they are "not the arbitrary creations of 'poets', but the natural expression of man's being and consciousness at the time. These primary 'meanings' were *given*, as it were, by Nature, but the very condition of their being given was that they could not at the same time be apprehended in full consciousness; they could not be *known*, but only experienced, or lived" (Barfield, *Poetic Diction*, 102).

125. For example, "[Barfield] followed Rudolf Steiner, who tried to make a synthesis

of Christianity and gnostic thought. [Lewis], like his friend [Tolkien], explored pre-Christian paganism, seeing how far its imaginative insights pointed to the truth of Christianity" (Duriez and Porter, *Inklings Handbook*, 78).

126. Ibid., 68.

127. In *Surprised by Joy*, Lewis has this to say about Barfield and his work: "... I think he changed me a good deal more than I him. Much thought which he afterward put into *Poetic Diction* had already become mine before that important little book appeared" (p. 200). In his letters, Lewis also cited Barfield as a contributor to his conversion: "I was brought back [to Christianity] . . . (d.) By argument with an Anthroposophist. He failed to convert me to his own views (a kind of Gnosticism) but his attack on my own presuppositions smashed the ordinary pseudo-'scientific' world-picture forever" (*Collected Letters*, 2:703).

128. Barfield, *Poetic Diction*, 177.

129. Ibid., 52.

130. Ibid.

131. Ibid., 52–53.

132. Ibid., 54.

133. Pascal noted something similar when writing about the imagination, though he was much more skeptical here (calling it an enemy of reason) of the role of imagination: "That is the part of the human being which dominates . . . I am speaking of the wisest, and it is amongst them that imagination has the overriding right to change their minds. . . . This proud, powerful enemy of reason, which enjoys believing that it controls and dominates it to show how much it can achieve in every realm, has established a second nature in man. Imagination has those it makes happy and unhappy, its healthy and sick, its rich and poor. It makes reason believe, doubt, deny . . ." (Pascal, *Pensees*, 16–17).

134. Lewis, *Mere Christianity*, 104.

135. As a related aside, a sense of God lurking around every corner is also described by Andrew Greeley in *The Catholic Imagination*. Greeley notes that (particularly in the Protestant imagination) there is reluctance to use analogical language—for example, to somehow equate human love with the divine. He notes that when such language (i.e., language that equates) is used there is the natural Protestant response of negating it: "If one says in this tradition that human sexual union is like the union between God and Her people, there is an immediate need to insist that God's passion is also very different from human passion. Thus, the Protestant imagination . . . stresses the 'unlike' dimension of a metaphor and is in fact uneasy with the idea of metaphor" (Greeley, *Catholic Imagination*, 8). A possible explanation for this reluctance is in the fear of false notions. Greeley notes that the Reformers focused on the "unlike" dimension of metaphor because of a fear of peasant superstition. This focus on the dialectical imagination was powerfully championed by the Reformers because it was not taken seriously by the Catholic leadership, and this dialectical imagination is an all important corrective to the analogical imagination (ibid., 8). However, the absence of the analogical imagination can be extremely destructive, for then it is difficult to find justification for any metaphorical language about God. And Greeley notes the extremity of the position in Tillich's rejection of anthropomorphic language: "[Tillich] tried to sweep [anthropomorphic language] away by talking about a God beyond God, about whom nothing at all could be said or known except negatively. All God talk then is not only metaphorical but also idolatrous. We must live out our lives knowing that there is God but knowing nothing about God" (ibid., 8–9). Marcus Borg also talks about this problem in his book *The God We Never*

Knew: "I found... Tillich very appealing. [His] attacks on supernatural theism legitimated the difficulties I was having.... But I was still unable to understand [his] affirmations very well.... Tillich's characterizations of God as 'the ground of being' or 'Being-Itself' or 'ultimate reality' seemed to make God very impersonal. There were jokes about praying to 'the ground of being'" (Borg, *God We Never Knew*, 24). Greeley sees the Catholic churches themselves as strongholds of the analogical imagination: there are stories there of God's presence in the human struggle. Greeley finds that an approach which focuses on the analogical imagination is, for obvious reasons, more readily accepting to the arts and to story: there is an "assumption that religion is story (narrative image) before it is anything else and after it is everything else..." (Greeley, *Catholic Imagination*, 45). There is the habit of storytelling and of being treated to storytelling in the Catholic imagination that lends itself to imaginative fruits, so that however "imperfect the story told, however inartistic its rendering, however unimaginative its exercise of the Catholic imagination, this storytelling still works" (ibid., 46). Greeley also insists that there can be a combining of the analogical imagination and the dialectical imagination. He notes a particular novel, *Therapy*, which does just such a thing. In this novel author David Lodge writes of the "pilgrimage of his protagonist to the Festival of Santiago de Compostela, a pilgrimage which, together with reading Kierkegaard, heals the man's soul. Combining the two imaginations, analogical and dialectical, in the same 'therapy' is a deft touch, evidence that the two imaginations need not exclude one another" (ibid., 49–50). In Lewis' fiction, too, there is always the dialectical and the analogical. The two imaginations appear as expressions of the same truth: Lewis both looks along (analogical) and looks at (dialectical). But the received content is at once reasoned—a delivered reason beyond mere rationalistic conceptions. Though, of course, the Protestant imagination (which Greeley thinks tends to focus more on dialectical language) does not necessarily require a severe negation of the analogical imagination. Greeley highlights the power of the analogical imagination and its importance today. He notes that the "enchanted imagination is alive and well among... young people" today, and that its importance and effectiveness in young Catholics is visible, for example, in their concern for the poor (ibid., 185). Furthermore, the analogical imagination gives the prosaic a sense of enchantment: we "may not want to imagine a world in which God lurks everywhere and people respond to Him as a community. Fair enough.... But at least you should be willing to admit that it is a legitimate way of imagining reality..." (ibid., 186).

136. "Recovery, in Tolkien's sense of the term, is a key to the Chronicles as fairy tales. The stories take the readers out of the Primary World and allow them to experience a Secondary World that changes their outlook, so that as they re-enter the Primary World, they see new things in it and see old things in fresh ways. Visiting Narnia gives readers a revitalized awareness and appreciation of things that to us may have come to be mundane..." (Schakel, *Way into Narnia*, 117).

137. Lewis, *Letters to Malcolm*, 22.

138. For example, anthropomorphic language is dangerous: if we talk about "meeting" God, this "talk of 'meeting' is, no doubt, anthropomorphic; as if God and I could be face to face, like two fellow-creatures, when in reality He is above me and within me and below me and all about me. That is why it must be balanced by all manner of metaphysical and theological abstractions. But never, here or anywhere else, let us think that while anthropomorphic images are a concession to our weakness, the abstractions are the literal truth. Both are equally concessions; each singly misleading, and the two together mutually corrective" (Lewis, *Letters to Malcolm*, 21).

139. W. G. Kummel also argued that the Gospels in particular, when seen as a literary form, were a new creation: "They are in no way lives after the manner of Hellenistic biographies, since they lack the sense of internal and external history (as in lives of heroes), of character formation, of temporal sequence, and of the contemporary setting. Neither do the Gospels belong to the genre, memoirs, in which the collected stories and sayings from the lives of great men are simply strung together. Nor do they belong to the genus, miracle stories, in which the great deeds of ancient wonder-workers are glorified in a more or less stylized manner" (Kummel, *Introduction to the New Testament*, 37).

140. "Lewis, though he never used the term, [held] a literary view of inspiration. The Bible is inspired literature carrying a divine message. Human in its origin, biblical literature has been 'raised by God above itself, qualified by Him to serve purposes which of itself it would not have served'" (Christensen, *C. S. Lewis on Scripture*, 90).

141. Ibid., 77.

142. "Some people when they say that a thing is meant 'metaphorically' conclude from this that it is hardly meant at all. They rightly think that Christ spoke metaphorically when he told us to carry the cross: they wrongly conclude that carrying the cross means nothing more than leading a respectable life and subscribing moderately to charities. They reasonably think that hell 'fire' is a metaphor—and unwisely concluded that it means nothing more serious than remorse. They say that the story of the Fall in *Genesis* is not literal; and then go on to say ... that it was really a fall upwards—which is like saying that because 'My heart is broken' contains a metaphor, it therefore means 'I feel very cheerful.' This mode of interpretation I regard, frankly, as nonsense. For me the Christian doctrines which are 'metaphorical'—or which have become metaphorical with the increase of abstract thought—mean something which is just as 'supernatural' or shocking after we have removed the ancient imagery as it was before" (Lewis, *Miracles*, 78–79).

143. For a look at Lewis' advice to modern biblical critics, one would certainly want to see his essay in *Christian Reflections*, "Modern Theology and Biblical Criticism." Lewis respected the learning of New Testament scholars, but he was often skeptical about their claims: "The authority of experts in that discipline is the authority in deference to whom we are asked to give up a huge mass of beliefs shared in common by the early Church, the Fathers, the Middle Ages, the Reformers, and even the nineteenth century" (*Christian Reflections*, 153).

Lewis gave four reasons why he was doubtful of modern New Testament criticism. First, whatever these people may be as biblical critics, he distrusted them as critics (ibid., 154). He claimed critics do not often seem to understand the literature they are studying. They seem imperceptive about the *quality* of the texts they are studying: "It sounds a very strange charge to bring against men who have been steeped in those books all their lives. But that might be just the trouble. A man who has spent his youth and manhood in the minute study of New Testament texts and of other people's studies of them, whose literary experiences of those texts lacks any standard of comparison such as can only grow from a wide and deep and genial experience of literature in general, is, I should think, very likely to miss the obvious things about them" (ibid., 154).

Lewis' second problem with modern biblical criticism was the claim "that the real behaviour and purpose and teaching of Christ came very rapidly to be misunderstood and misrepresented by His followers, and has been recovered or exhumed only by modern scholars" (ibid., 157). Lewis had already met this type of criticism in his own field long before he saw it in New Testament criticism. While he was studying philosophy (while reading for Greats) he was taught to believe that Plato had been misunderstood by Aristotle who in turn had been misunderstood by the neo-Platonists, and that it was only through the recovery efforts of modern scholarship that the true meaning had been found—so that when it had been recovered, it was found that Plato had really been an English Hegelian all along (ibid.). Lewis also saw this type of criticism in his dealings with literature: ". . . every week a clever undergraduate, every quarter a dull American don, discovers for the first time what some Shakespearian play really meant" (ibid., 157). He saw how these revolutions in thought could not really be possible: "I see—I feel it in my bones—I know beyond argument—that most of their interpretations are merely impossible; they involve a way of looking at things which was not known in 1914, much less in the Jacobean period. This daily confirms my suspicion of the same approach to Plato or the New Testament. The idea that any man or writer should be opaque to those who lived in the same culture, spoke the same language, shared the same habitual imagery and unconscious assumptions, and yet be transparent to those who have none of these advantages, is in my opinion preposterous" (ibid., 158).

For his third concern with modern biblical criticism, Lewis took issue with the use of an *a priori* assumption that the prophetic or miraculous does not and cannot occur: "Thus any statement put into our Lord's mouth by the old texts, which, if He had really made it, would constitute a prediction of the future, is taken to have been put in after the occurrence which it seemed to predict" (ibid.). He asserted that this assumption is a very helpful and sensible one if we know that these types of things never really occur, and similarly, the rejection as unhistorical of all passages that narrate miracles is sensible if we start by knowing that the miraculous in general never occurs (ibid.). The question of whether the miraculous ever occurs is really a philosophical question: "Scholars, as scholars, speak on it with no more authority than anyone else. The canon 'If miraculous, unhistorical' is one they bring to their study of the texts, not one they have learned from it. If one is speaking of authority, the united authority of all the Biblical critics in the world counts here for nothing. On this they speak simply as men; men obviously influenced by, and perhaps insufficiently critical of, the spirit of the age they grew up in" (ibid.).

Lewis' fourth problem with modern biblical criticism was the daunting task of reconstructing the genesis of texts. It is attempting an almost impossible task of searching and postulating "what vanished documents each author used, when and where he wrote, with what purposes, under what influences—the whole *Sitz im Leben* of the text." And Lewis freely admitted that this is done with "immense erudition and great ingenuity" (ibid.). He also admitted that it is very convincing. He felt as if he might have been greatly influenced by it if he hadn't had a personal experience which guarded him against accepting it outright. He had seen this practice from the other side, having been the subject of critical review. Lewis found that when he was being reviewed very little reviewing was actually going on. The reviews seemed to contain more talk about "imaginary histories" than it did evaluation, praise, or censure of the book itself: "The very terms which the reviewers use in praising or dispraising often imply such a history. They praise a passage as 'spontaneous' and censure another as 'laboured'; that is, they think they know that you wrote the one *currente calamo* and the other *invita Minerva*" (ibid., 159). Another such example was of Tolkien's *Lord of the Rings* trilogy. Some reviewers postulated that "the Ring in [the books] was suggested by the atom bomb. What could be more plausible? Here is a book published when everyone was preoccupied by that sinister invention; here in the centre of the book is a weapon which it seems madness to throw away yet fatal to use. Yet in fact, the chronology of the book's composition makes the theory impossible" (ibid., 160).

144. See Lewis, *Letters to Malcolm*, 52.

145. See ibid.

146. That is we must never think that we "bring beauty or wisdom" into existence "which did not exist before," but we must see ourselves "simply and solely as trying to embody in terms of [our] own art some reflection of eternal Beauty and Wisdom" (Lewis, *Christian Reflections*, 7).

147. Christensen, *C. S. Lewis on Scripture*, 88. It might also be noted that Lewis did not appear sympathetic to the theology of Karl Barth. In his letters, Lewis mentioned Barth's followers while discussing his encounters with Christians within Oxford: "They've all been reading a dreadful man called Karl Barth, who seems the right opposite number to Karl Marx. 'Under judgement' is their great expression. They all talk like Convenanters or Old Testament prophets. They don't think human reason or human conscience of any value at all: they maintain, as stoutly as Calvin, that there's no reason why God's dealings should appear just (let alone merciful) to us: and they maintain the doctrine that *all* our righteousness is filthy rags with a fierceness and sincerity which is like a blow in the face" (Lewis, *Collected Letters*, 2:351). He also remarked in his letters, "Yes, I have read *Agape and Eros*, and I don't like it at all, indeed I very heartily dislike it. It seems to me the last word of the most abominable form of Protestantism in a straight line from Luther through Barth" (ibid., 2:165).

148. Lewis, *Letters of C. S. Lewis* (1993), 480. Lewis' remarks here clearly resemble those of St. Bonaventure in *On the Reduction of the Arts to Theology*: "*Every good gift and every perfect gift is from above, coming down from the God of lights,* writes James in the first chapter of his epistle. This text speaks of the source of all illumination; but at the same time, it suggests that there are many lights which flow generously from that fontal source of light" (Bonaventure, *On the Reduction*, 37).

149. McGrath, *Christian Theology*, 169.

150. Frei, *Eclipse of Biblical Narrative*, 267.

151. Lewis, *God in the Dock*, 67.

152. David Brown also recognizes the problems modern biblical criticism has raised for Christians, but despite these possible problems, he still sees the biblical-critical method as vital and complimentary to Christian thought: ". . . so far from Christianity being undermined by post-biblical developments in its self-understanding, it has been hugely enriched by them" (Brown, *Tradition and Imagination*, 5). Brown notes that biblical history is not alone in its problems; other early histories are replete with the same issues. "Obviously my particular interest here is biblical history, but I have deliberately spread the net this widely, to demonstrate that the problems that confront theology are by no means unique or idiosyncratic. Indeed, in terms of information available the New Testament period is as well off as many another period of early history, nor, as we have seen, are its problems of interpretation without parallel elsewhere. So retreat from historical questions would seem to me quite mistaken" (ibid., 23). Brown sees the issues of historicity as important but not necessarily decisive for the Christian tradition. "For if, as the Christian believes, Jesus is still alive, then the question has ceased to be merely what he did in the past, but how his presence and influence can be appropriated in the here and now. A better imaginative relation between believer and Lord, greater coherence to the story and so forth, all then become relevant questions" (ibid., 25).

If the Christian believes that Jesus is alive and active, then he is to be seen as a fully relational being. Biblical criticism is clearly useful, but, as Lewis warned, the possibility of 'over-reaching' is present. Lewis recognized that the Christian community saw Jesus as a fully alive, fully relational being. Lewis emphasized a personal relationship with Christ (and a need to live in the Christ-life). The continued existence of Jesus needs to be recognized, and the act of being a part of Christ's life (indeed a part of Christ's Body) is seen in the participation of the Christian within the community both inside and outside the church.

153. Frei, *Eclipse of Biblical Narrative*, 267.

154. See ibid., 268.

155. That is, "The difference . . . seemed to have something to do with greater history-likeness or simplicity, not necessarily with greater credibility" (ibid., 272).

156. See ibid., 273.

157. Ibid., 280.

158. Augustine, *On Christian Teaching*, 29.

159. Chesterton, *Everlasting Man*, 26–27.

seven

The Theological Imagination

To appreciate Lewis' view of imagination an understanding of his concept of transposition is necessary. It is through the transposition of the divine life to the so-called mundane life that the mundane is saved. Barfield, borrowing from Aristotle, talks of "saving the appearances,"[1] and this is what Lewis' theory of transposition expresses and advocates: it is precisely through the participation of the divine in the world by which the world gets brought up into the divine. This participation is present not only in the first creative act of the divine but also in the myriad appearances, expressions and signs of the divine in (and through) the world and in (and through) its inhabitants. In what follows, I examine Lewis' view of imagination through his essay "Transposition," wherein lies a veiled Lewisian theory of imagination. Lewis' argument there is to be seen as bolstering the idea that there is a necessary transposition of the higher, divine life to the lower, mundane life. In this process, however, the lower life is saved by being brought up into the higher life. Additionally, the imagination is the organ of meaning: we gain our *telos* and meaning from a reliance upon the participation of the divine, of transcendence. The "untheological" imagination is surreptitiously relying upon transcendence to fund its work: the "untheological" narrative framework is ultimately nihilistic, terminating on the merely phenomenologically given, and losing, in the long run, what it attempts to hold up. The "untheological" imagination is an unorthodox theological view, in that it is funded by a meaning-filled narrative structure while attempting to communicate a narrative of meaninglessness. Thus, the narrative framework is still theological in its reliance upon a transcendent meaning or *telos*.

Coleridgean Imagination

In Aristotle's short discussion of imagination in *De Anima*, chapter three, he described the imagination (*phantasia*) as "that virtue of which we say that an image occurs to us . . ."[2] As such it is the human faculty that produces images. Imagination also stores and is the means by which we recall images. Professor James M. Garrett notes that, in general, discussions of the imagination can be broadly separated into two common camps: what he terms the Platonic and the Aristotelian. The Platonic view "holds that imagination is the lowest form of cognition because it provides us with only the shadows, images, and reflections of objects."[3] The Aristotelian view holds that the imagination is a faculty that "mediates between sensation and thought, as depending on sensation for its supply of images, and in turn supplying these images as input to thought."[4] The argument of whether or not Plato and Aristotle fit these categories notwithstanding, the categories can be helpful as general sensibilities and as counterdistinctions. Imagination is not merely fancy or murky shadow, nor is it to be seen merely as a faculty that depends on sensation for its supply of images. There is, of course, a clear sense in which Garrett's Aristotelian assertion is proper: that is, we can receive the higher realities only through analogy, through sensible things; the finite can only approximate the infinite. However, there is an epiphenomenon that occurs with this activity: the special participation of the divine and the revelatory knowledge that can arrive through the analogies. Furthermore, the ability to imagine speaks to another strange phenomenon—that we can place ourselves in time and space through imagination, that the ability to ponder the future and remember the past requires imagining, that the faculty is undergirded by an implicit metaphysic that moves us beyond mere immanence.

Lewis explained the imagination in various places, but he never gave an explicit theory.[5] He noted in *Surprised by Joy* that often "imagination is a vague word. . . . It may mean the world of reverie, daydream, wish-fulfilling fantasy."[6] Lewis distinguishes between mere fancy on the one hand and creative invention on the other. In a creative invention, one is a "creator, not a candidate for admission to it. Invention is essentially different from reverie..."[7] Here we see clearly the echoing of Tolkien's theory of subcreation. Lewis did, however, lay out this distinction more explicitly elsewhere. In the essay "Psycho-analysis and Literary Criticism," Lewis follows Coleridge's theory of imagination—imagination "in the highest sense of all"—as laid out in *Biographia Literaria*.[8] Coleridge distinguishes between the primary imagination and the secondary imagination, with a third distinction of fancy. The primary imagination is the method of communication and participation, the revelatory power of the divine in the mind of humankind: "The primary imagination I hold to be the living Power and prime Agent of all human Perception, and as a repetition in the finite mind of the eternal act of creation in the infinite I AM."[9] The secondary imagination is the "echo" of the primary imagination—it is the same in kind but not in degree. That is, the

> secondary [is an] echo of the former, co-existing with the conscious will, yet still as identical with the primary in the *kind* of its agency, and differing only in *degree*, and in the *mode* of its operation. It dissolves, diffuses, dissipates, in order to re-create; or where this process is rendered impossible, yet still at all events it struggles to idealize and to unify. It is essentially *vital*, even as all objects (*as* objects) are essentially fixed and dead.[10]

Coleridge defines fancy as having

> no other counters to play with, but fixities and definites. The Fancy is indeed no other than a mode of Memory emancipated from the order of time and space; and blended with, and modified by that empirical phenomenon of the will, which we express by the word CHOICE. But equally with the ordinary memory it must receive all its materials ready made from the law of association.[11]

Here we see a similar concern over the merely self-regarding or self-serving images and desires as expressed by Plato, Augustine, and Lewis: fancy in this sense is dangerous precisely because it is a deceptive mode; it orients us only towards the phenomenologically given (but also losing the immanent in the process) and away from the divine. The images of fancy terminate on the merely material, whereas the proper image will revert back to the divine life, saved and suspended through transcendence. Similar to Coleridge, Lewis noted that there are

> Two activities of the imagination, one free, and the other enslaved to the wishes of its owner for whom it has to provide imaginary gratifications. Both may be the starting-point for works of art. The former "free" activity continues in the works it produces and passes from the status of a dream to that of art by a process which may legitimately be called "elaboration": it is a motive power which starts the activity and is withdrawn when once the engine is running, or a scaffolding which is knocked away when the building is complete.[12]

The "enslaved" imagination of fancy is contrasted with the "free" activity of the primary imagination: the reversion back to its source in the latter and the spiraling downward to self-gratification and, ultimately, to nihilism in the former. We also see here both the motivating and foundational power of imagination—and it is a further clue to its reasoned nature. That is, the faculty of imagination is also what gets the engine running in matters of reason—it fills the gaps of the unknown by reaching out beyond itself, acquiring the deliverance of a reason beyond the algorithms of rationalist conceptions of reason. While Lewis did not explicitly lay out a theory of imagination, it can be discerned in the above sources. But in the essay "Transpostion," we get what may be the clearest account of Lewis' theory of imagination, even though, as Owen Barfield noted, "imagination is not mentioned."[13]

Transposition

Lewis noted that one of our major difficulties in communicating the spiritual life through signs and symbols is the reappearance of the old elements of natural life in our spiritual life—that there appears an obvious continuity between things natural and things spiritual. It seems natural to assume that if we had a real experience of revelation from outside the world that we should expect something other than our natural experience to help communicate it.[14] Lewis admitted that skeptics and cynics have a good *prima facie* case for their assumptions that, for example, love and lust are the same thing because they both end in the same physical act. It may be true that the same acts occur in justice as in revenge, or in love as in lust. But can we put a case up against the skeptics' or cynics' case and see if it is true? Lewis suggested taking an empirical instance of "higher" and "lower" levels of experience, where the higher level is within most everyone's experience. As his example,

Lewis used the sensation of sickness that occurs with aesthetic delights and with physical suffering. What we find is that a very similar experience is had by both nausea (which presumably no one really enjoys) and an aesthetic pleasure (which can produce the same physical feeling but is experienced as pleasurable). Lewis noted that during an experience one cannot in that moment stop to analyze the experience thoroughly:

> For myself I find that if, during a moment of intense aesthetic rapture, one tries to turn around and catch by introspection what one is actually feeling, one can never lay one's hand on anything but a physical sensation. . . . If I were to judge simply by sensations, I should come to the absurd conclusion that joy and anguish are the same thing, that what I most dread is the same with what I most desire. Introspection discovers nothing more or different in the one than in the other. . . . These sensations . . . do not merely accompany very different experiences as an irrelevant or neutral addition.[15]

When we feel the sickness, we desire it in one context and despise it in another. The sensation does not merely signify the joy or anguish; it becomes that which it signifies.[16]

Lewis took the emotional life as higher than the life of sensations: not as morally higher but as a richer, deeper, more varied and more subtle.[17] Lewis asked us to consider for ourselves: we find that our physical sensations tend to respond most adequately and exquisitely to our emotions; our sense resources are much more limited than our emotional resources; our emotional life is far more varied and our sense life has far fewer resources than our emotional life. We use our senses to "compensate" for the varied nature of our emotion by using the same physical sensation for different emotional responses.[18] We cannot have a direct communication between things when one set is higher and richer than another set. We also find this in other aspects of our life. There must be a transposition of the higher to the lower: "The transposition of the richer into the poorer must, so to speak, be algebraical, not arithmetical. If you are to translate from a language that has a small vocabulary, then you must be allowed to use several words in more than one sense."[19] If we take drawing, for example, we will find that representing three dimensions on a two-dimensional piece of paper requires the use of perspective. In order to use perspective we must give more than one value to our two-dimensional drawing. So, the "very same shape which you must draw to give the illusion of a straight road receding from the spectator is also the shape you draw for a dunce's cap."[20]

Lewis noted two qualities of transposition we can see thus far. First, the lower medium can only be fully understood if we know the higher medium. For example, we can understand our three-dimensional drawings only because we live in a three-dimensional world. We can see the problem more clearly by imagining a creature who perceived only two dimensions. If our creature could perceive "only two dimensions and yet could somehow be aware of the lines as he crawled over them on the paper, we shall easily see how impossible it would be for him to understand [our three dimensional drawing]."[21] Secondly, the term "symbolism" is not completely adequate for all cases of higher and lower transpositions. For example, the relation between speech and writing is a symbolical one:

> The written characters exist solely for the eye, the spoken words solely for the ear. There is complete discontinuity between them. They are not like one another, nor does the one cause the other to be. The one is simply a *sign* of the other and signifies it by a convention. But a picture is not related to the visible world in just that way. Pictures are part of the visible world themselves and represent it only by being part of it.[22]

The signs in this case are only signs because they are more than just signs; the thing signified is also present in the sign. The relationship is not in this case what most might term "symbolical"; it sacramental in Lewis' view. If we take our first case—that of emotion and sensation—the problem of viewing their relationship in merely symbolical terms becomes clearer. For in that case we see that the same sensation does not only accompany the emotions but it becomes a part of them.[23]

In the case of nature and spirit or God and humankind, Lewis affirms the same difficulties. If the higher or richer elements descend to the lower or poorer elements we will naturally have difficulties in understanding the higher life. The charge of the cynic or skeptic that all our spiritual experience is really just repackaged, disguised natural experience is also to be expected. If we assume that the lower is the only known medium, the higher is going to seem difficult to take:

> The brutal man can never by analysis find anything but lust in love; the Flatlander never can find anything but flat shapes in a picture; physiology never can find anything in thought except

> twitchings of the grey matter. It is no good browbeating the critic who approaches a Transposition from below. On the evidence available to him his conclusion is the only one possible.[24]

The rationalist, materialist mind will only see what is physically given. But the imagination cannot service the merely phenomenologically given. The impoverished imagination will look at a person lying on a bed sleeping and may see only REM or a series of energy exchanges (and this, too, is a deliverance of unacknowledged imaginative reason). The full imagination might look at that same person lying sleeping on the bed and in addition to the above see wonder, knowledge, mystery, and enchantment. The imagination devoid of the theological is not really imagination at all. As Lewis says, this person will see all the "facts" but none of the "meaning."[25] This person will analyze the experience from outside (as if this were really possible) and judge his or her analysis as truer than the actual experience.[26] But if, as Lewis says, everything is different when we view transposition from above, then we must also recognize our limitations when dealing with the spiritual life.[27] Spiritual things are to be discerned by spiritual means.[28] But we still must rest in the affirmation that we know something of the higher life, the spiritual life. We must emphasize the limits of our knowledge out of necessity and not merely out of humility.[29]

We must still find meaning, however, in how we approach the higher life. The higher life is still embodied in the lower, still intimately connected. Lewis stated that our claims are not really that startling:

> We are only claiming to know that our apparent devotion, whatever else it may have been, was not simply erotic, or that our apparent desire for Heaven, whatever else it may have been, was not simply a desire for longevity or jewelry or social splendours. Perhaps we have never really attained at all to what St. Paul would describe as spiritual life. But at the very least we know, in some dim and confused way, that we were trying to use natural acts and images and language with a new value, have at least desired a repentance which was not merely prudential and a love which was not self-centered. At worst, we know enough of the spiritual to know that we have fallen short of it, as if the picture knew enough of the three-dimensional world to be aware that it was flat.[30]

These limitations, however, might also be seen in a positive light, especially when concerning art and aesthetics. As Lewis noted, in a sense, transposition can do anything.[31] So, the lower life can be seen as valuable.

Lewis returns to the example of the drawing. Our two-dimensional drawing on plain white paper which contains clouds and a sun might be seen as a terribly inadequate representation of real things. But taken in another sense it is perfect in its own way: "If the shadows are properly done, that patch of white paper will, in some curious way, be very like blazing sunshine; we shall almost feel cold while we look at the paper snow and almost warm our hands at the paper fire."[32] The art gains its real, deeper and larger value from participating in a reality that it suggests. By striving for a higher reality the art may be seen as representational of that reality by being a participant in it. So, too, might the natural life participate in the spiritual life, by being swept up into the higher life. God, as Aquinas noted, wills to become small and by so doing pulls us up: "To restore man, who had been laid low by sin, to the heights of divine glory, the Word of the eternal father, though containing all things within His immensity, willed to become small. This He did, not by putting aside His greatness, but by taking to Himself our littleness."[33] Lewis echoed this view when he wrote, ". . . it seems to me that there is a real analogy . . . that humanity, still remaining itself, is not merely counted as, but veritably drawn into, Deity. [This is what seems to happen] when a sensation (not in itself a pleasure) is drawn into the joy it accompanies."[34] The immanent is participating in the reality of the spiritual life not only through its inclusion in the reality of the world but by its attempt to represent the higher life. What implicitly follows is a theory of aesthetics: art is that which strives to suggest more than it is, always reverting back to its transcendent source.[35] The highest form of art is the one that attempts to point beyond itself. The familial ties between Plato, Augustine, and Lewis cannot be missed. While Lewis still valued form and the artist's craft, he also, like St. Bonaventure, saw the gifts of the artist (indeed all gifts) as given by God, ultimately, to point humankind back towards God.[36]

The Organ of Meaning

In Mary Warnock's book *Imagination*, she attempts to "trace a single thread which runs through different accounts of imagination" in order to "see whether certain features of imagination would emerge as essential and as universal, if the thread could, as I hoped, be followed."[37] Warnock finds that the thread may be stated in the following fashion:

> there is a power in the human mind which is at work in our everyday perception of the world, and it is also at work in our thoughts about what is absent; which enables us to see the world, whether present or absent as significant, and also to present this vision to others, for them to share or reject. And this power, though it gives us "thought-imbued" perception (it "keeps the thought alive in the perception"), is not only intellectual. Its impetus comes from the emotions as much as from the reason, from the heart as much as from the head.[38]

Warnock concludes with a comment on Lewis' account of "imaginative epiphanies" in *Surprised by Joy*. She concludes that Lewis "minimizes the importance of such experiences, on the grounds that in themselves they are not religious, at most a kind of image or reflection of religious experiences. But he is wrong to play them down."[39] But Warnock is wrong to say that Lewis does not recognize these experiences as religious or that he simply plays down such experiences. What Lewis was doing was protecting against the inclination to idolize such experiences, to equate such experiences with God (i.e., to say that these experiences *are* God as opposed to pointers *to* God). We must always sit to the task, saying, "Not thus, not thus, neither is this Thou."[40] The finite can ultimately only suggest the infinite.[41] But the imaginative realms pull us out of our "dumb immediacy, distancing us from an oppressively close present and disqualifying the primacy of the merely real here and now..."[42] In a real sense, the imagination for Lewis is equated with the soul and as such the soul is "chiefly the imagination and emotions."[43] Lewis also saw the soul as having three distinct aspects: imagination, intellect, and will. As such the soul has three "concentric circles: the imagination outermost, the intellect next, and the will innermost."[44] Here we see a correlation with Aristotle's theory of imagination.[45] Aristotle also designated the imagination as a part of the soul, as "a power or faculty of the soul..."[46] The faculty of imagination is a poetic movement. It is a bringing forth, and in this bringing forth there is a reaching out to a beyond—but there is also a return. As such, there may appear to be "no anterior paradigm directive of the process, no *look* to which one would look almost constantly in fabricating something to look like the paradigmatic *look*."[47] The question remains, however, "From where do the images come?" For neither "is imaginal bringing-forth a matter of [mere] copying, of replicating—that is of reproducing—something actually seen..."[48] Imagination bestows a constant bringing forth, a constant reimagining of the divine creative act; the imagination is not exhausted by retrospective and prospective images.[49]

One of the most open means through which images are conceived and reach us is in narrative. The narrative gives us meaning and what has "a meaning is the total story. . . . Also in a symbolical narrative the meaning usually cannot be stated in conceptual terms: it lives only in the story."[50] In a letter to Eliza Butler, Lewis explains the differences in and the costs of believing imagination and mythology to be (1) fictive or (2) pointers to reality. Lewis stated that mythic and artistic creations are important

> products of imagination in the sense that their content is *imaginative*. The more *imaginative* ones are "nearer the mark" in the sense that they communicate more Reality to us. Poetry "creates life" in the sense that its products are something more than fictions occurring in human minds, mere psychological phenomena, and can therefore be described as inhabiting a "spiritual world." Poets "proclaim the mystery" in the sense that they somehow convey to us an inkling of supersensual and super-intellectual Reality: which is a Mystery in the sense of *mysterium tremendum*, something not merely [which] we happen not to know but which transcends our common modes of perception. They produce the illusion of penetrating it in the sense that they make us feel we have *understood* when we have really been refreshed by contact of quite a different kind with Reality.[51]

According to Lewis, if we view the imaginative quality of art as mere fiction, it is a very clear view and it will not appear to interfere with our lives. But we pay a price for this view: at the very least, this view will never give us the excitement of seeing art as part of larger reality. Conversely, the price we pay for holding the view that art does indeed reflect a reality is that we will not be certain that it will not interfere with our lives; we must live with a "disquieting recognition that this Reality with a big R might interfere with [us] and that the whole thing may go further than [we] wished or intended."[52]

Lewis' interest in the imagination as the "organ of meaning" can even be seen before his conversion to Christianity. In a 1926 letter to a friend, Cecil Harwood, six years before his conversion to Christianity, Lewis champions the imagination:

> No one is more convinced than I that reason is utterly inadequate to the richness and spirituality of real things: indeed this is itself a

> deliverance of reason. Nor do I doubt the presence, even in us, of faculties embryonic or atrophied, that lie in an indefinite margin around the little finite bit of focus which is intelligence—faculties anticipating or remembering the possession of huge tracts of reality that slip through the meshes of the intellect. And so, to be sure, I believe that the symbols presented by the imagination at its height are the workings of that fringe and present to us as much of the super-intelligible reality as we can get while we retain our present form of consciousness.[53]

Lewis here is clearly echoing Plato's theory of the forms: the reality communicated to us is a transposition of the higher life to the lower life; a rationalistic conception of reason cannot get us closer to it and, in fact, it will do the opposite. The mystery must be grasped by supernatural light, the divinely gifted imagination, which brings its special knowledge that can be received and communicated (however inadequately) only in this way. The idea that the imagination might be able to give us more than rationalistic conceptions of reason is clearly a concern of Lewis' before the composition of his fictive novels or apologetic works. A reasoning beyond rationalist reason is present within the imaginings, and reason can also help us judge the meanings of our imaginings—e.g., can help us judge between conflicting images.[54] Imagination is the prelude to action and motivation and is the pre-existent algorithm of reason.

Strict rationalism taken to its extreme denies that there is more than the phenomenologically given. If we stop here, we find there is no ultimate meaning behind the strange images and phantasms of the imagination. Friedrich Nietzsche is arguably one of the most imaginative and poetic of philosophers. His writing combines the rigorous and grave nature of his interpretation of life with his extremely potent imagination. However, without meaning in imagination (or even life in general) what do his powerful imaginings come to? The bleak darkness of illusion . . .[55] But Nietzsche had the daring confidence to recognize what his viewpoint did to the meaning of his imaginings: the logical end is a complete (and frightening) loss of a reason to exist.[56] This loss of meaning is ominous and desperate. It is an agonizing and haunting bleakness. The last hope comes in the form of the *Ubermensch*, who might ascend to power.[57] However, the destruction is clear. But,

> Nietzsche then goes on to confront the problem that this act of destruction has created. . . . [If] there is nothing to morality but expressions of will, my morality can only be what my will creates.

> There can be no place for such fictions as natural right, utility, the greatest happiness of the greatest number. I myself must now bring into existence "new tables of what is good."[58]

Yet, what we have done is taken the notions of good and evil and only seemingly jettisoned them: for we have now placed a conjured meta-ethic over and above our previous set of ethics. That is, what is now deemed "good" is what we can will—power and the ability to transcend the conventions of morality and society. Can we now say that we have really left behind notions of good when merely something else has become "good"? But perhaps it is more important to consider whether, once we have lost all meaning, we can then meaningfully find a reason for being. Can we meaningfully express meaninglessness? This brings to mind Shakespeare's Macbeth and his haunted emptiness towards the end of the play:

> Life's but a walking shadow, a poor player / That struts and frets his hour upon the stage, / And then is heard no more. It is a tale / Told by an idiot, full of sound and fury, / Signifying nothing.[59]

But of course if this is true, what real and ultimate meaning do even these beautiful, tragic, and poetic words have?[60] None.[61] We would have been brought into a narrative structure that tells us all is meaningless—and we are told all is meaningless through a meaningful narrative structure. The narrative is still funded by theological means, by an unacknowledged or unrecognized *telos* and meaning—but it is a heretical theological funding. We can see clearly the problem of an implied theological interpretation and formation expressing an imaginative "untheological" framework.[62]

In his essay "Fictioning Things: Gift and Narrative," John Milbank observes the implicit theological method of fiction writers who present an "untheological" viewpoint. Milbank notes specifically Philip Pullman's *His Dark Materials*:

> As if in recognition that by this means Christianity still exerts a covert hold on the global imagination, Philip Pullman in *His Dark Materials* has written an anti-Christian fantasy trilogy, which to some extent is deliberately directed against certain key themes of the MacDonald tradition—in particular the privileging of the innocent, childish eye—while at the same time it is manifestly indebted to this tradition for its mode of construction. This is especially apparent in terms of its envisaging of a parallel universe with its own laws which is deployed both to point out the arbitrary contingency of the universe we inhabit *and* to indicate more

sharply an essence of *ethical* legality that might transcend arbitrariness and display its imperatives in any possible world whatsoever. Moreover, Pullman's ethical prescription remains a theological one of a sort—he offers a kind of materialist Gnosticism as an alternative to orthodox Christian faith.[63]

We see the problems of presenting the "untheological" to the imagination, in that there is an implicit theology of presentation. In order to envision and present as meaningful what the world is or would otherwise be like (whether a materialist Gnostic universe or a Christian one) we need to engage our imagination. In order to engage our imagination we imply a meaning within what we see and say: the imagination is theological in its implicit reference to a transcendent meaning or purpose. We have no ultimate reason to accept Pullman's imaginative universe (or a Christian one) if there is no meaning in the imaginings. The merely rationalistic, materialistic worldview gives us no hope for meanings behind our imaginings. We are all living in a narrative framework: we are imaging (fictioning) a narrative thread, whether a scientific narrative framework, a purely rational or secular framework, or an explicit theological framework. There is meaning inherent in this action, within the narrative, that is not explained merely through the "facts," through the phenomenologically given: the "facts" tell us this or that based upon our own chosen narrative.

We might put the meaning of imagination down to the practical, but the question of meaning really just moves ahead of us: "What now is the meaning of the practical?" The meaning of imagination, then, could become *merely* practical or rational or scientific—for example, in questions such as "How we can manipulate our current situation?" or "How can we manipulate our raw material?" Even here there is still an implicit reliance upon a transcendent *telos* or meaning—the meaning of the practical is appealing to something other than mere materiality. We also see the deeper foundation the imagination demonstrates. For example, as Lewis stated, the imagination "runs ahead of scientific evidence. 'The prophetic soul of the big world' was already pregnant with the Myth: if science has not met the imaginative need, science would not have been so popular. But probably every age gets, within certain limits, the science it desires."[64] Imagination does not survive in a sterile and stagnate environment, and neither does science. Literary critic Northrop Frye noted that when we use words properly, on any level, we must engage our imaginations, "otherwise they become mechanical cliches, and get further and further removed from any kind of reality."[65] This mechanical thinking is exemplified by mob mentality, where we all say the same thing without having to think about it. We are always either fighting against this or giving into it when we use words. When we are fighting it we are participating in genuine human civilization, and this is the world of philosophy, history, and science, all of which use highly organized wordplay. We do find knowledge and information in these disciplines. However, they are also structures. That is, they are "things made out of words by a power in the human mind that constructs and builds. This power is the imagination. When we think of their content, they're bodies of knowledge; when we think of their form, they're myths, that is, imaginative verbal structures."[66]

The dominant narrative structure of the modern industrial Western world has tended towards a scientific, secular one. However, many people in scientific fields have turned away from viewing science as

> narrow positivistic . . . empirical, inductive, certain and totally verifiable. . . . What one discovers again and again, both from creative scientists and from the theoreticians of science, is an appreciation of the imagination in science. For instance, Max Planck, the discoverer of quantum theory, insists that the pioneer scientist must have "a vivid imagination, for new ideas are not generated by deduction, but by *artistically* creative imagination."[67]

Huston Smith also notes that "Science and tradition agree . . . in insisting that the way things really are is radically different from the way they seem. They also agree in claiming that this 'other' than the way things appear lies in the direction of more rather than less."[68] However, in materialist structures the imagination is often viewed as deficient.[69] In an essentially Christian way, any human faculty is to be viewed as fallen and finite. Of course we are not up to the task of understanding the whole gamut of nature, let alone the divine. But when viewed in a larger and more positive sense this only means that our imaginings can be seen as inexhaustible because they are in some small way reflecting and reaching for the infinite. However, the ultimate consequence of viewing the imagination as utterly and foundationally deficient is that science somehow does not need or cannot use the imagination as any sort of basis for inquiry, does not use models for explanation. It also assumes a bottom-to-top reasoning, where the imagination is comprised merely of reworked images from the natural world and is then vaulted up; or that the imagination bases its content solely and merely upon the senses, upon the "facts" of the material. This also implies that our imaginations have severe limits, which does not bode well for science or much else. But clearly even science proves this false nearly everyday by bringing forth new models, new discoveries, and new theories that demonstrate the active scientific imagination.[70] Rationalism cannot account for all of reason: there is the story of inspiration and initialization of ideas and concepts—as well as the ability to create new ideas and concepts from existing ones, the ability to be the foundation of ideas and the primary connector between ideas, the metaphysical gap filler, that which moves us from idea to idea and delivers real insight. It is in this space that reason opens up beyond itself—even though reason may attempt to supersede or suppress the space—and "spaces reason out into a field, into various fields. . . . With the release of spacing there commences . . . a mixing of interior and exterior . . . a figuration at the limit. Spacing is this figuration. . . . As such, it is (the movement of) imagination. . . . Occlusion, the release of spacings, leads from reason to imagination."[71] There is a reaching out of reason beyond itself over an abyss—reason crosses an abyss of the unknown, the un-thought, the possible, and imagination travels through the abyss to unchartered shores and brings back a light from the darkness by which one may navigate.

The imaginings of the scientist or secularist must also be given a value of meaning, and this requires the use of an implicit theological framework (i.e., a reference to a transcendent *telos*, or a meaning-filled universe) to communicate this information. The mere act of naming, of sign making, seems to put us into a relationship with a larger world—a world that can be shared, known, and communicated.[72] And even in more positive accounts of imagination, such Ralph Gerard's famous line that "Reason can answer questions, but imagination has to ask them," there is a remainder left over that a limited reason cannot fully account for of itself: even in the answering of questions there is space to fill in, space to link thoughts together—the imaginative leap of inferences, the leap between premises and conclusions. The imagination gives us a place, a fountain source that allows reason to flow—a creation of timelessness within space and time. Imagination allows us to "figure" at the limits of understanding: the realm of the finite reaches out and touches the fringes of the infinite.

It is true that the faculty of imagination sends us images of our hopes and dreams—and even sends us "practical" information (e.g., treatments for ailments have been known to come from dreams and imaginings).[73] The deliverance of knowledge, however, is troubling and the shadowy apparition of meaning still haunts us. Are we then merely "good animals" as Walker Percy might say, responding to mere appearances, expecting phenomena in a strictly behavioralist fashion?[74] This is, however, the "assumption that things which have been conjoined in the past will always be conjoined in the future is the guiding principle not of rational but of animal behavior."[75] The real inference comes when one can move to a conclusion: "Repeated experiences of finding fire . . . where he had seen smoke would condition a man to expect fire whenever he saw smoke. . . . When you have discovered what smoke is you may then be able to replace the mere expectation of fire by a genuine inference. Till this is done reason recognises the expectation as a mere expectation."[76] The inference requires the imaginative leap. Even though we may get practical information from our imagination (e.g., a solution to a mathematical problem) this is hardly all we get. Our imagination gives us much more than a mere formula: it provides the source from which reason flows, it gives us pictures, image-blocks of information, knowledge of otherness, phantasm, enchanted fairy dust—not just a formula. The formula travels with a strange companion. What is left for imagination if it has no larger meaning, if it is merely rationalized? What is left is the merely practical and used, the entertaining and amusing, and the nonsensical and absurd, leading ultimately to nihilism—and even here there is an implicit theological framework because one is appealing to something other or more than the mere material: the meaning applied at usage is something other than the merely phenomenologically given.

In Plato's *Phaedrus* we encounter the image of the soul as a "natural team of winged horses and their charioteer," so that our "driver is in charge of a pair of horses . . . one of his horses is beautiful and good and from stock of the same sort, while the other is the opposite and has the opposite sort of bloodline."[77] The horse on the right is the noble, upright one, a "lover of honor with modesty and self-control; companion to true glory, he needs no whip, and is guided by verbal commands alone."[78] The horse on the left, however, is a "crooked great jumble of limbs . . . companion to wild boasts and indecency . . . and just barely yields to horsewhip and goad combined."[79] We see the noble spirit and the passions as leaders of the intellect in this metaphor. We literally get nowhere without the leading horses of spirit and appetite, the passions. There is also the notion of the danger present in the leading horses. One is virtuous and noble, leading the intellect down the correct paths; the other is wild, leading the intellect to mere appetite. The noble horse is the natural companion of reason, it leads reason where reason would like to go and should go. The passions as such are not merely the irrational workings of mere material or base desires: there is a sense in which the noble horse has a knowledge that precedes the intellect, a reasoning beyond reason. The other horse can be corralled into serving the intellect and harnessed in unison with the noble horse—it too has its place. However, what we see in materialist, Enlightenment programs of rationality is an amputated soul, a severing of the intellect from the prescient spirit.[80] In this case, rationalism does not have anything to do with the good, the true, and the beautiful and it cannot contemplate the spirit as a rationality, for it is a rationality beyond the algorithms of mere rationalism. It can then only manipulate matter— or abstract out of the physical an imagined space and time, which is then overlaid on the world, in an attempt to sever itself from transcendence. We lose meaning and purpose and hold to functionality—but even here we impart an implied meaning and purpose, failing to make the severance we wish to make. The horses of spirit and appetite are in this process both consigned to mere feeling—and since feelings are "irrational" we thus lose the charioteer's natural companion horse, the spirit.[81] The love of beauty that the noble horse possesses is lost, and we are left with mere desire or appetite. The prophetic reason that leads the charioteer is lost, and once we have done this, once we have rejected the spirit, we are in the service of mere appetite, reason led by base desire alone.

Notes

1. For Barfield's view, see *Saving the Appearances*. So it is that in order to "'save these appearances' (to use Aristotelian language), one must give an ontological account of how mind is a reality not arising from limited matter, of the kind given by Plato, Aristotle and Aquinas (or even, in the end, Kant)" (Milbank and Pickstock, *Truth in Aquinas*, 74.

2. Aristotle, *New Aristotle Reader*, 192.

3. Garrett, "Kant's Model of the Mind," 1. As we have seen, I have argued against this view of Plato and poetics (i.e., that of complete transcendence with immanence utterly negated), chiefly in chapter 4, by claiming that Plato's warning against *poesis* is that it does not, if not properly produced, revert back to its divine source—the danger lies in the concept that ". . . whereas the liturgical image *does* revert to the highest source . . .

the fictional 'image of an image' is simply cancelled out in favor of an illusory abstract message or private delusory consolation." Art is to be viewed liturgically. If not it sinks into fancy, "mere fiction and spectacle and can become a drug, a distraction, or an incitement to sadistic violence" (Milbank, "Foreword," 16).

4. Garrett, "Kant's Model of the Mind," 1.

5. "Lewis nowhere defines imagination explicitly, and he uses the term in a number of ways: as the image-making power . . . the creative or inventive power . . . the power to make up things . . . the power to create fiction . . . the mysteriousness and adventurousness of romance . . . and imagination in some high Coleridgean sense. The essential concept, however, is that expressed by Tolkien in 'On Fairy Stories': 'The human mind is capable of forming mental images of things not actually present. The faculty of conceiving the images is . . . called Imagination" (Schakel, *Reason and Imagination*, 183).

6. Lewis, *Surprised by Joy*, 15.

7. Ibid.

8. Ibid., 16.

9. Coleridge, *Biographia Literaria*, 304.

10. Ibid.

11. Ibid., 305.

12. Lewis, *They Asked for a Paper*, 125.

13. Barfield, *Owen Barfield on C. S. Lewis*, 103.

14. That is, "If we have really been visited by a revelation from beyond Nature, is it not very strange that an Apocalypse can furnish heaven with nothing more than selections from terrestrial experience (crowns, thrones, and music), that devotion can find no language but that of human lovers, and that a rite whereby Christians enact a mystical union should turn out to be only the old, familiar act of eating and drinking?" (Lewis, *Weight of Glory*, 56).

15. Lewis, *Weight of Glory*, 58–59

16. Ibid., 59.

17. Ibid.

18. Ibid.

19. Ibid., 60.

20. Ibid., 60–61.

21. Ibid., 61.

22. Ibid., 62.

23. Ibid., 63.

24. Ibid., 64. As noted earlier, there is a similarity to be found within Austin Farrar's *The Glass of Vision*, where Farrar maintains that images are the only way in which religious truth can be effectively communicated. For example, through an experience of Christ within the New Testament we can receive special knowledge: knowledge that imparts "an apprehension of divine mysteries, inaccessible to natural reason, reflection, intuition or wit. Christians suppose such mysteries to be communicated to them through the scriptures. In particular, we believe that in the New Testament we can as it were overhear men doing supernatural thinking of a privileged order, with pens in hand" (p. 35).

25. Lewis, *Weight of Glory*, 71.

26. Ibid., 71–72.

27. Ibid., 64.

28. Ibid., 65.

29. Ibid.

30. Ibid.

31. Lewis, *Weight of Glory*, 72.

32. Ibid.

33. Aquinas, *Aquinas's Shorter Summa*, 3.

34. Lewis, *Weight of Glory*, 71.

35. Additionally, David Brown observes that postmodern thought can offer some insights into this process: "In an impressive study of art and architecture in the twentieth century Mark Taylor has argued that the only proper conclusion to be drawn for theology from history is a postmodernist one, that art in our own day is at its most significant when it hints at the transcendent other without ever promising to deliver" (Brown, *Tradition and Imagination*, 368).

36. In *On the Reduction of the Arts to Theology*, Bonaventure begins, "*Every good gift and every perfect gift is from above, coming down from the God of lights*, writes James in the first chapter of his epistle. This text speaks of the source of all illumination; but at the same time, it suggests that there are many lights which flow generously from that fontal source of light" (Bonaventure, *On the Reduction*, 37). The world is bursting full with God's presence and mystery. Bonaventure encourages us to search through the world to find traces of God. Clearly Bonaventure uses the term *art* in a much broader sense than our modern connotations would suggest (i.e., more than merely the "liberal arts"). Bonaventure's project in the *De Reductione* was to retrace all forms of knowledge back to God: "The idea of *reduction* in Bonaventure's world of thought has both a metaphysical and a cognitive significance. As a metaphysical term, the word has to do with the circle of creation as it emanates from God eventually to return to its point of origin. The idea of the return is expressed in the word *reduction* which means literally *leading back* . . . As a cognitive term, the word refers to the way in which the human subject comes to know and understand the realities of the created order in the light of this metaphysical conviction" (ibid., 1).

37. Warnock, *Imagination*, 9.

38. Ibid., 196.

39. Ibid., 209.

40. Lewis, *Letters to Malcolm*, 22.

41. In *Surprised by Joy*, Lewis stated that "Joy itself, considered simply as an event in my own mind, turned out to be of no value at all. All the value lay in that of which Joy was the desiring. And that object, quite clearly, was no state of my own mind or body at all. In a way, I had proved this by elimination. I had tried everything in my own mind and body; as it were, asking myself, 'Is it this you want? Is it this?' Last of all I had asked if Joy itself was what I wanted; and, labeling it 'aesthetic experience,' had pretended I could answer Yes. But that answer too had broken down. Inexorably Joy proclaimed, 'You want—I myself am your want of—something other, outside, not you nor any state of you'" (pp. 220–21). The "aesthetic experience" can only suggest the mystery; it cannot itself be the mystery. The imaginative experience gains its value by participating in the higher life it is suggesting.

42. Brann, *World of Imagination*, 798.

43. Lewis, *Collected Letters*, 2:632.

44. Ford, *Companion to Narnia*, 243. Lewis' expression of this comes in *The Screwtape Letters*. Screwtape, our senior devil, instructs Wormwood, our young tempter, in the ways of the soul and the ways of corrupting it: "Think of your man as a series of concentric circles, his will being the innermost, his intellect coming next, and finally his fantasy. You can hardly hope, at once, to exclude from all the circles everything that smells of the Enemy: but you must keep on shoving all the virtues outward till they are finally located in the circle of fantasy, and all the desirable qualities inward into the Will. It is only in so far as they reach the will and are there embodied in habits that the virtues are really fatal to us" (p. 31). Lewis saw a real danger in the moving of all the virtues from the will out to the imagination—so as to make them mere products of fancy. The Chronicles of Narnia can be seen as an attempt to thwart this process or to reverse it: i.e., by taking the virtues as presented to the imagination and moving them inward through the "habit" and means of story.

45. See especially, Aristotle, *On the Soul* 3.3, in *New Reader*, 199ff.

46. Sallis, *Spacings*, 136. John Sallis gives a succinct summary of Aristotle's theory of imagination. He divides it into six theses: "The first thesis expresses something that is determined by Aristotle's very placing of imagination. . . . Imagination belongs to the soul. . . . More precisely, it is a power or faculty of the soul . . . The second thesis assigns to imagination a place within the soul. . . . Imagination is an intermediate faculty of the soul. The third thesis links this intermediate power of the soul to images. . . . [The] fourth thesis . . . [is that the ability to make images] broaches . . . the character of imagination as power of synthesis. The fifth thesis specifies the relation of imagination to sensation. . . . The process of sensation—sensing or, as one might better say, perception or sense-intuition—is a movement brought about by the actual operation of sensation" (ibid., 135–36).

47. Sallis, *Force of Imagination*, 215.

48. Ibid.

49. Eva Brann also notes, "I nevertheless feel a flat certainty that the inner world of the imagination is not exhausted by retrospective and prospective images—by memories of past perceptions and expectations of future fact. It has space for visible, audible, all-but-tangible images of things that never were and probably never will be seen in mundane time and ordinary space . . . Such durability as these imaginative epiphanies have in our lives is that of recurrence rather than of persistence. But in compensation they convey at each return a coalescence of meaning and appearance that the ever-available external phenomena forever lack. To these all-but-substantial imaginative visions, this book has been one tenacious, tentative approach: They above all shape the imaginative life as a prelude to action, an incitement to reflection, and an intimation of paradise" (Brann, *World of Imagination*, 798).

50. Lewis, *Collected Letters*, 2:438. Lewis recognized, with Barfield, that all diction is poetic. Or, as Tolkien's reversion goes, "'Languages . . . are a disease of mythology'" (Carpenter, *Inklings*, 42).

51. Lewis, *Collected Letters*, 2:445.

52. Ibid., 2:446.

53. Ibid., 2:670–71.

54. "But even if the imagination cannot necessarily tell us what is true, it can at the very least show us the *"real significance and profound implications* of truth" (Anacker,

"Narnia and the Moral Imagination," 132).

55. "The beautiful illusion of the dream worlds, in the creation of which every man is truly an artist, is the prerequisite of all plastic art, as we shall see, and an important part of poetry also. In our dreams we delight in the immediate understanding of figures; all forms speak to us; there is nothing unimportant or superfluous. But even when this dream reality is most intense, we still have, glimmering through it, the sensation that it is *mere appearance*: at least this is my experience, and for its frequency—indeed, normality—I could adduce many proofs, including the sayings of the poets" (Nietzsche, *Basic Writings*, 34).

56. Nietzsche recognized that images were ultimately false chimeras, and that the poets lied too much: "'I heard you say that once before,' answered the disciple; 'and then you added: "But the poets lie too much." Why did you say that the poets lie too much?'.... Yet what did Zarathustra once say to you? That the poets lie too much?—But Zarathustra too is a poet. 'Do you now believe that he spoke the truth? Why do you believe it?'" (Nietzsche, *Thus Spoke Zarathustra*, 149). Furthermore, he understood that he too was a poet: "But granted that someone has said in all seriousness that the poets lie too much: he is right—*we* do lie too much. We know too little and are bad learners: so we have to lie.... But all poets believe this: that he who, lying in the grass or in lonely bowers, pricks up his ears, catches a little of the things that are between heaven and earth.... And especially *above* heaven: for all gods are poets' images, poets' surreptitiousness!... Alas, how weary I am of all the unattainable that is supposed to be reality. Alas, how weary I am of the poets!" (ibid., 149–50).

57. "The Superman is the meaning of the earth. Let your will say: The Superman *shall be* the meaning of the earth!" (ibid., 42).

58. MacIntyre, *Dependent Rational Animals*, 113–14.

59. Shakespeare, *Norton Shakespeare*, 2613.

60. However, a theistic framework is present in Shakespeare's *Macbeth*. As Peter Kreeft notes, "... a theistic frame, or point of view, is present in.... *Macbeth* and is deliberately removed in Faulkner's *The Sound of Fury* (the title refers to Macbeth's great 'Tomorrow' speech). Faulkner shows us what the world and life look like from the point of view of Macbeth himself, a morally insane soul.... But when we read Shakespeare we *judge* Macbeth to be insane from an implicitly higher point of view, which 'frames' the portrait of Macbeth" (Kreeft, *Philosophy of Tolkien*, 24).

61 Interestingly, philosopher Antonio Rosmini wrote—assuming a Platonic origin of ideas— "Words without any meaning whatsoever are merely useless sounds and cannot be used to help forward an argument... But words with a universal meaning, such as common nouns, do not refer to determined individuals, and are therefore either meaningless or indicate universal ideas" (Rosmini, *New Essay*, 1:137).

62. However, we must recognize the truths of nihilism too, for nihilism is right "to the degree [that it notes] reality does exceed every idealization that would seek to domesticate it.... [Furthermore, we] are indeed sedated by the mindless chatter of gossip; call it politics, sport, economics, romance or whatever" (Cunningham, *Genealogy of Nihilism*, 256).

63. Milbank, "Fictioning Things," 1.

64. Lewis, *Christian Reflections*, 84–85.

65. Frye, *Educated Imagination*, 67.

66. Ibid.

67. McFague, *Metaphorical Theology*, 75. Madeleine L'Engle has something very crucial to add to science's need for rediscovering myth and the imagination: "In these strange and difficult years since man has learned to split, though not fathom the dark and dangerous heart of the atom, the attitude towards the language of myth has altered radically. It is the scientists themselves who have shaken our faith in their omnipotence, by their open admission that they have rediscovered how little they know, how few answers they really have. Before they discovered nuclear fission and fusion, before they discovered the terrible fallibility this power revealed to them, many scientists were atheists; we don't need God if everything is explainable—in which case we would not need the language of the imagination and there would be no poets or storytellers. . . . It is the scientists themselves who today are telling us that they cannot tell us everything—even as we walk on the surface of the moon, even as we probe into the strange and further field of genetics. The deepest scientific truths cannot be expressed directly. We hear this from men like Pollard, who has remained a distinguished scientist and has also become a priest. Fred Hoyle is a famous astrophysicist; but when he has an idea that goes beyond present knowledge (something very different from wisdom) or that might upset some tired old pragmatic scientist, he turns to writing fantasy, where he can communicate ideas that are too big, too violent, too brilliant to be rendered directly" (L'Engle, *Glimpses of Grace*, 145–46).

68. Smith, *Forgotten Truth*, 100.

69. Huston Smith notes that the problem might be put this way: "If modern science showed that our senses are false witnesses, postmodern science is showing that the human imagination is comparably defective. It simply was not devised to reflect nature's total gamut . . . imagination has no alternative but to build its scenarios out of photographic frames our senses provide, which frames draw from only a tiny band in matter's varied continuum. It was this that provoked Haldane's famous 'mutterance' that 'the universe is not only queerer than we suppose, but queerer than we *can* suppose.' David Finkelstein's sequel is that respecting nature 'we haven't the capacity to imagine anything crazy enough to stand a chance of being right'" (ibid., 106).

70. This can be seen from a philosophical perspective in Mary Midgley's book *Science and Poetry*, where she argues that the imagination is an essential tool in understanding our humanity and that science utilizes and depends upon imaginative elements. From a popular perspective, this can be seen in the work of Dr. Djoymi Baker. She uses the television show Star Trek as her prime example. She states that Star Trek "Heralded real developments in science and drew on the great classical myths . . ," and she also says that "scientists often dismiss science fiction for getting it wrong. But . . . it can foreshadow or even influence developments in science . . ." (Skatssoon, "Star Trek," 1–2). She also notes that the use of imagination is important as a spring board to new developments: "'Because it's gone on for so many decades ['Star Trek'] has] had a big impact on what people think about space and what might be possible in the future . . . A lot of NASA astronauts cite it as their inspiration; scientists have cited it as their inspiration for new technology'" (Skatssoon, "Star Trek," 2).

71. Sallis, *Spacings*, xv.

72. As a related aside, Walker Percy identified what he called the Delta Phenomenon (or, conversely, the Helen Keller phenomenon). Percy's work in this area can be seen as demonstrating the inherent meaning in words (showing that diction is poetic). Furthermore, it demonstrates that language, as inherently poetic, implicitly references something beyond mere materiality. Following Percy's theory, the nature of language

displays a curious fact: that something more than a simple causal line or chain of events is occurring when we use language. Language cannot simply be reduced to mere materiality. We are referencing an implicit *telos* or meaning that goes beyond the merely phenomenologically given: it moves us beyond pure immanence. The act of naming, of sign making, puts us into a relationship with a larger world.

Percy had the conviction that within a short section of Helen Keller's *The Story of My Life* there contained a great mystery, a secret, and that "if one could fathom it, one could also understand a great deal of what it meant to be *Homo loquens, Homo symbolificus*, man the speaking animal, man the symbol-monger" (Percy, *Message in the Bottle*, 30). On a summer morning in 1887, Helen Keller had her breakthrough into language. Prior to this breakthrough, Helen had learned to respond like the behaviorists predicted: i.e., like a good animal: "When she wanted a piece of cake, she spelled the word in Miss Sullivan's hand and Miss Sullivan fetched her the cake (like the chimp Washoe, who gives hand signals: tickle, banana, etc.) . . ." (ibid., 34–35). What had happened to Helen Keller when she had her breakthrough? Helen received both the sensory message from her hand under the water as well as the signing of Miss Sullivan in her opposite hand. But then what happened in Helen's head? "What dawned on me was that what happened between Helen and Miss Sullivan and water and the word was 'real' enough all right, no matter what Ogden and Richards said, as real as any S-R sequence. . . . but that *what happened could not be drawn with arrows*" (ibid., 37–38). Percy came to the conclusion that this relationship was a nonlinear, nonenergic phenomenon. In other words, it was a phenomenon that could not be explained as a series of energy exchanges or causal relations. There is something peculiar going on here, something that cannot simply be reduced to mere material causal relations. Once Percy stopped drawing arrows, expecting to see an illumination of a causal, energic relation, he saw that he was left with a triangle. He saw that there were certainly at least three elements involved in the event: Helen, the water itself, and the word *water*. The question was, "In what way does one perceive that this 'stuff' is water?? Percy's own breakthrough was the notion that this triangle was absolutely irreducible, that the breakthrough of the Delta Phenomenon could not be drawn or demonstrated through mere causal links or energy exchanges: "Here indeed was nothing less, I suspected, than the ultimate and elemental unit not only of language but of the very condition of the awakening of human intelligence and consciousness . . ." (ibid., 40).

If we compare Percy's Delta Phenomenon with the behaviorists "pseudo triangle" we see that it is not a triangle at all but a simple causal line or chain of events: buzzer-dog-salivation-food. It is a series of energy exchanges. However, in the Delta triangle we see something quite different. For example, if a father points to balloon and tells his young son, "'That's a balloon,' or perhaps just, 'Balloon' . . . Unlike the buzzer-dog-salivation sequence, one runs immediately into difficulty when one tries to locate and specify the Delta elements—balloon (thing), *balloon* (word), boy (organism). . . . The balloon is not the balloon out there. The word *balloon* is not the sound in the air. The boy is not the organism boy. . . . Where, what is the word *balloon*? Show me the word *balloon* as I can show you the sound of the buzzer. Unlike the dog 'understanding' the sound of the buzzer to 'mean' food, the boy does not understand the particular sound *balloon*—which his father makes and which enters his ear—to mean the balloon. . . . [It] is precisely the nature of the boy's breakthrough that he understands his father's utterance as a particular instance of the word *balloon*. Where is the word itself?" (ibid., 42–43). The word *balloon* is not a concrete thing but an instance of a universal rule or law. Furthermore, it cannot be said that what the boy means when he points to the balloon is 'this particular round, red, rubbery and inflated object.' The boy understands this object as a member of a class of inflated objects. The boy himself cannot be understood as an organism "within whose neurons and molecules certain interactions occur which lead to his uttering and the name," but, rather, he is understood as being more than just the site where certain energy exchanges occur (ibid., 43). Something more curious happens: "He couples *balloon* with balloon. But who, what couples? Who, what is the coupler? Do you mean some part of his brain does the coupling? I could not say whether it is his brain which couples, his 'mind,' his 'self,' his 'I'" (ibid., 43). What Percy is willing to admit is that in this sequence two things that were not once connected now are, and for two things unconnected to become connected overtly implies a coupler.

73. For example, "The German chemist Kekule found the solution to a difficult chemical problem that way. He was very tired when he slipped into a day-dream. The image of a snake swallowing his tail came to him—and that provided the clue to the structure of the benzene molecule, which is a ring, rather than a chain, of atoms. The German writer Goethe had been experiencing great difficulty organizing a large mass of material for one of his works when he learned of the tragic suicide of a close friend. At that very instant, the plan for organizing his material occurred to him in detail. The English writer Samuel Taylor Coleridge . . . awoke from a dream with 200–300 lines of a new and complex poem clearly in mind" (Ruggiero, *Beyond Feelings*, 15). Something else that Ruggiero notes from these types of intuitive perceptions is that intuition seems to favor the trained mind, the reasoned mind—i.e., one is more likely to receive this type of knowledge if one is a well reasoned, critical thinker: Or as "[F]rench chemist Louis Pastueur once said, 'Chance favors the prepared mind'" (ibid., 144).

74. See Percy, *Message in the Bottle*, 34–35.

75. Lewis, *Miracles*, 20. A comparison can be made here with Hume in his *An Enquiry Concerning Human Understanding*, section 9, "Of the Reason of Animals," especially where Hume points out that "the animal infers some fact beyond what immediately strikes his senses; and that this inference is altogether founded on past experience, while the creature expects from the present object the same consequences, which it has always found in its observation to result from similar objects . . . It is impossible, that this inference of the animal can be found on any process of argument or reasoning . . ." (Hume, *Empiricists*, 384).

76. Lewis, *Miracles*, 19–20.

77. Plato, *Complete Works*, 524.

78. Ibid., 531.

79. Ibid.

80. As Pope Benedict XVI notes, the philosophies inspired by Enlightenment rationalism are often considered to be the last word of reason—indeed, the last word of reason which is common to all human beings. However, they are "based on a self-limitation," which is a self-aggrandizement of humankind: "The result is that man no longer accepts any moral authority apart from his own calculations"; and, although containing important elements of truth, is still "based on a self-limitation of reason that is typical of one determined cultural situation, that of the modern West. . . . Although they may seem totally rational, they are not in fact the voice of reason. They, too, have their cultural ties. . . . Above all, however, we must affirm that this Enlightenment philosophy, with its related culture, is incomplete. It consciously cuts off its own historical roots, depriving itself of the powerful sources from which it sprang. It detaches itself

from what we might call the basic memory of mankind, without which reason loses its orientation, for now the guiding principle is that man's capability determines what he does. If you know how to do something, then you are also permitted to do it . . ." (Benedict XVI, *Christianity and the Crisis of Cultures*, 40–41).

81. Anthony Esolen also notes something similar: "Many of you will recall [Plato's] famous metaphor in the *Phaedrus*, where he compares the human being to a charioteer whose rig is driven by a pair of horses, one of them noble and high spirited, the other tending to be fiery and wayward. The charioteer represents the reason or intellect; the noble horse, *thymos*; the wayward horse, appetite. It's a brilliant metaphor, capturing the truth that without the passions we literally get nowhere. It also distinguishes passion from passion, inasmuch as there is something about the noble horse that is friendly to reason—in a sense it aspires to reason. It is wrong to call it simply irrational. But here is what modern man has done, in brief. The thoughts are by no means original to me—you can find them in Alasdair MacIntyre, or in John Paul II, or in Benedict XVI, or in Dostoyevsky: 1. 'Reason' is shouldered off the chariot. A small subset of reason—an amputated charioteer—is put in reason's place. What is now called 'reason' can no longer discuss, rationally, the nature of the good or the beautiful. It can do two things: it can spin out sentences of symbolic logic or mathematics, which, despite their complexity, it asserts are only tautological, without any real connection to the world of stars and mangrove trees and bicycles. Or it can manipulate matter according to the physical laws it imputes to the world, inferring them (as things that happen to 'work,' rather than as things that really do exist in themselves) from empirical observations and mathematical analysis. This 'reason' can thus tell you how to build a Gothic cathedral, but cannot even begin to tell you why you would want to. 2. All other discussion of the good, the beautiful, and the true (except for the sorts of truths mentioned above) is relegated to the status of 'feeling.' . . . 3. All feelings are regarded as irrational. So then, not only is most of the function of Plato's charioteer assigned to the horses, but the good horse, the horse representing the rationality-aspiring passion for beauty, is eliminated entirely, leaving us with nothing but appetite. And there it is, appetite in the service of an amputated reason . . ." (Esolen, Mere Comments).

Bibliography

Works by C. S. Lewis

The Abolition of Man. New York: Macmillan, 1947.
Christian Reflections. Grand Rapids: Eerdmans, 1967. Reprinted, 1996.
The Chronicles of Narnia. New York: HarperCollins, 2001.
Collected Letters of C. S. Lewis. Edited by Walter Hooper. 3 vols. New York: HarperCollins, 2004.
"Dates of C. S. Lewis Letters: 23 Dec. 1950, Magdalen College, Oxford." In *A Severe Mercy*, by Sheldon Vanauken, 91–93. New York: Harper & Row, 1977.
"*De Descriptione Temporum*: Inaugural Lecture from The Chair of Mediaeval and Renaissance Literature at Cambridge University, 1954." In *They Asked for a Paper; Papers and Addresses*, 9–25. London: G. Bles, 1962. Online: http://www.eng.uc.edu/~dwschae/temporum.html.
The Discarded Image: An Introduction to Medieval and Renaissance Literature. New York: Cambridge University Press, 1964.
"On Stories." In *Essays Presented to Charles Williams*, 90–105. Grand Rapids: Eerdmans, 1977.
The Essential C. S. Lewis. Edited by Lyle W. Dorsett. New York: Touchstone, 1996.
An Experiment in Criticism. Cambridge: Cambridge University Press, 1995.
The Four Loves. New York: Harcourt Brace Jovanovich, 1988.
George MacDonald: An Anthology. New York: Macmillan, 1947.
God in the Dock: Essays on Theology and Ethics. Grand Rapids: Eerdmans, 1970.
A Grief Observed. New York: HarperCollins, 1994.
The Great Divorce. London: HarperCollins, 1977.
The Horse and His Boy. New York: HarperCollins, 2002.
The Last Battle. New York: HarperCollins, 2002.
Letters of C. S. Lewis. Edited by W. H. Lewis. New York: Harcourt Brace, 1966.
Letters of C. S. Lewis. Edited by Walter Hooper. New York: Harcourt Brace, 1993.
The Letters of C. S. Lewis to Arthur Greeves. Edited by Walter Hooper. New York: Collier, Macmillan, 1986.
Letters to Children. Edited by Lyle W. Dorsett and Marjorie Lamp Mead. New York: Touchstone, 1995.

Letters to Malcolm. New York: Harcourt Brace, 1992.
The Lion, the Witch, and the Wardrobe. New York: Macmillan, 1970.
The Lion, the Witch and the Wardrobe. New York: HarperCollins, 2002.
The Magician's Nephew. New York: HarperCollins, 2002.
Mere Christianity. New York: Macmillan, 1952.
Miracles: A Preliminary Study. New York: Macmillan, 1960.
Of Other Worlds: Essays and Stories. Edited by Walter Hooper. New York: Harcourt Brace, 1966.
Perelandra. New York: Scribner, 2003.
The Personal Heresy. London: Oxford University Press, 1965.
The Pilgrim's Regress: An Allegorical Apology for Christianity, Reason, and Romanticism. Grand Rapids: Eerdmans, 1981.
Present Concerns. Edited by Walter Hooper. New York: Harcourt Brace Jovanovich, 1986.
Prince Caspian: The Return to Narnia. New York: HarperCollins, 2002.
The Problem of Pain. New York: Macmillan, 1962.
Reflections on the Psalms. New York: Harcourt Brace, 1986.
The Screwtape Letters. New York: Macmillan, 1960.
The Silver Chair. New York: HarperCollins, 2002.
Surprised by Joy: The Shape of My Early Life. New York: Harcourt Brace, 1955.
They Asked for a Paper; Papers and Addresses. London: Bles, 1962.
The Voyage of the Dawn Treader. New York: HarperCollins, 2002.
The Weight of Glory, and Other Addresses. New York: Collier, 1949.
The World's Last Night, and Other Essays. New York: Harcourt Brace, 1960.

Other Works

Abel, Stephanie Ann. "Metaphor and Meaning: The Problem of Translation in C. S. Lewis's Ransom Trilogy." MA thesis, University of Oklahoma, 1992.
Acree, Carol. "Abstraction in Language." PhD diss., Auburn University, 1984.
Adey, Lionel. *C. S. Lewis's "Great War" with Owen Barfield*. Victoria, BC: University of Victoria, 1978.
Aertsen, Jan A. "Aquinas's Philosophy in Its Historical Setting." In *The Cambridge Companion to Aquinas*, edited by Norman Kretzmann and Eleonore Stump, 12–37. New York: Cambridge University Press, 1993.
Anacker, Gayne J. "Narnia and the Moral Imagination." In *The Chronicles of Narnia and Philosophy: The Lion, the Witch, and the Worldview*, edited by Gregory Bassham and Jerry L. Walls, 130–42. Popular Culture and Philosophy 15. Chicago: Open Court, 2005.
Anscombe, G. E. M. *Metaphysics and the Philosophy of Mind*. Oxford: Blackwell, 1981.
———. "Modern Moral Philosophy." *Philosophy* 33.124 (January 1958). Online: www.philosophy.uncc.edu/mleldrid/SzCMT/mmp.html.
Anslem. *The Major Works*. New York: Oxford University Press, 1998.
Appasamy, A. J. *Sundar Singh, a Biography*. Cambridge: Lutterworth, 2002.
Aquinas, Thomas. *Aquinas's Shorter Summa: St. Thomas Aquinas's Own Concise Version of His Summa Theologica*. Translated by Cyril Vollert, SJ. Manchester, NH: Sophia Institute Press, 2002.
———. *Catechism of the Catholic Church, with Modifications from the Editio Typica*. New York: Image/Doubleday, 1994.

———. *Selected Writings*. Edited and translated by Ralph McInerny. New York: Penguin, 1998.

———. *Summa Theologiae*, vol. 1: *The Existence of God, Part One: Questions 1–13*. Edited by Thomas Gilby, OP. New York: Image, 1969.

———. *The Summa Theologiae of Saint Thomas Aquinas: Latin-English Edition*, vol. 1: *Prima Pars, Q. 1–64*. Scotts Valley, CA: CreateSpace for NOVANTIQUA, 2008.

———. *The Summa Theologiae of Saint Thomas Aquinas: Latin-English Edition*, vol. 2: *Prima Pars, Q. 65–119*. Scotts Valley, CA: CreateSpace for NOVANTIQUA, 2008.

Aristotle. *A New Aristotle Reader*. Edited by J. L. Ackrill. Princeton, NJ: Princeton University Press, 1987.

———. *The Nicomachean Ethics*. Translated by J. A. K. Thomson. New York: Penguin, 2004.

Athanasius. *On the Incarnation of the Word*. Grand Rapids: Christian Classics Ethereal Library. Online: http://www.ccel.org/ccel/athanasius/incarnation.html.

Augustine. *Augustine: Earlier Writings*. Translated and edited by J. H. S. Burleigh. Philadelphia: Westminster, 1979.

———. *Augustine: Later Works*. Edited by John Burnaby. Philadelphia: Westminster, 1980.

———. *On Christian Teaching*. Translation by R. P. H. Green. Oxford: Oxford University Press, 1999.

———. *The City of God*. Translated by Henry Bettenson. London: Penguin, 2003.

———. *Confessions*. Translation by Henry Chadwick. Oxford: Oxford University Press, 1998.

———. *Enchiridion on Faith, Hope, and Love*. Washington, DC: Regnery, 1996.

———. *Sermons on the Liturgical Seasons*. Translated by Mary Sarah Muldowney, edited by Roy Joseph Deferrari. The Fathers of the Church, a New Translation 38. New York: Fathers of the Church, 1959.

———. *Soliloquies: Augustine's Interior Dialogue*. Translated by Kim Paffenroth, edited by John E. Rotelle, OSA. Hyde Park, NY: New City, 2000.

Avis, Paul D. *God and the Creative Imagination: Metaphor, Symbol, and Myth in Religion and Theology*. New York: Routledge, 1999.

Barfield, Owen. "On C. S. Lewis and *The Great Divorce*." *Mythprint*, January 13, 1976, 2.

———. *Owen Barfield on C. S. Lewis*. Edited by G. B. Tennyson. Middletown, CT: Wesleyan University Press, 1989.

———. *Poetic Diction: A Study in Meaning*. Middletown, CT: Wesleyan University Press, 1973.

———. *Saving the Appearances: A Study in Idolatry*. 2nd ed. Middletown, CT: Wesleyan University Press, 1988.

Bassham, Gregory. "Some Dogs Go to Heaven." In *The Chronicles of Narnia and Philosophy: The Lion, the Witch, and the Worldview*, edited by Gregory Bassham and Jerry L. Walls, 273–85. Popular Culture and Philosophy 15. Chicago: Open Court, 2005.

Beattie, Mary Josephine. "The Humane Medievalist: A Study of C. S. Lewis' Criticism of Medieval Literature." PhD diss., University of Pittsburgh, 1967.

Bell, James, and Anthony Palmer Dawson, editors. *From the Library of C. S. Lewis: Selections from Writers Who Influenced His Spiritual Journey*. Colorado Springs, CO: WaterBrook, 2004.

Bell, James S. "'Parabolic Gestures': The Mythopoic Art of C. S. Lewis." MA thesis, Univer-sity College Dublin, 1977.

Bellah, Mike. "A Celebration of Joy: Christian Romanticism in the Chronicles of Narnia." MA diss., Texas A & M University, 1995.
Benedict XVI, Pope. *Christianity and the Crisis of Cultures*. San Francisco: Ignatius, 2006.
Benson, Iain T. "C. S. Lewis and Catholicism." Paper presented to the Oxford University C. S. Lewis Society, Pusey House, Oxford, May 11, 2001. Online: http://web.archive.org/web/20030604071945/http://ic.net/~erasmus/RAZ496.HTM.
Bevan, Edwyn. *Symbolism and Belief: The Gifford Lectures, 1933–34*. London: Collins, 1962.
Beversluis, John. *C. S. Lewis and the Search for Rational Religion*. Grand Rapids: Eerdmans, 1985.
Blomberg, Craig. *The Historical Reliability of the Gospels*. Downers Grove, IL: InterVarsity, 1987.
Boehner, Philotheus. "Introduction." In *Philosophical Writings: A Selection*, by William of Ockham, translated by Philotheus Boehner. New York: Bobbs-Merrill, 1964.
Boethius. *The Consolation of Philosophy*. Translated by Richard H. Green. Mineola, NY: Dover, 2002.
Boles, Maria D. "Everything Began with Images: A Study of the Imagination and Redemption in George MacDonald's Phantastes and C. S. Lewis's 'The Lion, the Witch and the Wardrobe.'" MA thesis, East Carolina University, 2003.
Bonaventure. *St. Bonaventure's "On the Reduction of the Arts to Theology"*. Translated by Zachary Hayes. Works of St. Bonaventure 1. Saint Bonaventure, NY: Franciscan Institute, St. Bonaventure University, 1996.
———. *Itinerarium mentis in Deum: Latin Text from the Quaracchi Edition*? Translated by Zachary Hayes, commentary by Philotheus Boehner. Works of St. Bonaventure 2. St. Bonaventure, NY: Franciscan Institute, St. Bonaventure University, 2002.
Borg, Marcus. *The God We Never Knew: Beyond Dogmatic Religion to a More Authentic Contemporary Faith*. San Francisco: HarperSanFrancisco, 1997.
Brann, Eva. *The World of Imagination: Sum and Substance*. Lanham, MD: Rowman & Littlefield, 1991.
Brewer, Lee Allan. "The Anthropology of Choice: A Critical Analysis and Comparison of the Doctrine of Man in the Theologies of Karl Barth and C. S. Lewis." PhD diss., Southwestern Baptist Theological Seminary, 1989.
Brightman, Edgar Sheffield, editor. *Personalism in Theology: A Symposium in Honor of Albert Cornelius Knudson, by Associates and Former Students*. Boston: Boston University Press, 1943.
Brown, David. *Discipleship and Imagination: Christian Tradition and Truth*. New York: Oxford University Press, 2000.
———. *Tradition and Imagination: Revelation and Change*. New York: Oxford University Press, 1999.
Bryant, David. *Faith and the Play of Imagination: On the Role of Imagination in Religion*. Studies in American Biblical Hermeneutics 5. Macon, GA: Mercer, 1989.
Bultmann, Rudolf. *Jesus and the Word*. Translated by L. P. Smith and E. H. Lantero. New York: Scribner, 1958.
———. "New Testament and Mythology." In *Kerygma and Myth: A Theological Debate*, vol. 1, edited by H. W. Bartsch. London: SPCK, 1953.
———. *Primitive Christianity in Its Contemporary Setting*. New York: World, 1956.
Burton, Scott R., and Jerry L. Walls. *C. S. Lewis and Francis Schaeffer: Lessons for a New Century from the Most Influential Apologists of Our Time*. Downers Grove, IL: InterVarsity, 1998.

Caldecott, Stratford. "Speaking the Truths Only the Imagination May Grasp." *Touchstone: A Journal of Mere Christianity*, September/October 1998, 1–9.

Candler, Peter. *Theology, Rhetoric, Manuduction, or Reading Scripture Together on the Path to God*. Grand Rapids: Eerdmans, 2006.

Carnell, Corbin Scott. "The Dialectic of Desire: C. S. Lewis' Interpretation of Sehnsucht." PhD diss., University of Florida, 1960.

———. "The Meaning of Masculine and Feminine in the Work of C. S. Lewis." *Modern British Literature* 2 (1977) 153–59.

Carpenter, Humphrey. *The Inklings: C. S. Lewis, J. R. R. Tolkien, Charles Williams and Their Friends*. London: HarperCollins, 1997.

Cavanaugh, William T. *Theopolitical Imagination: Discovering the Liturgy as a Political Act in an Age of Global Consumerism*. New York: T. & T. Clark, 2002.

Chadwick, Henry. "Introduction" and commentary in *Confessions* by Augustine, xiv–xxvi. New York: Oxford University Press, 1998.

Chambliss, J. J. *Imagination and Reason in Plato, Aristotle, Vico, Rousseau and Keats: An Essay on the Philosophy of Experience*. The Hague: Nijhoff, 1974.

Chesterton, G. K. *The Everlasting Man*. New York: Image, 1955.

———. *Orthodoxy*. New York: Image, 1959.

Chivvis, John Carlton. "C. S. Lewis, Jesus, and Plato: Rhetorical Strategies for the Defense of Christianity." MA diss., Texas A & M University, 1996.

Christensen, Michael J. *C. S. Lewis on Scripture*. Nashville: Abingdon, 1989.

Clark, David K. "Narrative Theology and Apologetics." *Journal of the Evangelical Theological Society* 36 (1993) 499–515.

Clark, Susan Ann. "Myth as a Conveyor of Theological Truth in the Work of C. S. Lewis." MA thesis, Wake Forest University, 1992.

Clement of Alexandria. "Philosophy the Handmaid of Theology." In *Ante-Nicene Fathers* 2.6.4.1.5. Online: http://www.ccel.org/ccel/schaff/anf02.vi.iv.i.v.html.

Cohen, Carl. "The Case for the Use of Animals in Biomedical Research." In *Environmental Ethics: Concepts, Policy, Theory*, edited by Joseph DesJardins, 301–7. Mountain View, CA: Mayfield, 1999.

Cohen, Martin. *101 Ethical Dilemmas*. New York: Routledge, 2003.

Coleridge, Samuel Taylor. *Biographia Literaria*. Edited by James Engell and W. Jackson Bate. The Collected Works of Samuel Taylor Coleridge 7. Princeton: Princeton University Press, 1983.

Collings, Michael. "Of Lions and Lamp-Posts: C. S. Lewis' *The Lion, the Witch, and the Wardrobe* as response to Olaf Stapledon's *Sirius*." *Christianity and Literature* 32.4 (1983) 33–38.

Como, James T., editor. *C. S. Lewis at the Breakfast Table and Other Reminiscences*. New York: Harcourt Brace Jovanovich, 1992.

Courtney, Charles Rusell. "The Religious Philosophy of C. S. Lewis." MA thesis, University of Arizona, 1955.

Cowie, John W. "The Poetic Theory of C. S. Lewis." MA thesis, University of Dallas, 1971.

Cox, John D. "Epistemological Release in *The Silver Chair*." In *The Longing for a Form: Essays on the Fiction of C. S. Lewis*, edited by Peter J. Schakel, 159–68. Grand Rapids: Baker, 1979.

Cuddon, J. A. *Dictionary of Literary Terms and Literary Theory*. New York: Penguin, 1991.

Cunningham, Conor. *Genealogy of Nihilism*. New York: Routledge, 2002.

Cunningham, Richard B. *C. S. Lewis: Defender of the Faith*. Philadelphia: Westminster, 1967.
D'Costa, Gavin. "Karl Rahner's Anonymous Christian—A Reappraisal." *Modern Theology* 1.2 (1985) 131–48.
Deinsen, D. R. "Paganism and C. S. Lewis: Rethinking Christian Attitudes." Online: http://franciscan-anglican.com/PaganismLewis.htm.
Descartes, René. *Descartes: Key Philosophical Writings*. Hertfordshire, UK: Wordsworth, 1997.
Detweiler, Robert. *Religion and Literature*. Louisville: Westminster John Knox, 2000.
DeWolf, L. Harold. *The Case for Theology in Liberal Perspective*. Philadelphia: Westminster, 1959.
Donaldson, Mara Elizabeth. "Narratives of Transformation: C. S. Lewis's *Till We Have Faces* and Paul Ricoeur's *Theory of Metaphor*." PhD diss., Emory University, 1984.
Dorrien, Gary. "The 'Postmodern' Barth? The Word of God as True Myth." *The Christian Century*, April 2, 1997, 338–42.
Downing, David C. *Into the Wardrobe: C. S. Lewis and the Narnia Chronicles*. San Francisco: Jossey-Bass, 2005.
Duncan, John Ryan. *The Magic Never Ends: The Life and Work of C. S. Lewis*. Nashville: W Pub., 2001.
Dunn, Peter W. "The Question of the Validity of Miracles in *The City of God*." Online: http://www3.sympatico.ca/pwdunn/Augustine.pdf.
Duriez, Colin. *The C. S. Lewis Chronicles*. New York: BlueBridge, 2005.
———. *A Field Guide to Narnia*. Downers Grove, IL: InterVarsity, 2004.
Duriez, Colin, and David Porter. *The Inklings Handbook*. St. Louis: Chalice, 2001.
Easterbrook, Gregg. "In Defense of C. S. Lewis." *The Atlantic Monthly* 288.3 (2001) 46.
Eaton, Jeffrey C. "The Problem of Miracles and the Paradox of Double Agency." *Modern Theology* 1 (1985) 211–12.
Eco, Umberto. *The Name of the Rose*. Translated by William Weaver. New York: Harcourt Brace, 1983.
Edwards, Michael. "C. S. Lewis: Imagining Heaven." *Literature and Theology* 6.2 (1992) 107–24.
Eliot, Barklie W. "God as Storyteller: C. S. Lewis's Concept of Romance." MA thesis, Florida Atlantic University, 1987.
Engell, James. *The Creative Imagination: Enlightenment to Romanticism*. Cambridge: Harvard University Press, 1981.
Esau, Debra Laurie. "Nectar and Ambrosia for Tea: The Bringing Home of Myth in C. S. Lewis." MA thesis, University of British Columbia, 1984.
Esolen, Anthony. Mere Comments (blog of *Touchstone* editors). June 25, 2007. Online: http://merecomments.typepad.com/merecomments/2007/06/my-earlier-post.html.
Farrer, Austin. "An English Appreciation by Austin Farrer." In *Kerygma and Myth by Rudolf Bultmann and Five Critics*. London: SPCK, 1953. Online: http://www.religion-online.org/showchapter.asp?title=431&C=300.
———. *Faith and Speculation: An Essay in Philosophical Theology*. London: Black, 1967.
———. *The Glass of Vision*. London: Dacre Westminster, 1958.
———. *God Is Not Dead*. New York: Morehouse-Barlow, 1966.
———. *A Rebirth of Images*. 1949. Reprinted, Eugene, OR: Wipf & Stock, 2006.
Ferngren, Gary and Ronald L. Numbers. "C. S. Lewis on Creation and Evolution: The Acworth Letters, 1944–1960." *Perspectives on Science and Christian Faith* 48.1 (1996) 28–33.

Fesmire, Steven. *John Dewey and Moral Imagination: Pragmatism in Ethics*. Bloomington: Indiana University Press, 2003.
Filmer-Davies, Kathleen. "The Polemic Image: The Role of Metaphor and Symbol in the Rhetoric of the Fiction of C. S. Lewis." PhD diss., University of Queensland, 1985.
Forbes, Cheryl. "A Landscape for Imagination: A Study of the Narnia Tales of C. S. Lewis." MA thesis, University of Maryland, 1974.
Ford, Paul F. *Companion to Narnia*. New York: HarperSanFrancisco, 1994.
———. *Companion to Narnia*. Rev. ed. New York: HarperSanFrancisco, 2005.
———. "The Life of the World to Come in the Writings of C. S. Lewis." MA thesis, St. John's Seminary, 1974.
Fowl, Stephen E., and L. Gregory Jones. *Reading in Communion: Scripture and Ethics in Christian Life*. 1991. Reprinted, Eugene, OR: Wipf & Stock, 1998.
Fredrick, Candice, and Sam MacBride. *Women among the Inklings: Gender, C. S. Lewis, J. R. R. Tolkien, and Charles Williams*. Contributions in Women's Studies. Westport, CT: Greenwood, 2001.
Frei, Hans W. *The Eclipse of Biblical Narrative*. New Haven: Yale University Press, 1974.
———. *The Identity of Jesus Christ*. Philadelphia: Fortress, 1975.
———. *Theology and Narrative: Selected Essays*. Edited by George Hunsinger and William C. Placher. Oxford University Press, 1993.
———. *Types of Christian Theology*. Edited by George Hunsinger and William C. Placher. Yale University Press, 1994.
Freshwater, Mark Edwards. "C. S. Lewis and the Quest for the Historical Jesus." PhD diss., Florida State University, 1985.
Freud, Sigmund. *Civilization and Its Discontents*. Edited by James Strachey. New York: Norton, 1961.
———. *The Future of an Illusion*. Translated by W. D. Robson-Scott. New York: Liveright, 1953.
Fry, Karin. "No Longer a Friend: Gender in Narnia." In *The Chronicles of Narnia and Philosophy: The Lion, the Witch, and the Worldview*, edited by Gregory Bassham and Jerry L. Walls, 155–66. Popular Culture and Philosophy 15. Chicago: Open Court, 2005.
Frye, Northrop. *The Educated Imagination*. Toronto: Anansi, 1993.
———. *The Great Code: The Bible and Literature*. New York: Harcourt, 1982.
———. *Words with Power: Being Second Study of the Bible and Literature*. New York: Harcourt Brace Jovanovich, 1990.
Gaarder, Jostein. *Sophie's World: A Novel about the History of Philosophy*. New York: Berkley, 1996.
Gardner, Helen. *In Defence of the Imagination*. Cambridge: Harvard University Press, 1982.
Garrett, James M. "Kant's Model of the Mind." Online: http://www.calstatela.edu/faculty/jgarret/560/notes-kant.pdf.
Geivett, R. Douglas, and Gary R. Habermas. *In Defense of Miracles: A Comprehensive Case for God's Action in History*. Downers Grove, IL: InterVarsity, 1997.
George, Phyllis Burske. "Myth in the Narnia Chronicles of C. S. Lewis." MA thesis, California State University, San Francisco, 1973.
Gibb, Joycelyn, editor. *Light on C. S. Lewis*. New York: Harcourt Brace Jovanovich, 1976.
Gibson, Evan K. *C. S. Lewis, Spinner of Tales: A Guide to His Fiction*. Washington, DC: Christian University Press, 1980.

Gilkey, Langdon B. "Ordering the Soul: Augustine's Manifold Legacy." *The Christian Century*, April 27, 1988, 426–30.

———. "A Theology in Process: Schubert Ogden's Developing Theology." *Interpretation* 21 (1967) 449.

Gillespie, Steven John. "Narrated Thought and Sequential Argument: A Comparison of Two Texts by C. S. Lewis." PhD diss., University of Texas at Arlington, 1992.

Gilson, Etienne. *The Christian Philosophy of Saint Augustine*. Translated by L. E. M. Lynch. New York: Random House, 1960.

———. *The Philosophy of St. Thomas*. Cambridge, UK: Heffer, 1977.

Glaspey, Terry W. "Guardians of the Permanent Things: Tradition, Religion, Myth and Cultural Criticism in the Work of T. S. Eliot and C. S. Lewis." MA thesis, University of Oregon, 1991.

Glenny, Jacqueline. *C. S. Lewis's Cambridge: A Walking Tour Guide*. Cambridge: Christian Heritage, 2003.

Glover, Donald E. *C. S. Lewis: The Art of Enchantment*. Athens: Ohio University Press, 1981.

Glyer, Diana Pavlac. *The Company They Keep: C. S. Lewis and J. R. R. Tolkien as Writers in Community*. Kent, OH: Kent State University Press, 2008.

Gousmett, Chris. "Miracles: Signs of the Kingdom Coming." Online: http://www.freewebs.com/reformational/Miralces as signs of the kingdom.pdf.

Grace, Kevin Michael. "Praising God in Myth." *Newsmagazine* 29.1 (2002) 33–34.

Grandin, Temple, and Catherine Johnson. *Animals in Translation*. New York: Harcourt, 2005.

Greek, David J. "Inklings of Spiritual Imagination: C. S. Lewis, J. R. R. Tolkien, and Robert Jordan; Theological Inquiry in Contemporary Fantasy and Fairy Tale." MA thesis, Stetson University, 1994.

Greeley, Andrew. *The Catholic Imagination*. Los Angeles: University of California Press, 2000.

Green, Garrett. *Imagining God: Theology and the Religious Imagination*. San Francisco: Harper & Row, 1989.

———. *Theology, Hermeneutics, and Imagination: The Crisis of Interpretation at the End of Modernity*. New York: Cambridge University Press, 2000.

Green, Roger Lancelyn. *C. S. Lewis*. London: Bodley Head, 1963.

Greene, Brian. *The Elegant Universe: Superstrings, Hidden Dimensions, and the Quest for the Ultimate Theory*. New York: Vintage, 2000.

Gregory, Eloise Cheney. "C. S. Lewis: Fantasy as an Illumination of Reality." MA diss., University of the Pacific, 1967.

Gregory of Nyssa. "Oration on the Deity of the Son and the Holy Spirit." In *Patrologia Graeca* 46, 554–76. Paris: Garnier Fratras, 1857–66.

Gresham, Douglas. *Jack's Life: The Story of C. S. Lewis*. Nashville: Broadman & Holman, 2005.

Griffith, Jean D. "Morality and Faith in Fantasy: Exploring the Lion and Harry." MA diss., University of North Carolina at Wilmington, 2005.

Haigh, John D. "The Fiction of C. S. Lewis." PhD diss., University of Leeds, 1962.

Hammond, Guy B. "The Primacy of Ethics: Relationality in Buber, Tillich, and Levinas." *Bulletin of the North American Paul Tillich Society* 30.3 (2004) 24–30.

Hancock, Cassandra N. "Immanence and Transcendence in the Chronicles of Narnia." MA thesis, Florida Atlantic University, 1977.

Hannay, Margaret. "'Surprised by Joy': C. S. Lewis' Changing Attitudes Toward Women." *Mythlore: A Journal of Tolkien, C. S. Lewis, and Charles Williams Studies.* 4.1 (1976) 15–20.

Happ, Edward Gordan. "A Commentary on C. S. Lewis' 'The Four Loves' from the Perspective of His Doctrine of Transposition." BA thesis, Drew University, 1975.

Harrison, Jennifer P. "'And a Child Shall Lead Them': C. S. Lewis' Mythopoeic Art in the Chronicles of Narnia. MA thesis, Georgia State University, 1994.

Hart, Dabney Adams. "C. S. Lewis's Defense of Poesie." PhD diss., University of Wisconsin, 1959.

Hartt, Julian Norris. *Theological Method and Imagination.* New York: Seabury, 1977.

Harwood, A. C. "The Recovery of Man in Childhood." In *From the Library of C. S. Lewis: Selections from Writers Who Influenced His Spiritual Journey*, edited by James Stuart Bell, 301. Colorado Springs, CO: WaterBrook, 2004.

Hasker, William. *The Emergent Self.* Ithaca, NY: Cornell University Press, 1999.

———. *Metaphysics.* Downer's Grove, IL: InterVarsity, 1983.

———. "The Transcendental Refutation of Derterminism." *Southern Journal of Philosophy* 11 (1973) 175–83.

Hauerwas, Stanley. *The Hauerwas Reader.* Edited by John Berkman and Michael Cartwright. Durham, NC: Duke University Press, 2001.

Hauerwas, Stanley, and L. Gregory Jones, editors. *Why Narrative?: Readings in Narrative Theology.* 1989. Reprinted, Eugene, OR: Wipf and Stock, 1997.

Haugen, John T. *C. S.* "Lewis's Trilogy: Models, Modern and Medieval." MA diss., St. Cloud State University, 1979.

Hazlerig, James Alvin. "Recovering the Discarded Image: The Function of Medievalism in Two Cycles by C. S. Lewis." MA thesis, Stephen F. Austin State University, 1992.

Hemming, Terry E. "An Ignored Option: C. S. Lewis's Contribution toward an Alternative to the Matthew Arnold-F. R. Leavis View of English Studies and Its Relevance for a Christian Literary Theory." MA thesis, Calvin College, 1984.

Herndon, Charles A. "Understanding C. S. Lewis: The Medieval Model as Foundation and Eschatology as Mythical Form." MTS thesis, Samford University, 2001.

Hibbs, Thomas. "Introduction." In *Enchiridion on Faith, Hope, and Love*, by Augustine. Washington, DC: Regnery, 1996.

Hick, John. *The Fifth Dimension: An Exploration of the Spiritual Realm.* Oxford: Oneworld, 1999.

Hilder, Monika Barbara. "Educating the Moral Imagination: The Fantasy Literature of George MacDonald, C. S. Lewis, and Madeleine L'Engle." PhD diss., Simon Fraser University, 2006.

Hillegas, Mark R., editor. *Shadows of Imagination: The Fantasies of C. S. Lewis, J. R. R. Tolkien, and Charles Williams.* Carbondale: Southern Illinois University Press, 1970.

Hinten, Marvin D. *The Keys to the Chronicles: Unlocking the Symbols of C. S. Lewis's Narnia.* Nashville: Broadman & Holman, 2005.

Hirshberg, Jeffrey Alan. "C. S. Lewis: The Integrity of a Literary Mind." MA thesis, Bucknell University, 1971.

Hoey, Mary Amy. "An Applied Linguistic Analysis of the Prose Style of C. S. Lewis." PhD diss., University of Connecticut, 1965.

Hollwitz, John C. "The Mythopoeic Art of C. S. Lewis." PhD diss., Northwestern University, 1980.

Holub, Robert C. *Crossing Boarders: Reception Theory, Poststructuralism, Deconstruction.* Madison: University of Wisconsin Press, 1992.

———. *Reception Theory: A Critical Introduction.* New York: Methuen, 1984.

Hooper, Walter. *C. S. Lewis: A Complete Guide to His Life and Works.* New York: HarperCollins, 1996.

———. "Narnia: The Author, the Critics, and the Tale." In *The Longing for a Form: Essays on the Fiction of C. S. Lewis,* edited by Peter J. Schakel, 105–18. Grand Rapids: Baker, 1979.

———. *Past Watchful Dragons: The Narnian Chronicles of C. S. Lewis.* New York: Collier, 1979.

Hope, Jonathan. *The Authorship of Shakespeare's Plays: A Socio-Linguistic Study.* Cambridge: Cambridge University Press, 1994.

Houtman, Marcia K. "C. S. Lewis's Interplanetary Trilogy: 'An Imaginative Realization of Doctrine.'" MA thesis, South Dakota State University, 1978.

Howard, Thomas. *The Achievement of C. S. Lewis.* Wheaton, IL: Harold Shaw, 1980.

———. "The Moral Mythology of C. S. Lewis." *Modern Age* 22.1–4 (Winter–Fall 1978) 384–92.

Hume, David. *The Empiricists. John Locke: An Essay Concerning Human Understanding. George Berkeley: A Treatise Concerning the Principles of Human Knowledge. Three Dialogues between Hylas and Philonous, in Opposiion to Sceptics and Atheists. David Hume: An Enquiry Concerning Human Understanding. Dialogues Concerning Natural Religion.* New York: Anchor, 1990.

———. *Enquiries Concerning Human Understanding and Concerning the Principles of Morals.* Edited by L. A. Selby-Bigge. 3rd ed. Oxford: Clarendon, 1975.

Inchausti, Robert. *Subversive Orthodoxy: Outlaws, Revolutionaries, and Other Christians in Disguise.* Grand Rapids: Brazos, 2005.

Irenaeus. *The Writings of Irenaeus.* Vol. 1. Ante-Nicene Christian Library 5. Elibron Classics. Boston: Adamant Media, 2005.

Ivanov, Andrea. "The Silver-Breathed Barrier Breaker: Myth in the Literary, Theological, and Fictional Works of C. S. Lewis." PhD diss., University of Redlands, 1983.

Jacobs, Alan. *The Narnian: The Life and Imagination of C. S. Lewis.* New York: HarperCollins, 2005.

James, William. *The Varieties of Religious Experience.* New York: Modern Library, 2002.

Jantz, James D. "Tinidril's Temptation: The Un-Man's Attack on Reason, Imagination, and Will in C. S. Lewis's *Perelandra.*" MA thesis, Central Missouri State University, 1989.

Jarrett, Mitzi M. *The Theological World-View of a Fantasy: C. S. Lewis' Chronicles of Narnia.* Diss., Lenoir-Rhyne College, 1982.

Jasper, David. *Images of Belief in Literature,* New York: St. Martin's, 1984.

Jeffrey, David Lyle. "C. S. Lewis, the Bible, and Its Literary Critics." *Christianity and Literature.* 50.1 (2000) 95–109.

Johnson, L Kay. "Through the Wardrobe: An Epic Journey to Innocence and Imagination." BA thesis, Echerd College, 1991.

Johnson, Luke Timothy. *Living Jesus: Learning the Heart of the Gospel.* New York: HarperCollins, 1999.

———. *The Real Jesus: The Misguided Quest for the Historical Jesus and the Truth of the Traditional Gospels.* New York: HarperCollins, 1999.

Johnson, Mark. "The Body in the Mind." Online: http://www.arch.columbia.edu/Projects/Courses/Image.schemata/johnsoncenter.html.

Johnson, William G., and Marcia K. Houtman. "Platonic Shadows in C. S. Lewis' Narnia *Chronicles*." *Modern Fiction Studies* 32.1 (1986) 75–87.

Johnston, Robert K. "Image and Content: The Tension in C. S. Lewis' *Chronicles of Narnia*." *Journal of the Evangelical Theological Society* 20 (1977) 253–64.

Jones, L. Gregory, and James Joseph Buckley. *Theology and Scripturual Imagination*. Oxford: Blackwell, 1998.

Jordan, James. "Determinism's Dilemma." *Review of Metaphysics* 23 (1970) 48–66.

Jordan, Mark D. "Theology and Philosophy." *The Cambridge Companion to Aquinas*, edited by Norman Kretzmann and Eleonore Stump, 232–51. New York: Cambridge University Press, 1993.

Jost, Walter. *Rhetorical Invention and Religious Inquiry: New Perspectives*, New Haven: Yale University Press, 2000.

Justin Martyr. "The Word in the World before Christ." In *Ante-Nicene Fathers* 1.8.2.46. Christian Grand Rapids: Classics Ethereal Library. Online: http://www.ccel.org/ccel/schaff/anf01.viii.ii.xlvi.html.

———. *The Writings of Justin Martyr and Athenagoras*. Ante-Nicene Christian Library 2. Elibron Classics. Boston: Adamant Media, 2006.

Kant, Immanuel. *Basic Writings of Kant*. Edited by Allen W. Wood. New York: Modern Library, 2001.

———. *Critique of Pure Reason*. Translated by Norman Kemp Smith. New York: Palgrave Macmillan, 2003. Online: http://humanum.arts.cuhk.edu.hk/Philosophy/Kant/cpr/.

Kawano, Roland Mamoru. "The Creation of Myth in the Novels of C. S. Lewis." MA thesis, University of Utah, 1969.

———. "Reason and Imagination: The Shape of C. S. Lewis." PhD diss., University of Utah, 1974.

Kearney, Richard. *The Wake of Imagination: Toward a Postmodern Culture*. Minneapolis: University of Minnesota Press, 1988.

Keating, Daniel. "Subcreation in J. R. R. Tolkien and Dorothy Sayers." *The Chronicle of the Oxford University C. S. Lewis Society* 3.2 (2006) 11–20.

Keller, Helen. *The Story of My Life*. Edited by John Albert Macy. New York: Doubleday, 1905. Online: http://digital.library.upenn.edu/women/keller/life/life.html.

Kelso, Denise A. "Glimmers of Transcendent Truth: Mythic Philosophy and Symbolism in C. S. Lewis's *That Hideous Strength*." MA thesis, Florida Atlantic University, 1987.

Kerlin, Matthew S. "The Possibility of Theodicy: C. S. Lewis and the Role of Imaginative Texts in the Justification of Human Suffering." PhD diss., Baylor University, 2004.

Kierkegaard, Soren. "Is There Such a Thing as a Teleological Suspension of the Ethical?" In *Existentialism*, edited by Robert C. Solomon, 14–17. New York: Modern Library, 1974.

Kilby, Cylde S. *The Christian World of C. S. Lewis*. Grand Rapids: Eerdmans, 1964.

———. *Images of Salvation in the Fiction of C. S. Lewis*. Wheaton, IL: Harold Shaw, 1978.

Kilby, Cylde S., and Marjorie Lamp Mead, editors. *Brothers and Friends: The Diaries of Major Warren Hamilton Lewis*. New York: Ballantine, 1982.

King, Don W. "Narnia and the Seven Deadly Sins." Online: http://cslewis.drzeus.net/papers/7sins.html. 1st ed. published in *Mythlore* 10 (Spring 1984) 14–19.

Kingsmill, Patricia. "C. S. Lewis on Metaphor: A Study of Lewis in the Light of Modern Metaphor Theory." MA thesis, McGill University, 1996.

Kirby, William Joe. "Image and Order: A Study of C. S. Lewis' Critical Theory and Method." MA thesis, Memphis State University, 1973.

Knickerbocker, W. E., Jr. "The Myth That Saves: C. S. Lewis & the Doctrine of *Theosis*." *Touchstone: A Journal of Mere Christianity*, July/August 2000, 1–8. Online: http://www.touchstonemag.com/archives/article.php?id=13-06-031-f.

Kreeft, Peter. *The Philosophy of Tolkien: The Worldview behind The Lord of the Rings*. San Francisco: Ignatius, 2005.

Kreeft, Peter, and Ronald K. Tacelli. *Handbook of Christian Apologetics*. Downers Grove, IL: InterVarsity, 1994.

Kress, Robert. *A Rahner Handbook*. Atlanta: John Knox, 1982.

Kummel, Werner Georg. *Introduction to the New Testament*. Nashville: Abingdon, 1975.

LaMar, Erin K. "C. S. Lewis: Myth Lover, Myth Maker." MA thesis, Ball State University, 1989.

Landy, Timothy. "Nature, Myth, and Meaning in the Stories of C. S. Lewis: A Selected Annotated Bibliography." MA thesis, California University of Pennsylvania, 1992.

Larmer, Robert A. H. *Water into Wine: An Investigation of the Concept of Miracle*. Montreal: McGill-Queen's University Press, 1988.

Lash, Nicholas. *Easter in Ordinary: Reflections on Human Experience and the Knowledge of God*. Notre Dame: University of Notre Dame Press, 1988.

———. "Where Does Holy Teaching Leave Philosophy? Questions on Milbank's Aquinas." *Modern Theology* 15.4 (October 1999) 432–44.

Lavine, T. Z. *From Socrates to Sartre: The Philosophic Quest*. New York: Bantam, 1984.

L'Engle, Madeleine. *Glimpses of Grace: Daily Thoughts and Reflections*. Edited by Carole F. Chase. New York: HarperCollins, 1998.

Leyland, Margaret M. "Lewis and the Schoolgirls." *Lamp-Post of the So. California C. S. Lewis Soc.* 1.3 (1977) 1–2.

Lindaman, Robert E. "The Literary Criticism of C. S. Lewis." MA thesis, Mankato State College, 1965.

Lindsey, F. Duane. "An Evangelical Overview of Process Theology." *Bibliotheca Sacra* 134 (1977) 15–32.

Lindsley, Art. "C. S. Lewis on Absolutes." *Knowing & Doing*, Fall 2002, 1–4. Online: http://www.cslewisinstitute.org/files/webfm/knowing_doing/LewisAbsolutes.pdf.

———. "C. S. Lewis on Miracles." *Knowing & Doing*, Fall 2002, 1–5. Online: http://www.cslewisinstitute.org/pages/resources/publications/KnowingDoing/2004/Miracles.pdf.

———. *C. S. Lewis's Case for Christ: Insights from Reason, Imagination and Faith*. Downers Grove, IL: InterVarsity, 2005.

Lindskoog, Kathryn. "A. N. Wilson Errata." Into the Wardrobe. Online: http://cslewis.drzeus.net/papers/anwilsonerrata.html.

———. "C. S. Lewis: Reactions from Women." *Mythlore: A Journal of Tolkien, C. S. Lewis, and Charles Williams Studies* 3.4 (1976).

———. "Links in a Golden Chain: C. S. Lewis, George MacDonald and Sadhu Sundar Singh." *Lewis Legacy* 69 (Summer 1996). Online: http://www.george-macdonald.com/resources/sundar_singh.html.

———. *The Lion of Judah in Never-Never Land: The Theology of C. S. Lewis for Children*. Grand Rapids: Eerdmans, 1974.

Lochhead, Marion. *Renaissance of Wonder: The Fantasy Worlds of C. S. Lewis, J. R. R. Tolkien, George MacDonald, E. Nesbit and Others*. San Francisco: Harper & Row, 1977.

Loney, John Douglas. "Reality, Truth and Perspective in the Fiction of C. S. Lewis." PhD diss., McMaster University, 1985.

Long, D. Stephen. *Divine Economy: Theology and the Market*. Radical Orthodoxy. New York: Routledge, 2000.

Longacre, Judith Evans. "The Imagination in Education and the Contribution of C. S. Lewis." MA thesis, McGill University, 1987.

Loughlin, Gerard. *Telling God's Story: Bible, Church, and Narrative Theology*. Cambridge: Cambridge University Press, 1999.

Lovell, Steve. "C. S. Lewis and the Euthyphro Dilemma." July 14, 2002, 1–30. Online: http://www.theism.net/article/29.

———. "Philosophical Themes from C. S. Lewis." PhD diss., University of Sheffield, 2003.

———. "Steve Lovell Reviews Erik Wielenberg's *God and the Reach of Reason*." Dangerous Idea. July 31, 2008. Online: http://dangerousidea.blogspot.com/2007/10/steve-lovell-reviews-erik-wielenbergs.html.

Lubac, Henri de. *Medieval Exegesis*. Vols. 1, 2. Grand Rapids: Eerdmans, 1998, 2000.

Ludolf of Saxony. "Ludolf of Saxony on Reading Scripture Imaginatively" (from *Vita Christi*). In *The Christian Theology Reader*, edited by Alister McGrath, 90–91. 2nd ed. Oxford: Blackwell, 2001.

MacDonald, George. "The Fantastic Imagination." Introduction to *The Light Princess and Other Fairy Tales: Being the Complete Fairy Stories of George MacDonald*. Edinburgh: Canongate, 1987. Online: http://www.george-macdonald.com/etexts/nonfiction/fantastic_imagination.html.

———. "The Imagination: Its Function and Its Culture." In *A Dish of Orts, Chiefly Papers on the Imagination and on Shakespeare*. London: Low, Marston, 1985. Online: http://www.george-macdonald.com/etexts/nonfiction/the_imagination.html.

MacIntyre, Alasdair. *After Virtue: A Study in Moral Theory*. 2nd ed. Notre Dame: University of Notre Dame Press, 1984.

———. *Dependent Rational Animals: Why Human Beings Need the Virtues*. Chicago: Open Court, 1999.

———. "Virtue Ethics." In *Ethics: Contemporary Readings*, edited by Harry J. Gensler, Earl W. Spurgin, and James C. Swindal, 249–56. New York: Routledge, 2004.

———. *Whose Justice? Which Rationality?* Notre Dame: University of Notre Dame Press, 1988.

Macky, Peter. "The Role of Metaphor in Christian Thought and Experience as Understood by Gordon Clark and C. S. Lewis." *Journal of the Evangelical Theological Society* 24.3 (1981) 239–50.

Manganiello, Dominic. "The Mythic Christ: Frazer's Dying God in C. S. Lewis's *Till We Have Faces*." Touchstone: *A Journal of Mere Christianity*. December 2002, 1–9. Online: http://www.touchstonemag.com/archives/article.php?id=15-10-032-f.

Maniscalco, James. "Inklings and Myth: The Apologetic Method of C. S. Lewis." MA thesis, Ashland Theological Seminary, 1991.

Maritain, Jacques. *Art and Scholasticism with Other Essays*. 1930. Reprinted, N.p.: Filiquarian, 2007.

Markos, Louis. *Lewis Agonistes: How Lewis Can Train Us to Wrestle with the Modern and Postmodern World*. Nashville,: Broadman & Holman, 2003.

Marshall, Michael. *The Restless Heart: The Life and Influence of St. Augustine*. Grand Rapids: Eerdmans, 1987.

Marti, Joe. "Who Is the Lord (of the Rings)? God, Himself, Says Tolkien Biographer." *San Francisco Faith* 6.4 (2002) 1–8.
Martin, Robert Edwin. "Myth and Icon: The Cosmology of C. S. Lewis' Space Trilogy." PhD diss., Florida State University, 1991.
Matthews, Gareth B. "Knowledge and Illumination." In *The Cambridge Companion to Augustine*, edited by Eleonore Stump and Norman Kretzmann, 171–85. Cambridge: Cambridge University Press, 2001.
McClelland, Richard T. "The Mythopoeic World of C. S. Lewis." BA thesis, Reed College, 1970.
McClinch, Christopher C. "Reason, Imagination, and Universalism in C. S. Lewis." MA thesis, Virginia Polytechnic Institute and State University, 2002.
McConnell, Stephen D. "Knowledge by Acquaintance: Relational Spirituality in the Chronicles of Narnia." DLitt. diss., Drew University, 2004.
McDowell, Josh. *Evidence That Demands a Verdict*. Nashville: Nelson, 1979.
McFadyen, Alistair. *Bound to Sin: Abuse, Holocaust, and the Christian Doctrine of Sin*. Cambridge: Cambridge University Press, 2000.
McFague, Sallie. *Metaphorical Theology: Models of God in Religious Language*. Philadelphia: Fortress, 1982.
McGrade, A. S. "Natural Law and Moral Omnipotence." In *The Cambridge Companion to Ockham*, edited by Paul Vincent Spade. Cambridge: Cambridge University Press, 1999.
McGrath, Alister. *Christian Theology: An Introduction*. 3rd ed. Malden, MA: Blackwell, 2001.
Mckenzie, Patricia Alice. "The Last Battle: Violence and Theology in the Novels of C. S. Lewis." PhD diss., University of Florida, 1974.
McLaughlin, Sara Park. "*The City of God* Revisited: C. S. Lewis' Use of an Augustinian Vision in Selected Fiction." MA thesis, West Texas State University, 1982.
McLuhan, Marshall. *The Medium and the Light: Reflections on Religion*. Edited by Eric McLuhan and Jacek Szklarek. Toronto: Stoddart, 1999.
McMillan, Lex O. "C. S. Lewis as Spiritual Autobiographer: A Study in the Sacramental Imagination." PhD diss., University of Notre Dame, 1986.
Meilaender, Gilbert. "The Social and Ethical Thought of C. S. Lewis." PhD diss., Princeton University, 1976.
———. *The Taste for the Other*. Grand Rapids: Eerdmans, 1978.
Meynell, Hugo Anthony. "An Attack on C. S. Lewis." *Faith and Philosophy* 8 (1991) 305–16.
Midgley, Mary. *Science and Poetry*. New York: Routledge, 2002.
Milbank, Alison. *Chesterton and Tolkien as Theologians: The Fantasy of the Real*. London: T. & T. Clark, 2007.
———. "Knowledge and Truth in *The Lord of the Rings*." The Lord of the Rings Fanatics Plaza. January 24, 2009. Online: http://www.lotrplaza.com/forum/forum_posts.asp?TID=231144.
Milbank, John. *Being Reconciled: Ontology and Pardon*. New York: Routledge, 2003.
———. "Foreword." In *Introducing Radical Orthodoxy: Mapping a Post-secular Theology*, by James K. A. Smith, 11–20. Grand Rapids: Baker, 2004.
———. "Faith, Reason and Imagination: The Study of Theology and Philosophy in the 21st Century." Centre of Theology and Philosophy. Online: http://www.theologyphilosophycentre.co.uk/papers/Milbank_StudyofTheologyandPhilosophyinthe21stCentury.pdf.

———. "Fictioning Things: Gift and Narrative." Centre of Theology and Philosophy. Online: http://www.theologyphilosophycentre.co.uk/papers/Milbank_Fictioning Things.pdf.

———. "The Shares of Being or Gift, Relation and Participation: An Essay on the Metaphysics of Emmanuel Levinas and Alain Badiou." Centre of Theology and Philosophy. Online: http://www.theologyphilosophycentre.co.uk/papers/Milbank_Metaphysics-LevinasBadiou.pdf.

———. *Theology and Social Theory: Beyond Secular Reason*. Oxford: Blackwell, 2006.

———. *The Word Made Strange: Theology, Language, Culture*. Oxford: Blackwell, 1997.

Milbank, John, and Catherine Pickstock. *Truth in Aquinas*. New York: Routledge, 2001.

Milbank, John, Catherine Pickstock, and Graham Ward, editors. *Radical Orthodoxy: A New Theology*. New York: Routledge, 1999.

Mills, David. "Imaginative Orthodoxy." *Touchstone: A Journal of Mere Christianity*. November–December 1999, 1–21. Online: http://www.touchstonemag.com/archives/article.php?id=12-06-024-f.

———. *The Pilgrim's Guide: C. S. Lewis and the Art of Witness*. Grand Rapids: Eerdmans, 1998.

Miles, Jack. *Christ: A Crisis in the Life of God*. New York: Vintage, 2002.

Milheim, Sarah Jane. "An Examination of the Relationship Between: The Theological and Fictional Works of Clive Staples Lewis." BA thesis, Lenoir-Rhyne College, 2002.

Mitchell, Christopher W. "University Battles: C. S. Lewis and the Oxford University Socratic Club." In *C. S. Lewis: Lightbearer in the Shadowlands*, edited by Angus J. L. Menuge. Wheaton, IL: Crossway, 1997. Online: http://www.cslewisinstitute.org/cslewis/universityBattles.htm.

Monick, Stanley. "C. S. Lewis: An Approach to Christian Myth." *Lantern* 27.3 (1978) 62–69.

Moorman, Charles. *Arthurian Triptych*. New York: Russell, 1973.

Moreland, J. P. "God and the Argument from Mind." *Scaling the Secular City: A Defense of Christianity*. Grand Rapids: Baker, 1987.

Moreland, J. P., and William Lane Craig. *Philosophical Foundations for a Christian Worldview*. Downers Grove, IL: InterVarsity, 2003.

Morris, Frank Joseph. "Metaphor and Myth: Shaping Forces in C. S. Lewis' Critical Assessment of Medieval and Renaissance Literature." PhD diss., University of Pennsylvania, 1977.

Muncherian, Stephen. "You Shall Call His Name Jesus." December 23, 2001. Online: http://www.muncherian.com/s-mt1v21.html.

Mullin, Robert Bruce. *Miracles and the Modern Imagination*. New Haven: Yale University Press, 1996.

Murphy, Francesca Aran. *Christ, the Form of Beauty: A Study in Theology and Literature*. Edinburgh: T. & T. Clark, 1995.

Nash, Edith A. "The Rhetoric of C. S. Lewis: Apologia through Metaphor." MA thesis, Wichita State University, 1997.

Nelson, Dale. "Imagination & the Health of the Soul." *Touchstone: A Journal of Mere Christianity*. November 2002, 1–4. Online: http://www.touchstonemag.com/archives/article.php?id=15-09-047-b.

Nelson, Judith A. "The Doctrine of God Taught Through Symbolism: A Study of Aslan in C. S. Lewis's Chronicles of Narnia." MA thesis, Trinity Evangelical Divinity School, 1974.

Nelson, Michael. "'One Mythology Among Many': The Spiritual Odyssey of C. S. Lewis." *Virginia Quarterly Review* 72 (1996) 619–33.

Neuleib, Janice Witherspoon. "The Concept of Evil in the Fiction of C. S. Lewis." PhD diss., University of Illinois at Urbana-Champaign, 1974.

Newell, Roger J. "Participatory Knowledge: Theology as Art and Science in C. S. Lewis and T. F. Torrance." PhD diss., University of Aberdeen, 1983.

Nicholi, Armand M. *The Question of God: C. S. Lewis and Sigmund Freud Debate God, Love, Sex and the Meaning of Life*. New York: Free Press, 2002.

Niebuhr, H. Richard. *The Responsible Self: An Essay in Christian Moral Responsibility*. New York: HarperCollins, 1978.

Nietzsche, Friedrich. *Basic Writings of Nietzsche*. Translated by Walter Kaufmann. New York: Modern Library, 2000.

———. *Thus Spoke Zarathustra*. Translated by R. J. Hollingdale. New York: Penguin, 1969.

Norwood, William Durward. "The Neo-medieval Novels of C. S. Lewis." PhD diss., University of Texas, 1965.

O'Connell, Robert J. *Imagination and Metaphysics in St. Augustine*. Milwaukee: Marquette University, 1986.

O'Hare, Colman. "Charles Williams, C. S. Lewis and J. R. R. Tolkien: Three Approaches to Religion in Modern Fiction." PhD diss., University of Toronto, 1973.

Ockham, William. *Philosophical Writings: A Selection*. Translated by Philotheus Boehner, O.F.M. Indianapolis: Hackett, 1990.

O'Conner, Flannery. *Mystery and Manners: Occasional Prose*. Edited by Sally and Robert Fitzgerald. New York: Farrar, Straus & Giroux, 1969.

Oliver, Naomi Glenn. "The Higher and Lower Mediums of Meaning in Three Models Presented by C. S. Lewis: The Medieval, Modern, and Incarnational Models." PhD diss., Drew University, 1992.

Oliver, Rebecca. "The Rhetorical Function of Metaphor in C. S. Lewis: Beyond Persuasion." MA thesis, University of Guelph, 1994.

Oliver, Simon. *Philosophy, God and Motion*. New York: Routledge, 2005.

———. "Radical Orthodoxy: A Review." In *Faith and Freedom: Exploring Radical Orthodoxy*, edited by Jeremy Morris, 49–59. London: Affirming Catholicism, 2003.

O'Neil, Onora. "Vindicating Reason." In *The Cambridge Companion to Kant*, edited by Paul Guyer, 280–308. Cambridge: Cambridge University Press, 1992.

Origen. *The Writings of Origen*. 2 vols. Ante-Nicene Christian Library 10, 23. Elibron Classics. Boston: Adamant Media, 2005.

Ormsbee, Elizabeth H. "A Rhetoric of Reconciliation between Reason, Imagination and Faith in C. S. Lewis' Apologetic Works." MA thesis, University of Georgia, 1991.

Otto, Rudolf. *The Idea of the Holy*. London: Oxford University Press, 1958.

———. "Mysterium Tremendum." *Parabola*, Fall 1998, 72–76.

Oury, Scott. "'The Thing Itself': C. S. Lewis and the Value of Something Other." In *The Longing for a Form: Essays on the Fiction of C. S. Lewis*, edited by Peter J. Schakel, 1–19. Grand Rapids: Baker, 1979.

Owen, David W. D., editor. *Hume: General Philosophy*. Burlington, VT: Ashgate, 2000.

Paden, William E. *Religious Worlds: The Comparative Study of Religion*. Boston: Beacon, 1994.

Pascal, Blaise. *Pensees*. New York: Oxford University Press, 1999.

Pauck, Wilhelm and Marion. *Paul Tillich His Life & Thought*. Vol. 1. New York: Harper & Row, 1976.
Pearce, Joseph. *C. S. Lewis and the Catholic Church*. San Francisco: Ignatius, 2003.
Percy, Walker. *Lost in the Cosmos: The Last Self-Help Book*. New York: Picador, 2000.
———. *The Message in the Bottle: How Queer Man Is, How Queer Language Is, and What One Has to Do with the Other*. New York: Picador, 1975.
Peters, James R. *The Logic of the Heart: Augustine, Pascal, and the Rationality of Faith*. Grand Rapids: Baker, 2009.
Peterson, Jeffrey. "A Pioneer Narrative Critic and His Synoptic Hypothesis: Austin Farrer and Gospel Interpretation." Institute for Christian Studies, Austin, Texas. Online: http://personal1.stthomas.edu/dtlandry/peterson.html.
Peterson, Michael, William Hasker, Bruce Reichenbach, and David Basinger. *Reason and Religious Belief: An Introduction to the Philosophy of Religion*. 3rd ed. New York: Oxford University Press, 2003.
Phillips, Michael R. *George MacDonald: Scotland's Beloved Storyteller*. Minneapolis: Bethany, 1987.
Pickstock, Catherine. *After Writing: On the Liturgical Consummation of Philosophy*. Oxford: Blackwell, 1998.
———. "Is Orthodoxy Radical?" In *Faith and Freedom: Exploring Radical Orthodoxy*, edited by Jeremy Morris, 5–16. London: Affirming Catholicism, 2003.
Placher, William C. (1989) "Hans Frei and the Meaning of Biblical Narrative." *The Christian Century* 106.18 (1989) 556–59.
Plank, Robert. "Some Psychological Aspects of Lewis's Trilogy." In *Shadows of Imagination: The Fantasies of C. S. Lewis, J. R. R. Tolkien, and Charles Williams*, edited by Mark R. Hillegas, 26–40. Carbondale: Southern Illinois University Press, 1970.
Plantinga, Alvin. *Warrant and Proper Function*. New York: Oxford University Press, 1993.
Plato. *Complete Works*. Edited by John M. Cooper. Indianapolis: Hackett, 1997.
———. *The Great Dialogues of Plato*. Translated by W. H. D. Rouse. New York: Penguin, 1984.
———. *The Laws*. London: Penguin, 1975.
———. *Parmenides*. New Haven: Yale University Press, 1997.
Purtill, Richard. *Lord of the Elves and Eldils: Fantasy and Philosophy in C. S. Lewis and J. R. R. Tolkien*. Grand Rapids: Zondervan, 1974.
———. *Reason to Believe*. Grand Rapids: Eerdmans, 1974.
Pyles, Franklin A. "The Language Theory of C. S. Lewis." *Trinity Journal*. 4.2 (1983) 82–91.
Quammen, David. *Natural Acts: A Sidelong View of Science and Nature*. New York: Avon, 1996.
Quinn, Dermot. "G. K. Chesterton, C. S. Lewis, and the Uses of Enchantment." *The Chronicle of the Oxford University C. S. Lewis Society* 3.2 (2006) 4–10.
Rachels, James. *The Elements of Moral Philosophy*. 3rd ed. New York: McGraw-Hill, 1999.
———. "The Ethics of Virtue." In *Ethics: History, Theory, and Contemporary Issues*, edited by Steven M. Cahn and Peter Markie, 645–52. New York: Oxford University Press, 2002.
Rahner, Karl. "An Interview with Karl Rahner on the State of Catholic Theology Today." Online: http://www.innerexplorations.com/chtheomortext/kr.htm.
———. *Theological Investigations*. Translated by Edward Quinn. Vols. 1–20. New York: Crossroad, 1983.

Rauch, Sylvia M. "A Study of the Critical and Imaginative Achievement of Clive Staples Lewis." MA thesis, Canisius College, 1951.
Reddy, Albert Francis. "The Else Unspeakable: an Introduction to the Fiction of C. S. Lewis." PhD diss., University of Massachusetts, 1972.
Regan, Tom. *The Case for Animal Rights*. Berkeley: University of California Press, 2004.
———. "The Case for Animal Rights." In *Environmental Ethics: Concepts, Policy, Theory*. Edited by Joseph R. DesJardins. Mountain View CA: Mayfield, 1999.
Reilly, R. J. *Romantic Religion: A Study of Barfield, Lewis, Williams, and Tolkien*. Athens: University of Georgia Press, 1971.
Reindi, Darren Scott. "Myth and Meaning in C. S. Lewis' Chronicles of Narnia: Master's and Pupil's Metaphors in Christian Narrative." MA thesis, University of Georgia, 1991.
Reppert, Victor. *C. S. Lewis' Dangerous Idea: A Philosophical Defense of Lewis's Argument from Reason*. Downers Grove, IL: InterVarsity, 2003.
———. "The Lewis-Anscombe Controversy: A Discussion of the Issues." *Christian Scholar's Review* 19 (September 1989) 58–80.
Ricoeur, Paul. *Figuring the Sacred: Religion, Narrative, and Imagination*. Minneapolis: Fortress, 1995.
Rigoulot, Lois. "A Gift of Joy: The Use of Myth in the Fiction of C. S. Lewis." MA thesis, Adelphi University, 1967.
Rilstone, Andrew. "Fool, Charlatan or Evangelist? C. S. Lewis, Josh McDowell, and the 'Trilemma.'" Online: http://www.aslan.demon.co.uk/trilemma.htm.
Rist, John. "Faith and Reason." In *The Cambridge Companion to Augustine*, edited by Eleonore Stump and Norman Kretzmann. Cambridge: Cambridge University Press, 2001.
Riter, Eleanor Mildred. "Severity and Tenderness in Lewis's Imaginative Universe." MA thesis, San Francisco State College, 1971.
Rogers, Deborah Webster. "The Fictitious Characters of C. S. Lewis and J. R. R. Tolkien in Relation to their Medieval Sources." PhD diss., University of Wisconsin, 1972.
Rogers, Eugene F. "The Narrative of Natural Law in Aquinas's Commentary on Romans 1." *Theological Studies* 59 (1998) 254–77.
———. "Thomas and Barth in Convergence on Romans 1?" *Modern Theology* 12 (1996) 57–84.
Rosmini, Antonio. *A New Essay Concerning the Origin of Ideas*. 3 vols. Translated by Robert A. Murphy, Denis Cleary, and Terence Watson. Durham, UK: Rosmini House, 2001.
Ross, James Bruce, and Mary Martin McLaughlin, editors. *The Portable Medieval Reader*. New York: Penguin, 1977.
Rossi, Lee D. "The Politics of Fantasy: C. S. Lewis and J. R. R. Tolkien." PhD diss., Cornell University, 1972.
Ruggiero, Vincent Ryan. *Beyond Feelings: A Guide to Critical Thinking*. 5th ed. Mountain View, CA: Mayfield, 1998.
Russell, Bertrand. "The Value of Free Thought: How to Become a Truth-Seeker and Break the Chains of Mental Slavery." In *Bertrand Russell on God and Religion*, edited by Al Seckel, 239–70. New York: Prometheus, 1986.
Rusthoven, Jennifer Rae. "C. S. Lewis: The Great Myth." BA thesis, James Madison University, 1993.
Ryan, Tim. "The Influence of Platonic and Aristotelian Philosophy on the Evangelism of C. S. Lewis." MA thesis, Wheaton College, 2003.

Sallis, John. *Force of Imagination: The Sense of the Elemental.* Indianapolis: Indiana University Press, 2000.

———. *Spacings—of Reason and Imagination in Texts of Kant, Fichte, Hegel.* Chicago: University of Chicago Press, 1987.

Sammons, Martha C. "God Within: Reason and Its Riddle in C. S. Lewis' *Till We Have Faces*." *Christian Scholar's Review* 6.2–3 (1976) 127–39.

Sawdon, Veronica T. "C. S. Lewis's Concept of Myth in the Space Trilogy and the Narnia Chronicles." BA thesis, Maryville College, 1977.

Sayer, George. *Jack: A Life of C. S. Lewis.* Wheaton, IL: Crossway, 1994.

Sayers, Dorothy L. "The Lost Tools of Learning." Lecture presented at Oxford, 1947. Online: http://www.gbt.org/text/sayers.html.

———. *The Mind of the Maker.* New York: Coninuum, 2004.

Schakel, Peter J., editor. *The Longing for a Form: Essays on the Fiction of C. S. Lewis.* Grand Rapids: Baker, 1979.

———. *Reason and Imagination in C. S. Lewis: A Study of "Till We Have Faces."* Grand Rapids: Eerdmans, 1984.

———. *The Way into Narnia: A Reader's Guide.* Grand Rapids: Eerdmans, 2005.

———. *Word and Story in C. S. Lewis: Language and Narrative in Theory and Practice.* 1991. Reprinted, Eugene, OR: Wipf and Stock, 2008.

Schakel, Peter J., and Charles A. Huttar, editors. *Imagination and the Arts in C. S. Lewis: Journeying to Narnia and Other Worlds.* Columbia: University of Missouri Press, 2002.

Schleiermacher, F. D. E. *Friedrich Schleiermacher: Pioneer of Modern Theology.* Edited by Keith W. Clements. Minneapolis: Fortress, 1987.

Schrodt, Paul. "Augustine in Recent Research." *American Theological Library Association Summary of Proceedings* 55 (2001) 169–85.

Scotus, Duns. *Philosophical Writings: A Selectoin.* Translated by Allan Wolter. Indianapolis: Hackett, 1987.

Shakespeare, William. *The Norton Shakespeare.* Edited by Stephen Greenblatt. London: Norton, 1997.

Shelley, Bruce L. "Miracles Ended Long Ago or Did They?" *Christian History* 67 (2000). Online: http://www.christianitytoday.com/ch/2000/issue67/10.36.html?start=6.

Shoemaker, Steven Robert. "Beyond the Walls of the World: Practical Theology in the Fantasy Novels of C. S. Lewis." PhD diss., Duke University, 1979.

Shumate, Robbie Gayle. "Emotion, Reason, and the Tao of C. S. Lewis: A Theory of Pathos." MA thesis, University of Georgia, 1995.

Simpson, Margo Lee. "The Anti-Modern Imagination: C. S. Lewis and the Cosmic Trilogy." MA thesis, University of Ottawa, 2001.

Singh, Sadhu Sundar. *Sadhu Sundar Singh: Essential Writings.* Maryknoll, NY: Orbis, 2005.

Skatssoon, Judy. "'Star Trek' behind Many Tech Advances." Discovery Channel. September 27, 2006. Online: http://www.dsc.discovery.com/news/2006/09/27/startrek_tec.html?category=technology&guid=20060927111500.

Slack, Michael Dean. "An Air That Kills: C. S. Lewis's Fictive Use of Platonism." MA thesis, Ball State University, 1981.

Smalley, William E. "'Footprints of the Divine': A Study of Imaginative Literature as a Guide to the Spiritual Journey, with an Emphasis on *Prince Caspian* by C. S. Lewis." DMin diss., Wesley Theological Seminary, 1987.

Smith, Huston. *Forgotten Truth: The Common Vision of the World's Religions.* New York: HarperCollins, 1992.

Smith, James K. A. *Introducing Radical Orthodoxy: Mapping a Post-secular Theology.* Grand Rapids: Baker, 2004.

———. *Speech and Theology: Language and the Logic of Incarnation.* New York: Routledge, 2002.

———. *Who's Afraid of Postmodernism: Taking Derrida, Lyotard, and Foucault to Church.* Grand Rapids: Baker, 2006.

Smith, Mark Eddy. *Aslan's Call: Finding Our Way to Narnia.* Downers Grove, IL: InterVarsity, 2005.

Springer, J. R. "'Beyond Personality': C. S. Lewis' Concept of God." MA thesis, Wheaton College, 1969.

Stahl, John. "The Nature and Function of Myth in the Christian Thought of C. S. Lewis." *Bulletin of the New York C. S. Lewis Society* 7.3 (1976) 3–8.

Stock, R. D. "Dionysus, Christ, and C. S. Lewis." *Christianity and Literature* 34.2 (1985) 7–13.

———. "The *Tao* and the Objective Room: A Pattern in C. S. Lewis's Novels." *Christian Scholar's Review* 9 (1980) 256–66.

Strawbridge, Gregg. "Karl Barth's Rejection of Natural Theology, or an Exegesis of Romans 1:19–20." Paper presented at the 1997 Evangelical Theological Society meeting in San Francisco. Online: http://www.wordmp3.com/gs/barth.htm.

Stump, Eleonore. "The Mechanisms of Cognition: Ockham on Mediating Species." In *The Cambridge Companion to Ockham*, edited by Paul Vincent Spade, 168–203. Cambridge: Cambridge University Press, 1999.

Swafford, Dale William. "There Is Good Rock Here: Literary Formation of Myth and Faerie in C. S. Lewis and J. R. R. Tolkien." MA thesis, Wichita University, 1987.

Taliaferror, Charles, and Rachel Traughber. "The Atonement in Narnia." In *The Chronicles of Narnia and Philosophy: The Lion, the Witch, and the Worldview*, edited by Gregory Bassham and Jerry L. Walls, 245–59. Popular Culture and Philosophy 15. Chicago: Open Court, 2005.

Tanner, Georgia L. "Religious Allegory or Sacramentalism in the Works of C. S. Lewis." MA thesis, East Carolina University, 1996.

Tarrant, Melissa P. "Myth and Archetype as Meaning in C. S. Lewis's *Till We Have Faces*." MA thesis, Baylor University, 1993.

Taylor, Charles. *A Secular Age.* Cambidge, MA: Belknap, 2007.

Templeton, Mary Ann. "Leaving the Wardrobe Open: A Study of the Dialectical C. S. Lewis." MA thesis, Northeast Missouri State, 1982.

Thomas, Jesse J. "From Joy to Joy: C. S. Lewis and the Numinous." *Journal of Interdisciplinary Studies* 12.1/2 (2000) 109–24.

Thompson, Marie Alena. "C. S. Lewis and a Christian View of Myth." MA thesis, University of West Florida, 1997.

Tillich, Paul. *Biblical Religion and the Search for Ultimate Reality.* Chicago: University of Chicago Press, 1972.

———. *The Courage to Be.* New Haven: Yale University Press, 1979.

———. *Systematic Theology.* 3 vols. Chicago: University of Chicago Press, 1951–63.

Tolkien, J. R. R. *The Letters of J. R. R. Tolkien.* Edited by Humphrey Carpenter. New York: Houghton Mifflin, 2000.

Torrance, Thomas F. *The Ground and Grammar of Theology.* Charlottesville: University Press of Virginia, 1980.

Tracy, David. *The Analogical Imagination: Christian Theology and the Culture of Pluralism*. New York: Crossroad, 1981.
Urang, Gunnar. "Shadows of Heaven: The Uses of Fantasy in the Fiction of C. S. Lewis, Charles Williams, and J. R. R. Tolkien." PhD diss., University of Chicago, 1969.
Van Duren, Susan Cleveland. "The Incomprehensibility of God: Its Influence Upon the Fiction of C. S. Lewis." MA thesis, Georgia State University, 1984.
Vanauken, Sheldon. *A Severe Mercy*. New York: Harper & Row, 1977.
Vaus, Will. *Mere Theology: A Guide to the Thought of C. S. Lewis*. Downers Grove, IL: InterVarsity, 2004.
Veatch, Robert M. *The Basics of Biomedical Ethics*. 2nd ed. New Jersey: Prentice Hall, 2003.
Walczuk, Anna. "Thought and Imagination in the Selected Fiction of G. K. Chesterton and C. S. Lewis." PhD diss., Jagiellonian University, 1988.
Walker, Andrew, and James Patrick, editors. *A Christian for All Christians: Essays in Honour of C. S. Lewis*. London: Hodder & Stoughton, 1990.
Walker, Andrew. "Scripture, Revelation and Platonism in C. S. Lewis." *Scottish Journal of Theology* 55 (2002) 19–35.
Ward, Benedicta. *Miracles and the Medieval Mind: Theory, Record and Event, 1000–1215*. Philadelphia: University of Pennsylvania Press, 1982.
Ward, Graham. "Barth, Hegel and the Possibility for Christian Apologetics." In *Faith and Freedom: Exploring Radical Orthodoxy*, edited by Jeremy Morris, 17–38. London: Affirming Catholicism, 2003.
———. *Theology and Contemporary Critical Theory: Creating Transcendent Worship Today*. 2nd ed. New York: St. Martin's, 1999.
Ward, Michael. "Our Faith Observed: The Three-Fold Cord of Imagination, Reason and Will in C. S. Lewis." *Touchstone: A Journal of Mere Christianity*, July–August 2006. Online: http://www.touchstonemag.com/archives/article.php?id=19-06-022-f.
———. *Planet Narnia: The Seven Heavens in the Imagination of C. S. Lewis*. New York: Oxford University Press, 2008.
———. "The Son and the Other Stars: Christology and Cosmology in the Imagination of C. S. Lewis." PhD diss., University of St. Andrews, 2005.
Warnock, Mary. *Imagination*. Berkeley: University of California Press, 1979.
Wartenberg, Thomas E. "Reason and the Practice of Science." In *The Cambridge Companion to Kant*, edited by Paul Guyer, 228–48. Cambridge: Cambridge University Press, 1992.
Weger, Karl-Heinz. *Karl Rahner: An Introduction to His Theology*. New York: Seabury, 1980.
Wettstein, Howard. "Awe and the Religious Life." *Judaism*. Vol. 46 (1997) 387–407.
Wielenberg, Erik. *God and the Reach of Reason: C. S. Lewis, David Hume, and Bertrand Russell*. New York: Cambridge University Press, 2007.
Wilcox, Steven Michael. "Reality, Romanticism, and Reason: Perspectives on a C. S. Lewis Pedagogy." PhD diss., University of Colorado, Boulder, 1982.
Williams, Charles. *The Place of the Lion*. Vancouver, BC: Regent College Publishing, 2003.
Williams, Julia M. "Concepts of Love: An Analysis of the Elements of Platonic Thought in the Work of C. S. Lewis also Reflected in the Work of Augustine." MA thesis, Georgetown University, 1999.
Williams, Rowan. *On Christian Theology*. Challenges in Contemporary Theology. Oxford: Blackwell, 1999.

———. "Language, Reality and Desire in Augustine's De Doctrina." *Literature and Theology* 3 (1989) 138–50.

———. "Sapientia and the Trinity: Reflections on De Trinitate." In *Collectanea Augustiniana: Mélanges T. J. van Bavel*, 1:317–32. Bibliotheca Ephemeridum theologicarum Lovaniensium 92. Leuven: Leuven University Press, 1990.

Willis, John Randolph. *Pleasures Forevermore: The Theology of C. S. Lewis*. Chicago: Loyola University Press, 1983.

Wilson, A. N. *C. S. Lewis: A Biography*. New York: Norton, 1990.

Wilson, John. "Why There Are Seven Chronicles of Narnia." *Christianity Today*, April 1, 2003, n.p. Online: http://www.christianitytoday.com/ct/2003/aprilweb-only/4-21-52.0.html.

Wittgenstein, Ludwig. *Culture and Value*. Edited by G. H. von Wright, translated by Peter Winch. Oxford: Blackwell, 1980.

Woerner, Jody R. "The Quest for Joy: C. S. Lewis's Use of the Quest Narrative in His Fiction." PhD diss., Arizona State University, 2001.

Wolfe, Gary Kent. "The Symbolic Fantasy in England." PhD diss., University of Chicago, 1971.

Wolfe, Nathan. "Faith, Reason, and Belief in God: A Comparison of St. Anselm and C. S. Lewis." BA thesis, Southern Connecticut State University, 1998.

Wood, Allen W. *Kant's Ethical Thought*. Cambridge: Cambridge University Press, 1999.

Wright, Marjorie Evelyn. "The Cosmic Kingdom of Myth: A Study in the Myth-Philosophy of Charles Williams, C. S. Lewis, and J. R. R. Tolkien." PhD diss., University of Illinois, 1960.

Yoder, John Howard. *The Politics of Jesus: Vicit Agnus Noster*. 2nd ed. Grand Rapids: Eerdmans, 1994.

Ziegler, Mervin Lee. "Imagination as a Rhetorical Factor in the Works of C. S. Lewis." PhD diss., University of Florida, 1973.

Zogby, Edward Gabriel. "C. S. Lewis: Christopoesis and the Recovery of the Panegyric Imagination." PhD diss., Syracuse University, 1975.

———. "Triadic Patterns in Lewis's Life and Thought." In *The Longing for a Form: Essays on the Fiction of C. S. Lewis*, edited by Peter J. Schakel, 20–39. Grand Rapids: Baker, 1979.

Subject Index

Please note: References to individuals can be found in Name Index.

Absolute Idealism, 36–37n24
Abstraction, 111, 122, 155, 157, 163, 168
  Concretizing, 72n18, 139, 158, 178n36
Actions, 116, 182–83n75, 195
  Moral, 112, 114, 130n25, 131n32, 143
  See also Conduct, Right
Aesthetics, 43n124, 73n28, 198–99, 210n41
Allegories, 72n18, 73n22, 157, 184n97
  Lewis's Use of, 68–69, 126, 182n70
  See also Myth(s)
Anagogy, 184n97
Analogies, 55n1, 140, 160–63, 185n120, 193
  Language of, 50, 168, 186–87n135
  Lewis's Use of, 34–35n6
  See also Metaphors
Anamnesis, 18, 85, 89, 97, 98
Animals, 119, 130n19, 213–15n72, 215n75
Anscombe Debate, 9, 11–15, 35n14, 36n18, 36n21, 37n32, 37n33, 38n35, 59, 66, 75–76n49, 76n51
Anthropology, Christian, 43n125
Anthropomorphism, 186–87n135
Anthroposophy, 17, 164, 177n24
Appetite(s), 46, 47, 133n60, 208, 216n81
A Priorism, 62, 108, 111, 188–90n143

Argument(s), 25, 76n50, 85–86
  Lewis's Use of, 18–19, 26, 27, 34–35n6, 36n19
  Rational, 22, 23, 30–31, 40n63, 40n65, 40n68, 120
  Reasoning and, 20, 166–67, 212n75
  See also Anscombe Debate; Persuasion, Platonic; Trilemma Argument
Argument from Desire, 98–99n4
Argument from Reason, 12, 16, 37n31
Art/Artists, 26, 43n125, 74n32, 83–84, 96, 138, 167, 182–83n75, 190n146, 212n55
  Creation of, 55n1, 173, 174–75n2, 177–78n32, 210n36
  Divine Influences in, 140, 142, 170, 208–9n3
  Imagination's Role in, 5, 48, 195, 199, 201
  Meaning in, 176n13, 210n35
  Plato on, 87–89, 102n57
  Reality and, 88, 89–90, 198–99
  Telos of, 5, 77
  See also Literature; Poetry/Poets; Writing
Atheism, 20, 213n67
  Lewis's, 1–2, 3, 70, 154
Authority, Reason's Relationship to, 23–24

Subject Index

Authors, Intended Meanings of, 60–64, 71n14, 73n22, 73–74n28, 144, 158–59, 170, 183n92, 183n93
Autobiographies, 148

Barfield-Lewis Great War, 2, 164–65, 186n127
Beauty, 208, 216n81
    Creation's, 78–79, 95, 139
    Imaginative, 72n17, 174–75n2, 190n146
    Language's Conveyance of, 165, 169
Being, 48, 82, 185n124
    See also God
Belief(s), 21–22, 29–30, 35n12, 36n21, 40n68, 103n69, 153
Beneficence, Laws of, 117–18, 131n33, 137n89
Bible, 158, 163, 168–74, 179n49, 183n93, 188n140
    See also Gospels; New Testament; Scripture
Biographies, 58, 148
Broadcast Talks (Lewis), 17, 19

Categorical Imperative, 108, 112–13, 115, 119
Causes, 32–33, 133n60
Cave, Plato's Allegory of, 69, 82–83, 87
Character(s), 150–51, 178n34, 182–83n75
    Building of, 85, 86, 87, 135n77
    Moral Education through, 86, 125, 127, 143–44
    Traits of, 114, 131n32, 131n33
Children, 61–62, 101n30, 147–48
    Becoming Like, 92, 144–45, 173, 174, 177n24, 177n25, 177n26
    Moral Education of, 72–73n19, 75n48, 77, 80–82, 85, 89, 125–28, 134–35n74, 153
    Teaching Christianity to, 67, 74n44
Christianity, 39n53, 44n145, 149, 168
    Augustine on, 90, 183n93
    Doctrines of, 19–21, 29–30, 171, 183n94, 188n142, 190–91n152
    Epistemology of, 43n124, 43n125

Lewis as Apologist for, 1, 3, 9–11, 34–35n6, 35n12, 35n13, 36n19, 36n21, 40n64, 133–34n65, 185–86n125
    Morality of, 115–18, 121–24
    Symbolism in, 160–61, 185n107
    Teaching Children about, 67, 74n44, 181–82n64
    Theology of, 30–31, 115–16, 159, 190–91n152
    See also Christ; Church, Christian; Lewis, Clive Staples, Conversion to Christianity; Roman Catholic Church
Chronicles of Narnia (Lewis), 1, 76n55, 145, 211n44
    Christianity in, 34n5, 136n85, 155
    Imaginative Qualities in, 61–62, 187n136
    Lewis's Key Ideas in, 153–54, 177n25, 178n36
    Literary Criticism of, 59, 71n13
    Moral Education through, 84, 85, 125–27, 137n88, 153, 181n62
    Motivations for Writing, 10, 14–15, 66–68, 69, 177n25
    Rationality in, 148
    Symbolism in, 72n17, 122, 146–47, 151–52, 174–75n2, 184n97
    Women's Treatment in, 137n87
    See also Narnia
Chronos, 147, 179n42
    See also Time
Church, Christian, 48, 103n69, 161, 181n59
City, Ideal, 88, 102n57
Cognition, 43n125, 56n34, 129n10, 210n36
    Imagination's Relationship to, 46–48, 51, 129n10, 193
Communication, 182n73, 182–83n75
Comprehension. See Understanding
Conduct, Right, 121, 135n77, 136n80
    See also Actions, Moral
Conscience, 44n146, 115, 143, 167, 172, 183–84n95, 190n147

Consciousness, 17, 97, 110, 128n3, 139, 176n14
  Human, 99–100n6, 129n11, 164–67, 185n124
  Liberation of, 53, 183n87
Consequences, 111, 112, 131n31, 131n33, 143
Contemplation, 48, 104–5n98, 155–56, 182n71
Courage, 117, 118, 119, 125, 126–27, 150–51
Creation, 106n109, 181n59
  Act of, 55n1, 141–42
  Artistic, 55n1, 173, 174–75n2, 177–78n32, 210n36
  Beauty of, 78–79, 95, 139
  Human, 55n1, 109, 118, 126, 173, 175n7, 194
  Meaning Found in, 50, 117, 153
  Myths of, 183n93
Creator, the, 16, 50–51, 78, 140, 183n93
  See also God
Culture, 48, 61, 115, 130n18, 131–32n35, 132n42

Deduction, 48, 53
Deism, 129–30n16
Delta Phenomenon, 213–15n72
Demythologizing, 158, 159–60, 163, 172
Deontology, 22, 114, 115
Desire, 6, 32, 47, 85, 98n2, 112, 133n60, 208
  Lewis's Concept of, 79–80, 156, 186n127, 193–94, 200, 210n41
  Platonic-Augustinian Concept of, 18, 77–79, 93–95, 96, 139, 173
  See also Longing, Sense of
Dialectics, 10, 28, 168, 186–87n135
Divine, the, 61–62, 63, 85, 95
  Experience of, 32, 80, 81–82, 123
  Participation in, 73–74n28, 78, 193
  See also God
Divine Life, Transposition with Mundane Life, 7, 49, 62, 77, 89, 174–75n2, 192, 194, 196, 199, 202
Divine Simplicity, Doctrine of, 121–22

Drama, 89, 182n73
Dreams, 103n75, 165, 178n39, 179n39, 195, 207, 212n55
Dualism, 91, 100n15, 111
Duty, Sense of, 112, 114–15, 123, 124, 125–26

Education. *See* Moral Education
Eisegesis, 169
Elaboration, 195
Emotions, 60, 76n56, 200
Enchantment
  Meaning Found in, 146, 153
  Reading's Effects on, 62, 149, 167
  Sense of, 79, 143, 168, 186–87n135
  See also Children, Becoming Like
Enlightenment, the, 41n87, 57n44, 58
  Imagination Theories of, 5, 46, 51–54
  Moral Theory of, 119, 135n77
  Philosophy of, 161, 215–16n80
  Rationality Paradigm, 4, 9, 23–26, 30, 48, 54, 75–76n49, 98–99n4, 106n109, 110, 208
  Reason in, 46, 51–54, 151
  Religious Views of, 129–30n16
Epiphenomenon, 6, 55n1, 139, 193
Epistemology, 31, 43n125, 43n126, 45, 46, 48–49
Escapism, 83, 101n30, 168
Eschatology, 184n97
Ethics
  Aristotle's Concept of, 124, 133n60, 136n80
  Christian, 115–16
  Enlightenment, 119
  Kant's Concept of, 111
  Kierkegaard's Concept of, 123, 132–33n59
  Lewis's Concept of, 107–37, 138
  Rationalist, 108, 118–19, 124, 138
  Relational, 6, 108, 125, 126, 138
  Story's Conveyance of, 85, 127, 136n81
  See also Morality; Virtue Ethics
Eucatastrophe, 175n3
Evil, 86, 96, 101n43, 124, 132n48, 180n55, 181n62, 203

Existentialism, 182–83n75, 184n99
Experience/Experiencing
    Imagination's Relationship to, 96, 129n11, 210n41
    Immediate, 91
    Kant on, 129n9
    Meaning in, 110, 198, 207
    Myths' Relationship to, 145
    Religious, 81, 99–100n6, 100n15, 129–30n16
    Story's Presentation of, 34–35n6, 139, 155–56, 182n71

Fact(s), 36n15, 171, 198, 204, 206
    Myths vs., 171, 172, 185n107
Fairy, 6, 140–45, 174–75n2, 207
Fairyland, 2, 111, 126
Fairy Tales, 62, 72–73n19, 73–74n28, 74n46, 101n30, 138, 142–43
    Chronicles as, 187n136
    Lewis's Use of, 67, 69, 100n20, 175n3, 176n8, 178n36
    Teaching Christianity through, 74n44, 81, 83–84
    See also Myth(s)
Faith, 54, 118, 132–33n59, 151, 183–84n95
    Augustine's Concept of, 4, 10, 28–30, 92, 103–4n78, 172
    Christian Experience of, 129–30n16
    Gift of, 40n60, 43n128
    Imagination's Relationship to, 28, 34–35n6
    Reason's Relationship to, 21–22, 28, 29, 30, 31, 44n152, 48
    Truth and, 122, 123
Fancy, 3, 49, 52, 142, 175n7, 176n10, 193–94
    Imagination as, 56n34, 95, 98, 109
Fantasy, 52–53, 83–84, 142, 154, 168, 213n67
    Lewis's Concept of, 2–3, 61, 76n51, 101n30, 177n26, 178n36, 181n62, 186–87n35, 211n44
    Tolkien's Concept of, 53, 177–78n32
Fears, 40n64, 86, 101n43

Feelings, 75n47, 86, 99–100n6, 101n44, 112, 182n70, 208, 216n81
    See also Sensations
Fiction, 39–40n57, 89, 102–3n65
Fiction, Children's, 52, 95–96, 177n24, 203–4
    Lewis's Retreat into, 5, 10–17, 34n3, 34n5, 35n14, 36n18, 58–59, 67, 69, 153–54, 174
    Lewis's Writing of, 71–72n16, 76n55, 83, 85, 86, 141
    Moral Education through, 72–73n19, 75n48, 77, 89, 125–28
    see also Chronicles of Narnia; Lewis, Clive Staples, Works of
Fideism, 21, 23
Finite, Expressing the Infinite, 6, 32, 99–100n6, 110, 140, 144, 163, 193, 200, 206
Forgiveness, 116, 122–23
Formalism, 73–74n28
Forms, Platonic, 81, 82, 84–85, 88, 102–3n65, 202
    See also Platonism
Framing, 22–23, 26
Freedom, 96, 112, 180n55
Freudianism, 60, 70n3, 70–71n7, 74n32, 98n2

Games, 77, 81, 186–87n135, 187n138
Gnosticism, 185–86n125, 186n127, 204
Good Faith, Law of, 118
Good/Goodness, 107, 136n80, 144, 203, 216n81
    Aristotle's Concept of, 125, 133n60
    Augustine's Concept of, 96, 172
    Christian, 115, 118
    God's, 33, 117, 121–22, 162
    Knowledge of, 81–82, 84, 86, 123
    Lewis's Concept of, 126–27, 152, 181n62
    Longing for, 46, 79, 86
Gospels, 106n109, 149–50, 170–71, 179n48, 179–80n50, 188n139
Grace, 33, 43n128, 103–4n78, 122–23, 167

Greeks. *See* Philosophers/Philosophy, Greek

Habit, 85, 135n77, 211n44
Happiness, 32, 43n137, 79, 94–95, 100n9, 112, 133n60
  See also Joy
Heart
  Head and, 34–35n6, 69, 111
  Purity of, 78, 159, 172, 183–84n95
  Reason and, 42–43n123, 43n124
History, 38n41, 48, 61, 65
Honesty, 131n32, 131–32n35
Hope, 123, 172, 183–84n95, 184n97, 207
Human Beings, 36n15, 54, 100n15, 130n19, 146
  Creative Abilities of, 55n1, 118, 126, 173, 175n7
  God's Relationship with, 6–7, 50–51, 87, 123–24, 126–27, 135n85, 140, 152, 161–62, 168, 181n59
  Imagination of, 68, 173, 186n133, 213n69
  Reason as Faculty of, 43n128, 106n109, 108, 109–11, 190n147
Humility, 92, 103–4n78, 163

Ideas
  Communicating in Story, 3, 139–40, 206
  Imagination's Relationship to, 110, 154
  Kant's Concept of, 128n1, 128n3
  Platonic, 102–3n65, 212n61
Idolatry, 79
Illuminati, the, 18
Illumination, 33, 190n148, 210n36
Images, 33, 90, 97, 169, 193, 194, 212n56
  Kant on, 129n9
  Lewis's Use of, 34–35n6, 74n44, 97, 209n5
  Liturgical, 89, 208–9n3
  Meaning in, 55n1, 176n10, 202
  Story's Conveyance of, 3, 89, 139, 201
Imagination, 39–40n57, 106n109, 147–48, 168, 174–75n2, 182n74, 201, 213n67
  Analogical, 186–87n135
  Aristotle on, 193, 200, 211n46
  Artistic, 164, 165, 174–75n2
  Augustine's Concept of, 95
  Baptism of, 140–41, 167, 174, 175n3
  Cognition and, 46–48, 51, 129n10, 193
  Coleridge's Concept of, 194
  Consciousness Affected by, 164–67, 213n67
  Desire's Relationship to, 77, 85
  Dialectical, 186–87n135
  Enlightenment View of, 5, 15–16, 51–54, 70
  Epiphanies in, 200, 211n49
  Experience of, 96, 129n11, 210n41
  Faith's Relationship to, 30, 34–35n6
  Functions of, 45–57, 89, 135n77, 176n10
  Human, 68, 173, 186n133, 213n69
  Ideas' Relationship to, 110, 154
  Kant's Concept of, 56n34, 108, 109–10, 128n8, 129n9, 129n10
  Knowledge's Relationship to, 52, 174, 205, 207
  Lewis's Concept of, 1–4, 7, 14–15, 17, 34–35n6, 49, 53, 58, 60, 68–69, 98, 110, 142, 153–55, 168, 192–95, 200, 204, 209n5
  MacDonald's Concept of, 140
  Meaning Conveyed through, 7, 49, 55n1, 174, 192, 198–208
  Memory's Relationship to, 96, 98
  Moral, 77, 126, 135n76, 167
  Myth's Relationship to, 6, 139, 158, 201, 205
  Perception and, 49, 75–76n49, 158, 194, 200
  Plato's Concept of, 193
  A Priori, 128n8, 129n9
  Protestant, 186–87n135
  Reason's Relationship to, 11, 15–19, 35n13, 46–49, 51, 55n1, 75–

Imagination (*continued*)
  76n49, 108–11, 129n10, 129–30n16, 169, 186n133, 198, 206
  Revelation's Relationship to, 33, 34
  Science and, 206, 213n70
  Senses and, 31, 43n125, 47, 48, 52, 206, 213n69
  Soul and, 18, 181–82n64, 200, 207–8, 211n46
  Story's Relationship to, 61, 63, 187n71
  Theological, 138, 167, 192–216
  Thought's Relationship to, 5, 6–7, 49, 104n97, 139–40, 193, 200
  Transcendence of, 18, 52, 128
  Truth's Relationship to, 52, 104n97, 161, 164, 172, 175n7, 211n54
  Understanding's Relationship to, 34, 129n10, 129n11, 141, 206
  Untheological, 7, 192–93, 198, 203, 204
Immanence, 6, 144–45, 167
  Brought into Divine Life, 82, 84, 95, 199
  Transcendence and, 16, 19, 82, 140, 163, 193, 194, 199, 208–9n3, 213–15n72
Incarnation, 29, 48, 91, 167, 199
  See also Christ; God, Word of
Inclinations, 112, 130n23, 130n25
Individualism, Liberal, 41n77
Infinite, the, Finite Expressing, 6, 32, 99–100n6, 110, 140, 144, 163, 193, 200, 206
Influence, Aristotle's Concept of, 85–86
Inspiration, 58, 206
  Divine, 49–50, 169–70
  Literary, 63, 168–69, 173–74, 188n140
Intellect, 17, 18, 104–5n98, 200, 208, 216n81
  Imagination's Influence on, 31, 166–67
  In Lewis's Writings, 76n56, 211n44
  Truth and, 46–47, 141
Intuition, 113, 128n3, 128n8, 215n73

Joy, 6, 96
  Lewis's Concept of, 98–99n4, 99–100n6, 100n9, 154, 156, 183n87, 186n127, 193–94, 196, 199, 200, 210n41
  Platonic-Augustinian Concept of, 78–80, 94–95, 139
  See also Happiness
Justice, 23, 41n77, 120, 195
  Law of, 118, 119
Justification, Rational, 23–24, 25

Kairos, 147, 179n42
  See also Time
Kingdom of Heaven, 96
Knowledge, 18, 51, 128, 168, 208
  Attaining, 32, 97, 128n1
  Augustine on, 29, 91, 106n107
  God's, 29–30, 120
  Imagination's Relationship to, 52, 174, 205, 207
  Intellect's Relationship to, 47, 48
  Kant on, 128n7
  Myths' Conveyance of, 6, 158, 159–60
  Plato on, 81, 82, 84–85
  A Priori, 111
  Reason and, 28, 150, 215n73
  Revealed, 111, 193
  Senses as Source of, 32, 91, 103n74, 108
  Story's Conveyance of, 61, 154–55
  Truth and, 43n125, 123, 141

Language
  Analogical, 50, 168, 186–87n135
  Anthropomorphic, 187n138
  Divine, 50
  Meaning Conveyed by, 213–15n72
  Mythic, 158, 159–60, 163–64, 211n50, 213n67
  See also Poetic Diction, Barfield's Concept of; Speech; Words
Law, 88, 112–14, 132n48, 175n7
  Moral, 20, 107, 111, 117–18, 122–23, 125, 127–28, 142–43, 181n62

Learning, 18, 39n49, 83, 85, 97, 105n105, 106n107
Legends, 158, 172
    See also Myth(s)
Literalism, 184n97, 184n105
Literary Criticism, 58–66, 73–74n28, 188–90n143
    Lewis on, 5, 10, 60–63, 65–66, 71n14, 76n56, 169
    Psychoanalytic, 74n32, 194
Literature, 9, 48, 71–72n16, 101n30, 136n86, 167, 182–83n75
    Inspired, 168–69, 173–74, 188n140
    see also Fiction; Myth(s); Poetry/Poets; Story
Logic, 23, 52, 53
Longing, Sense of, 143, 146–47, 158, 167, 182n70
    Lewis's, 79–80, 94, 99–100n6
    Platonic-Augustinian, 77–98
    See also Desire
Love, 30, 43n128, 186–87n135
    Augustine's Concept of, 97, 172, 183–84n95
    God's, 29, 104n96, 106n109, 115, 186–87n135
    Lewis's Concept of, 114–15, 123, 125–26, 134n66, 152, 195, 198
Lying, 113–14, 131n32, 131–32n35

Magnanimity, Law of, 118, 119
Material, the, 58, 89, 142
Materialism, 106n109, 160
    Imagination and, 48, 205
    Lewis's Concept of, 38n35, 70n3
    Reason and, 15–16, 61, 208
Meaning, 70n3, 82, 176n13, 179n39, 185n124, 208
    Imagination as Organ of, 55n1, 174, 198–208
    Language Conveying, 213–15n72
    Lewis's Fiction, 58, 153
    Reason's Role in, 201–2
    Story's Conveyance of, 74n45, 86, 140, 143–45, 154–56, 171, 176n10, 176n16, 201, 202
    See also Author(s), Intended Meanings of; *Telos*; Universe, Meaning Found in
Memory, 94, 95, 96–98, 104–5n98, 105n105, 105–6n106, 194, 211n49
    See also Remembering
Mercy, Law of, 118, 119
Metaphors, 50, 127, 135n77, 154, 169, 176n14, 188n142
    See also Analogies
Metaphysics, 40n60, 45, 133n60, 174–75n2, 193, 210n36
    Reason and, 54, 56n34, 129n10
Mind, 3, 16, 72n18, 106n109, 208n1
    Human, 42–43n123, 52, 123, 200
    Imagination's Influences on, 49, 53, 55n1, 205, 209n5
    Rational, 48, 198, 215n73
    Sensations of, 34, 42
    See also Heart, Head and; Thinking
Miracles, 61–62, 160, 171, 188–90n143
Modernity, 51–54, 57n44, 58, 70n3
Moods, 151, 165
Moral Education, 86, 87, 135n75
    Characters' Conveyance of, 125, 127, 143–44
    See also Children, Moral Education of; Story, Moral Education through
Morality, 184n97
    Aristotle's Concept of, 124
    Christian, 115–18, 121–22, 123–24
    Kant's Concept of, 111–12, 119
    Lewis's Concept of, 107, 114–15, 117, 124, 126
    Nietzsche's Concept of, 124, 202–3
    See also Ethics; Tao, Moral; Virtues
Mundane Life, Transposition with Divine Life, 7, 49, 77, 174–75n2, 192, 194, 196, 199, 202
Murder, 115, 118, 131n31, 131–32n35
Mysterious, the, 39–40n57, 146–47, 148, 201, 209n24
Myth(s), 67, 97, 145, 152, 182–83n75, 183n87, 185n124, 213n70

Myth(s) (*continued*)
    Biblical, 163–64, 169, 170–71, 178n34, 183n93
    Christian, 3, 103n69, 181n59, 185n107
    Facts *vs.*, 171, 172, 185n107
    Imagination's Relationship to, 6, 139, 158, 201, 205
    Language of, 158, 159–60, 163–64, 211n50, 213n67
    Lewis's Crafting of, 9–11, 62, 71n13, 156–64, 165–66, 172–74, 174–75n2, 177n24, 177n26, 178n36, 204
    Modernist Ideas of, 70n3, 184n99
    Platonic, 88–89, 102–3n65, 129–30n16
    Power of, 2, 167, 182n74
    Truth Conveyed by, 2, 158, 172
    See also Allegories; Fairy Tales
Mythopoeia, 52–53
    Lewis's Use of, 3, 10, 69–70, 138–39, 174
Mythos, 52–53, 156

Naming, 206, 213–15n72
Narnia, 97, 177n25, 178n35, 181n59, 187n136
    Emergence into New Narnia, 77, 174–75n2
    Symbolism of, 146–47, 153, 180n55
    See also Chronicles of Narnia
Narrative. *See* Story
Narrative Framework, 6–7, 108, 119–20, 138, 182–83n75, 192–93, 204–5
Naturalism, 12, 13, 16, 20, 37n32, 38n35
Nature, 54, 129n9, 185n124, 206, 213n69
    God as Origin of, 48, 209n14
    Worldviews Influenced by, 61, 62
Neoorthodoxy, 169–70
Neo-Platonism, Augustine's, 97
    See also Platonism
New Testament, 159, 160, 188–90n143, 190–91n152, 209n24
    See also Gospels

Nihilism, 7, 16, 82, 98, 142, 167, 192, 195, 207, 212n62
Noesis, 43n124
Numinous, the, 99–100n6, 138–39, 140, 146–47, 148, 157

Obedience, 122, 134n66, 142, 180n55
Objects, 49, 55n1, 73–74n28, 78
Obligation. *See* Duty, Sense of
Occlusion, 129n13, 206
Orpheus, Story of, 156–57, 174–75n2
Other, the, 53, 134–35n74, 163, 210n35
    Longing for, 18, 146
    Myths' Conveyance of, 156, 158
    Sense of, 6, 138–39, 142, 173, 207
Oxford Movement, 4

Parables, 170–71, 185n108
Participation, 51, 168
    Divine, 33, 62, 81, 170, 174–75n2, 193
    Metaphysics of, 174–75n2
    Readers', 34–35n6, 62–63
Particularities, 22–23, 107, 117, 136n80
Passions, 207–8, 216n81
Perception, 211n49, 215n73
    Imagination and, 49, 75–76n49, 158, 194, 200
    Sense, 96, 97
    Transcending, 47, 201
Persuasion, Platonic, 4, 10, 26–28, 75–76n49, 84, 98–99n4
Phantasia, 95, 104–5n98, 193
Phantasm, 34, 47, 95, 104–5n98, 202, 207
    MacDonald's Theory of, 6, 138, 140–44
Philosophers/Philosophy, 26, 37n33, 102n57, 103n67, 116
    Aquinas on, 31, 43n137
    Christian, 39n53
    Enlightenment, 161, 215–16n80
    Greek, 4, 52
    Imagination's Relationship to, 19, 129–30n16
    Lewis's Teaching of, 9, 36n21, 36–37n24, 37n26, 107

Modern, 2, 14
Moral, 135n77
Naturalistic, 37n32
Rational, 54, 56n34, 129n10
Piety, 29, 104n80
Planets, in Chronicles of Narnia, 72n17
Platonism, 91, 97, 102–3n65, 104n81, 174–75n2, 193, 212n61
  See also Forms, Platonic; Persuasion, Platonic
Pleasure, 79, 86, 89, 94, 100n9, 101n44, 112, 182n71, 195
Poesis, 89, 141, 169, 208–9n3
Poetic Diction, Barfield's Concept of, 6, 139–40, 163–68, 186n127, 211n50, 213–15n72
Poetry/Poets, 52, 136n86, 165, 182–83n75, 201, 212n55, 212n56
  Imagination's role in, 200, 213n67
  Lewis's, 1, 2, 10, 34–35n6, 69, 158
  Plato on, 87–90, 102n57, 208–9n3
  See also Orpheus, Story of
Poiema, 182n70
Positivism, 14, 54
Productivity, 63, 109, 110, 128n8
Projection, 13
Prophecy, 147, 178–79n41
Psychoanalysis, 58, 59–66, 74n32
Psychology of Deliberation, Theory of, 135n77
Punishment, 86, 101n43
Pure Reason, 18, 110–11
  Augustine's Concept of, 90
  Enlightenment Concept of, 24, 29, 98–99n4, 106n109
  Kant's Concept of, 128n7
  Lewis's Concept of, 21, 126
  See also Reason
Purpose, 82, 86, 140, 208
  See also Telos

Rational Certainty, 21, 22
Rational Enquiry, 4, 24–26
Rational Inference, 15, 207, 215n75
Rationalism, 61, 81, 89, 99–100n6, 151, 167, 202
  Critical, 21–22, 179n48
  Enlightenment Paradigm of, 44n152, 68–69, 70, 98–99n4, 106n109, 215–16n80
  Imagination and, 109, 206
  Lewis's Concept of, 20, 107
  Limits of, 17–21, 36n15, 38–39n47
  Philosophical, 54, 56n34, 129n10
  Reason beyond, 53, 174, 186–87n135, 195, 208
Rationality, 21–26, 41n77, 166–67
  Augustine's Concept of, 28
  Enlightenment Paradigm of, 10, 28–29, 41n87, 48, 54, 208
  Kant's Concept of, 108, 110, 130n19
  Lewis's Concept of, 3, 4, 17, 36n21, 68, 69–70, 119, 154–55
  Practical, 23, 41n74, 120
  Reasoning Beyond, 3, 6, 15–16, 18, 202
  See also Universal Rational Consent
Readers, 60, 155, 182n70
  Participation of, 62–63, 71–72n16, 73–74n28, 144, 158–59, 167
  Scriptural, 169, 172, 173
Reality, 26, 82, 84, 106n109, 120, 146, 176n10, 177–78n32
  Aristotle's Concept of, 133n60
  Art and, 88, 89–90
  Fiction and, 52, 201
  God as Ultimate, 17, 186–87n135
  Lewis's Concept of, 146
  Spiritual, 169, 173–74
  Symbolism of, 60–61, 154
Reason, 47, 50, 88, 128, 182–83n75, 200
  Aquinas's Concept of, 4, 10, 30–34
  Arguments and, 20, 98–99n4, 166–67, 212n75
  Augustine's Concept of, 104–5n98
  Authority's Relationship to, 23–24
  Beyond Rationalism, 53
  Descartes' Concept of, 91–92
  Divine, 16, 124, 125, 141
  Enlightenment Paradigm of, 9, 28–29, 51–54, 151
  Faith's Relationship to, 21–22, 29, 30, 31, 44n152, 48

Subject Index

Reason (continued)
 Human, 43n128, 106n109, 108, 109–11, 190n147
 Imagination's Relationship to, 11, 15–19, 35n13, 46–49, 51, 55n1, 75–76n49, 108–11, 129n10, 129–30n16, 169, 186n133, 198, 206
 Kant's Concept of, 108–15, 128n3, 129n10, 130n17, 130n19
 Knowledge and, 28, 150, 215n73
 Lewis's Concept of, 15–16, 26, 31, 33–34, 34–35n6, 35n13, 58, 68, 70, 77, 99–100n6, 154, 201–2
 Limits of, 31, 206, 215–16n80
 Materialism and, 15–16, 61, 208
 Metaphysics and, 54, 56n34, 129n10
 Moral, 111–15, 126
 Rationalistic, 11, 15–16, 20, 47, 202
 Reasoning beyond, 3, 6, 139, 174, 208
 Revelation's Relationship to, 29, 31, 33
 Secular, 17, 19, 111
 Story's Relationship to, 4, 139, 145–46
 Truth Conveyed through, 42–43n123, 54, 216n81
 See also Pure Reason
Reception Theory, 73–74n28
Redemption, 29, 91, 95, 152, 180n55, 181n59
Reduction, 40n64, 109, 144–45, 210n36
Reformers, 186–87n135
Relativism, 22, 135n77
Religion, 21–22, 44n145, 72n18, 84, 126, 186–87n135
 Enlightenment Views on, 129–30n16
 Experience of, 99–100n6, 100n15
 Freud's Concept of, 98n2
 See also Christianity
Remembering, 105n99, 193
 Lewis's Concept of, 97–98
 Plato's Concept of, 18, 39n49, 80, 85, 96, 106n107
 See also Memory
Repentance, 16, 180n55, 198

Repetition, 93–94, 177n24, 194, 207
Representations, 55n1, 129n11
Respect, 67, 112, 117–18
Return, the, 146, 210n36
Revelation, 44n145, 91
 Aquinas's Concept of, 4, 10, 33
 Christ as, 117, 170
 Christian, 72n18, 209n14
 Experience of, 193, 195
 God's, 29, 44n146, 48, 50, 94, 106n109, 167
 Imagination's Relationship to, 33, 34
 Kant's Concept of, 108
 Reason's Relationship to, 29, 31, 33
 Theology of, 31, 163
Revenge, 78, 195
Roman Catholic Church, 4, 186–87n135
 See also Christianity
Romance, 14, 69, 99–100n6
Rules, 85, 109, 124, 131n32, 131–32n35
 See also Law

Sacra Doctrina, 31, 43n128
Salvation. See Redemption
Science, 36n15, 53, 125, 204–6, 213n67, 213n69, 213n70
Scripture, 44n145, 159–60, 184n97, 209n24
 Augustine's Belief in, 29, 90–91
 Demythologizing, 158, 172
 Lewis's Views on, 6, 139
 Story in, 166, 168–74
 See also Bible
Secularism, 17, 19, 39n53, 111, 206
Sehnsucht, 78, 80, 98n2
 See also Longing, Sense of
Sensations, 56n34, 199
 Emotions and, 183n87, 196, 197
 Imagination's Relationship to, 49, 129n10, 193, 211n46
 Mind's, 34, 47
 See also Feelings
Senses, the, 89, 97, 130n17, 196, 215n75
 Imagination and, 31, 43n125, 47, 48, 52, 206, 213n69
 Knowledge through, 32, 91, 103n74, 108

Sensibility, 110, 128n3, 128n8, 129n9
Signs. *See* Symbolism/Symbols
Sins, 72n17, 96, 116, 122, 132n48, 152
   See also Murder
Skepticism, 91, 150–51, 195
Society, 115, 133–34n65, 134n66, 203
Sonatas, Fairy Tales Compared to, 143, 176n14, 176n15, 176n17
Soul, 78, 106n109, 133n60
   Augustine's Concept of, 91, 93
   Excitement of, 139, 142, 173
   Imagination's Relationship to, 18, 181–82n64, 200, 207–8, 211n46
   Kant's Concept of, 129n9
   Lewis's Concept of, 62, 80, 144, 211n44
   Plato's Concept of, 26–28, 43n125, 82–83, 84, 88
Source Criticism, 71n14
Spacing, Metaphysical, 110–11, 206
Speech, 26–28, 42n99, 158, 197
Spirit, the, 34, 47, 48, 106n109, 195, 198–99, 208
   See also Holy Spirit
Spiritual, the, 58, 60, 150
Star Trek (TV series), 213n70
Stoicism, 129–30n16
Story
   Christian, 19, 44n145, 127
   Experiences Presented in, 60, 155–56, 167
   Form of, 34–35n6, 73–74n28, 74n45
   Lewis's Crafting of, 9–11, 62, 69, 71–72n16, 107–8, 138–40, 145–56, 182n70
   Moral Education through, 67, 72–73n19, 77, 81, 85–86, 125–28, 134–35n74, 136n81, 143–44, 153, 176n11, 211n44
   Plato's Concept of, 129–30n16
   Qualities of, 182n71, 182n72, 182n73
   Religious, 152, 186–87n135
   Scriptural, 166, 168–74
   Theology's Role in, 140
   Truth Conveyed by, 4, 145
   See also Fiction; Literature; Meaning, Story's Conveyance of; Myth(s); Narrative Framework
Storytellers/Storytelling, 3, 108, 143, 158, 186–87n135, 213n67
Subcreation, Tolkien's Theory of, 174–75n2, 177–78n32, 194
   See also Creation
Summa Theologica (Aquinas), 14, 135n79
Sun, Metaphor of, 82–83
Supernaturalism, 11, 45, 62, 140
Symbolism/Symbols, 154, 195, 197, 213–15n72
   Biblical, 160, 163, 169
   Christian, 72n18, 185n107
   Imagination's, 17, 202
   Platonism and, 102–3n65
   Story's Conveyance of, 10, 141, 182n70, 202
   See also Chronicles of Narnia, Symbolism in

Tao, Moral, 20, 107–8, 111, 115–25, 128, 130n21, 137n90, 143, 153
   See also Morality
Teleology, 79, 109, 133n60
Telos, 80, 85, 123, 124, 132–33n59, 133n60, 203
   Artistic, 5, 77
   Imagination as Organ of, 7, 49, 192–93
   Transcendent, 19, 77, 92, 204, 206
   See also Meaning; Purpose
Texts, Interpretation of, 60, 63–64, 65–66, 73–74n28
   See also Literary Criticism
Theft, 118, 131n31
Theism, 40n63, 186–87n135, 212n60
Theologians, 129–30n16, 169–70, 171, 182–83n75, 190n147
Theology, 9, 54
   Christian, 30–31, 115–16, 159, 190–91n152
   Imagination and, 192–216
   Lewis's, 3, 7n8, 38n41
   Modern, 188–90n143

Subject Index

Theology (*continued*)
  Narrative, 140, 170
  Philosophical, 35n12, 36n21
  Rational Arguments in, 30–31, 48
  Revelation's Role in, 31, 163
Theosis, 152, 181n59
Thinking, 16, 34, 105n105, 110, 166–67, 182n71
Thought(s), 47–48, 51, 82, 126, 139, 158, 182–83n75, 210n35
  Imagination's Effects on, 5, 6–7, 49, 55n1, 104n97, 139–40, 193, 200
  Platonic, 18, 96
Thymos, 216n81
Time, 25, 147–48, 179n42
Tradition, 23–26, 44n145, 107, 126, 136n85
Transcendence, 18, 45, 47, 58, 141, 160, 163, 208–9n3
  Ethical, 122–23
  God's, 5, 6–7, 38n36, 183n93
  Imagination and, 18, 52, 128
  Immanence and, 16, 19, 82, 140, 163, 167, 193, 194, 199, 208–9n3, 213–15n72
  Meaning through, 7, 192–93
  Telos from, 19, 77, 92, 204, 206
Transposition, 7, 49, 55n1, 95, 174–75n2, 192, 195–99, 202
Trilemma Argument, 149–50, 179n48
Trinity, the, 29–30, 33, 182n73
  See also Christ; God; Holy Spirit
Trust, 40n63, 96, 104–5n98, 118, 131–32n35, 148–49, 150–51
Truth, 88, 103n67, 104n80, 104n81, 105n99, 118, 131–32n35, 213n67
  Aquinas's Concept of, 43n126, 46–47, 48
  Augustine's Search for, 46, 90, 103n74
  Claims of, 25, 26–28
  Contemplation of, 133n60
  Divine, 31–32, 44n146
  Embodiment of, 174–75n2
  Faith and, 22, 123

  Imagination's Relationship to, 52, 104n97, 161, 164, 172, 175n7, 211n54
  Knowledge of, 43n125, 123, 141
  Lewis's Concept of, 154, 172
  Logical, 52, 91
  Mind's Grasp of, 16, 18
  Myths' Conveyance of, 2, 158, 172
  Reason's Relationship to, 4, 42–43n123, 54, 110
  Scriptural, 169–70, 171
  Spiritual, 170, 209n24
  Story's Conveyance of, 43n125, 95–96, 145

Unconscious, the, 53, 97
  See also Consciousness
Understanding, 32, 41n87, 56n34, 88, 97, 105–6n106, 111, 140
  Human, 43n128, 43n136, 118
  Imagination's Relationship to, 34, 129n10, 129n11, 141, 206
  Kant's Concept of, 128n3, 129n9, 130n17
  Pursuit of, 29, 54
  Story's Conveyance of, 144, 145, 153
Universal Ethical Imperative, 132–33n59
Universal Rational Consent, 6, 108, 119, 124
Universe, 51, 71–72n16, 78, 92, 181n59, 213n69
  Meaning Found in, 72n17, 203, 204, 206
Utilitarianism, 22

Values, 131–32n35
Virtue Ethics, 114, 131n32, 131n33
  See also Ethics
Virtues, 124, 125, 133n60, 211n44
  Children's Acquisition of, 80–81, 84–87, 127, 134–35n74
  See also Morality

Will, 43n128, 105–6n106, 180n55, 200, 211n44
  Acts of, 30, 49, 202–3

Augustine's Concept of, 96–97, 103–4n78
God's, 119–20, 121, 123, 124, 125, 199
Good, 111–12, 130n23, 131n33
Wisdom, 104n80, 158, 174–75n2, 190n146, 213n67
Augustine's Search for, 29–30, 90
Women
Lewis's Treatment of, 36n18, 137n87, 137n89
Rights of, 117
Word of God. *See* God, Word of; Incarnation
Words, 26, 33, 182n70, 204–5
Meanings of, 60, 64, 143, 164, 176n16, 178n39, 182n70, 212n56, 212n61, 213–15n72
Myths' Use of, 157–58, 174–75n2
Scriptural, 170, 171
See also Language; Speech
Worldviews, 60–61, 127, 153, 163
See also Lewis, Clive Staples (C. S.), Medieval Worldview of
Writing, 27–28, 39–40n57, 74n45, 76n55, 142–44, 197, 203–4

Name Index

Abraham, 123, 124, 132–33n59
Ambrose, Saint, 90
Anacker, Gayne J., 135n76
Anscombe, G. E. M. (Elizabeth), 9, 11–15, 35n14, 36n18, 36n19, 36n21, 37n31, 37n32, 37n33, 38n59, 59, 66, 75–76n49, 76n51, 113, 114, 115, 119, 131n31
Aquinas, Thomas, Saint, 4, 5, 8n13, 10, 14, 16, 30–34, 43n126, 43n137, 46–47, 48, 108, 109, 118, 123, 135n79, 161, 162, 199, 208n1
Aristotle, 23, 84, 85–86, 107, 109, 124, 125, 126–27, 133n60, 135n79, 136n80, 188–90n143, 192, 193, 200, 208n1, 211n46
Arnold, Matthew, 78
Aslan (Character), 66–67, 70n3, 97–98, 122, 125, 146–47, 151–52, 178n36, 178n39, 178–79n41, 180n55, 180n57, 181n58
Augustine, Saint, 4, 5, 8n11, 10, 28–30, 31, 32, 43n124, 43n126, 43n136, 46, 62, 77–79, 89, 90–97, 103n74, 104n96, 104–5n98, 106n107, 139, 159, 160, 169, 172, 173, 180n55, 183n94, 194, 199

Bach, Johann Sebastian, 181–82n64
Bacon, Sir Francis, 106n109
Baker, Djoymi, 213n70

Banez, Domingo, 54
Barfield, Owen, 2, 6, 10, 34n3, 75–76n49, 139, 154, 163–64, 165, 166, 177n24, 185n124, 185–86n125, 186n127, 192, 195, 208n1, 211n50
Barth, Karl, 38n41, 190n147
Basinger, David, 21
Becker, Carl, 44n152
Benedict XVI, Pope, 54, 57n44, 215–16n80, 216n81
Bennet, Jack, 13
Bentham, Jeremy, 24
Beversluis, John, 13, 35n12, 36n21, 39n53
Blake, William, 106n109
Boethius, 159
Bonaventure, Saint, 190n148, 199, 210n36
Borg, Marcus, 186–87n135
Brann, Eva, 55n1, 211n49
Brewer, Lee Allan, 12–13
Brown, David, 44n145, 129–30n16, 136n85, 190–91n152, 210n35
Bultmann, Rudolf, 184n99, 184n105, 185n107
Burton, Scott, 75–76n49
Butler, Eliza, 201

Calvin, John, 190n147
Carpenter, Humphrey, 11, 12, 36n18

Caspian (Character), 108, 150, 152
Chapman, George, 71–72n16
Chesterton, G. K., 19, 173, 174–75n2
Christ, 17, 118, 125, 134n73, 174, 179n48, 182n73
    Aslan's Parallels with, 151–52, 180n55, 180n57
    Baptism of, 33
    Coming of, 147, 181n59, 185n107
    Death and Resurrection of, 29, 75n47, 94, 175n3, 180n55, 190–91n152
    Personal Relationship with, 19, 136n85, 149–50, 190–91n152, 209n24
    Revelation through, 117, 170
    Story of, 2, 160–61
Christensen, Michael J., 168–69
Coleridge, Samuel Taylor, 48–49, 55, 174–75n2, 194, 209n5, 215n73
Cunningham, Conor, 38n36

Dante Alighieri, 7–8n10
Descartes, Rene, 16, 91–92, 100n15, 103n75, 106n109
Devil. *See* Satan
Dewey, John, 135n77
Dickens, Charles, 181–82n64
Dostoyevsky, Fyodor, 38n36, 181–82n64, 216n81
Duriez, Colin, 34n5, 69
Dyson, Hugo, 2, 154

Edmund (Character), 108, 122, 148, 150, 151, 152, 178n39, 180n55
Esolen, Anthony, 216n81
Euhemerus, 161
Eustace (Character), 108, 109, 122, 150, 152

Farrer, Austin, 5, 8n13, 14, 37n33, 40n68, 46, 119–20, 159–60, 163, 184n108, 209n14
Faulkner, William, 212n60
Fesmire, Steven, 135n77
Finkelstein, David, 213n69
Ford, Paul F., 182n71

Frei, Hans W., 63–64, 170, 171
Freud, Sigmund, 60, 70–71n7, 70n3, 74n32, 98n2
Frye, Northrop, 136n86, 178n34, 184n120, 204–5

Garrett, James M., 193
Geach, Peter, 37n31
Gerard, Ralph, 206
God
    Attributes of, 121–22
    Augustine's Search for, 90–95
    Belief in, 36n21, 43n136, 153
    Desire for, 78, 79, 96
    Essence of, 32, 33, 43n137
    Gifts of, 174–75n2, 199, 210n36
    Goodness of, 33, 117, 121–22, 162
    Humanity's Relationship with, 6–7, 50–51, 87, 123–24, 126–27, 136n85, 140, 152, 161–62, 168, 181n59
    Knowledge of, 52, 120, 149
    Love of, 29, 104n96, 106n109, 115, 186–87n135
    Mystery of, 91, 92
    Proofs of, 38n36, 40n60, 40n63
    Revelation from, 29, 44n146, 48, 50, 94, 106n109, 167, 170
    Speaking of, 3, 50, 161–62, 186–87n135, 187n138, 213n67
    Symbolized in Chronicles, 151–52, 178n35
    Transcendence of, 5, 6–7, 38n36, 183n93
    Will of, 119–20, 121, 123, 124, 125, 199
    Word of, 29, 158, 169–70, 185n107, 199
    Worship of, 30, 75n47
    See also Creator, the; Divine, the; Trinity
Goethe, Johann Wolfgang von, 215n73
Gower, John, 71–72n16
Grahame, Kenneth, 176n8
Greeley, Andrew, 186n135
Green, Roger Lancelyn, 71n13
Greeves, Arthur, 69

Name Index

Gregory of Nyssa, Saint, 180n55

Haldane, J. B. S., 213n69
Harwood, A. C. (Cecil), 17, 177n24, 201
Hasker, William, 15, 21
Hauerwas, Stanley, 127, 136n81
Havard, Robert, 13
Heidegger, Martin, 56n34
Herbert, George, 7–8n10
Hinten, Marvin D., 76n51
Holbrook, David, 70–71n7
Holy Spirit, 33, 103n72, 141, 182n73, 183n93
Hooker, Richard, 8n11
Hooper, Walter, 34n3, 70–71n7
Hoyle, Fred, 213n67
Hume, David, 215n75

Inchausti, Robert, 106n109, 182n74, 182–83n75
Iser, Wolfgang, 73–74n28

Jadis (Character), 154
James, William, 99–100n6, 100n15, 190n148, 210n36
Jauss, Hans Robert, 73–74n28
Jesus. *See* Christ
John, Saint, 184n105
John Paul II, Pope, 216n81
Johnson, Samuel, 181n62
Jordan, James, 15

Kant, Immanuel, 24, 52, 56n34, 108–15, 119, 124, 128n3, 128n7, 129n9, 129n10, 129n13, 130n17, 130n19, 130n25, 131n31
Kearney, Richard, 51–52, 56n34, 129n10
Keats, John, 71–72n16
Kekule, Friedrich August, 215n73
Keller, Helen, 213–15n72
Kierkegaard, Soren, 123, 129–30n16, 132–33n59, 186–87n135
King, Don W., 72n17
Kirkpatrick, W. T., 17
Kreeft, Peter, 102–3n65, 212n60
Kummel, W. G., 188n139

Lash, Nicholas, 100n15
Law, William, 8n11
Lawson, Sister Penelope, 141
L'Engle, Madeleine, 147, 213n67
Letitia (Character), 154
Lewis, Albert (father), 1
Lewis, Clive Staples (C. S.)
　Childhood Experiences, 79, 100n20
　Childlike Qualities of, 177n23, 177n25
　Conversion to Christianity, 2–3, 7–8n10, 19, 29, 34n3, 69–70, 75–76n49, 90, 186n127
　Dichotomy of, 9, 10–11
　Loss of Faith by, 1–2, 154
　Medieval Worldview, 4, 60–62, 69, 70, 71–72n16, 72n17, 75–76n49, 77, 126, 135n75, 164, 184n97
　Psychology of, 58, 59–66, 70–71n7
　Theology of, 3, 36–37n24, 38n41
　Wilson's Biography of, 11, 36n18, 58, 59–60
Lewis, Clive Staples (C. S.), Works of, 27–28, 34n5, 34–35n6, 35n13, 186–87n35
　The Abolition of Man, 20, 107
　The Allegory of Love, 102–3n65
　Chronicles of Narnia (*See* Subject Index)
　An Experiment in Criticism, 158
　The Great Divorce, 10, 140
　"Is Theology Poetry?", 103n75
　The Last Battle, 26, 77, 80, 102–3n65
　The Lion, the Witch and the Wardrobe, 66, 97–98, 146–47, 148, 151–52, 178–79n41, 180n55
　The Magician's Nephew, 154, 159
　Mere Christianity, 18–19, 107
　Miracles, 11–12, 13, 16, 36n21
　"Modern Man and his Categories of Thought," 34–35n6
　"Modern Theology and Biblical Criticism," 188–90n143
　Out of the Silent Planet, 125
　The Personal Heresy, 59
　The Pilgrim's Regress, 68–69

"Psycho-analysis and Literary Criticism," 194
"Rejoinder to Dr. Pittenger," 20
The Screwtape Letters, 211n44
The Silver Chair, 36n18, 59–60, 70n3, 145, 151
Space Trilogy, 34–35n6, 61–62, 66, 136n86
Surprised by Joy, 79–80, 186n127, 193–94, 200, 210n41
That Hideous Strength, 125
"The Weight of Glory," 78
"Transposition," 7
The Voyage of the Dawn Treader, 108–9, 122, 150, 152, 178–79n41
Lewis, Flora Hamilton (mother), 1
Lindskoog, Kathryn, 70–71n7
Locke, John, 106n109
Lodge, David, 186–87n135
Lovell, Steve, 98–99n4
Lubac, Henri de, 184n97
Lucas, John R., 15, 37n31, 37n32, 180n55
Lucy (Character), 108–9, 148, 149, 150, 178n39
Ludolf of Saxony, 179–80n50
Luke, Saint, 184n105
Luther, Martin, 190n147

MacDonald, George, 5, 6, 46, 50, 51, 138, 140–45, 158, 173, 174–75n2, 176n11, 203
MacIntyre, Alasdair, 10, 22, 23, 24, 25–26, 29, 41n87, 120, 123, 124, 127, 216n81
Manichees, 90, 103n69
Marie de France, 71–72n16
Mark (Character), 125
Marx, Karl, 190n147
McLaughlin, Mary Martin, 72n18
McLuhan, Marshall, 130n18
Menon (Character), 39n49, 85, 106n107
Midgley, Mary, 213n70
Milbank, Alison, 52, 53, 174–75n2
Milbank, John, 46, 47, 54, 89, 115–16, 203–4
Miles, Jack, 179n49

Mill, John Stuart, 131n31
Milton, John, 7–8n10, 79
Mitchell, Basil, 15, 37n31
Mitchell, Christopher W., 12–13
Moreland, J. P., 15

Nelson, Dale, 181–82n64
Newton, Sir Isaac, 106n109
Nietzsche, Friedrich, 124, 202–3, 212n56

O'Conner, Flannery, 39–40n57, 64, 74n45
Ogden, Charles K., 213–15n72
Otto, Rudolf, 99–100n6

Pascal, Blaise, 30, 40n60, 42–43n123, 43n124, 186n133
Pastueur, Louis, 215n73
Paul, Saint, 30, 118, 132n48, 147, 172, 183–84n95, 198
Percy, Walker, 207, 213–15n72
Peter (Character), 178n39
Peterson, Michael, 21
Pitter, Ruth, 177n23
Planck, Max, 205
Plantinga, Alvin, 15, 37–38n34
Plato, 4, 5, 10, 18, 26–28, 39n49, 47, 69, 72n19, 75–76n49, 77–79, 80–90, 96, 98–99n4, 102–3n65, 104n81, 106n107, 107, 121, 126, 129–30n16, 134–35n74, 139, 140, 173, 188–90n143, 193, 194, 199, 202, 207–8, 208n1, 208–9n3, 212n61, 216n81
Pollard, William Grosvenor, 213n67
Professor Kirke (Character), 148
Puddleglum (Character), 70n3, 151
Pullman, Philip, 203–4
Purtill, Richard, 15, 35n13

Queen of Underland (Character), 70n3

Rachels, James, 131–32n35
Raines, Kathleen, 177n23
Ramandu (Character), 108–9

Reepicheep (Character), 108, 150, 178–79n41
Reichenbach, Bruce, 21
Reppert, Victor, 12, 14, 15, 21, 37n31, 38n35, 179n48
Richards, I. A., 213–15n72
Ricoeur, Paul, 56n34, 62–63, 109, 176n10
Rilian (Character), 70n3
Rose, Seraphim, 181–82n64
Rosmini, Antonio, 212n61
Ross, James Bruce, 72n18
Rousseau, Jean Jacques, 24
Ruggiero, Vincent Ryan, 215n73
Russell, Bertrand, 40n64

Sallis, John, 110, 211n46
Samuel (Old Testament), 132–33n59
Sartre, Jean-Paul, 179n42
Satan, 121, 180n55
Saul (Old Testament), 132–33n59
Sayer, George, 12–13, 40n65, 70–71n7
Sayers, Dorothy L., 5, 8n13, 46, 50, 51, 76n51
Schakel, Peter J., 75–76n49
Schleiermacher, F. D. E., 99–100n6
Schumacher, E. F., 36n15
Scotus, Duns, 54
Screwtape (Character), 211n44
Selig, Robert, 38n41
Seneca, 129–30n16
Shakespeare, William, 102–3n65, 203, 212n60
Singh, Sadhu Sundar, 38–39n47
Smith, Huston, 205, 213n69
Smith, James K. A., 43n124, 43n125, 163
Socrates, 26, 27, 28, 39n49, 84, 85, 87, 89, 106n107, 121

Spencer, Edmund, 7–8n10
Steiner, Rudolf, 185–86n125
Susan (Character), 137n87, 178n39

Taliaferro, Charles, 180n55
Taylor, Mark, 210n35
Tillich, Paul, 186–87n135
Tillyard, E. M. W., 59
Tolkien, J. R. R., 2, 34n3, 53, 65, 75–76n49, 83, 102–3n65, 137n88, 146, 154, 173, 174–75n2, 175n3, 177–78n32, 185–86n125, 187n136, 188–90n143, 194, 209n5, 211n50
Traherne, Thomas, 8n11
Traughber, Rachel, 180n55

Uncle Andrew (Character), 154
Urs von Balthasar, Hans, 182n73

Vanauken, Sheldon, 19
Virgil, 156, 174–75n2

Walls, Jerry, 75–76n49
Ward, Michael, 14, 15, 16, 35n14, 72n17
Warnock, Mary, 199–200
Weston (Character), 125
White Witch (Character), 36n18, 125, 146, 151, 180n55
Wielenberg, Erik, 98–99n4
Williams, Charles, 8n13, 21
Williams, Rowan, 29
Wilson, A. N., 10–16, 35n14, 36n18, 58, 59, 70n3, 70–71n7, 76n51
Wittgenstein, Ludwig, 11, 14
Wood, Allen W., 130n19
Wormwood (Character), 211n44

www.ingramcontent.com/pod-product-compliance
Lightning Source LLC
Chambersburg PA
CBHW050436240426
43661CB00055B/2406